D0021088

DATE DUE

APR 19			
MAY 02			
GAYLORD			PRINTED IN U.S.A.

WITHDRAWN
UTSA LIBRARIES

The Population Crisis
and Moral Responsibility

EDITED BY
J. PHILIP WOGAMAN

PUBLIC AFFAIRS PRESS, WASHINGTON, D. C.

LIBRARY
University of Texas
At San Antonio

Published by Public Affairs Press
419 New Jersey Avenue, S. E., Washington, D. C. 20003
Printed in the United States of America
Library of Congress Catalog Card No. 72-97588
Copyright 1973 by The Population Institute

PREFACE

The rapid growth rate of world population, unparalleled in all human history, is today perceived by many thoughtful people in crisis terms. While not all experts agree about the extent of the crisis, many believe that the rate of growth already poses a serious threat to human economic and social well being and that the threat is likely to increase. A widespread debate has commenced on what response society should make.

This volume seeks to clarify fundamental ethical issues which are emerging in that debate. It is frankly exploratory in nature. The thirty-four authors of these essays attempt to shed new light on a problem which mankind is facing in new ways. Included among the authors are some of the nation's leading ethicists, theologians, and population experts. In their explorations they grapple with the problems of applying major Western traditions of ethics to our social dilemmas.

The history of thought on the subject of population is a long one, but the widespread effort to enlist governmental policy in limiting the growth rate is largely new. Hence there are not enough direct parallels or precedents in the religious and ethical traditions to guide us now without our having to engage in creative new thinking. Since the discussion is so largely a fresh one, we must expect sharp disagreements among those who participate in it—an expectation which will not be disappointed in the pages that follow. Indeed, half of these essays were written as responses to the other half. All of the essays are published here for the first time.

The writers diverge widely in their methods of approaching ethical issues and of interpreting basic factual information. In the preparation of this book no attempt was made to be inclusive of all human traditions, not because any is considered to be unimportant but because complete inclusiveness would have been unmanageable. In particular, most of the contributors reflect a basically Western heritage. Nevertheless, within that limitation there is great variation, and the volume may contain helpful clues for those who wish to relate the non-Western religious and ethical traditions to the population problem. Protestant, Catholic and Jewish religious traditions are more or less explicitly represented here; but even among scholars directly associated with particular faiths there is some disagreement as to whether ethics should be considered from a confessional religious standpoint or from a philosophical perspective inclusive of all faith traditions. While such differences may make it more difficult to interpret these materials as a whole, they may also reflect more realistically the complexity of ethical thinking. Ethicists and theologians do not, of course, think alike. There are points of general agreement and disagreement among reflective people in all fields. Confronting such diversity actually helps us to clarify and increase our understanding of issues.

In coming to terms with the different writers one should bear in mind several kinds of questions:

Is there in fact a population problem or crisis? Does the present growth rate portend danger to important ethical values? Is population growth basically self-regulating so that its size will remain consonant with essential human values without any need for governmental intervention?

What is the most promising method of ethical analysis? Is it a philosophical approach which seeks some common denominator of viewpoint acceptable to people of varying religious and moral traditions? Or is it an approach which attempts to base ethical judgments explicitly on such traditions—while trusting in dialogue to reconcile contrasting views?

When there is uncertainty (as there almost invariably is in situations calling for ethical judgment) what approaches to policy should be given the benefit of the doubt? Where should the burden of proof lie? Which authorities should be trusted most (for example, on ecological or economic questions)?

There is certainly not a consensus on such matters in this book, but reading the essays with such questions in mind may help every reader to clarify his own thinking.

A number of individuals and institutions have helped make this exploration possible. I wish to single out for special thanks the Population Institute of Washington, D. C., and its president, the Rev. Rodney Shaw, for providing the substantial financial support which made the cooperative process of study, consultation, and writing of this book possible. This process developed over a period of more than two years, involving regional and national consultations. Dozens of population experts, governmental figures, ethicists, and theologians of varying kinds and viewpoints participated. In undergirding this effort financially, the Population Institute guaranteed the fullest freedom of inquiry, desiring only to engage as many American thinkers as possible in active wrestling with the emerging ethical issues in population policy.

Many sources of information have been helpful, but I am especially indebted to the Population Council of New York, the Population Reference Bureau of Washington, D. C., the Institute of Society, Ethics and the Life Sciences at Hastings-on-Hudson, New York, and the Population Institute itself. These organizations provided a wide variety of reference materials for use by the writers whose work is contained in this volume and by others participating in the various consultations.

Several research and secretarial assistants—Virginia F. Wood, Lorraine Van Dine, Judy Birch, Dorothy Mills Parker, Edith B. Furgeson, and Carolyn Schneider—have borne much of the burden of clerical, research, and organizational detail. M. B. Schnapper, the editor of Public Affairs Press, has been a dependable source of wise counsel and direction in the publication process.

A project advisory committee included Eugene Borowitz, Daniel Callahan, Evans E. Crawford, Charles Curran, Alan Geyer, Major J. Jones, Robert Lee, Richard A. McCormick, Paul Ramsey, Harvey J. D. Seifert, Roger L. Shinn, and Seymour Siegel.

I wish, finally, to record my deep appreciation to the colleagues whose words appear in this book. In identifying each of them on pages vii - x so much more could be said than we have space for that purpose. They have done their work well, and they have borne with patience the editorial surgery and stylistic modifications which a volume of this kind inevitably requires, even when there may have been disagreement with the editor's judgment.

J. Philip Wogaman

Wesley Theological Seminary
Washington, D. C.

About the Contributors

JAMES E. ALLEN is associate professor in the Department of Health Administration and lecturer on medical ethics in the Department of Religion at the University of North Carolina. A senior research associate at the Carolina Population Center, he has studied population problems both in the United States and abroad.

W. FRENCH ANDERSON, M.D., is head of the section on Molecular Hematology of the National Heart and Lung Institute of the National Institute of Health, a member of the faculty of the Department of Genetics in the NIH Graduate Program, and a professional lecturer in biochemistry at George Washington University.

W. WALDO BEACH is professor of Christian ethics at Duke University Divinity School. His books include *Conscience on Campus*, *Christian Community and American Society*, and *Christian Ethics* (co-edited with H. Richard Niebuhr). A member of many learned societies, he was chairman of the council on Graduate Studies in Religion in 1962.

JESSMA O. BLOCKWICK is acting director of the Department of Population Problems of the United Methodist Board of Church and Society in Washington, D. C. Her career has included service as an editorial assistant for *Changing Times*, The Kiplinger Magazine, and extensive travel and writing.

DANIEL CALLAHAN is director of the Institute of Society, Ethics and the Life Sciences. A Roman Catholic layman and philosopher, he was editor of *Commonweal* from 1961-1968. His published books include *Abortion: Law, Choice and Morality*, *The American Population Debate* (editor), and *Ethics and Population*.

GEORGE CONTIS, M.D., is director of the Family Planning Program of the Office of Economic Opportunity. He was chief of the Family Planning/Population Division of the Bureau for Near East and South Asia of the U. S. Agency for International Development, 1966-1969.

EVANS E. CRAWFORD is Dean of the Chapel and professor of social ethics at the Howard University School of Religion. He has served as a visiting professor at Boston University and Wesley Theological Seminary. He is a member of the National Committee of Black Churchmen and the Society for the Study of Black Religion.

RICHARD D. N. DICKINSON, JR. is professor of Christian social ethics at Christian Theological Seminary, Indianapolis, Indiana. He has served as associate director of Quaker Conferences in Southern Asia and as Senior Research Officer in a study of the developing continents sponsored by the World Council of Churches. He is author of *Line and Plumet*, a report on the role of the churches in socio-economic development in the Third World.

ARTHUR J. DYCK is Mary B. Saltonstall Professor of Population Ethics and a member of the Center for Population Studies and of the Divinity School Faculty at Harvard University. His research and writing has been concentrated primarily in the area of ethics and population problems.

RICHARD M. FAGEY is Executive Secretary of the Commission of the Churches on International Affairs of the World Council of Churches. He has served in a wide

vii

variety of ecumenical positions over the past three decades, most of them concerned with world peace, economic development, and population problems. He is author of *The Population Explosion and Christian Responsibility* and other books.

DAVID M. FELDMAN is Rabbi of the Bay Ridge Jewish Center in Brooklyn, New York. He is chairman of the Committee on Marriage and Divorce of the Synagogue Commission of the Federation of Jewish Philanthropies and author of *Birth Control in Jewish Law: Marital Relations, Contraception, and Abortion, as Set Forth in the Classic Texts of Jewish Law.*

E. CLINTON GARDNER is professor of Christian Ethics at Candler School of Theology at Emory University. A past president of the American Society of Christian Ethics, he is author of *Biblical Faith and Social Ethics* and *The Church as a Prophetic Community.*

CATHERINE L. GUNSALUS is associate professor of historical theology at the Louisville Presbyterian Theological Seminary. She has been a member of the United Presbyterian General Assembly Committee on the Status of Women and a delegate to the Assembly of the National Council of Churches. She is an ordained Presbyterian minister.

PHILIP M. HAUSER is Director of the Population Research Center and professor of sociology at the University of Chicago. A past president of the Population Association of America and the American Sociologist Association, he has been a prominent member of and consultant to many national and international organizations in the population field. He is former Deputy Director and Acting Director of the U. S. Bureau of the Census and author of many books, including *Population Perspectives* and *The Population Dilemma* (ed.).

ANDRE E. HELLEGERS, M.D. director of the Joseph and Rose Kennedy Institute for the Study of Human Reproduction and Bioethics and director of Population Research at Georgetown University. A Roman Catholic layman, he was a member and Deputy Secretary General of the Papal Commission on Population and Birth Control, 1964-1966 and a member of President Johnson's Committee on Population and Family Planning, 1968.

JIMMYE KIMMEY is executive director of the Association for the Study of Abortion. Trained in political science, she has been a research associate at the Institute of War and Peace Studies at Columbia University, and she has taught at Barnard College in the field of international relations and American foreign policy.

JAMES C. LOGAN is professor of systematic theology at Wesley Theological Seminary in Washington, D. C. and national vice-chairman of the Faith/Man/Nature Group, an organization concerned with the relationship between ecological problems and theology. He has been a delegate to Faith and Order Conferences of the World Council of Churches and a consultant to other church bodies.

EDWARD LEROY LONG, JR. is professor of religion at Oberlin College. Elected president of the American Society of Christian ethics in 1972, he is author of *A Survey of Christian Ethics, Religious Beliefs of American Scientists, Science and Christian Faith,* and other works. He is a member of the Faith/Man/Nature Group, and he has participated as a member of or consultant to many national academic and ecclesiastical organizations.

RICHARD A. MCCORMICK, S.J. is professor of moral theology at Ballarmine School of Theology of Loyola University in Chicago. A past president of the American Catholic Theology Society, he is an associate editor of *America* and has contributed to *The Problem of Population, Norm and Context in Christian Ethics*, and other works.

EDWARD POHLMAN is professor of counseling psychology at the University of the Pacific in Stockton, California. Born and reared in India, he returned to that country from 1967-1969 to teach and direct research on population problems under the sponsorship of the Pathfinder Fund and the Carolina Population Center. He is author of *The Psychology of Birth Planning, Incentives and Compensations in Population Programs, Population: Hawks and Doves* (ed.), and other books.

RALPH B. POTTER, JR. is professor of social ethics at Harvard Divinity School and a member of the Harvard Center for Population Studies. He has been Secretary of Social Education and Evangelism of the United Presbyterian Board of Christian Education. His writings include *War and Moral Discourse* and various articles and papers on ethics and population.

ANNE B. RAPER is research assistant at the Carolina Population Center of the University of North Carolina.

ROSEMARY RADFORD RUETHER is assistant professor of historical theology at Howard University School of Religion. A contributing editor of *Christianity and Crisis* and member of the editorial boards of *Soundings* and the *Journal of Religious Thought*, she is author of *The Church Against Itself, The Radical Kingdom: The Western Experience of Messianic Hope*, and other works.

HARVEY J. D. SEIFERT is professor of Christian Ethics of the School of Theology at Claremont in California. His published books include *Ethical Resources for Political and Economic Decision, Power Where the Action Is, Conquest by Suffering*, and (with Howard J. Clinebell) *Personal Growth and Social Change*.

ROGER L. SHINN is Reinhold Niebuhr Professor of Social Ethics at the Union Theological Seminary in New York. A member of and consultant to many denominational and ecumenical agencies and conferences he is co-chairman (with Margaret Mead) of the U.S.A. Task Force on the Future of Mankind and the Role of the Churches in a World of Science-based Technology. His published books include *Wars and Rumors of Wars, Tangled World*, and *Man: The New Humanism*.

SEYMOUR SIEGEL is professor of theology and of ethics and rabbinic thought at The Jewish Theological Seminary of America in New York. He is a member of the board of the Synagogue Council of America and other national Jewish bodies. His published writings include *The Jewish Dietary Laws*, which he co-authored with Samuel Dresner.

HARMON L. SMITH is associate professor of moral theology at Duke University. His published writings include *Ethics and the New Medicine*, and *The Christian and His Decisions* (with Louis W. Hodges). He is associate director of the Inter-Seminary Church and Society Program.

JOSEPH J. SPENGLER is professor of economics and director of the Population Studies Program at Duke University. An internationally prominent scholar on population and economics for the past forty years, he is author of *The Population Crisis and the Use of World Resources, France Faces Depopulation*, and other works.

DOUGLAS E. STURM is professor of religion and political science and chairman of the religion department at Bucknell University, Lewisburg, Pennsylvania. He was executive secretary of the American Society of Christian Ethics, 1968-1972, and his published writings and research fellowships have been concerned primarily with the relationship between ethics and law and political science.

JOSEPH D. TYDINGS was United States Senator from Maryland, 1965-1971. A member of the President's Commission on Population Growth and the American Future, he has been an active leader in the development of legislation on population issues. Author of *Born to Starve*, he is a special consultant to the United Nations Fund for Population Activities. He was recipient of the Margaret Sanger Award for Distinguished Public Service, Planned Parenthood-World Population in 1970.

STEWART L. UDALL was Secretary of the Interior throughout the administrations of Presidents Kennedy and Johnson. A former Congressman from Arizona, he has long concerned himself with problems in conservation. His published writings include *The Quiet Crisis* and *1976: Agenda for Tomorrow*. He is presently chairman of Overview, an international environmental consulting firm.

ROBERT M. VEATCH is associate for medical ethics and associate director of the program on population and ethics of the Institute of Society, Ethics, and the Life Sciences. In 1971 he prepared several working papers on ethics and population for the U. S. Commission on Population Growth and the American Future.

CHARLES C. WEST is professor of Christian ethics at Princeton Theological Seminary. He is vice president of the American Society of Christian Ethics and a member of the ecumenical Task Force on the Future of Man and the Role of Churches in an Age of Science-Based Technology. His published books include *Communism and the Theologians, The Power to be Human*, and *Ethics, Violence and Revolution*.

J. PHILIP WOGAMAN is dean and professor of Christian social ethics at Wesley Theological Seminary and director of the Project on Ethics and Population Policies of the Population Institute, Washington, D. C. His published books include *Guaranteed Annual Income: The Moral Issues* and *Protestant Faith and Religious Liberty*.

CONTENTS

Part I

THE MORAL BASIS OF POLICY OBJECTIVES

Clarity on public policy begins with clarity on the objectives of policy. Essays in this part of the volume seek to develop such clarity by exploring the moral roots of the goals implied by discussion of population questions. In the history of thought on these questions, debate has often centered around conflicting views of "optimum population." In effect, this has really been a debate over policy objectives. These can be expressed in static terms (some fixed number of people in relation to some given conception of economic or ecological or other variables) or more dynamically (a raising or lowering of rates of growth without attempting to establish any fixed goal). In either case, an ethical or value component is inescapable as we seek to show why a particular size or rate of growth (or decrease) is better than some other. Most of the contributors to this section do take the question of an optimum population seriously, although they attempt to develop fresh sources of insight. Their views on the fruitfulness of a search for optimum population may be contrasted interestingly with those of a leading demographer, Philip Hauser, in Part III.

The first essay below, "The Contribution of Ethics," explores the relevance of ethics to population issues. It contrasts several typical models of optimum population with a more explicitly ethical one, and it argues the necessity of a religious or theological foundation for such ethical thought. In that regard it can be compared with Ralph B. Potter's more general philosophical exploration of "Alternative Approaches to Optimum Population Theory," although both writings can be understood as attempts to clarify the methods by which we arrive at value judgments in determining the optimum. Dr. Potter, professor of ethics at Harvard Divinity School and a member of the Harvard Center for Population Studies, carefully reviews the issues logically manifest in the traditional consideration of the major questions and attempts then to demonstrate the inadequacy, from an ethical standpoint, of this debate of the past two centuries. Charles C. West's paper, "A Theological Perspective," is written as a response to Potter from West's standpoint as a theologian. Dr. West is particularly critical of what he considers to be Potter's failure to move directly to a wrestling with immeasurable qualitative factors.

1

Daniel Callahan's "Population and Human Survival" should be considered from the standpoint of how the value of survival, expressed on different levels, can contribute to determining a basis for optimum population. It is not concerned simply with "survival" as a physical question, but with the ways in which survival is invoked in population discussions, the survival of group identity and the survival of certain cultural values. A well-known author of works on population questions, abortion, and medical ethics, Dr. Callahan is a Roman Catholic lay philosopher.

Rabbi Seymour Siegel's related essay addresses, mainly from a Jewish perspective, the hard question of the effect of a conception of optimum population upon the status of minority groups. Since size has often been regarded as an index of power, any effort to limit growth seems to be an effort to make permanent an existing unsatisfactory social situation. The issue is particularly pointed for groups which depend primarily or solely upon natural increase for their size. It raises the question whether such groups have a special moral claim in the determination of population policies by a whole society. Ethical assessment in this area must take into account the relative merits of social identity and universal meaning. While Rabbi Siegel's paper is largely focused on the experience of the Jewish community—of which he is himself a leader and teacher—its import can be generalized to include racial minorities and many other religious bodies. However, Jessma Blockwick's response takes sharp issue with his conclusion. She is acting director of the Department of Population Problems of the United Methodist Board of Church and Society. Both her paper and Rabbi Siegel's can usefully be compared with the black perspective of Evans Crawford in Part IV.

Catherine Gunsalus' feminist views focus on the tension between qualitative and quantitative factors in human existence. One of the few women theologians teaching in American theological seminaries, Dr. Gunsalus considers the different reference points from which these two factors can be understood, and she reflects upon the relative moral claims of life after birth, prior to birth, and in potentiality prior to conception. Waldo Beach, a professor of theology at Duke University, responds from his own theological perspective and questions her way of handling the conflict of values.

In his paper on "Ecological Considerations," James C. Logan takes cognizance of the relationship between environmental problems and current concern over population growth. A professor of theology at Wesley Theological Seminary, he explores the ultimate issues of man's relationship to nature and confronts the fact that there are no self-evident ecological norms. One should bear in mind, while reading his chapter, such questions as How much space do people need in order to be fully human? To what extent does a truly human life depend upon forests and wild animals and an abundance of physical beauty in the environment? Does man have a moral right to formulate his optimum population in terms of purely humanistic considerations? Does nature apart from man have any moral claims? Dr. Logan's respondent, former Secretary of the Interior Stewart Udall, supplements this essay with some of his own observations on ecology.

Harvey Seifert's "Economic Considrations" is concerned with the relationship between population size and the production and distribution of scarce economic values. During the nineteenth century this kind of question was central, and it remains very important today. A professor of social ethics at the School of Theology at Claremont, Dr. Seifert attempts to deal with the issues in more specifically ethical fashion than has generally been charactristic of the literature of population economics.

Some of the following questions may usefully be borne in mind while reflecting upon Seifert's essay: What are the basic economic needs of man and society—if man and society are to be whatever we think they ought to be? Should population be stabilized at a level consistent with the needs of any particular form of social organization? Is continuing population growth necessary for the stimulation of economic production or, to the contrary, does increased population tend to undermine the economic well-being of all? Is economic growth itself desirable? Answers to such questions entail ethical as well as economic judgments. Joseph J. Spengler's response to Seifert is from the standpoint of a classical economist and long-time student of population issues. Both his paper and Seifert's may well be compared with parts of Ralph Potter's discussion in which the "economic" and "welfare" definitions of optimum are reviewed in historical perspective.

1

THE CONTRIBUTION OF ETHICS

J. Philip Wogaman

The unprecedented size and growth of world population has clearly emerged as one of the most basic problems facing mankind in the closing decades of the twentieth century. The basic facts concerning this problem are well enough known, and most of them need not be reviewed here. It is sufficient to remember that world population has doubled in the last half century and that, at present growth rates, it will continue to double every thirty-five years until either nature or human action intervene. This rapid growth rate affects nearly every aspect of man's social, economic, political and cultural life. It creates some new problems and greatly exacerbates old ones. It can be argued that population size is already a factor in the suffering of hundreds of millions of people in the developing countries and in the environmental problems of more highly developed areas.

In the past, human increase has largely been kept within bounds by the natural forces of disease and famine, supplemented occasionally by war and primitive forms of birth control. But disease, famine and war are immensely destructive of human values. Medical and agricultural revolutions have to some extent limited disease and famine for twentieth century man. Therefore, despite some diminishing of crude birthrates in many countries, the world population has been moving ahead dramatically. While the carrying capacity of the planet for humans has yet to be determined, that capacity may have already been stretched to the breaking point from the standpoint of quality of life.

This basic situation has evoked widespread discussion among population experts, ecologists,, governmental officials, and others. Many thoughtful people believe that a *laissez faire* approach is a luxury we can no longer afford. They are beginning to ask how mankind will be able to halt population growth by using means which are not dehumanizing, and whether we shall be able to do so in time to prevent further suffering and hardship. Some twenty-one governments of developing countries have responded to what they regard as the population crisis by adopting official policies.[1] Governments of more highly developed countries, such as the United States, have been slower to respond, but even here official concern has increased notably in the past few years. The report of the U. S. Commission on Population Growth and the American Future in 1972 [2] signaled greater interest in official as well as unofficial circles. Many different kinds of governmental policies have been proposed in the United States and in other parts of the world.[3] Even without such evidences of interest, the objective consequences of the population growth rate are likely to create pressures to which governments must react in some way.

Population problems and policies are not purely practical or technical. At most points they also require consideration on the humanistic levels where our values become involved. Our very definition of problems suggests the points at which we believe our values to be threatened, and our approach to policy questions is usually dominated by our efforts to achieve or protect these values. For this reason, I do not believe we can bypass serious consideration of ethical issues in dealing with population problems and policies.

Ethics can be understood as the attempt to clarify the source and meaning of basic values and to apply them to the world of practical experience. All people have values and seek, in one way or another, to apply them. But the clarification of values and the analysis of practical problems in applying them demands considerable acquaintance with the great religious and humanistic traditions and with past and present approaches to ethical analysis. People who take ethics seriously must be concerned simultaneously with a deeper understanding of value traditions and with accurate factual understanding of problems. They must work constantly at the task of relating the one to the other. Where this is not done, we may be led to believe that we cannot deal with our problems successfully without abandoning our values, or that faithfulness to our values requires us to ignore the practical problems. Either way, the result is likely to produce personal and cultural crisis and disintegration rather than increased integrity and maturity.

The population crisis poses unusual new problems for ethical analysis. Issues of population policies which we now face have too largely been neglected heretofore by ethics. It is important that we not neglect them any longer. Increasingly, society will have to develop realistic policies. The question is whether these policies will be consonant with important moral values. I believe that where social policies are widely regarded as being both necessary but also immoral, some cultural disintegration is a likely consequence.

It cannot be assumed in advance that any particular policy approach is either ethical or unethical apart from examining it carefully in the light of important values. Our formulation of basic values can itself change in the interaction with policy. But where done carefully, ethical inquiry can clarify the value implications of alternative solutions to problems for the guidance of policy-makers and laymen alike.

The concept of "optimum population" tests most directly whether ethics has a contribution to make to population policy questions. The term optimum itself is meaningless apart from value judgment. It suggests that some number of people is "best" or "better" in relation to a physical or social environment. Moreover, any given viewpoint of optimum population provides an important clue to its author's basic ethical and even religious assumptions—whether he or she is conscious of this or not. The point can be illustrated by referring to several discernible "models" of optimum population in recent debate.

One quite widely accepted model could be called *the laissez faire position:* it is the view that that population size is optimum which results from the uncoerced decisions and activities of all potential parents. Occasionally in recent debates the point has been expressed that it is both disruptive and unnecessary for government to attempt any planning in this field. People can be counted upon to do what is desirable for them, and the sum total of the results of this will be what is desirable for society as a whole. The "Family Planning" movement emphasizes that its sole aim is to make it possible for each individual family planning unit to have the number of children (no more and no less) that it wishes to have. It is assumed that the results of this will be beneficial to society as a whole. That assumption may or may not be well-founded factually in a particular instance. In any case it is a *non sequitur* to suppose that *because* individual families find a particular family size desirable *for them* it is therefore desirable for society that they have that family size. This approach is in fact similar to the classical economic faith in the "invisible hand." It tends to absolutize the value of freedom, to neglect the possibility that freedom can be used for selfish as well as benevolent ends. It may be based on the view that whatever is done by people is good (in the literature of ethics this is called the "naturalistic fallacy") or on the view that whatever is done by people does not matter. Or it may simply hold that what happens to society as a whole is unimportant. Such views touch ethics and religion at the root.

Another model is based upon *maximization of national power*. It is an old assumption that group size is an index to social power. A column by economist Henry C. Wallich illustrates the continuing popularity of the viewpoint. While contesting the attitude of the Zero Population Growth movement, Wallich developed a picture of an America increasingly overwhelmed by the growth of other countries and predicted "we would be less well-prepared to defend our position as we became increasingly outnumbered." "A nation's power does not depend exclusively on population size," he wrote, "but numbers obviously have something to do with it." [4] To some extent this thinking is parallel to that of ethnic spokesmen who regard all talk of population limitation as being genocidal. There are, of course, factual difficulties in equating mere numbers of people with social power. (Were this not the case, China and India would be the leading superpowers simply because of their numbers.) Even were this not so, its chauvinistic ethical roots are more than evident. The power supremacy of a particular nation or group is not self-evidently a good at all—much less the supreme good. When treated as the basic value, it is a form of what H. Richard Niebuhr has called henotheism: a form of idolatry which takes some aspect of humanity as the organizing center of value and which correspondingly neglects the *whole* of reality. I am not suggesting that this is not a popular ethical viewpoint but that it is not self-evidently the right one.

Another model is based upon *maximization of economic productivity*. It treats as best that population size which contributes most to production. There are overtones of this in Joseph J. Spengler's argument that "the optimum population is that which enables a people 'to obtain, in return for whatever expenditure of effort [they] may regard as normal and proper, the largest, permanently practicable *per capita* product.'" [5] Others have noted the relationship between population growth and expanding labor pools and markets, urging continuing population growth as a means of maintaining the upward movement of the Gross National Product. This, of course, implies that products are of greater importance than people. A reasonable theory of optimum population must surely regard economic productivity as an important variable, but this is not the same thing as treating it as the central point in a theory of value.

Another model is based upon *happiness and pleasure:* that number of people is best which contributes most to maximization of pleasure and avoidance of pain. Wayne H. Davis recently referred to America as being overpopulated because "we have far more people now than we can continue to support at anything near today's level of affluence" [6]—thus implicitly regarding a high level of affluence as the governing moral norm. In more elaborate fashion, S. Fred Singer has devised a formula for determining the optimum based upon the same kind of assumption. He writes that "one definition often proposed defines optimum as the 'highest quality of life for the largest percentage of population.' This puts the burden on defining 'quality of life,' and on devising a yardstick for measuring it. In our society, where material comforts are important and contribute to what people perceive of as happiness, a loose definition might be 'having as much money as possible left over after taking care of the basic necessities, and having the necessary time and opportunities for spending it in a pleasant way.' It means also having the maximum range of choices for a way of life. This definition . . . tells you how to measure quality of life in terms of dollars by calculating the potential consumption and assigning a monetary value to free time." [7]

The nineteenth and early-twentieth century discussions of optimum population are replete with comparable appeals to the happiness principle. While happiness as such is difficult to oppose, it also raises difficulties when taken by itself as the basis for other values. If the objective of individuals in approaching questions of population policy should be their own *private* happiness, the goal would be quite understandable, though selfish and of doubtful ethical standing in the long run. If on the other hand, the goal should be the happiness of the greatest number of people, some ethical principle broader than happiness itself would be required to account for the obligation to make *other* people happy. That broader ethical principle has been assumed, in a rather confused way, by thinkers who try to use the utilitarian formula ("greatest good for the largest number") while basing it upon pleasure as the ultimate norm.

Still another model is based upon *minimum disruption of the environment*. The attempt to correlate population optima with ecological considerations may be the most novel contribution of recent discussion. It has emerged with force in the writings of Paul Ehrlich, Garrett Hardin and others. It is illustrated by Walter Orr Roberts' statement that "the optimum is that level of population at which the growth of population has ended and society has firmly established its determination to live in harmonious balance with the environment." [8] The well-being of the environment surely must also be a consideration in any defensible approach; but if the well-being of nature per se should become the governing consideration (as it is not quite in the Roberts statement, but as it sometimes seems to be in the more visceral contributions of the ecology movement), then it is clearly the case that the fewer people there are the better off nature will be. On this basis we might fittingly declare that the optimum population is really no population at all. Short of this, the term "harmonious balance with the environment" is both helpful and inconclusive. It is helpful because it acknowledges that whatever dangers there are from over-population do in fact accrue from disruptions and over-uses of the natural world and that man's life on this planet does in fact depend upon his living in harmony with nature. But it is inconclusive because it cannot tell us what a "harmonious balance with the environment" might be without introducing other value questions. The word "harmonious" begs the question of what *kind* of harmony.

There is a very wide range of possible balances between man and nature between the point where man is completely excluded and the point where man's overwhelming numbers threaten the very existence of nature. Furthermore, the concept of harmony with nature presupposes some theory as to the moral significance of nature. Of what intrinsic value is a tree or a bird or water and air? Are these to be regarded simply as human life-support systems and does "harmonious" mean that relationship between man and environment which best provides for human support? Or does it refer to some degree of human respect for different aspects of nature, regarded as value in their own right? A defensible theory of optimum population must begin, not end, with such questions.

These various models illustrate and pose the problem. How are we best to apply ethical insight to the determination of optimum?

A striking note in recent population discussions is the emergence of some explicitly ethical writing. Daniel Callahan's writings are particularly worthy of mention. His small monograph *Ethics and Population Limitation* [9] reviews a number of the basic problems and proposes several formal criteria for ethical decision-making in this field. He suggests that three formal values (freedom, justice, and security/survival) should be treated as norms and that "in cases of conflict, one is obliged to act in such a way that any limitation of one or more of the three fundamental values . . . continues to respect the values and can be justified because it promises to increase the balance of good over evil." It is unclear in context whether good and evil are defined by the presence or absence of the three values or whether good and evil have a meaning related to but also transcending those values.

This approach is interesting for our purposes because while explicitly ethical it is also apparently successful in avoiding religious or theological questions. It raises the question whether religion or theology have anything in particular to add. General values, such as freedom and justice, belong to the mainstream of Western ethical tradition and can be given meanings concerning which persons of differing faiths can agree. One does not need to be a Christian or a Jew or, for that matter, the adherent of any other particular religious tradition to acknowledge the importance of freedom and justice. Nevertheless, a problem develops when we wish to say why we regard such general values as normative. We can, along with Callahan, validate them through reference to still other values: "Freedom," he writes, "is a prized value because it is a condition for self determination and the achievement of knowledge. Justice, particularly distributive justice, is prized because it entails equality of treatment and opportunity and an equitable access to those resources and opportunities necessary for human development. Security/survival is prized because it constitutes a fundamental ground for all human activities."

But why, then, are self-determination, knowledge, equality of treatment, etc. important, and why, in particular, should we be concerned about whether *other* people have such values?

This kind of question suggests to me that until we have come to terms with our *center* of value—the ultimate object of all our valuing—we cannot really validate any lesser or abstract value-claim. Freedom, justice, security/survival, or any other such general values must be viewed in their ultimate context. The question is, what view of ultimate reality do particular ways of understanding and applying these values presuppose?

Such a question is properly called theological. It is an inquiry into the center of value in which we place our faith. Does it require intellectual arrogance? Quite the opposite. Theological views cannot in the final analysis be validated with certainty. Since they pertain to the nature of the whole of reality and since the whole of reality cannot be known by anyone, such views are based upon those experiences and symbols which people consider to be decisive as clues to the nature of the whole. It is by faith that we acknowledge that the character of the whole is most fully disclosed in this or that part. The way we understand or utilize abstract values, like freedom and justice, necessarily owes much to our overall view of things. Therefore, the attempt to treat such values as universal apart from theological dependency merely conceals what is in fact operative. I do not mean to say that there is no place in ethics for appeal to particular values which are not in themselves theological. I mean only that such values are incomplete until they can be related explicitly to central theological foundations.

If this is true, we cannot offer a satisfactory theory of optimum

population until we have in some fashion begun to relate population
size to ultimate concerns. This is not to say that optimum population
must be Christian or Jewish or based on any particular theological tradition in order to be satisfactory. No particular tradition can prove its
final superiority. It is to say that *some* theological commitment must
be made in an adequate theory of optimum population. The ecumenical and inter-faith movements of our time have partially validated the
hope that the dialogue among persons who are clear about their differing theological commitments greatly contributes to the foundations for
practical cooperation on common concerns while at the same time
clarifying the genuine, as distinct from merely apparent points of
difference. Perhaps this can also be true in discussions of ethics and
population policies. In any event, I wish in the remainder of this paper
to wrestle a bit with what I take to be the implications of Christian
faith commitments—recognizing that this is not the only possible
Christian interpretation and that theological interpretations based
upon other faith traditions may also justly be regarded as plausible.

Historically, Christian consideration of population matters has only
rarely concerned itself with limiting population. More frequently it
has been preoccupied with increasing the birth rate. This historical fact
is based upon more than a proof-texting use of "be fruitful and multiply," and it cannot simply be regarded as an irrational "pro-natalist"
bias. One can, on Christian grounds, argue the case for the maximum
possible number of births. In Christianity that case would seem to be
well-founded on the affirmation of the very great value which each life
has in terms of God's creation and grace. If each life has a transcendant
source of value—a point which can be made in several ways in Christian theology and as an outgrowth of a number of non-Christian perspectives as well—then each additional life is an incomparable addition to the sum of value. If that is so, then it is no accident that
Christian tradition has tended to place the burden of proof against
limiting the growth-rate. Every potential life which is not in fact permitted to become actual is an immense loss to itself, to God, and to
humanity.

On this basis, the optimum number of people might be the maximum possible number. In our time this would involve an acceptance
and acceleration of the present rapid population growth rates. In due
course, as I have said above, we might well expect the point of population stabilization to appear in the form of disease and famine, possibly along with war and psychological disorders. Such things are
deeply destructive. But disease and famine at least do not involve

human actions depriving potential human beings of the incomparable gift of life itself. Therefore, we seem to have a trade-off between quantity of lives and quality of life, in which an increase in the number of lives will ultimately (through disease and famine) increase suffering and vitiate the quality of life and in which an assured maintenance of better conditions of human existence can only be gained by self-imposed limitations upon the growth rate. But are there any "conditions" which are more deplorable than the condition of never having the chance to be born at all? Can the "quality of life" be used as justification for limiting the number of lives to be born?

A kind of nutritional reduction to absurdity may help to illustrate why it not only can but must. Complete maximization of the possible number of people would finally drive us to the point where the number of calories of food intake would be reduced to the maintenance level. (I cannot enter into the question of what that point would be.) Calories used to do anything other than increase and perpetuate the species would have to be regarded as luxury calories. Those calories might best be used to provide still further lives with the opportunity to exist. Calories used to fuel the enrichment of civilization through the development of the arts, the cultivation of philosophy, or even the preaching of the gospel would have to be considered as detracting from the main enterprise of creating new lives. In short, a kind of biological reductionism would have transformed the whole human enterprise into a deadly serious venture in survival. If one is not willing to accept this *reductio ad absurdum*, there must be *some* point beyond which the "quality" of human life cannot be subordinated to the increasing "quantity" of human lives. How are we to understand this point theologically?

To put this in traditional terminology, it seems to me that our problem is one of relating a Biblical understanding of covenant and grace on the one hand to an understanding of creation on the other. I am greatly influenced here by the well-known way in which Karl Barth has formulated this relationship in speaking of "creation as the external basis of the covenant" and "covenant as the internal basis of creation." God's covenant, his loving relationship with the whole human family, is the meaning of created existence; but created existence is necessary as a precondition for the covenant. Following the general direction indicated by this distinction, it can be said that the whole purpose of created existence is to render possible the coming to realization of God's covenant of love. The structures of created exist-

ence provide the frame of reference, the content, the ground, the substance in and through which "spiritual" life can acquire definiteness
of being. Without created existence, covenant is inconceivable. Without covenant, created existence is meaningless.

Deeper ecological sensitivity, such as that offered by James Logan's
essay in this volume, requires a further observation. To speak of covenant as the meaning of creation is not the same thing as regarding the
whole of reality as man-centered, with everything other than man
solely instrumental to human well-being and fulfillment. We have had
enough of that! If, by faith, we can ascribe the whole of creation to
divine intention, we may equally say that the whole of creation has
a goodness which is celebrated by God and that its goodness is not
dependent upon man. For instance, while the aesthetic richness of a
sunset or a forest does not register with the sunset or the forest themselves, the fact that such things have their existence from God means
that they have their value there and not only in man's perceptions.
The meaning of covenant is that man can perceive all such richnesses
of creation as values which link him not only with the natural world
itself but more importantly with God. Man himself is not independent
of creation. He is a part of it. Nevertheless, he has an apparently
unique capacity to transcend it, to come to a point of consciousness
and sensitivity. Thus, he is not *simply* a part of the natural order, and
it is proper to speak of his capacity for covenant.

How can this perspective be related to the question of optimum
population? The crucial question must always be what kind of relationship between human beings and the physical and social structures
of existence best undergird what God has intended for life in covenant.
Were life purely "spiritual"—whatever that might mean!—the question might be unnecessary; but since life is inescapably bound up in
natural and social structures, it is a question which cannot be avoided.
Thus, it is entirely conceivable that the whole ultimate purpose of
a given life might be frustrated by deprivation of conditions necessary
for its created existence. Beyond a not easily identifiable point, it
would be better that possible lives not be born than that the natural
and social resources of existence should be spread so thin as to deprive
some human beings of the conditions necessary for their fulfilling the
purposes of existence. Creation itself implies limitation. If it is to be
regretted that there cannot be an infinite number of lives, the author
of creation himself bears the responsibility!

All this has implications in relation to economics, politics, and all the forms and structures of man's natural and social existence. I wish here to illustrate the implications mainly from an economic standpoint. It can be argued that if people are best to experience in life the realities of grace and covenant, two conditions are necessary. The first is *security:* a considerable degree of assurance that one will not be lacking in the basic necessities of life in the future—so that one can live with an open, hopeful, attractive prospect and not regard the future basically as danger and threat. Basic economic security is a fitting symbol of the security all men possess in God's gracious love, and it may well be that for many people it is next to impossible to believe in the latter without experiencing the former. The second condition is enough abundance of material resources to liberate life from pure drudgery to creative opportunity. To be in a situation of sufficient abundance is to be freed from excessive manipulation, either by the forces of nature or fellow man. Both security and sufficient abundance help to undergird that freedom which is proper to man's becoming fully responsible.

But I do not believe that such points set aside the belief with which we began—namely, the very great value of each life. A strong presumption must be kept in force in favor of the creation of new life. The burden of proof must be against, not for, the limitation of population. But since, in the real world, unlimited population growth does undermine those conditions necessary for the fulfillment of life, we must at some point consider that the burden of proof has been met. This point may well vary in accordance with changes in technology and, perhaps to some extent in accordance with cultural change, and our perceptions of it will certainly be different. The remaining essays in this volume illustrate differing perceptions, just as they represent differing ways of formulating the basic ethical issues themselves.

1. Thomas C. Lyons, Jr., *Population Policies: A World Overview* (U.S. Agency for International Development, March 1971).

2. *Population and the American Future* (The New American Library, 1972).

3. Cf. Bernard Berelson, "Beyond Family Planning," *Studies in Family Planning* (The Population Council, February 1969), for an excellent summary and critique of the proposals.

4. Henry C. Wallich, "On Population Growth," *Newsweek* (June 29, 1970), p. 70.

5. Joseph J. Spengler, "Population Optima," in Daniel O. Price, ed., *The 99th Hour* (University of North Carolina Press, 1967), p. 31.

6. Wayne H. Davis, "Overpopulated America," in Daniel Callahan, ed., *The American Population Debate* (Doubleday Anchor, 1971), p. 165).

7. S. Fred Singer, "Government Policies," in Singer, ed., *Is There an Optimum Level of Population?* (McGraw-Hill, 1971), p. 552. Spengler is here quoting A. B. Wolfe.

8. Walter Orr Roberts, "There is an Optimum Population Level," in *ibid.*, p. 345.

9. The Population Council, 1971.

2

ALTERNATIVE APPROACHES TO

OPTIMUM POPULATION THEORY

Ralph B. Potter

The term "optimum" may be taken to mean "the amount or degree of something that is most favorable to some end." [1] "Optimum population" would be a population having a size or character most favorable to the proper end of mundane existence, which may be spoken of as "the good life" or "well-being."

Actual population may diverge from the supposed optimum. If all relevant values are incorporated into the definition and calculation of the optimum, any discrepancy between the actual and the optimum population may be seen as a potentially remediable limitation upon well-being. A government dedicated to the fullest well-being of its constituents might, then, be held to be obliged to implement population policies designed to influence demographic processes in a manner calculated to bring the actual and the optimum populations into adjustment. If, however, the optimum is defined in relation to a narrowed set of ends, if it becomes, for example, merely an "economic optimum" or a "national power optimum," rather than a comprehensive "human optimum," the obligation to intervene on a given occasion to achieve a closer approximation of the actual and the optimum population can be forcefully challenged by those who invoke values, ends, or considerations ignored or neglected in the definition of the narrowed versions of the optimum. Critics can then assert the equal or superior importance of elements neglected in any partial definition of the optimum. They may substitute rival limited versions or insist upon the overriding priority of a single higher, more comprehensive account of the "true," or "synthetic," or "integral" optimum purporting to allow a more inclusive and balanced evaluation of the determinants of well-being.

A theory of population functions as a guide to action in the realm of public policy. It is sought as an aid to ranking and selecting policies which influence the terms of human existence at a particular time and place. Interest in optimum population theory is a consequence of the beliefs that demographic processes are open to a degree of manipulation through purposeful intervention and that variations in population size and character thus induced may have bearing upon the wellbeing of men and women.[2]

Optimum population theory is a "pragmatic and frankly normative concept."[3] Its construction requires the completion of intellectual tasks within the normative realm of ethical theory and within the pragmatic sphere guided by social scientific knowledge. Difficult questions are encountered in both domains.

The determination of an optimum can take place only in relation to a given end. The selection of an end entails judgments in the realm of ethics. Elaboration of a theory of optimum population cannot proceed apart from the adoption of some assumptions concerning answers to questions such as: "What is the good life for man in this world?" "What are the conditions conducive to well being?" or "What does a man need to live well?" "Whose well-being ought to be of concern to those formulating policy likely to have an influence upon demographic factors?" "What justifies intervention that may destroy the conditions prerequisite for the realization of certain preferred forms of living well?" "What degree of predictive certainty concerning the longterm consequences of policies should be required of a prudent policy maker?"

The determination of the end of policy is a logically prior task. But once the end is defined, formidable obstacles still present themselves within the domain of social scientific assessment of the probable consequences of alternative courses of policy. "How will specific policies affect various demographic processes?" "How will these demographic processes affect, in turn, the complex, interrelated social, economic, ecological, political, cultural, aesthetic, spiritual, and psychological conditions that together form the environment within which men seek to live well?" "What reciprocal impact will developments in these several realms have upon demographic processes?" "What will be the subsequent, long-term, net effect upon the conditions of life?"

The ethical and the social scientific tasks are both indispensable. They are, moreover, interlinked. When optimum population theorists pose the question, "If we were fewer, or if we were more numerous, should we be better off?",[4] their reply assumes an answer to the ethical question of what it means to be "better off" and projects a social scientific forecast of conditions anticipated under the alternative circumstances of increased or decreased population. In accounting for the past frustrations of optimum population theory and in assessing its future prospects, we must examine more closely the problematic elements encountered in the performance of the ethical task and in the social scientific realm.

The ethical problems confronted by any version of optimum population theory arise out of the necessity of deciding what constitutes human well-being and how best to promote the well-being of those affected by policies designed to influence demographic processes. The possibilities of existence are limited by many restraints, a number of which are aggravated by maladjustment of the number, distribution, age structure, or rate of growth of population in relation to the given circumstances. The effects that may be attributed to demographic factors may be great or small, but, in either case, it makes sense to ask whether the situation would be improved if demographic factors were to be varied this way or that through purposeful intervention. The questions of optimum population theory come to be raised in the context of anticipated intervention designed to change the total circumstances of life through induced variation in the demographic processes that help shape the environment within which men must seek their vision of well-being.

Purposeful change of policies affecting population variables entails the risk that some men will be deprived of the conditions necessary for the realization of their preferred version of the good life. Such harm to the life prospects of some requires justification. It would be arbitrary to bring about changes that may enhance the well-being of some while subverting the well-being of others without the provision of plausible reasons justifying apparently unequal treatment. The idea of justice establishes a baseline of expectation that "beings of one and the same essential category must be treated in the same way." [5] All men are members of the same essential category of "human beings," and, *prima facie*, each man's vision of his well-being constitutes a claim of equal force with all others upon the community to facilitate or at least not to hinder its realization, unless good reasons for some pattern of preferential treatment can be given. The question of optimum population is, at its core, a moral problem. Specifically, it is a problem of justice, concerned with the adjudication and adjustment of "conflicting claims upon the advantages won by social cooperation." [6] If the policies assessed in the framework of optimum population theory were thought to have no effect, or no differential effect upon the prospects of realizing one or another form of well-being, the theory itself would be otiose. But what is at stake in optimum population policy is the question of whose good, and whose version of the good, is to be served by the power of the state and other agencies to influence the circumstances of existence through whatever changes can be effected through population policies.

The nub of the problem underlying various versions of optimum population theory is that different men hold different concepts of what constitutes their own well-being and that of others. They differ in their portrayal of what they need to live well. Any given set of arrangements and conditions enhances the prospects for the attainment of certain forms of well-being and hampers others.[7] Demographic factors influence the conditions of life. The various contending concepts of well-being may be said to have differing demographic prerequisites and implications, prerequisites and consequences so incompatible that the creation of conditions conducive to one version may entail the sacrifice of prospects for that attainment of another. Given this conflict of claims for the opportunity to live out one's preferred mode of living, optimum population theory purports to tell us which population size and character would be "best."

The several varieties of optimum population theory that have been elaborated reflect various ways of coping with the clash among incompatible sets of demographic prerequisites. First, conflict might be reduced if certain of the claims for access to the conditions necessary to implement a particular version of the good life could be disqualified as "unreasonable." In extreme cases such a standard is applied to forestall the implementation of schemes that would allow a tiny minority to monopolize and hoard resources essential for the bare survival of fellow citizens. In light of existing inequalities of distribution within and among nations today, such an invocation of the principles of distributive justice can be brought to bear to disqualify claims to a complacent life of high consumption in a world in which many are malnourished or starving.

A second means of reducing the range of contending claims would be consciously to prefer one or another style of life on explicit grounds, asserting, perhaps, that it represented a more "truly human" manner of existence, or was ordained by God or by custom, or would eventually redound to the benefit of all. The reasons given in support of the preferment might seem plausible in one setting or to one generation while carrying little weight with others.

A third tactic would be to assert that the appraisal of what is truly desirable for members of a community rests not with individuals or groups, who may harbor desires that do not effectively promote their own true interests, but with the "consensus among those who have special qualifications for judging the effect on welfare of the consumption of this or that commodity in this or that quantity."[8] Such an approach rests on the contradiction of the assumption that well-being depends upon maximum economic welfare seen as the maximization of the satisfaction of actual desires. It trades upon the distinction between the desired and the desirable. One can anticipate a widespread reluctance to surrender to some "more competent authority" the capacity to define "what one truly desires."

A fourth approach is to affirm that the good is the satisfaction of rational desire and that social policy is to aim at the greatest possible sum of satisfied desires, regardless of the "quality" or the distribution of the satisfactions. In such a Utilitarian scheme the desires of individuals are conflated into a single coherent system of desire to be pursued as "the social good." A persistent difficulty arises from the inclination to view desires of certain qualities as more worthy of fulfillment than others and from the tendency of most to see the fulfillment of their own desires as constituting an especially worthy cause warranting exceptions from the theoretical indifference to the distribution of goods.

We shall give special attention to a fifth method which can be elaborated from the fourth by narrowing the focus to the needs, wants, and desires common to all reasonable men in an attempt to expand the supply of primary goods which constitute the functional prerequisites for the attainment of virtually every plausible version of a decent mundane existence. An effort is made to sidestep the perennially controversial question of "What is ultimately good for man?" by substituting the question, "What is indispensable for the fulfillment of any likely version of the good life?" Attention is focussed upon the provision of common necessities conducive to, or, at least, not incompatible with any version of well-being. If a solid economic foundation can be established, each individual may embellish as he wishes that which he constructs upon the common economic substructure. Whatever else one may choose to pursue, prospects for attaining the goal will be enhanced by the creation of a strong economic base which will free everyone from enslavement to the niggardliness of nature, multiply powers and options, widen the margin of resources, increase physical security, create the possibility of leisure for "higher pursuits," etc.[9]

The theory of optimum population thus becomes narrowed to the theory of the *economic* optimum of population. The clash among contradictory concepts of the preconditions necessary for the realization of contrasting visions of the good life is submerged by the assumption that increased economic productivity will benefit all and harm none in a manner for which they cannot be compensated. It is enough, therefore, to focus upon "the most productive ratio between population and natural resources. Productivity is to be measured by the *per capita* income of ultimate consumers' goods. This ratio is called the *optimum,* and a population of this most efficient size the optimum population." [10] The theory comes to have a very specific focus: "Optimum theory searches for a maximum output by (hypothetically) varying population size." [11]

The theory of the economic optimum is eminently suited for the purpose of providing seemingly precise directives for policy. The theory is simple in structure and "liberal" in tone. It offers a measurable index of the satisfaction of common wants readily accounted for by observation of the most basic facts of human existence and does not require a probing of the nature and origin of the more elaborate and variable idiosyncratic desires of individuals. Yet, "the notion of the optimum is frankly a utilitarian end and an individualistic concept. It assumes that the function of the economic process is to serve individuals." [12] It allows for the measurement in quantifiable units of changes brought about by purposeful intervention with respect to factors that may be claimed to have significant bearing upon the well-being of every member of the community. The effects of policy can thus be evaluated with the aid of indices that provide simple and quantifiable measurement of "improvement" in relation to a factor that is both open to influence and of decisive import.

The narrowed theory of an economic optimum of population has been subjected to criticism by authors of very diverse orientations who are frequently lumped together as proponents of a "welfare optimum." [13] In preparing his rebuttal to these assorted critics, Manual Gottlieb sketches the nature of their attack: "Among certain circles it has become popular to belittle a 'purely economic optimum'; to search for all sorts of possible conflicts between an output optimum and 'health,' 'spiritual,' 'aesthetic,' and 'ethnic' factors and to 'deepen' the research with sociological considerations. . . . We are warned that the concept of an economic optimum 'is somewhat narrow and partial,' 'fails to appreciate the nature and complexity of human personality and culture.' " [14]

Gottlieb's reply to the "welfare criticisms" indicates the narrowed purpose of the economic optimum:

"[The criticisms] mostly represent a romanticist and nationalist backwash which seeks protective 'scientific' coloration for adherence to conventional or traditional notions. The economic population optimum involves no 'subordination' of ethical or moral values to 'sordid' material welfare or any postulated 'equivalence' of welfare and economics. All that is modestly claimed is that limited productivity universally imposes an actual or potential restraint on economic welfare; that improvements in productivity are desirable; and that the improvements have non-self-reversing effects on welfare. It is not argued that economic productivity cannot be increased by many other means, or that economic welfare cannot be improved with existing productivity, or that the richness and intensity of life could not be raised with constant economic welfare." [15]

It is necessary to differentiate more carefully among the criticisms of the economic optimum and be more precise in discerning the various types of questions critics impose. Few challenge the assumption that improvements in economic productivity are desirable, although many would insist that the assessment of the net advantages of increased production must include a more precise accounting of ecological and human costs. Economic factors are readily recognized as significant determinants of well-being. But, critics aver, they are not decisive. It is possible for individuals and for groups to enjoy a very high level of economic prosperity and to fail to attain well-being. Conversely, others are able to live well at a relatively low level of economic productivity. The most zealous proponent of the theory of the economic optimum would admit that economic development is, at most, a condition and not a guarantee of well-being. Other considerations enter in. The quarrel is concerning what account should be taken of these "other considerations" in the construction of a theory concerning the optimal population for a territory.

Closer examination indicates that there may be two different reasons for taking or not taking account of a particular consideration. A factor held by some to be an important element in a theory designed to guide policy formulation may be neglected by others either because it is held to have insignificant bearing upon the attainment of well-being or because it is thought to be immeasurable. Theorists differ concerning which considerations they assign to the categories of significant and measurable, significant but immeasurable, measurable but insignificant, and immeasurable and insignificant.

Theoretically, all significant factors affecting the conditions of well-being should be taken into account. In practice, however, some con-

siderations acknowledged to be significant are excluded by some theorists because their measurement is elusive and attention to them
would clutter the conceptual apparatus and render its results less statistically certain. The exclusion of some factors acknowledged to have
significant bearing upon well-being is characteristic of every version
of optimum population theory and is not merely a foible of proponents
of the economic optimum of population.[16] The purpose for which a
theory is intended influences its shape. A strong desire to attain statistical precision thought necessary for the immediate guidance of
policy imposes constraints upon the range of considerations that can
be taken into account. Within the category of significant determinants
of well-being, attention comes to be limited to those that are thought
to be at least potentially measurable.

Proponents of the theory of the economic optimum of population
wish to narrow the indices as far as possible, taking, in most cases,
changes in *per capita* real income as the basis for evaluating the effects
of population policies upon the general well-being of a community.
Their critics reply that such an index may permit precise measurement but that what it measures falls so far short of having a decisive
consequence for well-being that assessments of the impact of policy
upon the ultimate goal may be mistaken. They would accept a trade-
off of a decrease in statistical precision for a wider accounting of factors presumed to impinge upon the conditions of well-being. The
debate is about the convenience and accuracy of various indices. The
question is, "What measures best enable one to assess the impact of
policy upon the conditions thought to be conducive to well-being?"
The issue should not be confused with the dispute over what conditions are most conducive to well-being. Presumably, as the state of
the art of measurement improves, more and more factors should be
taken into account in the calculus of the optimum population until
every factor within the category of significant determinants of well-
being has been weighed.

It is ironic that the theory of the economic optimum, frequently
criticized as too narrow and defended against those who would substitute more expanded indices, itself represents a broadening of considerations in relation to earlier inchoate versions of optimum population
theory which focussed only upon the relation of population to food
supply. The economic theory strives to preserve statistical precision
while applying a more comprehensive index of economic welfare, which
is taken to be a crucial determinant of well-being. Lionel Robbins,
a vigorous advocate of the theory of the economic optimum, inveighs

against the "fodder optimum," but presses his point to a paradoxical conclusion:

"It is still possible to hear even educated people discussing the problem of population as though it were only a problem of food supply. . . . The optimum is not a fodder optimum. It has nothing to do with subsistence. On the modern theory an area is over-populated when total returns per head are less than they would be if the population were a little smaller, and this is a point which may be reached long before there is any question of 'pressure on the means of subsistence.' Theoretically it is possible to imagine a community, all of whose members enjoy the standard of life of millionaires, which was yet over-populated in the economic sense. If the elimination of one millionaire would increase returns per head to the efforts of the others, over-population would be present. [17]

Robbins says, in effect, that even though food may be the most basic necessity on the scale of the urgency of wants, men desire many things in addition to food, and since we can measure with the aid of refined economic indices the effect alternative population policies have upon the satisfaction of many of these additional wants, we should take their satisfaction into account in calculating the size of optimal population. "Welfare critics" would urge that strenuous efforts be made to refine indices for elements not yet included in Robbins' accounting and that, in the meantime, an intuitive assessment be substituted for the unavailable statistical measures of factors having significant bearing upon well-being. There is no good reason for limiting the expansion of considerations other than the claim that, given the state of the art of measurement, a particular balance between scope and precision offers the most accurate basis for estimating the effect of population factors upon whatever is held to be of value.

Robbins' conclusion concerning the "overpopulation" of a community all of whose members enjoy the standard of living of millionaires is paradoxical enough to stimulate reflection upon what is meant by the term "overpopulation" and the links between that concept and the idea of an optimum population. Most abstractly, the word "overpopulation" must mean something like "a circumstance in which a value held dear is jeopardized by effects attributed to demographic factors." The term binds together ethical affirmations concerning what is of value and social scientific analyses of the source of deleterious effects upon that which is valued. For a consistent theorist, the value jeopardized in the state of overpopulation would be the same as that sought through the establishment of an optimum population. In speaking of the optimum, the theorist says to the policy maker: "Choose policies that will bring demographic effects most favorable to value X." On particular occasions he might declare, "A state of over-population (or, perforce, underpopulation) now exists because value X is jeopardized by demographic effects." Similar problems of social scientific and ethical analysis confront the theorist in defining and applying either the concept of "overpopulation" or "optimum population." The problems are to isolate the influence of population factors and to justify policies designed to influence demographic processes in light of the possibility that other variables may be more significant determinants of well-being and less costly targets of intervention.

For the social scientist, increased analytical sophistication has made it more difficult to have confidence in the capacity to isolate and measure the specific effects that demographic factors have either in shaping the conditions within which value X is to be optimized or in generating the pressures which jeopardize value X in the state of "overpopulation." Sharpened awareness of the interrelatedness of demographic, economic, ecological, social, psychological, cultural, and religious factors has destroyed the theoretical simplicity of the centuries-long debate among those who supposed that population size and rate of change were dominant determinants of social and economic existence and exercised an inherent and constant influence for good or for ill upon the condition of societies.[18] Given a fuller appreciation of the reciprocal interrelatedness of a widened set of demographic factors with an indefinite number of non-demographic variables, it becomes exceedingly difficult to trace any change in the conditions of life back to a specific demographic cause. The effects of demographic factors vary according to the influence of the manifold non-demographic elements with which they are interlinked. A given type of change in any set of demographic processes can have no single, knowable effect predictable apart from knowledge of the full constellation of impinging factors.

Fuller acknowledgment of the interrelatedness of demographic and non-demographic factors diminishes the independent effect that can be ascribed to policies aimed at influencing demographic variables. In light of such awareness, the optimum population must be seen as being highly volatile, capable of fluctuating more rapidly than actual population as a result of changes in economic variables such as the level of technology, the quality of natural resources, the distribution of goods, patterns of domestic economic organization, the terms of foreign trade, the capacities of the work force, and habits of consumption, plus modifications in countless non-economic factors that may vary independently. Most population policies require a long period of time to have full effect. It is risky to implement sharp changes in population policy in quest of the conditions that will optimize value X unless the many other factors that contribute to the formation of the total environment can be reasonably well forecast.[19]

In performing the social scientific task of optimum population theory the analyst encounters difficulty in forecasting the specific effects that population policies may have in interaction with all other significant determinants of the condition of society within which men must seek their version of the good life. In dealing with the question of overpopulation, a parallel problem is met in the elaboration of a *post factum,* causal analysis of the role demographic maladjustments may have played in the creation of circumstances that menace value X. What evidence can support the assumption that demographic factors are the predominant cause of the undesired state and the inference that demographic change is the most obvious "cure"? What makes it more reasonable to refer to a particular circumstance as "overpopulation" rather than "productive insufficiency," "uncharitable maldistribution," or simply, "injustice"?

In the development of optimum population theory it has been recognized that the isolation and estimate of the effects of demographic variables requires either the empirically false assumption that all other possible determinants of the condition of society have relatively insignificant effect or a resort to the hypothetical formula, *ceteris paribus,* enabling one to say, "Other things being equal, value X would be enhanced if the following adjustments were to be made in demographic processes . . ." A similar artificial freezing of other determinants, which allows one to be systematically inattentive to the significance of the non-demographic factors shaping an undesired situation, is a generally unacknowledged feature of many diagnoses of "overpopulation," which say, in effect, "Given the way things are arranged, value X is jeopardized by the effects of certain demographic processes." Such a statement is not a simple, "value-free," "social scientific" utterance. The special prominence that the term "overpopulation" gives to demographic factors needs to be justified in light of the actual interrelatedness of demographic, economic, social, political, religious, cultural, psychological and other variables in the causal nexus which forms society at any point in time.

Focus of attention upon demographic factors as the predominant cause and cure of the jeopardy of value X may be a consequence of a supposition that other determinants are more firmly fixed and less open to purposeful manipulation than demographic processes. Supposing that the most effective point of intervention is in relation to demographic factors, theorists may reason backwards to discover the demographic "causes" of maladjustments. The use of the term "overpopulation" to characterize a situation tends to discourage analysis of the causal effects of non-demographic variables and to restrict the capacity to envision the extent to which adjustment might come about through changes in elements that need not be frozen under assumptions concerning "the way things are arranged." A different manner of characterizing a situation would bring to the forefront of consciousness potentially variable elements other than demographic processes.

Application of the label "overpopulation" to a situation actually formed by the intricate interaction of innumerable processes has the important moral consequence of focussing past and future responsibility upon local inhabitants. "Overpopulation" implies that their procreative habits are the determinative factor in generating the undesired circumstances and the ineluctable barrier to a successful intervention by others. Use of the term invites a train of reasoning that reduces the responsibility of all outsiders to make significant sacrifices for the sake of proffering aid: demographic factors are the decisive determinants of the situation; decision upon demographic events properly rests with couples in the afflicted region; therefore, there is little we as outsiders can do; hence, we may continue in good conscience to enjoy our relative comfort.

The more decisive demographic factors are seen to be on "social scientific" grounds, the less prospect there seems to be for ameliorating the situation through changes in non-demographic factors. Outsiders may, in fact, have many means of temporary or more permanent relief at their disposal. In particular circumstances, the shipment of food supplies, permission of migration, aid in the development of means of production and other conventional proposals might be put into effect. Or, a variety of more radical responses might be made, some of which might require sacrifice of economic goods by more affluent societies, a blurring of customary beliefs concerning the relation between national boundaries and obligation to assist, a leveling of standards of living throughout the world, an increase in economic and political interdependence, and other significant changes in "the way things are arranged."

As long as any combination of changes in non-demographic factors could bring about a reduction in the jeopardy to value X, it is reasonable to argue that the situation should be described not as one of "overpopulation" but as "unjust distribution," "arbitrary restraint of migration and exchange," "reactionary nationalism," "selfish unconcern for others," "limited moral sympathy," etc. Each label focusses attention upon a particular set of presumed determinants and presents implicit recommendations concerning the factors that ought to be changed in the search for correctives. Such labels shape awareness; they operate as pointers locating possible points of change. Their application is likely to stimulate controversy. But quarrels over the appropriateness of the labels employed to describe a situation in which value X is threatened serve to expose the network of hidden assumptions that underlie the formulation and application of the term "overpopulation" and the concept of an optimum population.

Once it is noted that there are many things that might be done to relieve the jeopardy to value X in a circumstance popularly designated as one of "overpopulation," reasons for doing or not doing particular acts must be given. If the question is pressed persistently, "Why do we not do this?" the giving of reasons will eventually make it clear that an entire constellation of beliefs touching all the elements of a philosophy of life is necessary to sustain a seemingly simple diagnosis of "overpopulation." Debate concerning the most appropriate manner of characterizing a situation and what should or should not be done in response to it rapidly extends beyond the boundaries of any single discipline or area of competence. Disputants must assess demographic and other social scientific findings, define the limits of loyalty and obligation with the aid of political philosophy, weigh claims arising from moral principles and duties, and reflect upon the more ultimate context shaping the nature and destiny of man.

A demonstration that a particular form of intervention by A to relieve the unhappy symptoms of "overpopulation" in the territory of B would entail a sharp decline in the standard of living of A, a disruption of established economic and political relationships, or some other set of "costs," does not settle the question as to whether or not these policies should be implemented and the cost paid for the sake of aiding even an improvident neighbor. If people persist in asking, "Why do we not do these things?" discussion must eventually be

driven to the boundary of philosophical, religious, or theological interpretation of human existence which provides the framework within
which what is good and obligatory for men must finally be assessed.
To attempt to disallow such reflection as "irrelevant," "superstitious,"
"pre-Newtonian," or "unscientific," is to assume a particular "religious" stance based on indemonstrable convictions concerning the
range of factors impinging upon human life. In the face of persistent
inquiry into the bases for preferring one set of actions to another,
there is no reasonable means of evading "religious discourse." One's
entire "worldview" is eventually submitted to scrutiny.

When actual policy choices must be made, choices that redistribute
benefits and costs among men who disagree upon what constitutes
well-being, the futility of the attempt to evade the necessity of expli-
cating the premises sustaining the concept of "overpopulation" and
theories of optimum population becomes evident. It is not enough to
know that a policy would be most favorable to a particular end or
value. We need to know what would be most favorable to an entire
schedule of ends that include all of the significant aspects of well-
being. Robbins' vivid illustration of the economic optimum, previously cited, sharpens the point: "Theoretically it is possible to
imagine a community, all of whose members enjoy the standard of
life of millionaires, which was yet over-populated in the economic
sense. If the elimination of one millionaire would increase returns per
head to the efforts of the others, over-population would be present." [20]
Are we to conclude that a conscientious citizen, concerned that the
"best" state of affairs should be reached, should forthwith assassinate
one or more of the millionaires? If not, why not? The circumstance
Robbins describes may represent overpopulation "in the economic
sense." That informs us that, within the limited, partial perspective
of economic concern, the existing situation is not optimal. But if
other human concerns, such as the desire to be secure from threat of
assassination for economic motives, are taken into account, the situation might prove, on balance, to be the best obtainable at the moment. We must look far beyond the particular economic optimum to
discover the bases for rational decision concerning concrete policy
issues.

The debate that was to be narrowed bursts open again when it
becomes necessary to weigh important human concerns that are incommensurable in relation to a simple economic standard. There are
obvious restraints upon the single-minded realization of the economic

optimum, restraints created by the persistence of human concern for non-economic interests. In the history of debate concerning optimum population theory many of these concerns have been advanced as correctives and crystallized as rival criteria of optimum population. The result has been a cacophony of "criteria." In completing the formula, "Other things being equal, value X would be enhanced if the following adjustments were to be made in demographic processes . . ." theorists have nominated for the role of value X concerns such as happiness, individual welfare, health and long life, the development of character, eugenic selection, ecological integrity, national economic or political or military power and prestige, religious or ethnic interests, employment, man-hour productivity, real wages per capita, per capita consumption, real income per capita, the standard of living, beauty, an economy of nature in which life is not wasted by high birth and high death rates.[21] Lately, the phrase "quality of life" has served as a vague successor to earlier efforts to formulate criteria for a "synthetic optimum of population."

These goods, variously and confusedly referred to in the literature of optimum population theory as "goals," "aims," "ends," criteria," "values," represent "other considerations" it would be foolish to ignore totally in formulating policy designed to create conditions most favorable to well-being. The optimum theorist says to the policy maker: "Chose policies that will bring demographic effects most favorable to value X." The identity of value X may differ. But there are logical restraints upon what can function as a plausible candidate for value X. It must be a value so important in some coherent view of the world that one can reasonably recommend policy measures designed to influence population size, distribution, character, or rate of change on its behalf, mindful that such policies will entail, to a greater or lesser degree, disappointment of existing expectations and new restraints upon established liberties. A sense of proportionality rules out trivial claimants. Value X must be weighty enough to offset whatever harm is wrought by the implementation of policies designed for its promotion. The only source of such weight can be the contribution the advancement of value X will make to well-being. The choice of value X cannot be totally capricious. The only reason that can be given to support its crucial role in the definition of overpopulation and the determination of optimum population is its immediate and decisive bearing upon welfare.

Even with such restraints, a variety of candidates have been put forward as rival claimants to the status of that which the policy maker should seek first to advance in formulating population policies. It is not possible to be certain as to whether advocates have had clearly in mind the claims they wish to make for the value they have proposed. With regard to each and every item on the list of contending values, it is sensible to say that a policy maker should take this consideration into account. The necessary social scientific calculations demonstrating which demographic characteristics will be most favorable to a particular value will be easier in some instances and more difficult in others. But the demographic features most favorable to per capita real income, say, may be highly unfavorable for the attainment of military prestige and power. Or, that which serves a strong ethnic interest in a situation in which intense intergroup rivalry is compounded by highly disparate rates of differential fertility may clash with the fullest realization of individual welfare. The policy maker needs to know not simply what population characteristics would be optimal for this or that particular value, but what relative weight he should assign to each of these several values in planning his course within specific circumstances. Theories that yield many optima yield none that is useful.

A partial, narrow argument concerning the economic optimum or any other particular optimum of population can provide only a partial, narrow guideline for policy, a guideline that is always vulnerable to being challenged and overridden by a more comprehensive account of the nature of well-being, the conditions conducive to it, and the effect of population policies upon the diverse factors influencing those conditions. Optimum population theory must ultimately deal with what is "humanly best" in particular circumstances and not merely with what is generally best in an economic, aesthetic, eugenic, military, or any other partial perspective.[22]

A concise statement of the besetting problem of optimum population theory is given inadvertently by Radhakamal Mukerjee in his book, *The Political Economy of Population*: "As we rise from level to level, from the ecologic through the economic to man's institutional and ethical environment, the adjustment of numbers yields different kinds of optima, both from the standpoint of the individual and that of society. These have to be harmonised in order that we may have a sound population policy. The problem is not only the reconciliation of the individual and the social optimum, but also of working out a compromise between ecologic, economic and ethical ends. The quality of the population, the stability of resources, the continuity of employment, the standard of comfort as well as national

security and individual happiness have all to be safeguarded in popu-
uation planning." [23]

The above passage restates the classical issues of political and ethical philosophy. All that is relevant to problems in those areas bears
also upon a theory of optimum population that does not take refuge
in the device of estimating what would be "optimum in this particular sense" while leaving unanswered the question of how this particular concern is to be weighted by a policy-maker acting in specific
circumstances in a manner calculated to affect the well-being of
many men of diverse philosophies and aspirations.

Mukerjee goes on to construct a concept of the "integral optimum"
and delimit its utility:

"Accordingly the true optimum of population is the integral optimum which is based, as we shall find, on a harmonious co-ordination
of the optima in the successive levels of ecology, economy and state
in respect of (a) the expectation of life, (b) personal happiness and
self-expression,—all these from the individual standpoint, and of (a)
the stability of the economic base and occupational balance, (b) the
regularity and continuity of employment, and (c) national security,
and power,—all of the latter from the collective standpoint.

"Such an integral optimum is, however, a mere hypothesis or a
social aspiration. It is a problem for the economic and social order.
The ecologic and the economic optima can be quantitatively expressed and measured. But not the integral optimum. The realistic
integral optimum numbers cannot be precisely determined since several factors which determine this optimum and also the trend of
population are imponderable and immeasurable. Besides there is in
the whole process a mutual dependence of causes and effects." [24]

Mukerjee's delineation of the elements of the "integral optimum"
and parallel efforts to define a "synthetic optimum" invite the question as to why just these considerations should be drawn together.
A strong element of intuition binds the elements of such theories
together. If the ecologist's intuition of what constitutes a relevant
consideration differs from that of the economist, or the military
leader, or the artist, or the ethicist, or the rabbi, who then is the
expert to whom appeal shall be made concerning the proper identity
of value X? The definition of the "integral optimum," which is that
which is important for policy decisions, is, finally, a political enterprise in which knowledge of the particular optima most favorable to
this or that special concern may or may not play a significant role in

determining the choice arrived at by whatever clumsy processes govern political decisions in a given society.

The guidance to be gained for policy making from any and all versions of optimum population theory has been so meager for so many decades that one must account for the periodic revival of interest in the concept. It may be that the theory recurs because it is a useful antidote to simplistic, dogmatic teachings which attribute a consistently good or universally evil consequence to population change of one type or another. The optimum theory requires a case by case examination and evaluation of the effects of population changes. It permits no rigid certainties concerning the beneficial or harmful results of particular population policies. It bars all demographic panaceas. The *locus classicus* of the theory of the economic optimum, set forth by Edwin Cannan in 1888 in his volume, *Elementary Political Economy*, exhibits the polemical utility of all versions of optimum population theory:

"It is not true that an increase of industry or that a decrease of population must always increase the productiveness of industry. No more is it true that an increase in population must always increase the productiveness of industry, or that a decrease of population must always diminish it. The truth is that the productiveness of industry is sometimes promoted by an increase of population and sometimes by a decrease of population." [25]

E. P. Hutchinson concludes his lengthy survey of *The Population Debate* with the following observation concerning the theoretical importance of optimum population theory and its limitation:

"Another by-product of the new development was a resolution of the old theoretical debate, whether the socio-economic consequences of a large and growing population are beneficial or harmful. According to the new optimum theory, the problem does not really exist, for population growth may be desirable under some conditions, undesirable under others. Whereas previous theory had regarded population and its growth as forces having an inherent and constant influence, now it appeared that the significance of population varies with time and place. . . . The optimum theory was a step toward a fuller appreciation of the population problem but it left unanswered the question of the conditions in which population growth is beneficial and in which it is harmful." [26]

Optimum population theory has left the most important questions "unanswered" because among the elements logically implied in the theory are ethical and philosophical questions that are unanswerable in the logic and framework of discussion of the natural and social sciences. It is necessary to back up and think again in light of traditions of religious and ethical thought concerning what constitutes an "answer" to questions concerning what is best for men. Optimum population theory has been left mainly in the hands of economists. The issues logically entailed cannot be dealt with adequately in terms of the underlying ethical categories most economists have taken over from utilitarian moral philosophy. The major forms of optimum population theory thus far advanced are dependent upon the promise of utilitarian logic to render all human claims commensurable in relation to a single common principle. Optimum population theory needs what utilitarianism seems to offer: 1) a non-transcendental, secular account of moral reasoning plausibly suited to guide policy reflection in a pluralistic society; 2) a seemingly unproblematic interpretation of the basic aim of life as consisting in happiness; 3) a moral logic by which apparent controversy may, in principle, be removed by social scientific calculation of the empirical consequences of proposed policies; and 4) a single norm of the greatest good for the greatest number which forestalls the possibility of the existence of two valid but irreconcilable claims and permits the assumption that there will always be a single policy which, on balance, is the best thing to do on the whole in the given circumstances.[27]

The problems that have proved intractable for utilitarianism also subvert the utility of the several versions of optimum population theory: men persist in pursuing visions of their own well-being that cannot be reduced to a common term permitting comparability, calculation, and conflation into a single optimum. They affirm incommensurable values that have conflicting demographic prerequisites and consequences. Utilitarianism does not provide a reasonable, noncircular basis for narrowing the range of desires and claims that must be respected. The further development of optimum population theory must await clarification of the elements of ethical theory that form the core of reflection upon what is "most favorable."

1. *Webster's Seventh New Collegiate Dictionary* (G. and C. Merriam Company, 1963), p. 593.

2. The intended bearing of optimum population theory upon policy is well expressed by Hugh Dalton in speaking of the relationship of optimum population (O) to actual

population (A): "Since there is no natural harmony between the movements of our two variables O and A, our practical aim must be a harmony deliberately contrived. It is obvious that A may be controlled to some extent by deliberate policy, especially as regards the number of new births, which policy may either stimulate or depress, and as regards migration. It is less obvious, but true, that O also may be influenced in the future by present policy." Hugh Dalton, "The Theory of Population," *Economica*, (March, 1928), p. 45.

3. Manuel Gottlieb, "Optimum Population, Foreign Trade and World Economy," *Population Studies*, III (1949-50), p. 151.

4. Dalton, p. 31.

5. Chaim Perelman, *The Idea of Justice and the Problem of Argument* (London: Routledge and Kepan Paul, 1963), p. 16. The search for reasons justifying changes intended to improve circumstances may well serve to expose injustice in existing arrangements that discriminate unfairly against the prospects of attaining certain aspirations of well-being while preferring others without evident due cause.

6. John Rawls, *A Theory of Justice* (Harvard University Press, 1971), p. 16.

7. For an application of cost-benefit analysis to the problem of the redistribution of benefits and burdens through changes of values, see Nicholas Rescher, "What is Value Change? A Framework for Research," in *Values and the Future: The Impact of Technological Change on American Values*, Kurt Baier and Nicholas Rescher, editors (The Free Press, 1969), pp. 68-109.

8. E. F. Penrose, *Population Theories and Their Application: With Special Reference to Japan* (Palo Alto: Food Research Institute, Stanford University, 1934), p. 75. For a critique of Penrose, see Manuel Gottlieb, "The Theory of Optimum Population for a Closed Economy," *The Journal of Political Economy*, (December, 1945), p. 294f.

9. John Maynard Keynes notes that Alfred Marshall, the most influential economist of the early twentieth century, "never departed explicitly from the Utilitarian ideas which dominated the generation of economists which preceded him." There is, according to Keynes, no passage in Marshall's works "in which he links economic studies to any ethical doctrine in particular. The solution of economic problems was for Marshall not an application of the hedonistic calculus, but a prior condition of the exercise of man's higher faculties, irrespective, almost, of what we mean by 'higher.' The possibility of progress 'depends in a great measure upon facts and inferences, which are within the province of economics; and this it is which gives to economic studies their chief and their highest interest.' This remains true even though the question also 'depends partly on the moral and political capabilities of human nature; and on these matters the economist has no special means of information; he must do as others do, and guess as best he can.'" John Maynard Keynes, "Alfred Marshall: 1842-1924," in *Essays and Sketches in Biography* (Meridian Books, 1956), pp. 46f.

10. A. B. Wolfe, "The Optimum Size of Population," Chapter V in *Population Problems in the United States and Canada*, Louis Dublin, editor (Houghton Mifflin, 1926), p. 68.

11. Gottlieb, "The Theory of Optimum Population for a Closed Economy," p. 297.

12. Wolfe, p. 68f.

13. See, for example, Imre Ferenczi, *The Synthetic Optimum of Population: An Outline of an International Demographic Policy* (International Institute of Intellectual Co-operation, League of Nations, 1938), pp. 48ff.

14. Gottlieb, "The Theory of Optimum Population for a Closed Economy," p. 295ff.

15. *Ibid.*

16. H. P. Fairchild, a "welfare critic" of the theory of the economic optimum argued that the optimum should be defined in terms of the "standard of living" and that "the content of the phrase should be restricted to material, tangible goods that are susceptible of observation and measurement, ignoring all those spiritual or intellectual enjoyments which however important, have no material basis and therefore are not susceptible of exact treatment. I therefore suggest, as a definition of the standard of living, simply the average level of comfort, including all material goods from the barest necessaries to the most elaborate luxuries, enjoyed by the people (most helpfully considered in family units) of a given society at a given time." H. P. Fairchild, "Optimum Population," in *Proceedings of the World Population Conference*, Margaret Sanger, editor (London: Edward Arnold and Company, 1927), p. 75.

17. Lionel Robbins, "The Optimum Theory of Population," in *London Essays in Economics: In Honour of Edwin Cannan*, T. E. Gregory and Hugh Dalton, editors (London: George Routledge and Sons, 1927), pp. 103-34, p. 120.

18. E. P. Hutchinson, *The Population Debate: The Development of Conflicting Theories up to 1900* (Houghton Mifflin, 1967), p. 450f.

19. For an example of a pessimistic view concerning forecasting and an indication of the consequences it has upon one's orientation to optimum population theory, see D. E. C. Eversley, "The Special Case, Managing Human Population Growth," Chapter VIII in *The Optimum Population for Britain* (Proceedings of a Symposium held at the Royal Geographical Society, London, on September 25 and 26, 1969), Symposia of the Institute of Biology, No. 19, L. R. Taylor, editor (London: Academic Press, 1970), pp. 103-116, especialy pp. 104f.

20. Robbins, p. 120.

21. For an example of an alternative list of the "various possible aims," see Alfred Sauvy, *General Theory of Population*, Christophe Campos, translator (Basic Books, 1969), p. 37-38.

22. Léon Buquet draws a distinction between the particular, partial, narrow concept of the optimum, illustrated by "the economic optimum," and the general optimum: "Avec la notion *d'optimum particulier de population*, il s'agit de trouver la relation qui existente entre la densité et la fin retenue: le bien-être individuel, par example. Nous nous trouvons alors en présence d'un probleme scientifique: une fin étantpréalablement proposée, l'esprit doit determiner l'organisation des moyens la mieux propre a l'atteindre. Au contraire, la notion *d'optimum général de population* met en jeu le choix des fins; elle implique un judgement de valeur; avec elle, nous quittons le plan strictement scientifique pour rencontrer celui du normatif." Léon Buquet, *L'Optimum de Population, Pragma*, VI (Paris: Presses Universitaires de France, 1956), p. 12.

23. Radhakamal Mukerjee, *The Political Economy of Population* (Longmans, Green, 1943), p. 13f.

24. Mukerjee, pp. 16f.

25. Quoted in Robbins, p. 114.

26. Hutchinson, pp. 405-406. See also pp. 392-393.

27. Bernard Williams, *Morality: An Introduction to Ethics* (Harper Torchbooks, 1972), pp. 90-93.

3

A THEOLOGICAL PERSPECTIVE

CHARLES C. WEST

It is always risky to comment from a theological perspective on an analysis which claims only to be an exercise in analytical logic. Differences in the method of two disciplines are too easily confused with disagreements on substance. Nevertheless, for the sake of deeper understanding, I shall take the risk.

In his essay, Dr. Potter wrestles with an insoluble problem on two levels. One level leads to a shrewd, sober, and I believe Christian insight. The other leads to a dead end. The problem is an adequate theory of optimum population. It is insoluble because the quantifiable elements in it, however many variables a computer can absorb, are subordinate to the qualitative decisions to be made on the level of cultural, religious, psychological, ecological or esthetic values. To discuss these qualitative choices, however, leads one into ideological conflicts which no science can reduce to a common denominator. Potter points out that this dilemma exists, but he does not take us into the realm of the qualitative. Instead he pulls back and suggests that policy makers be guided by a relative, experimental perception of the greatest good for the greatest number in a given situation. This is wise for theological among other reasons. Unfortunately he clothes this insight in utilitarian rationalism, as if its moral logic were somehow after all a *deus in machina*, a god in the machine which would always produce the best policy for the circumstances. Of all religious illusions, this one is the least functional.

In what follows I shall try to build on Dr. Potter's positive insight, using Christian theological resources to raise a few of the substantive issues which he left untouched. The result will not be an "optimum theory of population," but it may suggest a style by which we might live creatively with the insoluble.

First, the question of who holds the power. There is a tendency in American life to blur the distinction between public power undergirded by coercive force—the political power of the government—and the subtler forces of social attitudes and communities. Whose concept of optimum population is at stake here? An official commission has reported to the United States Congress on the subject. There has been much discussion of government-sponsored population policies in developing countries. Behind much thinking on this subject is the assumption that somehow the holders of coercive power in society must do something to limit or redistribute population, and that it is the task of the ethicist to advise them in making laws to this effect and enforcing them. This gets us theologically into the whole question of the role and limits of political power in realizing (or hindering) the promise of God for the community as a whole, which it is the church's task to discern and make known.

Let me come straight to the point on this issue. I believe that the Biblical-theological tradition of the Christian faith, after battling over this question for centuries, stands today shoulder to shoulder with the advocates of civil liberties in affirming sharp limits on the right of political powers to determine the ethos or the personal decisions and commitments of society as a whole. A government agency may *have* a policy of optimum population as a guide to such actions as it may take, just as it should have a positive vision of social justice or of world peace which it is pursuing. But this policy will be just one ideology among many possible ones. Government's task is not to *enforce* allegiance to one view of the good society, or of optimum population which is an element thereof, not even its own view which may have been approved by a majority of the people. When it attempts this, it usurps religious functions and moves toward totalitarianism. It is called by God to experiment with realizing justice among its people in relative ways, and with guiding principles of whose possible bias it must be constantly aware. It must use the coercive force at its disposal in such a way as to enlarge the areas of freedom and to provide the means whereby government power may be opposed, challenged and corrected. In the realm of population policy the tension between the majority and minority groups in our own country is an obvious case in point. Government has the task of policing the marketplace of societal tensions so that no group enslaves another by the use of private power, by denying hospital facilities for a legal abortion for instance, or contrariwise by forcing a doctor to perform an abortion against his conscience. It has the positive task of encouraging forms of community to emerge which do not rest on coercion, and of encouraging people toward the responsible exercise of their freedom.

Second, given these limits on what government may do, what is the role of the church (non-Christians may insert here whatever community of ultimate meaning they belong to) in forming the attitudes and communities that will bring about an optimum population? One cannot face this question without beginning with the problem of the relation between the value of human life as such to the quality of human life. What makes human life *human*? Wherein lies the image of God in human beings? Overpopulation may reach the point where this humanness, this image of God, is practically obscured, and in our age it will be human sin, not fate, nature, or Divine Providence which will be responsible if it does. It is we who have intervened in the age-old cycle of life and death by our technology, our medicine, and our biology.

The theological starting point I suggest here may seem to be at odds with much of traditional Christian and Jewish piety, yet it is, I believe, Biblical. The individual human life as such is *not* an absolute value. The image of God does not reside there. God created the physical environment including human life. It glorifies God to be sure, but in its cycle of life and death, and in the order of its processes. Man comes into existence as a living soul when God calls him. It is the relationship established by this calling that communicates the image of God. Karl Barth suggests that the first created illustration of this image is in the relationship between two inescapably different human beings, man and woman. Calling means that that which was merely biological becomes spiritual. Human beings gain a destiny, a direction, an area of relationships with each other to explore and develop. This is what it means for man and woman to live. The more they truly live in this relationship—with one another, and with God—the more their lives have an eternal quality and death becomes something not to be feared.

From this starting point, if we accept it, some consequences follow:

What makes human life human is the covenant which we enter in response to the calling of God. To be human is to live in relationships by which one's whole being is defined and redefined as one explores them, relationships which no human authority can circumscribe. No state, no ideology, nationalist or universal, no tyranny of economic power or any other human instance may use its coercion to force a limiting structure on humanity. Even God himself refused to use his power this way. Faced with human rejection and unfaithfulness to both calling and covenant, he came incarnate and powerless into human life to call men again and re-establish the relation. Out of this the Christian church was born and from the triumph of this covenant it lives and gives hope to the world.

This means that the attitudes and decisions out of which an optimum population policy will emerge must be formed in the covenantal communities of today's society, Christian or otherwise. They must come out of the way people understand themselves through their relationships with one another in mutual affirmation and support. They must grow from the meaning of life and its promise which people discover in dialogue with one another. If these covenantal communities are not there, or if they are self-enclosed units at war with others, no coercive power on earth can create them or enforce any vision of social justice or population policy. Nor can any logical calculus of the greatest happiness for the greaest number find a policy everyone will accept. If they are there, political power may reinforce some of them and weaken others, according to some rational standard. Dr. Potter's utilitarianism is then one option among others. But then the question arises whether reason and power do not unite to give special meaning to some lives at the expense of others, and to place some lives in the system of "happiness" and "meaning" dominated by others. It is the task of the church in this field of tensions to be a covenantal community which questions all the others and opens them up to their true humanness in the calling of God. The people of God, as Isaiah says, are called to offer a covenant to all the "nations," that is, to all those groups in the world which organize themselves into closed systems.

The image of God that makes human life human is expressed in a limitation that lies not at the periphery of life—out where human strength gives out—but right at its center. The other—first God, then the other human being—confronts a man (or a woman) in every moment. He (or she) is defined by this other, discovers what it means to be human in relation to him or her. God gives form to man by limiting him, and in this limitation and out of this form comes the freedom to be a person. Once again, no human authority can provide this limit. This is the meaning of the inevitably individualistic tenor of civil rights. But it does mean that to bring a child into the world and not care for it is disobedience to God. The image of God is developed in the freedom men and women discover in accepting the limits of their finitude, their mutual dependence, their very existence in response to the calling and command and gift of God, as grace and promise, not as restriction.

This means for society that the network of social relationships that form a child growing up, the channels of love and care, of faithfulness and truth which explain to him who he is *with* others, must be the matrix out of which a population policy must grow. Individualistic dogmas which tear this network and collectivist powers that regiment it, both undermine a responsible approach to childbearing. The church's task is to express the freedom which God's limitation of man brings to this network, over against all human absolutes.

There is nowhere in the Bible an unlimited right of human procreation. There are indeed blessings on children and many offspring are a part of the promise of God to Abraham and others in the Old Testament. But having children is a particular calling *not* a general right. It is subject to the first determination of humanity which is to live in and explore the covenantal relation in response to God's promise and command. To have children in another context is of course "natural," whatever that word may mean. But there is a poignant insight in the story of the expulsion of Adam and Eve from Eden, which places the birth of the first children in that "natural" setting outside paradise, in sorrow and pain, and resulting in the fratricidal strife of Abel with Cain. How may children become a blessing? By being born in response to God's command and promise says the Hebrew Bible, to people who give absolute priority to their response to God, not to home and family as such.

The New Testament way of dramatizing this is to point out, contrary to Jewish as well as pagan views of the time, that the promise of God is not tied to the genetic continuity of a race. Not the people as such, but Christ alone, is the fulfillment of the promise. The people of God are therefore to grow and spread over the earth not by having children, but by evangelism—by offering the covenant in God's name to the nations. In this new family and household of God, not dependent on biological relations, children may be welcome and blessed. The calling of fatherhood and motherhood is given honor. But the vocation of celibacy is also recognized, and the single woman has a place never before given her. Love between man and woman in marriage is given its own status and dignity as a reflection of the image of God, not subordinated to the procreative function. To have children may be a calling and a gift. It is not a desperate necessity on which the meaning of life depends.

This new orientation led to the most effective population control in history—in the late Roman Empire. It was exaggerated and overdone. The balance of New Testament insight was distorted by a neo-Platonic abhorrence of sex and exaltation of virginity. Today we are experiencing a justified revolt against that distortion. But the church today once again has the task of reminding human families and communities that life's meaning depends first upon the relation to God in the household of faith and that no one has a "right" to have a child apart from that relation and that community; though of course, once again, no human authority may usurp the Divine place and dictate who shall and shall not procreate.

The world and the church face an eschatological problem, in relation to population policy. If the vehicle of our hope is not the procreation of the race, what is that vehicle? The early Christians believed the eschaton to be much nearer than it was. Later Christians turned toward the dualism of a heaven above this world which made the question of the human future less acute. Today we are back in the this-worldly Hebrew-Christian context, placing our hope in the future, even when we believe in a transcendant God. Our society indeed lives with a kind of paradox: those who are most actively engaged in realizing the future, determining the form of society in spheres ranging from theology through politics, business, and professions to the sciences, tend to have fewer children. It is other people's children whose future they are planning. There is a parable in this. It is a New Testament spirit. The difficulty is that we have not extended the community of our covenant to include many groups of people who are producing the mass of the next generation. Increasing numbers of children are being born into families, or to people, who cannot care for them adequately, often because of the unjust social conditions in which they live. The attitudes of the next generation are being formed in isolation from much of the future planning which is going on, and often in resentful antagonism to it. Can the church break through this barrier? How can we translate the promise of the future which the elite are planning into hope for the children of tomorrow where they are? This requires eschatological faith, because death is involved—the death of our kind of world and our kind of people, and the surrender of the world to others. As middle and upper class professionals and as Christians we had better ask ourselves how we find God's promise in being a light to these Gentiles.

• One example of this tension is a differing attitude in different classes toward security. One of the criteria of optimum population is assumed to be the security—the assurance of survival—of those to be born. But it does not work this way in many a poor urban environment. Social workers cluck their tongues at the irresponsibility of mothers who keep on having children, whether married or unmarried. Suburbs quake at the population explosion down there. But a look at the Biblical story reveals an odd perspective on this.

Security has a very low priority in the history of the people of God. Abram was called to go out from his father's land, home, family, not knowing whither he went. And most dramatically, every Christmas we celebrate the story of a child born in a stable, while the parents were on a journey no woman nine months pregnant should have undertaken, at the dictate of a distant emperor. This family was forced a few days later to flee for its life to a strange country and to return to its home only some time—perhaps a year or two—later. Perhaps earlier generations, empathized with that story better than we. Many of them knew from personal experience what it means to bear children of promise in the midst of fear and danger. Perhaps some people in our urban ghettos or among the poor of the third world understand it better today. In any case it is the task of the church to proclaim promise not security, and to call people to the urgent, sacrificial responsibility which that promise offers and requires. This is not to say that the poor have the Gospel, but it is they who are in a position to receive it. Out of this interaction of risk and responsibility in conditions of real insecurity, a new approach to optimum population will arise.

What might result from such an approach? If what is needed is a picture of the ideal society accompanied by an ideal number of people, the church cannot be of much help. The place where St. Augustine went furthest astray was his effort to determine the number of the saved in the day of judgment. There are, however, some things Christians can say from their faith which suggest goals in population policy. For example:

• There should be few enough people in a given place so personal relations can develop among them and convenants be formed. Mass depersonalized society is dehumanizing.

• The church might embody certain communal styles of life which inspire the rest of society with ways of life in the context of which to determine their childbearing.

• There is a certain esthetic quality to the interaction between man and nature, and in the appreciation of the possibilities of human relations, which the church could help explore and out of which would emerge a sense of how many children and when and where are appropriate. Central to this esthetic sense would be the *agape*, the outflowing love of God in Christ.

• Economic justice is a negative imperative, but it is not all that is meant by justice. If people are hungry or enslaved to others by economic need their family choices will be unfree. But what fulfills human life cannot be reduced to economic terms. Different societies develop different styles of common life which must be allowed their autonomy in a creative interaction with others. These styles and not just economic adequacy will determine the number of children the society can support.

But when these things are all said, they do not amount to a policy. The number of people a society can support, consistent with all being truly human in their interaction with each other, is a function of the quality of the relations this society establishes. A whole nation may not be enough space for two people who hate each other strongly enough. There are heights of spiritual interaction and love which allow several people to live creatively in a one-room hut or flat. People can starve in the midst of abundance. Others can thrive in a shared poverty. The task of Christians is to size up the condition of human relations realistically, to fight the battle of the powerless and the poor until they can assert their human claims on the powerful and the rich, and at the same time to explore the possibilities of human relations in mutual covenants open to renewal and correction. Out of such covenants people may be able to discern and test their calling to have children or to give themselves to opening channels of hope for the children of others.

4

POPULATION AND HUMAN SURVIVAL

DANIEL CALLAHAN

No biological axiom is more firmly established than the instinct of survival. Every species seeks to live and to perpetuate itself. The history of existing species can be recounted as a drama of adaptation and survival. This history of extinct species, by contrast, can be told as a tale of adaptative failure and consequent demise. Tolstoy's observation, in the opening lines of *Anna Karenina,* that all happy families are alike and all unhappy families different, seems no less true of species. Those which survive share a common trait: they are able to adapt to changing circumstances. Those which die out do so in a variety of ways, some rapidly and spectacularly, and others by slow attrition. The history of the human species is of a piece with the history of other successful species. Human life goes on because, over tens of thousands of years, it has developed the biological capacity to adapt itself in a phenomenal way to almost every earthly environment.

But there are of course some distinctive notes in human survival. The most important is the fact that human beings, through the evolution of a superior brain, have been able to take conscious, intelligent control of their survival. Where other species have been dependent only the luck of an advantageous draw in the genetic and environmental lottery, the human species has, by means of wit and culture, been able to parlay its bet in a way impossible for other species. We have not, so far, gone the way of the passenger pigeon or the dinosaur, both lovely creatures, but to their misfortune rather stupid.

The relationship between population growth and survival is obvious. It is quite possible to conceive of a world in which there are too many people to be supported by the available psychological or environmental resources. One has only to make certain projections from the figures on existing growth and consumption rates to come up with some disturbing possibilities. Add to this the recollection of what happened to individual tribes and groups in the past, decimated or wiped out by starvation, war or disease, and it is easy to imagine something similar happening to the whole species. Just this kind of imaginative speculation has been a powerful impetus behind a concern for world population rates. In terms of force and potency it has overshadowed the myriad other arguments for population limitation, those which bear on economic development or the maintenance of a decent quality of life. The very notion of extinction, utter extinction, is the most unbearable thought of all.

How should we understand the drive for survival in human beings? And how, as both a drive and a value, should it be approached and weighed in the context of population growth? At the outset, some curiosities should be noted, which taken together point to deep mysteries. Unlike other animals, human beings are consciously able to kill themselves by suicide; some people choose to die. Unlike other animals, humans are able to give up their lives in the service of ideas, values and ideologies. Unlike other animals, human beings are not satisfied with mere adaptation and survival; they seem constitutionally predisposed to want more than life, and in general just to want more of everything. This is another way of saying that human beings want to be happy, a trait which leads them into religious and philosophical quests, the building of cultural and political systems, and an unabated pursuit of scientific knowledge and technological application.

The sum total of these species-specific quirks suggests that the usual biological models and scientific laws relevant to non-human living species will have their drawbacks; and in practice that seems to be the case. Models which work with ants do not work well when extrapolated to human beings. If nothing else, it is an offense to good biological order that while all species, including the human, want to survive, only the human species sits around talking about it. And it is a positive outrage that some of the talk leads to one group of human beings killing another group in the name of survival.

The central paradox of human survival is part of the paradox of human life. Why is it that, while human beings, as individuals, groups and species, want desperately to survive, they will not settle for *mere* survival? Why it is that human beings are able to treat survival as both the highest value and as the lowest value? Why, for the sake of goals other than survival, will they run the most extravagant gambles with survival? Why, when they increasingly know that unchecked population growth could lead to disaster or extinction, do they nonetheless give population control a low social priority?

It will not do to urge, as do some biologists and ecologists, that

human beings are just stupid and short-sighted in this respect, per-
versely refusing to consider the folly of their ways. Indeed there is
folly, if one wants to center on the need for survival as the sole
important bioligical value. But the evidence of human thought and
behavior suggests that human beings value many goods, of which
survival is only one. This is one of the critical respects in which
they differ from animals. Arguments which would work with ants,
whose aspirations are limited to survival, will not work with human
begins, who insist upon something more.

Nor, to use a more sophisticated model, will it do simply to say
that, while man's unique genetic makeup was invaluable in enabling
him to survive in the past, it must now be modified and subdued in
órder that it will continue serving him in the future. This is the
over-adaptation model, which compliments man for his good beginnings but then criticizes him for not knowing when he has got
enough of a good thing. But that also misses a critical point about
man, that he seems compelled to act for ends other than optimal
adaptation and a satisfactory mode of survival.

The point of these remarks is to see if, at the outset, the problem
of population growth and human survival can be set in some illuminating context. I do not think it altogether enlightening to be
told that all sorts of drastic steps must be taken if the species is to
survive. That is probably true enough, but it persupposes the aspiration level of an insect, who cares nothing about anything but
survival. Nor is it illuminating to be told that man has over-adapted.
That may also be true, but it presupposes that human beings ask
nothing other than optimal adaptation. In short, we are not likely
to understand human attitudes toward survival, much less influence
their procreative behavior, unless we understand the exceedingly
complex human response to the problem of survival in relationship
to all of the other ends human beings seek in addition to survival.

More importantly, if there is a need for an ethic of survival in
relationship to excessive population growth rates, this ethic must
be constructed from richer ingredients than the observation, however true, that population poses a dire threat to the survival of the
human race. Since human beings are not ants, it is doubtful they
will be very responsive to that kind of truth; and in fact they have
not been. Moreover, I would want to argue that, in order to remain
human, they should *not* be all that responsive. Or better, they should
be responsive only to those survival arguments which manage to
integrate the need for survival with a whole range of other human

needs, some of which would risk survival for the achievement of other values.

A beginning can be made toward this integration by noting some of the uses and abuses of the concept of survival. Historically, the uses have been more evident than the abuses. Among the uses are those of a fundamental perception of the biological reality-principle: unless one exists, everything else is in vain. That is why survival, the desire to live, is so potent a force, and why the right to life is such a basic part of any reasonably enlightened social, political and legal system. Politically, particularly in time of war, national survival has been a potent force for mobilization of community effort, transcendence of self-interest, and creation of patriotic espirit. For individuals, the desire to ensure the survival of offspring has been the source of great and selfless sacrifice and the voluntary acceptance of obligations to future generations. Within the private self, a will to live, to survive at all costs, has literally kept people alive, staving off a despair which would otherwise have been totally destructive. That individuals, tribes, communities and nations have committed so much will, energy and intelligence to survival has meant that they have survived, and their ancestors are present to tell the tale. Nothing is so powerful a motive force, for self or society, as the threat of annihilation, nothing so energizing as the necessity to live. Leaving aside the question of whether we need more enlightened attitudes toward suicide in our society, which we may, it is still not for nothing that suicide has been looked upon with abhorrence, whether from a religious or a psychological perspective. It seems to violate the most fundamental of human drives, and has always required a special explanation or justification.

The value of survival could not be so readily abused were it not for its evocative power. But abused it has been. In the name of survival, all manner of social and political evils have been committed against the rights of individuals, including the right to life. The purported threat of Communist domination has for over two decades fueled the drive of militarists for ever-larger defense budgets, no matter what the cost to other social needs. During World War II, native Japanese-Americans were herded, without due process of law, into detention camps. This policy was later upheld by the Supreme Court in *Korematsu* v. *United States* (1944) in the general context that a threat to national security can justify acts otherwise blatantly unjustifiable. Under the banner of survival, the government of South Africa imposes a ruthless *apartheid*, heedless of the most elementary human rights. The Vietnamese war has seen one of the greatest of the many absurdities tolerated in the name of survival: the destruction of villages in order to save them.

But is is not only in a political setting that survival has been evoked as a final and unarguable value. The main rationale B. F. Skinner offers in *Beyond Freedom and Dignity* for the controlled and conditioned society is the need for survival. For Jacques Monod, in *Chance and Necessity,* survival requires that we overthrow almost every known religious, ethical and political system. In genetics, the survival of the gene pool has been put forward as sufficient grounds for a forceful prohibition of bearers of offensive genetic traits from marrying and bearing children. Some have even suggested that we do the cause of survival no good by our misguided medical efforts to find means by which those suffering from such common genetically based diseases as diabetes can live a normal life, and thus procreate even more diabetics. In the field of population and environment, one can do no better than to cite Paul Ehrlich, whose works have shown a high dedication to survival, and in its Holy Name a willingness to contemplate governmentally enforced abortions and a denial of food to starving populations of nations which have not enacted population control policies.

For all these reasons, it is possible to counterpoise over against the need for survival a "tyranny of survival." There seems to be no imaginable evil which some group is not willing to inflict on another for the sake of survival, no rights, liberties or dignities which it is not ready to suppress. It is easy, of course, to recognize the danger when survival is falsely and manipulatively invoked. Dictators never talk about their aggressions, but only about the need to defend the fatherland, to save it from destruction at the hands of its enemies. But my point goes deeper than that, it is directed even at a legitimate concern for survival, when that concern is allowed to reach an intensity which would ignore, suppress or destroy other fundamental human rights and values. The potential tyranny of survival as a value is that it is capable, if not treated sanely, of wiping out all other values. Survival can become an obsession and a disease, provoking a destructive singlemindedness which will stop at nothing.

We come here to the fundamental moral dilemma. If, both biologically and psychologically, the need for survival is basic to man, and if survival is the pre-condition for any and all human achievements, and if no other rights make sense without the premise of a right to life—then how will it be possible to honor and act upon the need for survival without, in the process, destroying everything in human beings which makes them worthy of survival? To put it more strongly, if the price of survival is human degradation, then there is no moral reason why an effort should be made to ensure that survival. It would be the pyrrhic victory to end all pyrrhic victories. Yet it would be the defeat of all defeats if, because human beings could not properly manage their need to survive, they succeeded in not doing so. Either way, then, would represent a failure, and one can take one's pick about which failure would be worse, that of survival at the cost of everything decent in man or outright extinction.

Somehow we need to find better alternatives. We need to survive as a species, but in a way which preserves a wide range of other human values, and in a way which is as sensitive about means as about ends. Population limitation will be an essential means to survival of the species. Thus the problem is to find a way of controlling population growth, size and distribution which is as morally viable as it is demographically effective. This means, therefore, that the survival value of population limitation must be complemented by a sensitive regard for other values along the way. A balance will have to be devised, of the most delicate kind. A number of steps are necessary, the first of which is to analyze the various types of supposed threats to survival. At the very least, we need to know which are real and which are imaginary, which are of the essence and which are dispensable. We also need to have a sense of those other values human beings prize, especially those for which they are willing to risk survival, even to give it up altogether. In sum, we need to know just what it is we are trying to balance, and what would count as a good balance.

A number of types of survival can be distinguished, the most important of which are survival of the species, and the survival of nations, cultures, groups (racial, ethnic and religious), and individuals. Survival of the species provides the prototype concept of survival. Taken literally, it can be understood to mean a continuation of human existence, specifying nothing about the number of those existing or the quality of their existence. In that sense, the species could survive if only a handful of fertile humans existed, much as the bison or the California Condor exists, and even if the level of existence was that of a primitive tribe. If, then, survival of the species alone is the goal, understood in a minimal sense, it is reasonable to suppose that nothing less than a global, all-encompassing catastrophe, would suffice to bring about extincton. Nuclear warfare, together with a persistence of life-extinguishing levels of atmospheric radiation, might present that kind of threat. It seems to me difficult, however, to imagine any other kind of catastrophe which would have a like effect. Over-population would, well before human extinction, most likely be a self-correcting phenomenon. People would die until a supportable number remained, a state which could be reached well before extinction became an imminent reality. To be sure, excessive population growth could conceivably bring about a world-wide nuclear war, as people and nations struggled for more space and resources. And I suppose it is possible, in a world of concrete, to imagine oxygen shortages. But those are the only circumstances, I believe, in which it makes much sense to talk about the extinction of the species because of over-population. To be more blunt, the spectre of human extinction because of over-population is a chimera, providing a poor base upon which to build a concern for excessive population growth. It could happen, under some remote circumstances; but then any and all kinds of catastrophes are imaginable under some circumstances.

These remarks are not meant to dismiss survival as a concern, though. If the concept is understood in a wider, non-literal sense, it is serviceable and important. Let me stipulate that sense as the continuation of the human species at a level of health and subsistence which makes possible the development of culture and individual self-fulfillment. This definition of survival leaves open the question of the rate of growth and the number of people the earth can sustain. The optimum population of the earth, encompassing some optimal notion of survival, can not be a fixed figure. Too much depends upon the kind and quality of life desired or lived. If the ideal model is that of the affluent American, that will produce a very different degree of magnitude than if, say, the model of a healthy, middle-class Indian is used. The central question is not so much whether the human species will survive, but how it will survive. And this question cannot properly be answered without a consideration of what human beings actually need to live a life of dignity and fulfillment. At the least, with the possible exception of health care, it is doubtful that in any deep sense human life requires for its fulfillment all the goods that the affluent American thinks he needs. On the contrary, quite apart from population considerations, our version of technological affluence carries an excessively high psychological and social price.

Survival also remains an important concept if further extended to include the survival of nations, cultures, groups and individuals. Most people, one might guess, are actually more concerned about their own survival, the survival of their family and of the social group with which they most identify, than with survival of the species. They live in the world, but it is their psychological and social world which counts. A threat to that latter world will be far more immediately unsettling than a threat to something so abstract and impersonal as the species. How many of us would be desperately concerned about the fate of the species if, along the way, our family, our descendants, our culture and our social groups were certain to disappear?

A distinction can be made between personal and social survival, on one hand, and species survival, on the other. Personal-social survival refers not only to the survival of individuals, but to the survival of those groups which provide individuals with their culture, their values and their social identity. Since the rise of the nation-state and with the acceleration of world-wide nationalism, the nation has been added to older, traditional social groupings as a source of individual identity and as the primary economic unit supporting individual welfare. In the United States and elsewhere in the world, the survival of racial and other types of minority groups has taken on a new power. Conflicts among religious and ethnic groups are, as is well known, a major impediment to the development and implementation of population policies.

When survival is seen in this broader context, a variety of ambiguties can appear. The survival of a nation, for instance, can be understood in a number of senses. It can mean *literal survival,* often the focal point, real or imaginary, of debates over the amassing of weapons. It can mean *political survival,* that is, the survival of a particular set of political and legal institutions. It can also mean the *survival of a particular way of life,* as for instance in references to the "American way of life." The emphasis here can fall on the preservation of certain cherished values, such as freedom or economic individualism, or on certain levels of economic well-being and employment opportunities. It can also mean survival as a world power or, less pretentiously, survival as a political and economic entity which commands the respect of others. If a willingness to go to war is taken as one test of a nation's perception of a threat to its survival, then it is evident from history that all of the above senses of national survival have at one time or another come into play. Less dramatically, nations have established population policies, both pro and anti-natalist, on a similarly wide range of grounds.

Within nations, and often across national borders, the *survival of religious, racial and ethnic groups* has been a powerful motive in fostering or opposing population control policies. While the dynamic here requires considerably more research for a clear understanding of the forces at work, a few characteristics seem evident. For many individuals and groups, there is a far stronger sense of identity with their racial, ethnic or religious group than there is with the nation in which they happen to live or to have been born. This may happen either because, taken positively, these groups provide a stronger source of meaning and community bonding than national identities (particularly in pluralistic societies), or, negatively, because of a fear (often rational enough) that the majority populations in particular nations are hostile toward them. The fear of genocide among blacks in the United States is a case in point in this latter context. Genocide can be understood as physical extermination in its most extreme form, or as the stripping away from a minority group its culture, self-respect, political power, self-direction or distinctive identity.

Both types of genocide have an appalling number of historical precedents, and a fear of socio-cultural extinction is often as strong as a fear of physical extinction. For fearful minority groups, whose heritage is that of persecution, refutation of the charge that physical genocide is intended by no means suffices to show that sociocultural genocide is not at work. It is beside the point that sociocultural genocide is not consciously intended. The same result can occur if the policies devised and imposed by the majority impose a greater burden on minorities than on themselves. A population policy designed by middle-class whites, seeking the two-child norm per couple, will inevitably seem a piece of cultural imperialism. Blacks will be quick to note that this norm imposes few burdens on upward-mobile, affluent whites, who are not likely to want more than two children anyway, regardless of population control motives. They will no less quickly note that the values to be protected by the population policy, whether economic, political or environmental, are the values of that white majority, not their values.

So far I have tried to analyze the concept of survival and to note the various senses in which it is used and may be understood. Perhaps it can all be summed up in the following way. The power of the drive for survival draws on biological, psychological and social roots. As individuals, we fear death and extinction. That fear seems universal, attested to by literary, religious and philosophical evidence dating back to the beginning of human consciousness. But we also fear, perhaps no less strongly, the destruction of our psychological and social worlds of meaning and identity. A blow to the ego can be, in its perceived power, as strong as a blow to the body. A blow to our primary reference group—whether that group be racial, religious or ethnic—can be as threatening as a blow to the private self. For many or most of us, the private self cannot be sharply distinguished from the communal self which we share with others in our group. More people commit suicide because of a shock to their sense of self-worth and identity than because of dire physical illness. And human beings seem as willing to kill or be killed in defense of their social group as in defense of their individual life. In short, we simply cannot understand human motivation or behavior if we do not understand both the pervasiveness of the drive for survival and the great variety of ways, individual and social, in which it manifests itself.

At the same time, however, we will no less fail to understand the place of survival in human life and history if we do not also observe the way it can be complemented by, or subordinated to, a wide range of other values. I have already contended that few human beings, at least in the long run, will settle for mere physical survival. Prisoners will risk their life to escape from jail. Slaves are willing to die in attempts to be free of their masters. Colonial nations will revolt in the face of overwhelming odds to achieve their independence. Nations will go to war to preserve their sovereignty and some, however insane it appears to be, will build and store nuclear weapons in massive over-kill quantities rather than be losers in the nuclear arms race.

With some ingenuity, I suppose it would be possible to develop a theory to show how all such acts, despite their appearance, are no more than an adumbration on the theme and drive of survival, particularly in its social and psychological variants. Anyone who wants to develop such a theory is welcome to do so. I find it equally plausible, however, to understand such acts by seeing in them a manifestation of human needs and aspirations which, if they do not necessarily transcend survival in their force and weight, can certainly be as strong in many cases. The American revolution was not fought to preserve physical survival; colonial Americans were in no danger of physical extinction or even in danger of serious poverty. That revolution was fought to advance the values of freedom, justice and self-determination. When Israelis say "never again" and assert their willingness to die rather than accept subjection, they are making clear their need for something more than survival, their freedom and dignity as a people. The Jewish case is particularly significant in another respect also. The lesson which many Jews believed they learned from the holocaust is that the most ineffective way to guarantee survival is to passively be willing to settle for survival. Unless one wants more than survival, and is willing to die for it, even survival will be taken away.

A similar dynamic can be seen in the rise of black militancy in this country. The perception of the militants is that the passivity of an older generations of blacks, a hang-over from the years of slavery, is naive and counter-productive. Far from assuring the survival of blacks, it makes them easy prey for racists, whether the motives of the latter are literal or cultural genocide. Both Jews and militant blacks, whatever their other differences, have seen that survival will always be in jeopardy as long as it is dependent upon the good will and toleration of others. And if this is true of survival, it is no less true of the protection of freedom and justice.

There are two general points which can be drawn from the variety of examples I have offered. The first is that it is possible to conceive of a variety of circumstances in which an excessive emphasis on survival, casting aside other human needs and values in the process, can severely jeopardize survival. Nuclear weapons, originally developed for self-defense, can be seen as the great symbol of that thesis. Almost as powerful a symbol can be found in excessive population growth rates, which stem, we should recall, from the powerful success which medicine has had in meeting the need to reduce death rates, i.e., in meeting the demand of human beings to survive rather than to die. The second point is that a viable, human ethic of survival must encompass all the other values and goals human beings seek and prize. Otherwise, it will either be self-defeating or productive of a life which most people will not find worth living.

A third point also needs development, to complement the first two. Survival as a need and value will inevitably be perceived in different ways by different individuals and groups. While it is now possible to scientifically determine what people need in the way of nutrition to survive physically, and perhaps from that knowledge to project the kind of agricultural and environmental resources necessary to sustain minimally adequate diets for given numbers of people, not much else is known with any certainty. Important research is being done on the effects of crowding on behavior, on the limits of environmental pollution, and on the extent of natural resources. But so far I think it not unfair to say that little scientific consensus has been reached on any of these problems, each one of which effects human survival. The most we know is that the earth cannot support an infinite number of people infinitely exploiting natural resources and infinitely polluting the environment. But that does not tell us much about what an optimal population size or growth would be. One thing evident from debates about the limits of the earth's carrying power, and about optimal population size, is that the ideological values brought to bear on existing data are enormously diverse. There is little agreement on just what exactly is necessary for mere survival, on the one hand, and for survival with dignity, on the other.

The problem becomes even more complicated in the light of the great variety of habits, traditions and expectations which govern what various individuals and groups perceive as necessary for the kind of survival they can, so to speak, live with. The recent back-to-nature romanticism of some middle-class Americans is based on the premise that a happier life can be found in an existence close to the earth, spared the excesses of technology. Less-developed countries, more experienced in living close to the earth, are rarely subject to such romantic fits. High infant mortality rates and short life-expectancies do not exactly encourage the view that a technology-free life is conducive to high levels of survival. The fact, however, that there exists a revolt against technology in many places in the developed countries, while at the same time the drive for a more advanced technology continues apace in areas which do not yet have it, suggests that a middle-ground must be sought.

I would speculate that both a deficiency and an excess in the power of survival breed anxiety and discontent. Too low a survival level forces a constant confrontation with annihilation, an unbearable kind of burden. Yet too high a survival level seems to produce a very similar kind of response. In the former case, it is the fear of physical destruction which is paramount; in the latter it is that of psychological destruction. Technological societies have achieved physical security at the price of psychological and social insecurity. The combination of individualism, consumerism, the generation of unlimited material desires, competitiveness and anomie, together conspire to make psychological survival fragile and precarious. If this felt fragility had the effect of reducing the demands made on technology, a more rational balance might be found. Unfortunately, it seems to accelerate the demands, particularly in the development of drug and behavioral therapies which do not strike at the roots of the insecurities but seek only to ameliorate the symptoms. A parallel phenomenon appears to be at work on the national level. Each of the nuclear powers in the world displays anxiety about the adequacy of its power. The result is a constant spiral of nuclear arms and their delivery systems, with each nuclear nation subject to constant internal pressures for the development of ever more sophisticated methods of defense and deterrence. The net result is not a greater sense of security and survival, but less. One could hardly seek a better illustration of the tyranny of survival, a tyranny, it is clear, which can dominate the excessively rich as powerfully as it dominates the excessively poor.

The major difference between the rich and the poor, however, is that the culture of the rich has established an almost unattainable survival level. Its point of departure is a very high base line, one which appears unable to conceive of an acceptable survival which does not include all the comforts, power and symbols of advanced technologies. Moreover, these "benefits" of technology seem to need constant improvement even to keep pace with the ever more expansive, seemingly unlimited demands they have historically generated.

My point here is a variant on the familiar thesis that the consumption levels and style of life to be found in affluent, technological societies pose a global danger to the preservation of natural resources and to the environment. I believe that to be a reasonable position. But I am also asserting that the motive force behind this hazardous phenomenon is that same drive for survival which dominates the poor, non-technological societies. The difference is that the emphasis in the rich countries shifts from the physical to the psychological level. At that level, two things appear to happen. The first is that the survival demands become increasingly difficult to fulfill, mainly because so much more, an infinity more, is asked; frustration and dissatisfaction are generated. The second is that the means chosen to fulfill the survival drive tend to be increasingly counter-productive. Just as the survival potential of the nuclear powers is probably less, in the end, than that of the militarily weaker nations, so too the psychological survival power of individuals in technological societies is probably less than that of individuals in less-developed countries.

As I hope the foregoing discussion will have made clear, the relationship between survival and an optimal population growth and size is complicated by a number of shifting variables. The need for survival is modified by the need to realize other values as well, notably freedom, justice and a sense of dignity and worth. The meaning of survival, once one moves beyond the level of bare subsistence, will be subject to a variety of different national, group and individual interpretations, primarily because survival will usually be interpreted in terms of desired standards of living and the preservation of values seen as integral to a satisfactory self-identity. The problem which remains is to see if it is possible to set forth some general standards concerning the use of survival as a value.

The *first requirement* is that a way be found to respond to the need for survival without, at the same time, allowing that need to become a tyranny. The tyranny can result either because of a panic in the face of a genuine threat to survival, because survival is invoked for self-interested or totalitarian political purposes, or because of an unnecessarily or unrealistically high standard of acceptable survival. Perhaps it is possible to do no more in the face of the last two possibilities than to be aware of their potential force, and by political and cultural debate to neutralize or overcome their baneful effects. The panic which can result from a real threat to survival will be more difficult to cope with, a panic which can lead to draconian measures in the name of self-preservation. At that point, the question must be faced whether there can be such a thing as too high a price to pay for survival. I believe there can be, particularly when the proposed price would involve the wholesale killing of the weak and innocent, the sacrifice to an extreme degree of the values and traditions which give people their sense of meaning and identity, and the bequeathing to future generations of a condition of life which would be degrading and dehumanizing. In short, the price would be too high when the evil of the means chosen would be such as to create an intolerable life both for the winner and the losers. While it might be possible to conceive of individuals willing to have their lives sacrificed for the sake of group survival, it becomes more difficult to imagine whole groups being willing to make such a sacrifice. And there is a very serious moral question whether that kind of sacrifice should be asked for or accepted, even on a voluntary basis.

The worst problems, however, are likely to arise not at the extremes but at some intermediary points. Certainly it would be reasonable and ethical to ask an entire population to give up to some extent some of its cherished values in the name of survival. Which ones and to what extent would be for them to determine. A minimal requirement, though, if that kind of demand is to be made, would be mutual agreement. If the values to be sacrificed were central and essential to the population's sense of its own dignity, I believe near unanimity would ethically be required, with the burden equally distributed among the entire population. This is not a case where a plurality of votes or opinion should reign. It is much too easy to imagine a powerful majority happy to purchase its own survival by taking what it needs from a weaker minority. Nothing less than an almost total consensus should be required if the means of survival require the taking of severe action. To put it even more strongly, I think it would be well within the rights of a minority to jeopardize the survival of all if they correctly perceived that a majority intended to kill them to save its own skin. It would be no less the right of a minority to refuse to cooperate in a program designed to preserve a certain level of survival if that program was designed to require inequitable sacrifices from the minority.

The *second requirement* is that a way be found to determine when survival should (a) first be taken into consideration, and (b) when it should be allowed to become a social priority. My phrasing of the problem presumes the utility of understanding survival as a continuum, requiring points of demarcation in order that the right action may be taken at the right time. Survival should first be taken into consideration when there is evidence that either population growth rates or distribution patterns could, if unchecked, lead to a serious endangering of basic physical needs, a threatening of cherished national or group values, and a subverting of psychological security and identity. Note that I used the phrase "taken into consideration." The point of that wording is to suggest that too precipitate an action, when the hazard is still distant and problematic, may—given the possible tyranny of survival—do more harm than good. At the early stages, the wisest course may simply be that of public education about the possible consequences of present behavior and attitudes.

But let us assume that the stage of a dark cloud on some distant horizon has been passed, and the evidence is good that serious deterioration has already set in. At what point in the deterioration should survival become a priority? Observe that I said "a" priority; it should never become *the* priority if that means the sacrifice of all other values. But there are surely conditions under which it could become a priority, and a very high one. The most important of those conditions would be the existence of evidence that irreversibility was beginning to set in. That is, a state of affairs where it would become increasingly impossible to return to the original conditions. That situation, combined with visible evidence of serious present deterioration, would warrant a focus on survival; for that is just what would be at stake.

The *third requirement* is that a way be found to take account of the obligations owed to future generations. It is possible to conceive of present forms of behavior which, while in posing only minor hazards and inconveniences on the living, could in their cumulative effect over a long period of time pose a serious danger to those yet unborn. The test of irreversibility is again useful. Are present actions such that their consequences would not only be harmful to those not yet born, but also of a kind which could not be reversed by them? Destruction of irreplaceable natural resources, permanent contamination of the environment, and the bequest of an excessively large number of people would be apt illustrations of this possibility.

The most vexing problem here, however, bears on the degree of sacrifice which can be demanded of the living in the name of the survival of the unborn. That demand cannot, I believe, encompass the destruction of basic liberties of the living or a deprivation of those physical necessities of life required for their survival. But it could well encompass a radical shift in the style of living, in levels of consumption, and in the number of children they bring into the world. The sticking point here would be whether shifts of this kind could be made involuntary. In the end, I think not, if only because the rights of the living, not to mention their political power, will transcend the rights of those yet to be born. But a vigorous educational campaign, even of a propagandistic nature, would not be out of order.

This paper has displayed a certain degree of skepticism about the invocation of survival. The reason for this is the long history of evil which has been done in its name, and the fact that, even now, proposals are being put forward which would lead to comparable evils. The instinct for survival is a strong one; it is rarely necessary to stimulate people to worry about it. But it is necessary on occasion to curb the human appetite for it, and to take steps to make certain that survival is recognized for what it is—a basic requirement of human life, not the goal of that life.

5

GROUP COMPETITION AND SURVIVAL

Seymour Siegel

The Bible's first commandment is "Be fruitful and multiply." This is one of the few biblical commandments to be taken seriously. There is widespread concern that the commandment has been fulfilled so zealously as to endanger the human race. Focusing on the first part of the verse (be fruitful and multiply), the last part has been over-looked (and fill the earth). Since we have (it seems) filled the earth, perhaps it is time to repeal the call for fruitfulness and multi-plication. There seems little argument that somehow there must be achieved a stop in filling the earth with new progeny. The only argument is how this can be done without sacrificing other cherished values and traditions. The call for absolute population stabilization (or Zero Population Growth) is by no means unanimous. Some objectors are motivated by religious dogma, views about the sexual function, and by other considerations. While these objections can be countered by appeal to progressive views and by the nature of the crisis, such dissenting voices deserve respectful attention. They raise important issues, and they illustrate the truism that moral policy decisions involve tragic choices.

The tragic aspect of choice can be illustrated personally. I have a friend who has resolved to have at least six children. He and his wife believe that in this way they are helping to make up for the murder of six million fellow Jews. I have another friend who had a large family before World War II. He lost them all at Auschwitz. He determined that after his liberation from the death camps he would marry and replace his lost family. This was not only a way to fill the void in his life—but also a means to affirm the value of life and the grandeur of being a Jew. I have another friend who has emi-grated to Israel. He wishes to participate in the upbuilding of the ancient homeland. He and his wife are determined to have a large family. This—to his mind—is a way to guarantee the Jewishness of the reborn Jewish state.

These individuals represent an attitude within embattled minority communities that the general call for population control are certainly acceptable—in general—but that in particular cases, especially those involving ethnic and racial survival, a zero growth rate may be tantamount to group suicide. This view—though found within all groups—has been expressed vigorously in two of our minority communities—the Jews and the blacks. Several prominent rabbis have recently called upon their congregations to neglect the current calls for population control.[1] Rabbi Moshe Goldblum of Pittsburgh's Congregation Beth Shalom, a conservative synagogue, told his people that "we must replace the six million before we can even begin to discuss with the rest of the world the problems of population control." The conservative group to which the rabbi belongs has long held liberal views on contraceptives and abortion. Another rabbi, from a liberal constituency, is reported to have said "when we talk of population explosion today we must not speak of the Jew . . . We are confronted with a dilemma. Shall we be 'liberal' and control our birth rate in America and lead the world into zero growth or shall we remember the six million? Shall we first make up for the six million before we join the rest of the world in keeping the level?"

Rabbis are seldom obeyed by their congregations. Even several rabbis do not make a counter-movement. From statistics it is clear that the vast majority of the Jews do not accept the rabbis' argument. However, the rabbis have raised critical issues. If one takes into account the natural attrition resulting from assimilation and intermarriage, the prospects of a vanishing American Jew are too real to be ignored. In a widely quoted recent article, Milton Himmelfarb is sharply critical of the population movement in general.[2] He suspects that the leaders of the movement for zero population growth are willing to use totalitarian methods to bring about reduction in birth. After all, he argues, if you see the abundance of children as a plague then "reasonably advanced countries deal with plague by education, but also by sanitation, by vigilance, above all by compulsory inculation." Reviewing some of the methods proposed by population control advocates, Himmelfarb warns that the cure may be worse than the disease. Concerning the specifically Jewish situation, Himmelfarb reacts vigorously to pleas for population stabilization. Since the Jewish population of the world has dropped a fifth in one generation, he asks, is it not rational that Jews, at least, be exempted from the general commandment not to be fruitful and not to multiply?

"For every 1,000 people in the world 996 or 997 are not Jews. All the Jews in the world are fewer than two-thirds of the blacks in the United States and fewer than one-third of the Catholics in the United

States." Identifying himself with what he (tongue-in-cheek, to be sure) calls parochial Jews, Himmelfarb asserts that since zero population growth is for combatting the population explosion, it is the right thing for population exploders. "But Jews are not exploding. . . . It is not they who have too many children . . . they have too few children. They are imploding. For Jewish population imploders the right thing is not z/p/g, but m/p/g, maximum population growth."

Of course, Himmelfarb realizes that his argument is group-centered. It may sound ethnocentric and even selfish to some. But many Jews and others as well feel that a viable world should be a varied world, including different ethnic, racial and religious groups. Without such diversity, mankind would be vastly impoverished. Therefore, if it is evident that internal and external pressures continually diminish the ratio of, let us say, Jews in relation to the rest of the world, then the argument for absolute population stabilization sounds considerably less convincing. Taking the call for population stabilization seriously can endanger the future of Jewish culture and civilization.

From the Jewish point of view the argument becomes even more critical when it is related to the Jewish position in Israel. The Zionist enterprise was based on the notion that the Holy Land was to be re-established by creation of Jewish communities there. Though the recognition of the powers of the world was politically crucial, the real achievement of Zionism would be measured by the ability of the Jewish people to establish a Jewish majority. This would make it possible to have a Jewish homeland where Jewish life could flourish and be creative, unhampered by the disabilities of minority status. Therefore, it was obvious that it was absolutely vital to increase the number of Jewish inhibitants. Long before the establishment of the State of Israel, the *vishuv* (a name given to the Jewish community in Palestine) sponsored a program of "internal immigration." This meant increase through natural growth. This call was heeded mostly by families coming from oriental countries, whose level of education and sophistication was much less, in general, than their European brothers and sisters. The latter tended to have small families. Recently, it was reported that a new organization had been established in Israel to promote the interests, rights, and prospects of large families. Ten percent of Israel's families rear forty percent of the nation's children. The government of Israel applauds parents of large families. These, it is announced, "contribute to the national welfare." The new organization referred to above claims that if a fraction of the cost expended by Israel for the needs of immigrants were to be expended in aid to prolific parents, "we would build a stronger and happier country." The name of the new group is PROFF, Privileges and Rights of Fruitful Families." The high birth rate of the Arab minority within Israel and the growth of population of Israel's Arab enemies makes the drive for increased Jewish population literally a life and death issue as the Israelis see it.

These and other calls for a Jewish 'exception' from the general call for population control are prompted by a sense of loss, a sense of worth, and a sense of responsibiilty. The Jews who suffered heavy casulties during World War II, whose culture and faith is suppressed in the Soviet Union, whose youth is attracted away by assimilation and intermarriage, and who have a history of stubborn survival—feel a profound sense of loss. A painful void has been created. Some way must be found to fill this void.

This sense of loss is reinforced by a strong sense of worth. It is after all, a good thing for civilization that the Jews have survived. (This, is of course also true of other minorities). The record of their contributions to society has been quite remarkable. Why, then, it is asked in all seriousness, should a productive community risk extinction for the sake of the ideology of zero population growth. No one would urge population reduction upon families who have consistently produced men and women of significant productivity. If this is true about particular families (what if the Kennedy's, for example, had limited their family to two) it is also true for groups which have shown an ability to contribute to society in a significant way. By producing more offspring they do not endanger civilization. They enhance it. This does not imply that there are better and lesser breeds. It is certainly true that a proliferation of children makes it difficult for some nations and groups to fulfill their great promise. By all means let such groups regulate their population size. However, it is argued, mankind does not gain by diminishing the pool of productive people, whose numbers have been greatly decreasing in any case.

This sense of loss and sense of worth is associated also with a sense of responsibility. The heritage of Judaism (and this, of course, applies to others as well) has been carried forward with extraordinary tenacity and at a cost of incalculable sacrifice. This puts an added responsibility upon those who have survived. The experience of the European holocaust has heightened this sense of responsibility. One of the most widely quoted passages in recent Jewish religious literature was written by Professor Emil Fackenheim: "I believe that whereas no redeeming voice is heard at Auschwitz, a commanding voice is heard, and that is being heard with increasing clarity. Jews are not permitted to hand Hitler posthumous victories. Jews are commanded to survive as Jews, lest their people perish." [3] This sense of responsibility is extremely persuasive to committed Jews. It is the sense of an obligation toward survival. In the final analysis this obligation can be fulfilled through being heretical in the face of the Zero Population Growth dogma. This quest for survival is not permeated by a sense of competition with other groups. The number of non-Jews is inconsequential. What counts is that the people of Israel be given a chance for survival. It is not competition with other groups that is the issue; it is rather competition with the angel of death. A recent spokeman in *Shma* underscored this judgment with his comment that "Man's craze for self destruction is evident in Jewish involvement in population control and Zero Population Growth. . . . If we believe in Judaism's message, we must see that there are Jews to bear the message. Without Jews there can be no Judaism." [4]

It is noteworthy that among Jews today the largest families are produced among the ultra-orthodox, especially hasidim. These pietists do not recognize the legitimcy of artificial methods of birth control except under clearly defined threats to the health of the mother. [5] Of course it is true that when families make decisions about their family size, many factors other than their Jewishness or other ethnic identification are taken into consideration. However, it is true also that among the many factors Jewishness will be one and in some cases the crucial one.

The opposition to population control in the black community takes on a different character. Zero Population Growth is seen as a cheap means of solving the problems engendered by centuries of persecution and neglect. As such it is perceived as a "cop-out." It involves cutting down the number of welfare recipients through population control rather than finding a solution to the welfare problem. The propaganda for population control is also seen as a means of freeing the black proportion of the population and cutting off the chances black people have of improving their condition by political pressure strengthened by larger numbers.

In a position paper presented to the President's Commission on Population Growth and the American Future, [6] Professor Charles V. Willie reports that many people in the black community are deeply "suspicious of any family program initiated by whites." He insists that these charges are not "absurd nor hollow" and that blacks believe "that there are genocidal aspirations on the part of the white community" toward them. Among other things, the attack on black family structure expressed in the Moynihan Report reinforces the fears of black people that the program to limit population is another sally against their way of life. Professor Willie's research shows that fears of "black genocide" are found both among educated and uneducated blacks. "Unless American society can assure black people that it is committed to their survival with dignity and equality, they will refuse to cooperate with any national population plan." One way to allay the fears of black people would be to direct propaganda equally to all communities—not only to the minority groups. When it is perceived that a great deal of the effort to limit family size is directed to the minority sector of our population, suspicions are aroused that the real aim of the policy is to freeze the percentage which the various minority groups now enjoy and to make relative increase impossible. Professor Willie believes that since fertility is generally relative to economic and educational level, the correct way to appeal to the black community would be to intensify efforts to inhance the economic and educational level of all people, especially blacks.

Another study, conducted in a New England black community, uncovered suspicions that family planning programs were forms of "black genocide," "but not at a high level"[7] However, it was found that black males under thirty years of age agreed with the statement that "all forms of birth control are designed to eliminate blacks and that encouraging blacks to use birth control is comparable to trying to eliminate this group from society" in larger proportions than others in the community. The statement "all forms of birth control are designed to eliminate blacks: elicited the following responses: "Fourteen percent of all the blacks" agreed. While 100 percent of the males over thirty disagreed with the statement, 29 percent of the males thirty and under agreed with it." These researches clearly show that there is a growing feeling in the black community, especially among younger groups, that birth control, Zero Population Growth and the rest are plots perpretrated against them by the white majority.

Some of the same conclusions were reached at a national conference on the health needs of black Americans held in December, 1971, under the auspices of Meharry School of Medicine, Howard University School of Medicine, the National Dental and Medical Associations and the Congressional Black Caucus. These groups charged that "the government has been promoting family planning for the poor at the expense of maternal and child health services." The term family planning should mean not only limiting births but planning for a family's comprehensive health care.

Whether these fears are valid or not, they are perceived as valid by growing numbers of blacks, and it can be expected that they will act according to their perceptions of the situation. This observer believes that the term "genocide" is hardly applicable to the black situation. Even with the lamentable oppression visited upon blacks their percentage of the population in the United States has risen about two percent in the last decades. However, the critics of population control in the black community have a valid point to make. Family planning must not become a substitute for social justice. It should not blind our eyes to other needs. Any community under threat looks for large numbers as one way of promoting self-defense. Even racial minorities fear assimilation and the dismantling of their traditional cultures. Diminishing numbers makes this fear more realistic.

Thus we have seen that significant minorities within our culture find legitimate reasons to separate themselves from the general effort to limit population. What do we say to these minorities?

A common reaction would be to oppose the ideas of the minorities on the grounds that they represent exaggerated ethnic consciousness. This consciousness must yield, we argue, before world-wide needs. The common good is greater than any private good. In a world threatened by ruin through excess of people, purely parochial interested should be sacrificed. Such an attitude was expressed recently in a column by the political analyst, Joseph Kraft. He sees "the celebration of ethnicity" as "boastful self-glorification.: He views "ethnic narcissism" as setting group against group in "invidious competition." Implicit in Kraft's remarks are hopes that the "melting pot ideology" will again gain strength. When that happens all men will set the interests of the whole world above those of their own particular community. This is another way of stating the old dilemma of particularism versus universalism. Calls for universalism—usually coming from the majority—are perceived as lacking in good faith, since they result in everyone becoming like the majority. True community requires both poles—particularism and universalism. We are all of us the same, and different. Forgetting that "all men are created equal" is, of course, a bad thing. Overlooking the differences among men is equally wrong. It has been recognized increasingly that group identity is a basic element of human existence. We are born into our groups before we become citizens of the world. The "universal man"—

except for rare exceptions—is non-existent. To cut oneself off from these roots is to cut oneself off from an indispensible source of nourishment. This is the message of the "new ethnicity" so ably described recently by Michael Novak in *The Unmeltable Ethnics*.

Concomitant with appreciation of group identity is a desire for survival and continuity. Quantity does not, of course, guarantee equality. But there can be no quality unless there is some quantity; and, given the degree of group interaction, there must be substantial quantity if any kind of meaningful continuity can be achieved. This is a critical fact governing the life of nations and other groups. To neglect this reality is not possible. For Jews, blacks, American Indians and others it is an obvious fact that the human race can only be enriched if they continue to exist in large numbers. If there are people who believe that there are too many of their own—like Indians, Japanese or even Americans—let them, by all means, practice whatever limitations they wish. For those who feel that there are too few of their kind in the world, rather than too many, there is a good argument to be fruitful and to multiply.

Is the argument convincing? I believe it is. Group survival is a positive good for mankind. Even group competition enhances society. There is a talmudic saying: the competition among sages increases wisdom. The healthy rivalry among different groups can be beneficial if it is confined to creative areas and is limited by commonly agreed-upon ground rules.

Whether the above argument is convincing or not there is one other consideration that is of vital importance. However persuasive the arguments for population control might be, their very convincing quality is dangerous for it can lead to dogmatism and arrogance. Some of the proposals that are put forward to limit population are frightening indeed in their implications. The spectre of armies of bureaucrats deciding when and how couples can have children is frightening. Too often in the past events that seemed to be relegated to the realm of science fiction have turned out to be dreadful realities. To many people, the threats of freedom and conscience coming from population control advocates with power seem greater than the possible consequences of overpopulation. For this reason the claims of the minorities are warnings to over-zealous planning that they should stop to think about the implications of their proposals and their threat to conscience and freedom. In this way the claims of the minorities are paradigmatic of the whole problem revolving around the population planning effort. The program must be furthered at the utmost. But it cannot be furthered at the cost of compromising freedom or by invading human privacy. The dilemma of coercion versus the common good is as old as civilization itself. The dissent of the minorities in the population effort is valuable in reminding us of the bitterness and basic insoluability of the dilemma.

It is, of course, right and good that educational efforts be extended. It is vital that the best means of population control be made available to all who want to use them. But once we step beyond the bonds of persuasion and equal opportunity into coercion of conscience, freedom, and rights then we have destroyed something very precious in the human being.

1. *The Jewish Post and Opinion* (February 18, 1972).

2. Milton Himmelfarb, "A Plague of Children," *Commentary* (April 1971).

3. Emil L. Fackenheim, *Quest for Past and Future: Essays in Jewish Theology* (Indiana University Press, 1968).

4. *Shma: A Journal of Jewish Responsibility* (May 19, 1972), p. 23.

5. For a full discussion of the views of Jewish religious leaders on birth control see David Feldman, *Birth Control in Jewish Law* (New York University Press, 1968).

6. Charles V. Willie, "A Position Paper," *Population Reference Bureau Selection No. 37* (June 1971). Dr. Willie is a black sociologist.

7. William A. Darity et al., "Race Consciousness and Fears of Black Genocide as Barriers to Family Planning," in *ibid.*

6

GROUP SURVIVAL

THROUGH LIMITATION OF GROWTH

Jessma Blockwick

Even for those who believe that population growth is threatening to destroy any quality for human life on earth, and for many even life itself, it is tempting to agree that Jews should not be expected to take part in programs of population limitation. We can understand the longing, so eloquently voiced by Dr. Seymour Siegel, to replace the six million who died so horribly during the Second Great War. We all carry some burden of guilt, and might find this an opportunity to make a gesture of expiation. Additionally it is certainly true that for a tiny minority of the world's people to double in numbers would have very little effect on whether or not we face disaster from the population explosion.

Nonetheless, there are troubling questions raised by Rabbi Siegel's paper which need to be examined carefully. If an exception to the need for limiting population growth is made for the Jews as a matter of justice, how can we define this as an ethical paradigm for this area of concern? Since the issue of black fears of genocide is included in the discussion, it seems clear the Jews are not to be an isolated example. Then we must ask, what about the American Indian, who surely suffered genocide? What about other Indian tribes which are facing extermination in some Latin American countries, the Montagnards in Indochina, the Ibos, the Bengalis in Pakistan? Sadly, humankind's entire history is full of the slaughter of the weak by the strong. Should we then set a limit backward in time, beyond which the pain and suffering by a group would not entitle it to exemption from limiting growth in the future? Would we have to set up some measure of degree of suffering and killing which would be sufficient to permit exception? Who would be the judge of which groups are to be allowed to multiply and which are not?

There are still further complications. Groups, whether racial or religious, do not have babies. Individuals do. Yet it is the total of these individual acts which adds up to a population explosion. Few responsible voices argue that man's numbers can keep growing indefinitely. Rather the arguments center on how growth is to be stopped and when it must be done to avoid catastrophe.

Suppose we succeed in building a real awareness of the dangers from continued population growth and a general acceptance of the need to take action to stop it. In this climate, we then say to the black woman, "You may have as many children as you want because of past injustices"; to the Jewish woman, "You many have more than two because there are too few of you" to the Catholic woman, "You may have a large family because of your religious beliefs." But then to the white, Protestant, middle-class woman, "You can have only one or two children because of the population crisis." Surely Solomon in all his glory wouldn't have wanted to grapple with that one! The psychological and social hazards of such deliberate discrimination, not only for the individual woman, but for society in the immediate exacerbation of latent group hostilities, do not need spelling out.

Here another note of our times needs to be interjected. Rabbi Siegel quotes exclusively from Jewish rabbis and black men in discussing this right or need to have more babies. A common practice, as is the largely male composition of this volume's authorship! It is much as Claire Booth Luce remarks in reviewing a book on abortion: "Like so many of the books which learned men have written about 'women's problems,' this is really a book about the problem men are having with other men who refuse to see the 'women's problem' as they do." [1] It is all too easy to begin to speak of women en masse as counters to be moved about in power plays when population problems are talked about. Yet it is surely not an ethically defensible position to urge women to have more and more children on the ground that it will give the *group* more power, when the *personal* result may be to grind the individual woman deeper into poverty and powerlessness.

Apparently Jewish women are still having small families, in spite of exhortations to do otherwise. Similarly, studies show that black women do want to have access to family planning services. Perhaps women believe there are other contributions they can make to add strength to their group other than merely serve as a producer of more babies. Thus, Jewish women may understand, the magnificent gifts from their people have been entirely disproportionate to their numbers.

Thus, Francis Beale says: "Those who are exerting their 'manhood' by telling Black women to step back into a domestic submissive role are assuming a counter-revolutionary position. Black women likewise have been abused by the system and we must begin talking about the elimination of all kinds of oppression. If we are talking about building a strong nation, capable of throwing off the yoke of capitalist oppression, then we are talking about the total involvement of every man, woman and child, each with a highly developed political consciousness. . . . To wage a revolution, we need competent teachers, doctors, nurses, electronics experts, chemists, biologists, physicists, political scientists, and so on and so forth. Black women sitting at home reading bedtime stories to their children are just not going to make it." [2]

Sometimes family-planning programs have been coercive and aimed at the poor, particularly the black poor. The answer to the fears of genocide should be found in excellent general health-care programs for all rather than by any such divisive means as leaving certain groups out of the population picture entirely. Recently a black churchman pointed out to the United Methodist Department of Population Problems that to claim that population-limitation messages should only be directed to the white majority is patronizing. It implies that blacks are not really mature enough to accept their full responsibility in society.

In carrying his thesis outside our nation, Rabbi Siegel speaks to the need of Israel for more people in order to be more secure against the Arabs. Such nations as Egypt, however, are being seriously hurt not strengthened by rapidly growing numbers.

Breeding competitions are hard to control—or to win. Barring some strange development, blacks will always be in a minority in the United States. If they were able to increase family size precipitously as a conscious political ploy, the whites could easily counter by having more children themselves, or by increasing immigration quotas. The only result would be to heighten racial tension. Similarly, whites are a permanent minority in the world at large. There are people, such as the British economist, Colin Clark, who argue that the white race must have more and more babies to keep the world from being dominated by Asians. Today it is a common theme in certain Latin American countries that they must increase their numbers to achieve great power status and thereby overcome Yankee imperialism.

There used to be frequent articles in the United States warning that in x-number of decades the Catholics would take over in this country unless the Protestants stepped up their baby production. Jews are a minority faith—and so are Christians—or Buddhists. Any minority group which feels itself endangered could use this as a rationale for growing while others should not. Once we open the Pandora's box of suggesting that one group or faith or nation should try to increase its size vis-a-vis some other, then we are surely on the path to inevitable disaster from population pressures, including the likelihood of armed conflicts.

Similar dangers lie in Rabbi Siegel's statement that no one would urge population reduction upon families who have consistently produced men and women of significant productivity! We must ask the unavoidable question as to who is to be the judge of which people are producers with the right to have more children, and which the non-producers. One could speculate, for example, that a majority in this country might not rank professors of social ethics high in "significant productivity!" Would the number of children allowed be in proportion to the degree of productiveness—as decided by the unnamed judges? What and who would determine when a family had lost this special right? Rare indeed would be the individual who would declare himself or his family or group out of the useful category. This doctrine in effect would make any kind of stopping of population growth virtually impossible.

Justice and wisdom would seem to bring us down to a need to accord the same privileges and responsibilities to all. On the micro level of the family, and on the macro level of the group or nation, we have never been able to anticipate where the next flowering of science or philosophy or art will burst forth. As the United Nations is concerning itself with preserving a diverse genetic pool for plants, we need to be equally vigilant to preserve human diversity in all its richness. This means guarding fiercely the right to survive for every group, every religion, every tribe, every race. This guarding is not best accomplished by setting off a competitive battle of numbers.

The "ideology of zero population growth" does not imply extinction, but rather an eventual end to growth. In view of the fears of many that Jews and their religion may eventually disappear, there is every justification for urging Jewish women to be fruitful enough to replenish their numbers. Other groups similarly have the right to respect and a decent existence. But this is replenishment—not multiplication. By seeking to understand God's command in that light, we can assure the survival of the rich variety and the diverse values which are precious to man's heritage.

1. Claire Booth Luce, "Two Books on Abortion," *The National Review* (January 12, 1971).

2. Francis Beale, "Double Jeopardy: To Be Black and Female," in Toni Cade, ed., *The Black Woman* (New American Library, 1970).

7

QUALITY VS. QUANTITY: A FEMINIST PERSPECTIVE

Catherine L. Gunsalus

Quality and quantity are indeed opposed to each other at many points in the determining of optimum population. Their opposition, however, is not self-evident. Do we mean quantity of goods or of people? Do we mean quality of life-style interpreted by means of a certain quantity of consumer goods? Or do we mean quality of life determined by such non-quantitative values as self-realization and fulfillment? Do even these non-quantitative values depend in some fashion on population size?

The population question also appears quite different depending upon the social unit whose perspective is being used. There are basically five possible social units in this regard: (1) the world as a whole, (2) the nation as a political unit, (3) a cultural group, probably a minority racial or religious group, (4) the family, (5) the might-be mother. Frequently there are conflicts between a world-perspective that views unlimited population growth as a dire threat to all humanity and the attitude of the family or woman who sees a large family as a positive value. We can also understand conflict between minority groups which desire to increase their numbers in the face of national policies seeking to lower birth rates.

Obviously the levels of social units are not always opposed. Frequently the self-interests of different levels happen to coincide: a lowered birth rate may help the economic growth both of the nation and of the family. Sometimes loyalty to a larger unit affects a smaller one: concern for world population may cause a couple to limit their family even though they would prefer to have more children; group loyalty may cause a couple to increase family size, even at the expense of their standard of living.

As long as population control depends upon the voluntary compliance of the family, then it is these small social units that must balance self-interest and loyalty to larger groups. For this reason most of the publicity seeking voluntary birth control has been aimed at pointing out family self-interest or else it has appealed to a sense of national or world responsibility.

This convergence of self and national or world interest or this goading of a sense of loyalty is, however, an indirect approach. It has two major weaknesses. First, when the language is so clothed in our self-interest, it makes the cynics among and within us wonder what the "real" interest is of those who sponsor the programs. The fear of being manipulated is strong in many of us, particularly as we become more sophisticated about advertising techniques. Whether it is minority groups that fear genocide or the alienated middle-class white young who feel that reduced population is a ploy to have a greater consumer society without a real change in values, the population control campaign that tries to link everything to family self-interest has this serious limitation: it is not trusted. The second weakness is that the most significant reason at these smallest unit levels for limiting the birth rate may be basically contrary to the values of the larger groups. To this argument we shall return later.

Thus far only voluntary programs of birth limitations have been considered. But what of more drastic measures that might be undertaken by the state, some form of required limit on family size? Does the question of voluntariness also affect the quality of life as well as determining quantity? One factor is certain: if the state seeks to limit births, it is the perspective of the state that has determined that the birth rate is too high. As we have seen, the perspective of the state may or may not coincide with the views of other social units. What then becomes of the validity of these other perspectives? Only the state has the machinery for enforcing its decisions. The other four social units cannot compete in this regard. The world view and minority group opinions must depend on moral suasion. For many of us, an increase in the mandatory character of the views of the state as opposed to the views of the world or of sub-cultures or of individuals is in itself a decrease in the quality of life within the state. It is not a question of numbers, of the larger group benefiting at the expense of a small group. Each person is a part of more than one level. The world view is not composed of a larger number of people than the sum total of national views or of family views. Half of the world view is also composed of might-be mothers. It is not a matter of the greatest good for the greatest number. Rather, it is a matter of which is the most valid perspective for the determining of this issue.

Let us grant that in dire circumstances such a limitation on the freedom of smaller units were allowed by the people. We need to follow out what this could mean. If the perspective of the state

is used as the determinant of optimum population and if in any
degree the state is allowed to enforce its view, on what grounds could
this right of the state be used only to *limit* births? Coercive ability
given to the state must be viewed from the possibility of increasing
as well as decreasing population even though the one side seems unlikely at the moment. For some nations at some points in their history
it is not an unknown desire. Great danger lurks in allowing the
perspective of the state to have advantage over the perspectives of
the smaller social units. Nor can we guarantee that even the world
and national view will always coincide, and the world view has no
coercive machinery.

Birth and "the future" are intricately related. In one sense to
give birth to a new generation is an act of hope; it is assurance that
there will be a future for the world and for a specific group. This
positive character of birth and the future is often stressed and needs
little underlining. On the other hand, overpopulation is also a threat
to the future and the need for limitation on births is also cast in terms
of a negative future for the whole world. All of this is obvious. But
let us look at other ways in which the birthrate and the future are
related.

The closeness of "the future" is not self-evident. The future is not
simply all time yet to come. "The future" the scientist speaks of
may be generations away. The future I speak of for myself cannot be
that distant. When we talk about the effect of the birthrate on the
future, *the future being considered is closest in chronological time to
the smallest social units.* Or, conversely, the future being considered
is the most remote from the largest social units. For example, the
threats of overpopulation to the world are frequently put in terms
of a few generations from now. The problems at a national level
appear somewhat closer. The minority sub-cultures usually relate
themselves politically to the nation in which they live and therefore
deal in time-periods similar to those of the nation.

There is a great difference when we come to the family unit, however. The couple that considers the effect of another child on their
lives is not dealing in generations-long planning. They are considering the next eighteen years or so. The first child launches them into
parenthood and may well affect their life-style drastically. But an
increase in the birthrate in their family after this is most likely to
affect them economically and socially from four to twenty-two years
after the child's birth. Infancy may not have that much of an effect
on their lives as a couple as will the later period of their child's

life. A second or third or later child may not present a great change
in their life-style as a couple.

The smallest unit is not the couple but rather the might-be mother,
the woman who decides whether or not to have another child—or
the woman who fails to decide and therefore does have another child.
Usually the might-be mother is treated simply as one-half of the
couple who are deciding about their family. But so to consider her is
a serious mistake. In our culture it is the woman to whom falls the
greatest burden of child care, particularly during the pre-school years.
It is her life that will be the most dramatically affected by the birth
of a new child. In fact, the economic and social responsibilities of the
couple may begin to increase precisely at the point that the woman's
sole responsibility wanes: in our society, at the point of the child's
entrance into school.

A time-line can be constructed to show the immediacy of the future
for these different social units in our present culture:

Birth to 4 years	4-18 or 22 years	next generation 35 years	several gener- ations — 100 yrs.
might-be mother	couple	nation and sub- cultures	world

To ignore the difference in closeness of the future of the woman as
might-be mother and as one-half of a couple is to overlook the greatest immediacy and the pressure that goes with it as a point for decision-making regarding the birthrate.

Furthermore, to speak to women simple as part of couples is to
address those probably already involved in fairly traditional family-
oriented structures. To speak directly to women as might-be mothers
would mean also addressing those who have not yet married, and this
might alter their attitudes toward marriage and children. A program
aimed only at couples is fairly conservative and traditional, ex-
pecting no change in basic social institutions. A program whose
focus is the might-be mother could have no such limitation. One
could expect the most dramatic alteration in birthrates when the
rationale for such limitation is aimed directly at those whose immediate future is the most affected by a new birth. But to give such
rationale could conflict with other values deeply held by both national and even wider cultures. The greatest reasons to be given to
a woman as might-be mother in order to convince her that a new
birth would be detrimental have to do with her own freedom and

self-fulfillment in ways other than as a mother. Considering the great difficulty changes in social attitudes and in legal structures concerning women have faced in this country, it is highly unlikely that the reasons most closely affecting women could be stressed. It would involve altering the culture so that women were psychologically free to seek fulfillment and a sense of personal worth in ways other than motherhood. It would also mean that those other ways would have to be open to women in more than a token fashion.

As long as women are raised to believe that if they do not marry and have children somehow they are failures and social outcasts, and as long as the actual employment opportunities for women are not satisfying, little but tinkering will be done with the birthrate. The most cogent reasons for limiting births, as seen by the social unit whose future is most immediately touched by the decision, are not utilized by publicity that seeks to lower the birthrate. The modern state has considered its own welfare to be affected by the strength of the family units within it. For this reason the state has taken great interest in marriage and divorce laws, really replacing religious institutions in this regard. Tax laws, social security benefits, and myriad other legislative acts have been framed to support family units. A move that would create great numbers of unmarried people or childless couples might well be seen as a threat to national mores by those in power. These factors play an even larger role in cultures that have even more negative attitudes toward the full emancipation of women.

It amounts to the question of the quality of whose life is to be considered. It is one thing to base arguments upon the quality of life for my children's grandchildren. A world view tends to do this. It is something else to base arguments upon the quality of our life as a family, including the immediate lives of our children. Even more direct would be arguments based on the quality of *my* life this year and next. The smaller the social unit the greater the tendency to focus on the quality of lives now in existence, and the ways in which they would be altered by new births. The larger the social unit the greater the tendency to focus on the quality of life for future generations, for those not yet born.

How can we balance the claims of lives presently in existence with those yet to come? Usually it appears selfish to claim that present lives, my own included, have prior claims. Exploitation of the earth, forgetful of future generations is a clear argument against such selfishness. Many ecological problems can be traced to a lack of responsibility for the future on the part of past generations. But there is another side of this coin. Selfishness is a complicated term and not always is it rightly applied. This leads to another assertion.

Extreme hopelessness may well exclude any sense of the future at all and stress the present moment only. But hopelessness can also cause us to give up on the present and look only to the future. *Interest in the quality of life of future generations in contrast to concern for the quality of my own life may be a reflection of the sense of hopelessness I possess about my own possibilities.* To look mainly to future generations is a form of vicarious living caused not by altruism but by frustration. Religion has all too often encouraged this. It is not healthy nor can it lead to a healthy society in the future since the hopelessness is transmitted along with the concern. Women in our culture frequently suffer from lack of possibility for themselves and the consequent cultural pressure to live through their husbands and children. Much of the contemporary women's liberation movement is based on ending such vicarious living.

Positive self-valuation is a step forward from a negative self-image. An ethic that is derived from the experience of those who have a long history of self-valuation and whose positive identity is part of the culture may well reflect a need for humility, lack of exploitative actions, greater responsibility for the future, and so forth. In our society this has been the experience of white men. Our ethics have been written largely by this group. Our religious institutions have also reflected the same bias. Those who have not had this experience, particularly women and non-white men, who have been denied in many ways by law and custom a real future for themselves, and have been forced to live through their hopes for their children or their hopes for heaven beyond, cannot at the moment subscribe to an ethic which calls their new-found pride "selfishness." Calls for birth control that look exclusively to future generations therefore miss the mark with those who have only recently begun to consider the quality of their own lives to be as important if not a greater claim than the lives of those yet unborn.

Women and minority groups are not the only ones who have tended to live vicariously, however. Parents who feel that they have been kept from social and financial success by their own limited backgrounds may so stress their duty to their children that their children are overwhelmingly aware of the basic sense of failure and frustration in their parents' lives. This emphasis on the next generation is *not* self*less*ness. It is not a wholesome concern for the future. It is rather a clear message from the parents that their own lives are unsatisfactory. It lays great demands upon the children to satisfy the parents' need for success. It is not surprising that children frequently react against the tone of hopelessness and demand whereas the parents interpret their own actions as generous and unselfish. In reality it is selfishness on the part of the parents, but it can so easily pass for altruism.

A sense of personal worth allows me to assume that the quality of my own life is important. I may then opt to have fewer children or no children at all in order to preserve my present life-style or in order to gain the life-style I wish. To some degree this can be seen as selfish, but no more selfish than is the desire to have children so that they can achieve for me what I do not believe I can achieve for myself. In the case of the might-be mother the decision whether or not to have children may well depend on the availability and quality of child care facilities. It may also depend on a re-ordered society that places equal responsibility for child care on both male and female parents. Both measures would allow a woman to have a child and not alter drastically her own life. If the aims of much of the present feminist movements are realized, such incentives for women to have children may well be necessary.

The constant viewing of the population question from the world or national or even family level is indirect and unnecessary. If the perspective of women were the basic one, the birthrate would drop with no pressure needed. This has not been the approach because the drastic changes this would mean in our society have not been accepted or desired by those in power.

When we seek to find a balance between the quality of life of those now living and the quality of life of future generations, neither present nor future can be sacrificed for the other. A positive self-evaluation, a sense of hope for ourselves and our own future will help in this balancing, although an emphasis on the need to avoid exploitation must also continue.

There are two other expressions of this new emphasis on the priority of present lives over possible future lives. One is the trend toward the adoption of hard-to-place children by couples — and also by single people — who choose not to have children born to them or who choose to limit severely the number of their natural born children. Whether this is a trend found only in a small segment of our society, or whether it is a growing movement, only time will tell. It remains true, however, that the adoption of hard-to-place children is a way of saying that the quality of life of those already born takes precedence over the possibilities of those unborn.

The second expression of this new emphasis is the move to liberalize the abortion laws. It is a more difficult situation because a life conceived but not yet born fits neither category clearly. So much of the controversy stems from differing opinions as to whether a life conceived but not yet born is more to be viewed on the side of the presently living or on the side of future generations. But the arguments also reflect a difference in the degree to which the quality of life of those presently living is believed to take precedence in some ways over the quality of life of future generations. It is no accident that the new awakening on the part of women that their own lives are significant, can be fulfilling in themselves, has led also to a more open support for the liberalization of abortion laws. For most of us abortion is not a good form of birth control, yet it remains a necessary back-up measure to present forms of contraception and to present ignorance of contraceptive measures. Liberalized abortion laws may pressure research scientists to take more seriously the demands of growing numbers of women for safe, convenient, economical contraceptive means. When these are found, abortion will be a far less responsible choice than it now may be. Had the quality of the lives of women been taken with greater seriousness before this, the pressure for better contraceptive methods might well have led to positive results before the demand for more liberal abortion laws had arisen, and might have rendered such legislative changes less necessary.

All of this sounds highly individualistic, as though the might-be mother or the couple really should be the only planning level for the determination of optimum population. What has been said above is a corrective to what normally seems the perspective and therefore it needs to be kept in mind. The growing self-interest of women, which is a maturing positive event, could easily bring the population to manageable proportions without any larger group planning for population control. However, this is not to say that there need be no consideration of population at higher social levels. There are values to be reaped at both the national and world level that only conscious awareness and decision-making can insure. In other words, if, due to the changes in the situation of women, the birthrate were to drop rapidly, this would still leave many things to be done in order to take account of this fact, things that really can only be done at a national or world level.

If the population develops self-limiting characteristics because of the reasons stated above, then great efforts must be made to see that all those who are born reach the full development and age of which they are naturally capable. If the proportion of infants to the whole population is drastically smaller, then in order to maintain a stable optimum population, there must be great conservation of all infants and young persons so that they will indeed reach adulthood. Perhaps we assume that we do all we can now to see that the young are protected. But this is not the case on a society-wide basis. Families may do the best they can, but poverty, lack of medical services, all of these factors limit what is actually done. We have, as a society, assumed that the young were really the concern only of the family. If our society as a whole did not somehow deep in its psyche retain the idea that the young are to some degree expendable, that the only tragedy in the death or stunted growth of a child is to its family and not really to the whole society, then the priorities of the nation would be different than they are. A severely limited number of births could have the effect of prompting the whole nation to see its responsibility to all children in a way that it presently does not. There might ultimately be the same sense of responsibility at the world level. This need for concerted effort will be all the greater if the actual determination of population size remains in the hands of private citizens, women and families, and out from under the possible direct manipulation of the state, since the easy alternative of again increasing births cannot be used.

If the nation were to consider all children to be the concern of the whole society since even in objective terms of numbers no child could be thought expendable, what could this mean? Let us look briefly at several different areas:

I. *Before conception:* As long as we hold to the totally voluntary character of parenthood, the decision whether or not to have a child must be left to the prospective parents. The state ought not inflict its opinion as to who should be born or who should give birth. Yet it remains true that there are many who ought not to have children because of their own inability to produce or raise healthy children. Every condition that presently militates against responsible decision-making about parenthood must be eliminated as much as possible. In order to insure this, and in order to increase, before conception, the highest possibility of healthy children who will be properly cared for, the following would need to be done:

There needs to be solid, accurate sex education before an age at which adult sexual activity is possible. There must also be contraceptive information and materials available to any who desire them. We need a stress on physical fitness, especially for young women, so that maternal health is improved. This would require a revamping of several attitudes. If young women remain pressured to fit a social stereotype that sees them concerned about weight but not about nutrition and leads them to a serious lack of strenuous exercise because it is thought unfeminine, then we cannot anticipate healthier mothers and children. Sports in schools have become more and more a serious matter for boys only and even there they exclude many who are not natural athletes. Competitive sports for the few has replaced the original understanding of physical education for everyone. If a stress on health replaced the present beauty queen image for women, then a healthier young female population might be achieved. Concern for maternal health cannot begin after a woman conceives. It must be there long before.

There must be an alteration of social attitudes so that parenthood is seen as a task and not as a natural event for which no one needs training. If social attitudes did not assume that everyone *ought* to be a parent and that self-esteem and the fulfilling of society's expectations were part of the reason for having children, then the real choice for parenthood might be made on far better grounds than it is presently. Nor is it true that more money makes one a better parent. Greater social services, such as maternal and child health, available to all, could allow less affluent people who truly desire children, to produce and raise healthier children. We need greater research into the prevention of birth defects so that more of the children who are conceived are born healthy. We need the continued development of genetic counseling so that couples can make responsible decisions where there is a known possibility of a defective child.

II. *Before birth:* Greater social concern would mean that health care for the pregnant woman would be seen as a nation-wide concern so that all children are born as healthy as possible. At present this is too much a private concern of the family, too much related to their financial ability to pay for such care. If a society considered every pregnancy to be of great value to the whole community it might then see that the health of the mother during pregnancy and delivery is the concern of everyone and must be guaranteed to everyone. Again, the present lack of interest can be traced to the belief that some children are expendable, and some mothers as well. A greatly lowered birthrate could alter this.

Also needed is further research into safer methods of delivery, including the possibility of home delivery by mid-wives in some instances. Hospitals have not been proven to be the healthiest places for newborn children. On the other hand, hospitals are the best places in the case of any complication or difficulty. We need to be able to predict more accurately what births could safely occur at home.

III. *After birth:* Health care must be available for all children for the same reason it is needed for maternal health. There must be equal valuation of male and female children by both parents and society so that all children born can reach their full potential in terms of intellectual and interpersonal development. Part of the reason parents often value a son more than a daughter is that a son may well be expected to succeed in the world and, therefore, reflect well upon his parents. A daughter does this usually only in terms of whom she marries, which is a far less direct reflection. The very desire to have a son achieve for the parents is in itself a problem for the son, as we have seen. If success in the world were equally available to daughters it could add to the pressures to achieve that they feel, but it might also dilute some of the pressures felt by sons. On the basis of our present attitudes, if we develop the ability to conceive a child of a desired sex, it could wreck havoc in our society very quickly since the preference for male children would unbalance the sex distribution of the next generation. It could be interesting to see the kind of family institutions that might then develop.

In order to maintain a stable population the diseases and other conditions to which the young are particularly susceptible would need to be eliminated. In the category of "other conditions" three need to be mentioned. All three are conditions which many deplore, but society as a whole is not totally committed to their elimination. Perhaps if the absolute value of the lives of the young for the whole nation were more visible because of a lower birth rate, then these conditions might receive top priority. The three conditions are (1) drug-related deaths, (2) automobile accidents, (3) war-related deaths. In all three cases the greatest concentration of these deaths is on young men. If this group were not considered somewhat expendable, it is difficult to see why more public pressure has not been brought to bear on hard drugs and on auto safety. We seem to assume that as long as *our* children are not directly affected it is not our problem. In the case of combat deaths, the specific responsibility of fighting cannot be fairly given to one age and sex group. In a totally stable population, such a risk would have to be spread evenly across the population or, better yet, eliminated for everyone.

The educational system for the young would also need to be altered drastically. A rapidly growing population has meant that a disproportionate percentage of the population is young. The education of the young has taken on more and more the character of mass production. It has also involved the lengthening of time before a person can join the labor force. Because more people are entering the labor market from the young group than leaving it by retirement or death, education has the character of holding back greater and greater numbers by increasing the time spent in preparation. So much of our education has the effect of segregating the young from any meaningful contact with the wider society. Out of this segregation has come a youth culture which on the one hand rejects the idea that the young cannot or ought not to participate meaningfully in the decisions of the larger society or even in the decisions that affect their own lives and education. On the other hand, this youth culture has also increased the alienation that exists between the young and the rest of society because there is a difference in values.

If a society had a limited number of young people, then they might more easily be integrated into the rest of society. They could present little or no threat to the job market since the young would not be a disproportionate group in size. A return to an apprenticeship form of education would be possible in some areas. A higher proportion of adults to children in many forms of education would also make sense. Would this mean that the values of the youth culture would also end and that only traditional, older values would prevail? This need not be the case if the young are really integrated into the whole society with decision-making responsibilities at an early age. Then the viewpoints of this age group could be added to the whole. However, some strong peer group activity and orientation is needed for the formation of clarity and confidence in their views of the young, and this must be present. Too much integration can be dangerous. The present almost total segregation of the young, largely accomplished by our educational institutions with their rigid age groups and minute contact between teachers and individual students, has led to the formation of a peer group based on alienation; and this is not healthy.

Finally, were the quantity, at least in proportion, of the young in our society to decline, a drastic reorganization of our values could occur. We have mentioned the ways in which the vast numbers of the young have caused them to be segregated from the rest of society, and, in a way undervalued. This undervaluing could occur because of the patriarchal attitudes of older people as well as simply the sheer numbers of the young. They have been viewed as a threat on the job market, even as women and minority groups have been. Were their numbers lessened, both relatively and absolutely, then this segregation and threat could end and the young be integrated into society. It would also be necessary that their potential contribution be considered valuable by society, which would involve an end to the patriarchal value structure. Because of pressure from the youth culture this is beginning to occur.

The youth culture has also had the effect of causing society to overvalue youth, at least as a time of life. We see this constantly in the fear of aging and the desire always to be thought young. Whether we turn to the fashion industry or to music, the youth culture dominates. To be past thirty is a tragedy, not only as viewed by those who are under thirty but equally so by many who are past this magical limit.

In the past decade there has been much to disillusion. For a brief while, in the time of the political Camelot, it appeared that to be young might mean to be wise. The Civil Rights marches in which the young were involved had begun to produce a few results. It might be that the young had found some political ways and means that would accomplish their purposes. Even in the days of the Children's Crusade of the campaign of 1968, there seemed to be hope. The field of theology in this country also seemed to believe that to be young meant to be in tune with new trends, such as the Secular City. The old giants were gone, both in politics and in theology. There was a distrust of the old who brought with them the aroma of the dying world before the Second World War. It was necessary to think young in order to be relevant and alive to the issues of the day. But then assassinations and politics as usual, culminating in Chicago, 1968, left many with no place to go. To be young was as futile as to be old.

We can never go back before that. There is no possible way that age can ever again be venerated simply in itself. We can never return to a time when plodding along through the ranks of the organization can seem *ipso facto* worthy of reward. The youth culture has changed that. The newness of the vision of the young who have learned to trust their own insights and perspective, and the fact that our world continues to change so rapidly, will continue to force us to recognize that long experience may as easily disqualify us from future leadership as qualify us. If our experience has locked us firmly into the ways of the past, we may find adaptation to the new exceedingly difficult.

Yet the disillusionment of youth is also real, at least to the young, and music and fashion are just beginning to exploit this. If in the future there is no overwhelming youth culture, and yet if we cannot return to the more traditional structures of the past, what then is to be the future valuation of youth and age?

It must be something new. Even in our traditional society age has only been venerated to a point—until retirement age. Age, beyond employment years, is as much of a limbo as is youth in our society. In a culture that determines personal worth largely in terms of earning capacity, the old, women, and the young have all found themselves outside the circle of the significant in many ways. All have suffered from job discrimination and from paternalistic protective legislation in order to keep them out of the circle. The elderly also live increasingly in a segregated society. They are either isolated in urban or rural loneliness or else put together in retirement homes or villages. Whether elegant or poor in their living accommodations they remain so often away from other age groups.

Many of the ways suggested above regarding the integration of the young into the wider society could also be helpful in integrating the elderly. If education ceased to be a highly institutional system for the young and became instead a more personalized process for all age groups, then education might be a major leisure time activity. It could cease being simply drudgery to be endured in order to enter the job market at a certain level. The lengthening of the process of formal education seems to have as much to do with postponing entrance into the labor market as with preparation for it. There is such a functional character to much of our education that a more leisurely approach could overcome. Part of this is the utilitarian character of job-oriented schools. But some of it is the alienation of the young from anything that has preceded the moment in which they come to social consciousness. Were the segregation of the young to end then we might anticipate a lessening of their a-historical attitudes. If this occurred, then some of the antagonism between young and old might cease and they could find themselves involved together in the same educational experiences.

In small ways there is today a growing rapport between young and old. Both have in common that they are not beholden to an employer and are therefore free to advocate positions that fear, prudence, or position might have led them to hesitate about otherwise. Both groups also find themselves frequently in institutional situations where others control their lives—i.e. schools, retirement homes. Both groups are beginning to demand participatory democracy at these levels. The young have preceded the old in this. A group of retired persons previously employed by church agencies has been organized recently. It sees as two of its tasks the development of greater democracy in retirement homes and the development of liaisons with the young. This coalition of old and young bodes well for the future, if it can expand.

Our present American society stresses so totally economic grounds for personal value, and neither the old nor the young usually qualify. If our social values change so that contributions of a non-economic nature are also valued by society, then both youth and age might be seen as valuable to the whole community. Further, if non-productive leisure activities become valued, then again both young and old could find their place within an integrated society. If leisure time so increases that all employment would be considered part-time, then the segregation of these age groups could be lessened even more. It is the stress on productive, economic values that has alienated these two groups from the rest of society. It is fear of too many people competing for jobs that has kept these groups separated.

In summary, and in reverse order from the original presentation, three major points are to be made. First, an exceedingly positive change in our present value structure could occur if the growth of our population ceased and consequently, if the percentage of the population who were young were smaller. This would by no means be an automatic value change resulting from population shifts but would need to be accompanied by clear attempts to integrate all age groups of society. The main agency for such integration would be a drastically altered educational system that would not be tied directly to future employment. This could occur most easily if there were a far smaller proportion of young people to be educated and to be employed.

Secondly, a stable or even decreasing population would demand greater concern for the health and development of every child. This is a change in values greatly to be desired. It could only be accomplished if clear national policy to this affect accompanied a decrease in population. It could not be left to private, voluntary acts of concerned individuals.

Finally, the most rapid way to initiate such changes in our population and our values is by the total emancipation of women so that options for self-fulfillment other than motherhood are not only exceedingly positive but also socially acceptable. We are presently headed in this direction without any planning, at least in this country. How calmly and how rapidly remains to be seen and depends in no small measure upon the leadership of political and religious institutions in our society.

8

QUALITY AND QUANTITY: THE CONFLICT OF VALUES

Waldo Beach

Catherine Gunsalas' paper offers many fresh insights into the elusive dialectical problem of quality vs. quantity in the population problem. With many of her briskly-stated exceptions to conventional wisdom I would concur. I must, however, take sharp exception to many of the points she attempts to establish and her reasons for so doing.

I should make it clear that I come at this paper as a contextual Christian ethicist, standing between the Christian faith and the empirical facts. I am helped by a four-leveled approach to every policy question: (1) a descriptive analysis of the hard facts, (2) a sorting out of the values at stake, or the values in collision in the situation, (3) a normative statement of the relevant moral "ought" to be perceived and obeyed, and (4) an affirmation of the ultimate "why" or theological sanction of the moral "ought."

Level 2—i.e., the values in collision in the situation of the population explosion—can be sorted out in three dimensions: *what* values are at stake, *whose* values, and *when* the values prized or sought are anticipated. Miss Gunsalas quite rightly deals with *whose* values are at stake in her analysis of the five social units (world, nation, cultural group, the family, and might-be mother) to whom the problem looks of course very differently, as between the smallest and largest unit. She correctly alerts us to the time dimension (or the *when* dimension) of the value problem in her discussion of the temporal line stretching between concern for *now* values or the very near future, vs. posterity, or values in the far future. But what I miss in her descriptive analysis of the problem is an account of *what* values are at stake, a qualitative consideration of the range of psychological, spiritual, economic, educational, and personal values that impinge consciously or unconsciously on the choices of men and women to have more children, or less, or none at all. On these matters, other than in quick references to such "non-quantitative values as self-realization and fulfillment," Miss Gunsalas is quite elusive.

Yet these considerations are certainly as important as the quantifiable values. Let me put the matter in a dramatic and fantastic way: what if the federal government ordered that on the ceiling of every master bedroom of suburban American a graph should be posted showing the rising line of the world's population and the dropping line of the earth's resources to sustain that population? How much effect would this have on the birth rate of middle-America? Probably very little. In so far as people make deliberate and conscious choices over procreation, they do so out of immediate concerns for the well-being of their own close-in circle, rightly or wrongly. They will make their decision out of a complex of value-preferences, among which the considerations of a spiritual sort, both for themselves and for the children they want and whom they feel they can afford to raise, weigh quite more heavily than the population explosion.

This leads to a second point where I would demur from the paper: in the implication of her assertion that "interest in the quality of life for future generations in contrast to concern for the quality of my own life may be a reflection of the sense of hopelessness I possess about my own possibilities." She suggests, that the concern of parents for the well-being of their children, even at the expense of their own, is a form of "vicarious living" which is merely an inverted egoism and morally wrong. From the standpoint of a Christian ethicist, and as a parent and father, I would protest this generalization. One does not have to adopt a "doormat" view of the Christian life to affirm that there are strong spiritual values of personal fulfillment in the devotion and sacrifices of parents for the education and nurture of their children. The feminist bias of the author, celebrating the liberation of women from the fetters of child-rearing, has rather blinded her to some of the values that accrue to a life turned out from itself in consideration of one's children, and finding freedom of another sort. Further, her expectation that the crusade for Women's Liberation would do more than any other factor to lower the birth rate is much too simple a panacea.

If we could discern more exactly *what* values constitute good quality of life we might weigh into the balance-scale the factors to be reckoned with responsibly in setting normative policy, private and public. It seems evident to this critic that it is too simple to start with the premise that there is an exact inverse ratio between quantity and quality of life, between density of the mass and the quality of humane living. In determining "optimum" population (a qualitative term, not synonymous with "maximum") economic and ecological criteria weigh very heavily, to be sure, but they are not the only criteria; there are spiritual, aesthetic, and moral criteria which are more than derivative from the economic.

The valences of qualitative and quantitative values do indeed depend on the cultural circumstances of the social unit, as Miss Gunsalas rightly maintains. In a rural setting, the larger family may be an asset for all the persons in it; in an urban setting, a liability. In the United States the form of the population problem is drastically different from its form in the Third World. For an American family of moderate means to go beyond the 2.11 limit might be an expression of responsible love and yield certain qualitative values in the give-and-take of family enterprise, in the personal enrichment of the variety of persons, in the prospect of the children's support of parents in elder years, values not enjoyed by the couple who have no children. Nor does such a positive evaluation of the larger family unit reduce to second-class citizenship, as Miss Gunsalas suggests that it does, the unmarried person or the childless couple.

The prescriptive or normative part of her paper is addressed to what we ought to do as a nation *if* we had a lower birth rate and reduced the proportions of the young in our society. Her positive suggestions are almost all valid and incontrovertible. It would indeed be salutary for the quality of life if we had better sex education, health care, reintegration of youth and the elderly into our society, and more personalized education. But the big IF remains. These prescriptions are not addressed to the premise: *how* to lower the birth rate, except perhaps as a kind of "Promised Land" inducement. She has the cart before the horse. We are assured that there would be a healthy positive change in the value-structure if there were fewer young people. And if we had a "more limited number of young people, then they might more easily be integrated into the rest of society." The value structure is apparently the dependent variable for Miss Gunsalas, the population size the independent variable. Speaking in the normative vein, she seems to offer quantitative solutions to qualitative problems, which is rather unusual coming from a theologian. This observer would set the matter the other way around and claim that the problem is how to alter the value-structures of our society, and the inner religious faiths that lie behind them as their ultimate sanction. Speaking from a Christian standpoint, it means to me that there are qualitative approaches to quantitative problems. How to change the value-structure, the inner motivations of parents in the decisions about parenthood, toward conscientious and responsible choice: that is a task prior in urgency than to consider the beneficient consequences of having fewer young people.

To speak in cryptic terms, and to say nothing more than what is plain and obvious, the normative response to the population crisis I would advocate would be to create a public conscience for the voluntary limitation of birth, out of an ethic of responsible steward-ship. Retire from circulation the biblical verse "be fruitful and multiply." Put in its stead the Great Commandment, read in terms of the needs of the far neighbor—far both in a spatial and in a temporal sense—whose quality of life is as valuable as my own. In the private realm, this would mean a parenthood planned to a size proportionate to economic and cultural circumstances. In the public realm, it would mean the support of legislation for the dissemination of birth control data and devices, the liberalizing of abortion laws, the reduction of tax exemption for large numbers of children, and all the other measures of political constraint on family size.

9

ECOLOGICAL CONSIDERATIONS

JAMES C. LOGAN

While Ernst Haeckel, the German zoologist, coined it over a century ago, "ecology" became a common American word in 1970. The word took on reality for Americans as they discovered something of the condition of their habitation, their *oikos,* their "spaceship" earth. Through the various public media the basic, elementary lesson of ecology was set forth: earth is a finite web-of-life, and man in the midst of that web has been creating havoc by wantonly exploiting his environment and heedlessly multiplying himself.

There were the "prophets before their time" who had sounded the ecological forecasts, but for the most part the public had not heard or the message had not registered. As early as the 1950's John Stewart Collis argued that man had already lived through two basic periods in human relationship with the wider environment. First was the "Era of Mythology" when men believed that they should venerate the world because it was inhabited by spirits and gods. Second was the "Era of Economics" when the natural world was viewed as an economic commodity and its value calculated in terms of cash. Nature was desacralized or divested of its gods, first, through agricultural development and, then, through industrialization. Collis' argument was that the "Era of Economics" had "brought us to the edge of disaster." The only rational choice confronting *homo sapiens* was to enter a new era — "the Era of Ecology." [1]

The ecological crisis of the 1970s confirmed Collis' analysis. There rages today a conflict between value systems. The established system is one which through the centuries western man has developed, sometimes consciously and sometimes unconsciously. In many quarters this value system is taken for granted, but in some quarters it is today being challenged vigorously. The inherited value system goes something like this:

• *Earth is to be subjugated to the self-determined ends of the human species.* This attitude has recently been labled as the ideology of anthropocentricism.[2] Man is the center of all things earthly, and nature has been put under his feet. Man is the exclusive center of intrinsic value, and if the natural world outside of man possesses value, its value is purely instrumental. Much benefit has accrued from this interpretation. The emergence of the scientific spirit of inquiry, industrialization and technology are implicitly the products of a so-called "desacralized" and, hence, man-centered understanding of nature. Such a view of the natural environment, however, is not without implications for the interpretation of the human species. The human species is isolated and elevated to a realm above nature, and now in non-mythological freedom the human race can do with nature what it pleases. Lost is a holistic understanding of man; gone is that symbiosis between man and environment. Now there is an alienation between the human and the natural.

• *Concomitant with the subjugation ideology is the view of nature as essentially lifeless, inert matter.* It is not profitable to argue which came first the practice or the idea. The idea had had a long and venerable history in the philosophical tradition. What is important to see is that the eighteenth century picture of nature as a mathematical-mechanical system was used as a defence for advancing industrial and technological exploitation of nature.

Such a view has implications for the understanding of the human species. If, as Descartes had held, nature is simply extended matter, what is the uniqueness of the human? Philosophy and theology retreated to the subjectivity and interiority of man to answer that question. In the meantime the quantitatively overwhelming realm of the inorganic pressed more and more heavily upon the human species in the form of a reductive naturalism causing one to wonder if any distinction could be made between environment and man. Cut the cords which bind man to nature, and a reaction will simply absorb man into an undifferentiated whole. Neither isolation nor absorption are answers. Teilhard de Chardin constantly reminded us that there is a reciprocal interaction between man and his environment. An impersonal, lifeless universe soon robs man of his vital personal being. "The only universe capable of containing the human person is an irreversibly personalizing universe." [3]

• The subjugation of nature and the attendant picture of the lifeless, inert character of nature fed into another ideological factor. *Individuals and nations come to measure their success by the increased level of consumption and the demand for more products.* For example, the Gross National Product functions as an economic thermometer, and the same economic values are increasingly prevalent in the developing nations. The technological society thrives on the resources which it can extract from the earth. The economy of such a society is built upon rapid consumption and increased demand for more products. Technology until recently has been confined to the Western world, but today this is no longer the case. The stage is set for another understanding of human life and society. Some commentators are telling us that with the expansion of technology we can expect within a short time a savage competition between nations for raw materials. Whereas, in this brief descriptive analysis we began with man over nature, we can now see how this eventually leads to man against man. While the richer nations become richer, more and more people are left in the lurch without sufficient natural resources, food and water in the poorer nations.

• *Running through these three factors is a thread of a fourth, the political ideology of the individual.* John Locke was the one who expressed this so clearly and left its mark so deeply upon political philosophy. Man "is absolute lord of his own person and possessions . . . and subject of nobody." Community or government arises as the means to help one preserve his property rights, something the individual was unable to do on his own. Property therefore means power. The man with power is the man with property; he has the rights. In such a view human rights are relegated to a subordinate position, and property rights assume the dominant position. At precisely this point, the ecological concerns about the environment merge with the social concerns of the human community. The conservationist mentality in the past has not always reckoned with this. There is biting truth in the cynical observation that only the economically and property-privileged can afford the luxury of an ecological conscience. The protest movements for the civil rights of black, poor, women and the demand for a resolution of the bitter conflicts taking tremendous tolls of human and environmental life in warfare are fundamentally part of the scenario of protest against the older value system which made it simple to treat everything but self as impersonal objects to be manipulated. The concern for a viable future environment forces to center stage the centuries' old conviction that individual property rights are supreme, and therefore superior to human rights and nature's rights. In the Judeo-Christian tradition it is difficult to argue for such extreme individualism. In that particular faith perspective we have no property rights as such. "The earth is the Lord's. . ." A pressing question cannot be avoided by the ethically sensitive person. Can we expect a people who have elevated territorial rights above human rights and dignities to the extent that we wage wars, and who lock blacks, poor and women into stereotypes of inferiority to exercise any greater concern for nature and its own rights?

For those who have the eyes to see, it should be obvious that the coalescence of these basic attitudinal developments has placed the human family not only over nature but in a fundamental sense *against* nature. The human species has been removed from its symbiotic unity with nature, and the only value of the natural world is to be found in the utilitarian function whereby the natural world serves the benefit of man. While not discounting the positive role which instrumental value plays in the enrichment of human life, the question cannot be avoided: what will happen if we continue to extend our thoughts and attitudes on this course into the future? As I have pointed out in each of the above factors, these developments are not without consequences for the way in which we view human life itself. This in itself should be a constant reminder to us that the separation of man from nature is contrary to fact. Man is part of the "oikos" and not just an inhabitant in it. The reduction of nature to the exclusive status of instrumental value threatens to reduce man accordingly. In such a context of value the same technique employed to "subdue" nature can be applied in other directions toward the manipulation of individuals and groups. What happens to nature in the end also happens to man, for he is part of nature. If nature is divested of inherent meaning and significance, it is a very simple matter for man to become no more than an object for study and exploitation. This "absolutization of human life at the total expense of subhuman life," insists John Cobb, "seems to lead to a mode of being in which human existence itself would be subhuman in quality." [4]

It is possible, at least for the immediate future, to continue the ethical debate within the context of anthropocentrism. Prudential wisdom abounds in the popular and learned press to the effect that if we do not do such-and-such in relation to the environment, then such-and-such will happen to us humans. Prudential wisdom always has an "ad hoc" character to it. But can such prudential wisdom sustain us over the long haul? If we persist in this manner, then we may as well give up the ethical debate for all that is required is the reporting of scientific facts and the adjusting of our life-styles accordingly. It therefore seems imperative, if the ethical discussion on population and environment is to proceed in a responsible manner, to raise the question of inherent value in nature itself. A responsible ethic for the human community requires that such a question be considered.

If nothing is good which does not serve man, what saves us from the parochialism of defining the "good" as that which serves particular individuals or particular groups and nations? The motivation of self-interest, even if it be enlightened self-interest, militates against a responsible consideration of the quality of life essential for all peoples. Over the long distance a consideration of the inherent value of the natural environment will be necessary to save us from the myoptic vision of pragmatic self-interest.

To be sure, the quest for inherent values in the natural world is fraught with dangers. Paul Santmire has argued persuasively that the nineteenth century advocates of a return to nature and the practice of a "rustic piety" exemplified a social "cop-out" from the arena of the pressing human problems of urbanization, economics, and social justice.[5] Even more recently Richard Neuhaus has passionately claimed that there is a danger of "environmental imperialism" which is "anti-poor," "anti-people."[6] His protest is legitimate and should be heard. Bird-watchers rarely get concerned about rats! The historical analysis of Santmire and the prophetic protest of Neuhaus warn that the question of inherent value in the natural world is a pseudo-question if we continue to view the human and the subhuman as two distinct and separate families of value competing with one another. Indeed, it is to continue the old game with the same rules to inquire if nature has a value independent of man. This is the manner in which most of Western philosophy has played the game since Descartes. As a result the "great philosophical divide" today seems to be between the empircists and positivists on the one side (who claim primacy to sensory experience, which in turn creates the mind) or the idealists and existenitalists on the other side (who place emphasis first on the subjective experience of mind or existence itself). Neither tradition is really capable of supplying us with a philosophical means of getting at the issue. Fortunately there are other voices, though not a majority, who speak of another way.

This latter position claims that knowledge of the subhuman and human does not originate in a specific experience of the world as a locatable object but rather with a primal intuition of the worth of life. When this axiological intuition is critically examined it becomes clear that life is more than a single unit, namely, *my life*. Life is a continum ranging from the human to the subhuman. To divide life and to claim that knowledge begins with a concrete sensory experience of some locatable object is to commit what Whitehead once called *the fallacy of misplaced concreteness*. The natural world including the human family is not a collection of entities placed in a container called "time and space." The natural world including the human family is a continuous, multi-faceted process. The classic man/nature dualism is eschewed in such a view of reality. What emerges is a vision of life and matter within a single continuum.

This is not to reduce man to the subordinate position which he occupied in the older naturalisms. Man still possesses a distinctiveness —the distinctiveness that in the whole evolutionary process it is he who is selfconscious and therefore in a position to be a determiner of the future of that process. This is not to claim that man is no longer an historical being, but it is rather to extend the manifold of his history to include his kinship with the history of the cosmic order. Man is not a mere human cut off from nature, but he is the expression of evolving life in its as yet fullest attainment. In a unique way he exemplifies the categories of all of which he is part. This is not the place to set forth a programmatic metaphysics. It should be sufficient to point to the fact that not only philosophers but natural and social scientists, historians, poets and religionists from their varying perspectives point to a similar unified vision of reality. It is the awareness of which Loren Eiseley writes that "you are also a rag doll made of patches out of many ages and skins." [7]

And what about the question of value? If human life is valuable (and this symposium explicitly or implicitly is predicated upon that assumption) and if human life is distinctive in terms of degree and not of difference in kind from all else which is, then there is an inescapable reciprocity between the natural and the human. Man is the particular matrix of that reciprocity. This is not to say that there are no degrees of value. Such a claim would be a regression to primitivism where every distinction is lost in an undifferentiated whole. There is value to each stage of life in the evolving process, and there is value appropriate to each stage as it supports other stages of development.

Theologically, such a unified vision needs an ultimate ground of value. It may be possible to argue within such a unified framework without theistic reference, but the argument is certainly more plausible on theistic grounds. That the subhuman and human have a value in themselves is a perfectly rational affirmation in the light of evolutionary development. That the subhuman and human have value to God makes the ethical affirmation a mandate for responsible action. It was from this final court of appeals that the prophets of Israel derived their mandate to proclaim both judgment and hope for man and earth. Their hope was not unlike the one which I have attempted to sketch in a different way. In the midst of the ecological debate, there has been a kind of theological advocacy which calls for an either/or decision—either the God of Genesis or the God of the prophets. To say the least, this is bad biblical exegesis. The prophets recognized clearly that the God in whose name they spoke was the Creator of the ends of the earth *and* the Lord of history. To choose the natural without the social or vice versa would have been an anachronism to them, and it will be fatal for us today.

The natural inclination of the philosopher or theologian is to stop at this point. But life is lived as well as reflected upon. We, therefore, turn to some of the specific issues of population and environment.

Much of the environmental debate in recent times has focused on the factors of pollution and environmental deterioration. Pollution has been with us ever since man began attempting to control his environment, but today's greatly accelerated rate of change and our ability to detect and forecast the effects of such change inflate the problem to frightening proportions. But what are the causes of the situation? Here there is considerable disagreement.

At one end of the spectrum are the Paul Ehrlichs claiming that "too many cars, too many factories, too much detergent, too much pesticide, multiplying contrails, inadequate sewage treatment plans, too little water, too much carbon dioxide—all can be traced easily to *too many people.*" [8] S. Fred Singer has even coined the barbarism "populution" to describe the situation.[9] In more guarded rhetoric Lamont C. Cole sums up the position: "there is no way for us to survive except to halt population growth completely or even to undergo a period of population decrease if, as I anticipate, definitive studies show our population to be already beyond what the earth can support on a continuous basis. Just as we must control our interference with the chemical cycles that provide the atmosphere with its oxygen and nitrogen, so must we control our birth rate." [10]

At the other end of the spectrum are those who claim that lack of governmental control of the development and direction of technology, not increased population, has been the chief factor in pollution of the environment. Barry Commoner is probably the most competent proponent of this view: "Is it only a coincidence that in the years following World War II there was not only a great outburst of technological innovation, but also an equally large upsurge in environmental pollution? Is it possible that the new technology is the major cause of the environmental crisis?" [11]

Between these positions on the spectrum, but tending more in the direction of the latter, are those who point to the very complex nature of the relationship between population and pollution. These persons put more stress on the economic factors, such as increased per capita income, and the fact that, as could easily be predicted, the rich who have demanded even more, thereby creating more land, air, water, chemical, thermal, and radio-active pollution than poor people.

It is possible to state the causal relation between population and environmental deterioration in an oversimplistic manner. It is obvious that pollution entails polluters. Behind this self-evident fact lies a welter of factors which must be taken into consideration in any adequate assessment of the situation. Here it would be proper to pay attention to some observations of Barry Commoner:

• Since World War II the population of the United States has risen by 42 per cent. Productivity in areas where pollution is a major factor has risen dramatically above the percentage of population increase. For example, chemical productivity increased by 73 per cent between 1958 and 1968.

• The theory that urbanization, increased population density and internal crowding are major factors in the pollution picture needs more careful scrutiny. This theory does not account for the fact that many of the population problems are not urban in origin. Fertilizer, pesticides, mercury are hardly urban preoccupations. The automobile is certainly a major urban factor, and its contribution to pollution can hardly be underestimated. The pivotal question, however, is not so much the increase of urban population but the necessity of the automobile in urban areas. The compacting of the poor and minority groups in urban ghettos while affluent citizens migrate to suburbia is the general urban scene in terms of population shifts. The population criss-crosses in the morning and evening hours as suburbanites come and go to their offices in the city while many in the inner city commute to outlying industries. Commoner concludes, "the intensification of environmental problems associated with urbanization is not so much due to the increasing size of the population as it is to the maldistribution of the living and working places in metropolitan areas." [12]

• During the same period of 1946-50 certain key sectors of agriculture actually declined in productivity. Grain production per capita decreased by approximately 8 per cent; meat and lard production decreased per capita by approximately 6 per cent. Something of the same picture can be seen in clothes production. Between 1950 and 1968 per capita fiber use increased only 9 per cent.

"This over-all increase in total United States production" Commoner concludes, "falls far short of the concurrent rise in pollution levels, which is in the range of 200 to 2,000 per cent, to suffice as an explanation of the latter. It seems clear, then, that despite the frequent assertions that blame the environmental crisis on 'overpopulation,' 'affluence,' or both, we must seek elsewhere for an explanation." [13]

We might profitably look at the mushrooming technological advance. Since World War II we have experienced the introduction of many new technical processes, but these processes many times have been introduced without a full understanding of what some of the results may turn out to be. Unquestionably, one of the motivations for accelerated introduction of new technical process has been economic growth. In many instances the value of a short-term economic gain has far outshone concern for the ecological consequences of the long run. The public realities of "gullibility" and "ignorance" have to be factored into the picture. The public has been without the information and insight to know what was happening. Thanks to Rachel Carson in 1962 and her disciples since then the picture has become more intelligible. In addition to the public factor, there is what Jacques Ellul has pointed to: technology's inherent tendency to become autonomous and to become an end in itself. Technological growth becomes itself the "good," the value to be defended. That value permeates the industrial and public sectors without discrimination!

We cannot, however, allow technology to be a convenient scapegoat. It is as simplistic to argue that technology is the great "prime mover" and "first cause" of environmental deterioration as to argue the same for increasing population. While man is shaped by technology, he is also the shaper of technology. The demands of production placed upon the new technologies is a human demand. The statistical argument mustered by Commoner is a per capita argument. The picture changes dramatically when "per capita" is pluralized. What if population continues to expand? Obviously, this will place increased demand upon the physical environment for raw materials which in many cases are becoming less and less. While the pollution problem may be basically a problem of politics, economics and human values, the problems of scarcity and depletion remain to be faced. And these are basically problems of population.

The Western world has proceeded for centuries with the facile assumption that the finite earth has infinite resources. It is true that every decade has brought new discoveries of minerals and fossil fuels.

We know of more untapped pools of oil than we knew of thirty years ago. Our technologies of extraction constantly improve and enable us to develop deposits unreachable or uneconomic a few years ago. It is also true that agricultural techniques have advanced remarkably in recent years, and there is no reason to doubt still further advances. As yet, however, man has only a glimmering knowledge of the ecological picture and of the delicate balances that sustain him. He seems to have even less knowledge of the consequences of his intervention into, stimulation of and extraction from the web of life. At the present time the spaceship earth is flashing warning signals that indicate we cannot continue to assume an infinite supply of resources to meet the growing demands of consumption and expanding population. Already a large proportion of our present 3.5 billion neighbors are undernourished and thousands die daily of starvation. When increased levels of consumption are coupled with increased mouths to be fed, bodies to be clothed, and families to be housed, the full picture is almost overwhelming. For centuries man has practiced what the biologists call "competitive exclusion" in respect to various species of animals and in recent centuries that "competitive exclusion" has been extended to the inanimate world of material resources. This practice of "competitive exclusion" extends into the human community itself when the consumption levels continue to increase for rich minorities while the increasingly poor majorities suffer and in their suffering know that it is not the fickle-finger of fate which has dealt them their blow.

The Judeo-Christian tradition has long recognized the ethical imperative to feed the hungry and clothe the poor. For centuries we have operated, however, with a "trickle down" theory. That approach simply has not worked. Time has caught up with us, and we are confronted with a three-dimensional ethical and strategical dilemma. Three dimensions are (1) expanding population, (2) the limits of our eco-system, and (3) millions who lack a basic subsistance level of life. These three factors are interdependent. We cannot retard population growth until those millions are more secure in a material way, and we cannot do either effectively over the long range if we continue to ignore the limits of this little planet.

We have as yet made no mention of the problem of space as this relates to population and environment. The experience of space is fundamental for the quality of human and subhuman forms of life. It is difficult to deal with this matter, however, in quantitatively measurable terms. Here the variable of the human psyche is very important.

The statistics from a midtown Manhattan survey are informative and troubling. While the survey did not include ghetto life per se, it offered a sufficiently wide sampling to illustrate the point validly. Of the total persons surveyed (1,660), 18.5 per cent were found to be free of serious psychological symptoms. Of the total, 2.7 per cent were found to be incapacitated, though no hospitalized persons were included in the sampling. Between these extremes the term of social scientists found varying degrees of psychotic and neurotic symptoms.[14] While the studies on human population crowding have not yet been refined to the point of Calhoun's work with rats, the fact remains that a crowding population suffers increased internal stress. To what extent the factor of space figures into the recent outbreaks of frustration and violence in our cities, no one can yet say with accuracy. That there is some correlation seems to be beyond doubt.

The question of space cannot be dealt with in an absolutistic manner. Persons and populations have differing understandings and demands of space. The rapidly changing character of urban life throughout the world indicates, however, that "the implosion of the world populations into cities everywhere is creating a series of destructive behavioral sinks more lethal than the hydrogen bomb. Man is faced with a chain reaction and practically no knowledge of the structure and the cultural atoms producing it." [15]

We have pointed to three areas of ecological concern—pollution, depletion, and space. It is easy in confronting an ethical situation of the magnitude of the cosmos and the human race to commit the fallacy of single causation. Some environmentalists have committed that fallacy in their heavy-handed claims that over-population is the key to the mystery confronting us. Responsible ecological analysis demands that as many of the factors and variables as possible should be included in the process of analysis. Environment itself is not static, and in this sense is itself a variable. We have been unable to point to population as *the one cause*—though it is certainly one of the basic causes.

All analyses are perspectival. Attitudes and values are the context within which any analysis proceeds. For that reason I began with a preliminary exploration of attitudes and values regarding the natural world. In conclusion I return to that issue now in a more inclusive and at the same time more specific focus, namely, the implications for an environmental ethic in relation to the issue of optimum population. At the outset, it should be noted that the adjective "optimum" implies a value judgment. Objective analysis alone cannot supply an adequate definition of "optimum." A host of non-empirical considerations must be brought into relation with the scientific input. I take it that "optimum" in this case refers to the conditions which should be met to provide a quality life capable of sustaining an ecological balance mutually beneficial to both human and subhuman life forms. That places squarely before us the ethical question and the following observations:

• If all forms of life have value appropriate to their particular levels or stages of development and if human life is the apex of that continuous development, then within the confines of the population debate the burden of proof cannot be assigned simplistically. The burden of proof rests equally upon those who desire large families and those who advocate social and legal measures to control population expansion. If the distinctiveness of man within the evolutionary process is that he can reflect upon that process and to a great degree determine its future direction, the real distinctiveness of man lies in his exercise of responsibility for the future of that process. The ethical problem of responsibility for the future of the process is too complicated to permit single solution answers.

• If unlimited growth in population were to have serious repercussions on the eco-system to the extent that it could be shown that the eco-system cannot continue to sustain life capable of actualizing additional value, then measures of control and restraint would ethically be in order. At this point it is easier to state how optimum population should not be defined than how it should. A bare subsistence level is not an appropriate measure for optimum population. A bare subsistence level condemns man to perpetual warfare with his environment, and simply accentuates the age-old cleavage between man and nature. The eco-system including man must be capable of actualizing future potentialities for the enhancement of life.

• Concern for the present moment is not sufficient. Population levels should be maintained that will allow the earth to care for future generations. It is not just a matter that our children should have a future, but if the various forms of life express a value of their own, then we must be advocates of the values "without voices" for the future.

• The affirmation of value in all forms of life does not imply a non-interventionist attitude toward nature. The natural world is not to be left to itself, even if this were possible Nature is not maximally efficient. Lynn White in his well-known essay advocated the Franciscan model of reverence for nature. In contrast, Rene Dubos more recently has suggested that the Cistercians offer us a more viable model. It was they who built their monasteries on the low lands and swamps of Europe, forcing themselves to transform the land and make it maximally efficient. Dubos has called for a responsible, creative intervention with nature rather than passive reverence.[16]

• Population policy must express global and not special group interests. Self-interests and national interests must become subject to the broader welfare of the whole. Parochial interest will simply breed more of the havoc which we already experience in man's competition with nature and fellow humans.

• Closely allied with the above is the necessity to consider the perspectives and sensitivities of deprived segments of our society. "Having less and enjoying it more," which happens to be a slogan in some ecological quarters may be very appropriate ethical advice to those who already have more than their share. It is hardly appropriate advice to the poor and ethnic groups who have been victims of discrimination in our own society and the developing nations of the world.

1. John Stewart Collis, *The Triumph of the Tree* (London: Cape, 1950).

2. See Lynn White, Jr., "The Historical Roots of Our Ecologic Crisis," in Paul Shepard and Daniel McKinley, eds., *The Subversive Science* (Houghton Mifflin Co., 1968), pp. 341-350; Frederick Elder, *Crisis in Eden: A Religious Study of Man and His Environment* (Abingdon Press, 1970).

3. Teilhard de Chardin, *The Phenomenon of Man* (Harper and Row, 1959), p. 290.

4. John B. Cobb, Jr., "The Population Explosion and the Rights of the Subhuman World," *IDOC North-America* (September 12, 1970), pp. 42-43.

5. H. Paul Santmire, *Brother Earth: Nature, God and Ecology in Time of Crisis* (Thomas Nelson, Inc., 1970), pp. 6-12.

6. Richard Neuhaus, "Environmental Imperialism and the Third World," *American Report* (April 14, 1972), p. 11.

7. Loren Eiseley, "The Time of Man," in *The Light of the Past: A Treasury of Horizon* (American Heritage Publication Co., 1965), p. 38.

8. Paul Ehrlich, *The Population Bomb* (Ballantine, 1968), pp. 66-67.

9. Cited by Lawrence A. Mayer, "U.S. Population Growth: Would Fewer Be Better?" in Daniel Callahan, ed., *The American Population Debate* (Doubleday & Co., 1971), p. 8.

10. Lamont C. Cole, "Can the World Be Saved?" *New York Times Magazine* (March 31, 1968).

11. Barry Commoner, *The Closing Circle: Nature, Man and Technology* (Alfred A. Knopf, 1971), p. 133.

12. *Ibid.*, p. 135.

13. *Ibid.*, p. 139.

14. Reported in Marston Bates, "Crowded People," in Callahan, *op. cit.*, p. 78.

15. Edward T. Hall, "Human Needs and Inhuman Cities," in *The Fitness of Man's Environment* (Harper Colophon Books, 1968), p. 155.

16. Rene Dubos, *A Theology of Earth* (Smithsonian Institute, 1971).

10

THE NEEDED REVOLUTION IN VALUES

Stewart Udall

Environment and ecology are producing a ferment that is resulting in a revolution in human values. This is a deep conviction with me, and it goes to the heart of the morality of the outlook for humankind. I like the emphasis on "optimum human environment" in James Logan's essay. I have no serious disagreement with it, and my inclination is to buttress and support its major points. The very idea of "optimum" as a goal suggests tying our aims to ethical objectives of the highest order. It is increasingly clear that whatever problem we attack, unless we approach it holistically and humanistically we shall misdefine it and, in the end, fail to achieve solutions that are morally right. In tying together a goal or objective of optimum population or optimum environment or optimum relationship of human beings to the natural system of which they are a party we are forced to think holistically and humanistically. It is fragmented, "pragmatic" thinking linked to outdated concepts of "progress" that is at the root of the environmental crisis in 1972. Most of our ethical errors, in the broad historical sense, are related to the quantitative, materialistic approach to human affairs that has dominated the "modern societies of the Western world.

The religious leaders in this country and those who are the guardians of our ethics should rethink many of the concepts which have contributed to the evolving ecological crisis. It is a tragic paradox that in many parts of the world deeply imbedded religious concepts are responsible for creating demeaning, dehumanized social policies. For example, Moslem religious views in Bangladesh dictate that the thousands of women who were raped now should be considered wasted human beings who must be cast aside as non-persons. This is the end result of a cruel and outmoded religious doctrine. And so it is with the abortion issue in this country today when women who are not ready to carry out the high responsibilities of parenthood are told, "You must bear the child anyway, and it is criminal and sinful if you don't." I believe we are working against human nature—and against reverence for life—when people are forced to contravene their own deepest instincts.

One of the things that has bothered me most when I look at our concept of private property and our concept of progress is the fact that by concentrating on the materialistic yardsticks, by concentrating on measuring our well-being by our gross national product or the amount of consumer goods we have to satisfy our needs, we have left out something that economists like Joseph Spengler have been trying to get us to contemplate for a long time. By narrowing our aims to a materialistic standard of living we have ignored the "public standard of living" which embraces the condition of the community, the overall environments of cities and neighborhoods—as well as all of those amenities that determine the public happiness of a people. When we look at the sick and cancerous American cities today, we see that our cities have been allowed to go down the drain at the very period in our history when we were achieving great feats of technological development and materialistic growth.

I believe the time has come to formulate a population policy keyed to sound ecological and ethical aims. The dualism between Nature and Man must not only be discarded as outdated and dangerous, but we must see, as Aldo Leopold has put it, that "conservation will get nowhere until we stop treating Nature as a commodity to be bought and sold and treat it as a community to which we belong." Unless we change before this decade ends, I am convinced that the United States will be regarded as the world's most gluttonous society. It will find itself in a moral position which is increasingly indefensible insofar as the world community is concerned. The tentative conclusions of the MIT/Club of Rome Project, and its recent book *The Limits of Growth*, will force us to begin to think in terms of constraints on growth and ethical limits on our heretofore unbounded appetites. Professor Logan is right in saying that it is wrong for us to look at our population problem without relating it to the prospect of the world community as a whole. While the United Nations Stockholm Conference of 1972 on environment may have accomplished but little, at least it has helped start a dialogue about the limits of growth and the moral responsibilities of the individual nations.

A final point must be made. When they hear talk about "optimum environment" or "optimum population," some people look at the United States and its vastness and say "We have enormous space left, why do we have a population problem?" The answer is that we are already putting enormous pressure on our resources; we are already racing pell mell toward rationing the use of some of these resources. Furthermore, a counter question must be put: What's wrong with having a spacious country, with wanting to have spacious cities, with wanting to have a man/land ration that is good for the spiritual and mental health of its people? In terms of a life-giving environment, my own conviction is that even in this "spacious country" we have a population that already exceeds the optimum.

11

ECONOMIC CONSIDERATIONS

Harvey Seifert

Those who project ideal goals and laudable programs need also to confront the stern resistances of complex reality. Ethicists may talk about what is ultimately desirable, but economists may puncture their bright balloons by pointing to such things as scarce resources or unanticipated consequences. Those formulating population policy had better take seriously the kinds of factors that impress economists. No one can go very far in defining optimum population without determining what economic standard of living is desirable and what available economic alternatives will allow the earth to sustain varying numbers of people. On the other hand, those determining economic policies need increasingly to consider the demographic consequences of any particular economic decision. As the ethicist joins a three-cornered conversation with specialists in economics and population, his indispensable contribution is in the clarification and implications of general predispositions and ultimate goals. He helps to evaluate means in the light of ends consistent with our most inclusive conclusions about reality.

What do we want economic processes and population policies to accomplish? Even those who disagree sharply on specific measures are likely to agree on the general goal of the fullest possible actualization of the highest potentialities of persons. This includes the full range of values about which the economist is concerned as he tries to relate limited resources, including human power, to infinite human wants. Speaking in theological language, this is to say both that man is inherently good and that God's material creation is good. The Bible is full of ecstatic delight in the enjoyment of physical reality and human association. A higher standard of living, so long as it does not deprive others, is to be desired. Galbraith has quipped about the common wisdom at this point, "Wealth is not without its advantages and the case to the contrary, although it has often been made, has never proved widely persuasive." [1]

At the same time material things are not to be considered as ultimate value. Jesus warned against laying up treasurers on earth at the expense of spiritual growth. "A man's life does not consist in the

112

abundance of his possessions." (Luke 12:15). To give material goods a higher place than social and spiritual values is to place mammon before God. A certain quantity of material goods is indispensable to physical life and therefore to social and spiritual values on this earth. Even the saintly monastic requires food between his fasts. While some values are higher, others normally are prior. Public policy should therefore aim to maximize the full range of values at the same time that it subordinates those which are significantly means toward even more important ends. Our religious tradition is not ascetic in the absolute sense of regarding material goods as evil. It does nevertheless insist upon an asceticism of proportion in the sense of rigorous consistency in applying a scale of priorities. Values may be ranked from lower to higher on the basis of criteria which place intrinsic values above instrumental values, permanent above transient, and those more fully releasing human possibilities above those more partially involving the potentialities of persons. In the light of these considerations physical and material values may be placed at the bottom of the scale, social or relational values in intermediate position, with moral, intellectual, aesthetic, and spiritual values in the top position.

Another major ethical claim is that every person should have equal opportunity for access to the full range of available values. Universalism is to be joined to human fulfillment. Every child's right to grow and develop is as basic as his right to survive. This is a central social meaning of the overarching ethical norm of love. Such outgoing, active concern takes in also all generations yet unborn. When one asks "Who is my neighbor?" the answer includes not only every person now living on earth, but every person who may appear in the future.

As the definition of value involves a tension between the higher and the prior, so universalism of opportunity presents the antinomy of quality and quantity. The first tension raises the question of what it is important to provide from the limited resources of the environment. The second antinomy asks for how many persons such values should be provided. Is it better to apply resources to the greater good of fewer people or to the lesser good of more people? Whenever resources are limited there is obviously a contradiction, for example, between maximizing the welfare of the present generation and preserving a similar opportunity for future generations through an indefinite future.

It can be argued that at the present stage in human history quality is more important than quantity. This conclusion rests partly on the threat to the continued existence of all life which is posed by increasing quantity of the magnitude now confronting us. Another supporting reason is the availability of unprecedented possibilites for realizing higher human potentialities, which were previously not accessible. We now have psychological, cultural, and theological resources for developing a "new humanity," in a strikingly different "post-industrial" man. If the purpose of life is the full utilization of man's highest capacity, we should appropriate these enabling resources. This is not to propose a kind of elitism in which a chosen few shall now have superior opportunity at the expense of the rest of mankind. It is to say that all men now alive and anticipated in future generations should have opportunity for unprecedented development, which means that populations of necessity need to be limited in size.

Infinite growth in either quantity or quality is impossible within a finite universe. The earth and its ecosphere has limited natural resources and restricted capacity for absorption of polluting wastes. It is a crucial part of the vocation of man to devise the most creative balance possible between the complex factors involved. As a contribution toward that end I shall discuss the relationship of population size to economic growth, and the implications of alternative economic patterns and goals.

It has been argued that continued population growth is necessary to stimulate economic production. The more babies that are born the more baby carriages can be sold, and the more school buildings contractors and plumbers can build. But prosperity is not quite so simple. The more babies that grow up to young adulthood, the more jobs have to be provided and the more natural resources are depleted by the steel used in the school buildings. From an ethical standpoint the basic question is what happens to each baby that is born. Prosperity is to be defined not in terms of national wealth accumulated or speed with which the wheels of industry go round, but in terms of human fulfillment. More frequent and more destructive wars are also a way of stimulating economic growth, but we can surely find better ways which also allow preserving the humanity which we are trying to fulfill.

Numerous studies now indicate that under modern circumstances population size is inversely related to healthy economic growth. After a point which has already been passed by much of the world and is at least being rapidly reached by all of the world, increased population tends to undermine maximum economic well being. A variety of "cost-benefit" analyses of population growth have now shown that after this point additional births cost society more than is gained.[2] Where the marginal product of an additional worker is low his productive contribution is outweighed by social outlays for maintaining social services like health, education, and transport which he requires. Limiting populations raises available per capita income, which can be used to raise standards of living, or as savings to invest in more rapid economic development, or for both. In addition, savings are made by government as it needs to provide public services for fewer persons. Also, in developing nations, where caloric intake is substandard, the resulting improved diet may lead to productivity increases.

If an underdeveloped country reduced its fertility by 50% in a period of 25 years, Ansley J. Coale's studies indicated that at the end of 60 years it could double the income per consumer. In 90 years it could triple this income and after 150 years it could have an income per consumer six times as great as if the original population growth had remained unchanged.[3] Coale concluded that reduction of fertility "will be a major element in making possible the modernization and industrialization that every country must pass through in order really to join the twentieth century."[4]

Reducing population growth in developing countries would allow considerably larger returns from such economic assistance funds as become available to them. President Lyndon Johnson in his 1965 speech on the twentieth anniversary of the United Nations said, "Less than five dollars invested in population control is worth a hundred dollars invested in economic growth." While economists see this ratio varying in different situations, they are inclined to accept the general conclusion. After facing the complexities involved, Goran Ohlin concluded, "The purely economic case is convincing—so convincing that one is tempted to say that population control might bring the dawn of sustained economic growth within sight in the developing countries."[5]

This analysis is complicated by satisfactions which children may bring to specific families rather than to the country as a whole. To a considerable extent these satisfactions are cultural matters, modifiable by changing social standards or expectations. Companionship may be secured from fewer children, particularly if this is the relationship sustained by custom. As parents come to share higher social expectations for education and other opportunities, they are likely to gain greater satisfactions when they provide more for fewer children than when they provide less for more children. Relying on a large family as a source of security in old age becomes less important when society adopts more economical ways to provide an even higher old age income. For reasons such as these, societies which attain higher levels of prosperity tend to have lower birth rates. As expectations and costs for children become higher, satisfactions tend to be so defined that they are maximized within smaller families.

Nevertheless, there is still a danger that numerous individual families will shortsightedly make choices that conflict with the long run social interests of all families. Population growth is the result of millions of decentralized decisions. It is possible that the present generation will not weigh heavily enough the welfare of future generations. As Kenneth Boulding has suggested, "It is always a little hard to find a convincing answer to the man who says, 'What has posterity ever done for me?' "[6] Unless that man has a more altruistic ethical orientation he is likely simply to go on eating, drinking, and merrily polluting. Completely laissez-faire or anarchic procedures in the decisions of small family units may prove to be no more appropriate here than they are in economic or political decisions. Even democratic governments at some points need to move beyond education to pressure in order to guarantee the widest possible freedom and opportunity.[7]

This entire problem has somewhat different aspects in more industrially developed countries. Larger populations can more easily be sustained at a higher standard of living when there has been considerable technological development. Even developed nations, however, pass a point of diminishing returns where the problems become greater than the gains. They do not need population growth to sustain prosperity or aggregate demand. There are better ways to secure the same result, as, for example, by producing for the needs of less developed nations or by provision of additional services for their existing population.

A smaller group of economists would still argue that rapid population growth can be offset by an increased savings rate, more rapid technological progress, or lower costs of production since larger quantities are produced.[8] In addition to specific rebuttals to these assertions, a major rejoinder is that they overlook the threats of resources depletion and environmental pollution. These perils must be avoided or we will not sustain any population at all, no matter how developed or undeveloped a nation may be. The more people, the faster resources are used up and the more environmental poisons are produced. To be sure, there are also those who here place their confidence in new discoveries of substitute resources and of pollution control methods.

While these may somewhat postpone the final disaster, they are not likely to eliminate the necessities of a finite environment. Many essential resources are exhaustible. Particularly with a runaway population, there is no reason to believe that in all the areas involved adequate substitutes could be developed rapidly enough. Having taken such inventive possibilities into account, Kenneth Boulding still concludes that we have moved from a "cowboy economy" (with limitless plains and reckless behavior) to a "spaceman economy" (without unlimited reserves of anything). This transition he feels calls for economic principles and actions which are quite different from those of the past.[9] Industrial civilization could now come to an end through its own expansion—a lethal instance of the failure of success.

With the surprisingly rapid acceleration involved in exponential growth, as Herman Daly puts it, we will reach a point at which "the 'marginal' cost of one more step may be to fall over the precipice." [10] Because of the short doubling time in many of the factors involved, plus the immense quantities being doubled, exhaustion may come very suddenly. Within a few years we may move from a situation of great abundance to one of tragic scarcity. A classic illustration is that of a water lily which doubles in size each day and in thirty days can completely fill a particular pond, choking off all other forms of life. For a long time the plant seems small, and one may decide to do nothing about it until it has covered half the pond. Then he has only one day to save the pond.[11] Add to the acceleration of exponential growth the fact that some types of remedial action require a long lead time. In population control or resource development, for example, there is a lengthy lag between initiating a policy and reaping its effects. To expand the illustration of the half-filled pond, if there is no available method to clear out growth faster than the doubling rate is filling it in, even the most arduous labor during the last days can no longer prevent the plant from filling the pond.

The ethical thrust toward sharing the earth's resources as widely as possible, to both present and future generations, supports exploration into forms of greater economic efficiency. Even with early and effective efforts at population control, world population for a time will remain so large as to tax our capacities. At the same time it will always remain important to conserve more resources for the distant future. Moving alongside population controls must be those economic policies which utilize limited resources as effectively as possible toward maximum human fulfillment.

One of these possibilities is the increased spread of a humane modern technology. It is commonly recognized that division of labor, scientific invention, and the use of machines increases the productivity of an industrial civilization. It is not so widely admitted, however, among those who share the benefits of industrialization that theirs is also a costly obligation. Insofar as they are concerned about the well being and equal opportunity of all persons on earth they need to share the benefits which they have inherited. At this point certain cold hard facts of economic life become indispensable directives. Not only does raising standards of living in underdeveloped countries require industrialization, but such industrialization requires the investment of large amounts of capital. Such capital is obtainable only internally, by artificially depressing already low standards of consumption by totalitarian means, or externally through economic assistance programs from abroad. If we do not want developing people to live under tight totalitarian controls, we will need to supply much of the required capital. Such capital from external sources can come either from private investment, philanthropic agencies, or governments. Private investors are not likely to supply all that is necessary, particularly in view of the fact that some of the foundational development projects, like basic education or harbor improvement, will not yield profit returns. Philanthropic agencies like the church unfortunately do not have sufficient altruistic outpouring of support to begin to meet the need. This means that inevitably large amounts of capital will need to be raised through taxation by governments acting either unilaterally or through the United Nations. This is a moral obligation which our "aid weary" generation cannot escape. One of the most glaring immoralities of our time is our reluctance to increase our contribution to economic assistance programs.

Another consequence of this type of economic analysis is to underscore the futility of the protest against technology by the contemporary counter-culture. To oppose industrialization is to condemn millions of people on this earth to a desperate and dismal existence. One may retreat to a pre-industrial commune in the hills, but he is not thereby contributing to an alternative society which has any realistic promise for economic improvement. This becomes another illustration of individualistic action which must assume responsibility for suffering and starvation of countless numbers of one's fellow beings. The counter-culture is quite right in objecting to senseless products or dehumanizing processes in modern technology. Developing nations do not need to reproduce all the defects in western industrial civilization. Modern technology can be used to a much greater extent as the servant of mankind, to enhance human values rather than to destroy them.

A second reform which would allow improved support of a larger population is the elimination of much current waste. We use up more natural resources than are actually required through unnecessary duplication of services or undue variety in models, in manufacturing useless or harmful goods, or in premature obsolescence. One of our more immoral practices is the intentional use of "death-dating," or planned obsolescence. This includes purposely manufacturing goods of less durability, thus creating a junkman's paradise. It also includes a psychological version as in an emphasis on style changes which cause products to wear out in the owner's mind. Even though the closet is full of nearly new clothes, they must be discarded in favor of those which "everyone is wearing." For anyone who is ethically sensitive, bank robbery might be considered a misdemeanor in comparison with the major felony of planned obsolescence that steals from both present and future generations. Also criminally indicted might be those forms of advertising which manufacture the demand for those irrelevant gadgets which we foolishly and profusely produce.

Preparation for war promotes some of the most disastrous wastes by all major nations. As Senator Fulbright has put it, "Violence is our most important product." [12] While more than half of each federal tax dollar is used for past, present, and future wars, the world seems less secure because of the terror of modern weaponry. Armament expenditures for overkill capacities are particularly impossible to justify. Not only do such policies pillage natural resources, but they divert other essential factors of production from the agricultural improvement, engineering innovation, and other services which would better support the poor and the unborn.

A considerable redistribution of income and wealth is a third imperative in a world in which the 6% of the population in the United States uses up about 40% of the world's production of natural resources. Also, within the United States in 1962, 2% of the consumer units owned 43% of the country's wealth, while 95% of the less wealthy owned another 43%.[13] Reducing such inequities is a necessary application of justice apart from possible effects on population. It is also a matter of efficiency to direct resources to the point of greatest marginal utility. It is a form of waste to use resources for comparatively useless consumption by the rich.

Myrdal has argued that in underdeveloped countries radical reforms toward greater equality are almost a condition for more rapid economic growth, particularly since in such countries, instead of saving for constructive investment, the rich tend to squander their income in conspicuous consumption and investment, and in capital flight. Higher returns for the poor, on the other hand, would improve health and therefore ability to work, social equality and therefore national integration, hope for changing the status quo and therefore economic and political incentive.[14]

It is sometimes feared that such redistribution would affect savings for reinvestment in economic growth. For supplementing private savings, however, we could rely on internal generation of capital by business corporations or on social forms of saving through taxation. Less capital would be needed as limits were set to the indefinite expansion of gadgetry for the wealthy. The outdated answer to poverty was continued expansion of material production, with part of the general prosperity filtering down to the poor. When finite resources no longer allow such indefinite expansion, there is no just alternative to some form of sharing of the world's wealth. It may well be that the chief ethical problem for the United States today is how a rich man may enter the kingdom of heaven.

A fourth economic alternative is the introduction of larger measures of national and international planning for the more efficient utilization of resources. Genuine economies are possible by business firms as they carefully coordinate all the many preparatory steps as well as the final assembly of the product. For maximum utilization of resources the same kind of planning needs to be done by governments. This is the only way to deal with crucial dilemmas like the elimination of depressions, the maintenance of equity and stability in the total economy, or the provision of social services that do not lend themselves to profit-motivated competition. The agency for coordinated decision is inevitably more inclusive as problems become more complex and comprehensive. For a universal project, like the preservation of peace or the termination of pollution, the coordination required goes beyond national states to the United Nations. The view of national sovereignty which holds that a country's treatment of resources within its national boundaries is completely its own business is obsolete in view of the unity of the biosphere, the limited stock of natural resources, and the world wide effects of population—mismanagement of which may undermine the foundations of civilized society. While there are dangers in too much concentration of power, a pluralistic economy can minimize these by introducing similar kinds of checks and balances and of divisions of function that we are already familiar with in political matters. While preserving a major part of economic decision-making in local and private hands, we can maximize outputs for world populations only by an extension of the essential coordinating functions of national and international bodies.

This may involve an extension of liberty as well as of efficiency and opportunity. One of the best kept social secrets is the extent to which purely individualistic or anarchic definitions of liberty actually result in autocratic control over vast majorities. So long as men are neither completely wise nor altruistic, the absence of social controls soon results in dictatorial domination by the most unscrupulous, or accidentally fortunate, or immediately efficient in short-run terms. In unplanned situations, including population policy as well as economic production, long lists of important decisions are being made by a few individuals without the participation of the larger number affected by them. Insofar as state control gives citizens something to say where previously they had nothing to say, this becomes a grant of greater freedom. The invention of democracy allows maximum possible liberty along with order. As Karl Mannheim said, "The weakening and passing of controls also implies the weakening and passing of liberty." [15] Appropriate government controls become enabling and liberating rather than prohibiting and constraining.

A fifth economic alternative has loomed so large in recent discussions as to deserve separate extended treatment. This option could involve a new definition of economic goals emphasizing the quality of the more fulfilled life. At the same time it is seen as a necessity to any kind of prolonged life on this planet. The issues raised may well be approached through a consideration of recent proposals for a nongrowth economy.

With all the improvement that might be made in economic processes there are still limits to indefinite expansion. The more persons we try to bring to higher material standards of living the more quickly we will exhaust available resources. It is not enough to limit populations if those remaining continue to consume more and more. The exhaustion and pollution of resources will eventually bring the economy to a screeching halt and with much greater suffering than if we had slowed it down earlier. Therefore it is argued that the appropriate contemporary policy is one of planned retrenchment, or a non-growth economy. In economic production there is a point at which decreasing marginal benefit (the contribution of the last unit added) becomes less than increasing marginal cost. At this point we ought to recognize that we have enough and that continued increase in production figures is no longer progress. We would recognize this point of no return more quickly if we made a social audit as well as a financial audit of producing firms, or if we substracted from the gross national product the social costs of dead lakes or noisy streets. When the dirt from a factory soils the neighbor's curtains, the home-owner pays for the cleaning. If the laundry bill were charged to the factory, its owners might reassess their policies. If we did this for the economy as a whole we would sooner recognize the defects in our traditional enthusiasm about continuous economic growth. Her-man Daly has suggested that at this point the historic view of pro-gress is "a senile ideology that should be unceremoniously retired into the history of economic doctrines." [16] Replacing it should be the idea of a stationary-rate or zero-growth economy, which would parallel zero population growth.[17]

This proposal is sound insofar as it applies to the production of resource-depleting material goods. Suggestions that available re-sources are expandable are highly speculative and in an overall sense improbable. Most of the conceivable solutions merely defer the crisis or shift the threat from one point to another. In view of the sheer sizes of population involved in periodic doubling we are in a new situ-ation. Under these circumstances, as the range of our choices is in-creasing on trivial products like electric tooth brushes, fundamental conditions like a liveable atmosphere, which are necessary for any choice, are rapidly becoming uncontrollable. As Ezra Mishan has put it. "Business economists have ever been glib in equating economic growth with an expansion of the range of choices facing the individual; they have failed to observe that as the carpet of 'increased choice' is being unrolled before us by the foot, it is simultaneously being rolled up behind us by the yard." [18]

Along with this aspect of validity there are two other respects in which "zero-growth economy" is the wrong term which gives a dangerous impression. For one thing, it is understandable that zero-growth proposals should be greeted with dismay by representatives of the Third World. They see visions of slowing their own economic growth while a self-interested, affluent portion of the world also throttles down, but still maintains its vast superiority in an intoler-able neocolonialism. It must be said more plainly than advocates of a stabilized economy have usually done, that developing areas still require dramatic economic growth. The only way to stabilize world resources depletion therefore, is for advanced nations to cut back their standards of living. They need to eliminate the production of enough Cadillac type products to allow growth for poverty areas. Temporarily they might use their productive capacities to produce for the developing world. In the long run we cannot escape the necessity for international redistribution of productive wealth.

Racial minorities and the poor in developed countries are also frequently suspicious of such ecological proposals as have here been suggested. They fear that they will be the hardest hit by resulting unemployment or price increases, or by transfer of funds from poverty programs, or by discriminatory population control.[19] Unless environmentalists make abundantly clear their intentions with respect to poverty and inequality, we may suffer sniping between them and the poor, when both ought to be uniting against the real enemy. Two reform groups may argue over the crumbs from the economic pie while military and industrial producers of vast waste run away with most of the slices. There is no way of escaping the fact that any effective and ethical solution of our problem will require fundamental changes in major, traditionally-accepted aspects of our common life. Ecologists are belatedly learning that theirs is not a painless revolution that can by the mere cogency of argument easily mobilize the support of privileged and powerful groups.

Another factor, which is occasionally suggested but is not sufficiently emphasized by the proponents of a stabilized economy, involves an amazing new possibility for human growth which can now for the first time be more fully implemented. Of necessity the great preoccupation of past generations, absorbing the bulk of their working time and creative energies, was the production and distribution of material goods. As larger parts of the world are now becoming overdeveloped areas in this respect, we face either the end of history or an entirely new era in history. Simply to enjoy the possibilities won by our ancestors is now a prescription for disaster. It is also possible, however, that in terms of the hierarchy of values, our major preoccupation may increasingly become not physical and material values but social and spiritual values. We may now devote dramatically increased man hours to the solution of major social problems, the cultivation of resources in group relationship, and the release of the intellectual, aesthetic, moral, and religious capacities of man. Our preoccupation more largely may become politics and poetry and prayer. So long as the threat of war continues, for example, how many million peace workers around the world should be paid a decent livelihood for research in international relations and activity in changing public opinion? A larger proportion of the population working very hard on such matters would deplete comparatively few irreplaceable resources and cause considerably less pollution than would a continuation of more outdated forms of production.

The portion of gross national product due to the provision of services rather than material goods has already been expanding. This trend needs to go a great deal further as we take more seriously the enhancement of social and spiritual values. This would mean the appearance of new vocations, or in times of increased leisure, the possibility of a second simultaneous vocation for many people. It could rescue retirement from meaninglessness and provide ways for the elderly to continue to contribute to personal growth and social change. This would probably mean spending more through the public sector of the economy. At least in the initial stages, this sector is better suited for providing many of the requisite services, such as adult education or subsidized drama, art, and music, or mental health and personal growth clinics. In view of accepted patterns for separation of church and state, churches would need to provide for new religious explorations. They might be joined by other private agencies in moving beyond delinquency or marriage counseling to career counseling, ethical consultation, creative recreation, and spiritual life direction. Conceivably some of these might develop into private professions supported by clients' fees. Pressure groups or private foundations might employ more activists working on poverty, race, or war.

Such an expansion of services would require some additional material goods. Aesthetic expression calls for canvas or musical instruments, galleries or concert halls. Counselors have desks or couches. In comparison with other types of production these requirements can be quite modest. Many of the meeting rooms are already available in churches and schools, and the telephones for political canvassing are already installed in homes and offices. Furthermore, this development would be quite consistent with, or even aided by, reduction of material standards of living to the level of a simpler life including only what is functionally defensible. Along with limits to population growth this would make prospects for the future of mankind considerably more hopeful. At the same time that we consumed fewer material goods and shared more equally with the poor at home and abroad, all of us could still enjoy life more. The result of a reordering of priorities would be to raise our total standard of living. A better life on a higher level of human development would be more widely available than ever before. This would not be a "no-growth" but a selected growth economy.

Other desirable outcomes might be associated with this shift in our primary attention. Status would be assigned to "leading citizens" in the community not because they were rich or bureaucratically powerful, but insofar as they were humanly sensitive, socially creative, and aesthetically and spiritually alert. Similarly "great powers" among the nations would qualify not by military strength, but by ideological and sociological contribution. Size of population and material affluence would no longer be equated with group power. This will require a transformation of humanity's purposes, a revolution in values based on a profound conversion experience about ultimate matters. Such a transformation in accepted morality and life styles is impossible without ethical support and direction. It is quite unlikely that mankind can muddle through this sort of basic transition without the help of a vital, active church. Once again Judeo-Christian attitudes and guidelines may prove to point the way out of our recession of the spirit to a resurgence of creativity.

1. John Kenneth Galbraith, *The Affluent Society* (Houghton Mifflin, 1958), p. 1.

2. Summarized in Warren C. Robinson, "Population Growth and Economic Welfare," *Reports on Population/Family Planning*, a publication of the Population Council (February, 1971). For more popular treatments, see Stephen Enke, "Birth Control for Economic Development," Science (May 16, 1969), pp. 798-802, and Donella H. Meadows, et al., *The Limits to Growth* (Universe Books, 1972).

3. Ansley J. Coale, "The Economic Effects of Fertility Control in Underdeveloped Areas," in Roy O. Greep, ed., *Human Fertility and Population Problems* (Schenkman Publishing Co., 1963), p. 159.

4. *Ibid.*, p. 162.

5. Goran Ohlin, *Population Control and Economic Development* (Organization for Economic Cooperation Development Center, 1966), p. 120.

6. Kenneth E. Boulding, *Beyond Economics* (University of Michigan Press, 1968), p. 283.

7. On this problem see Paul Demeny in National Academy of Sciences, *Rapid Population Growth* (Johns Hopkins Press, 1971), pp. 214-15.

8. As examples, see T. Curtin, "The Economics of Population Growth and Control in Developing Countries," *Review of Social Economy* (September 1969), pp. 139-153, and Warren A. Johnson and John Hardesty, eds., *Economic Growth vs. the Environment* (Wadsworth Publishing Co., 1971), Part 3.

9. Boulding, *op. cit.*, pp. 281-82. For a discussion of the seriousness of the limits set by resources depletion and pollution, see Meadows *et al.*, *op. cit.*, especially Chapters 2 and 4.

10. Herman E. Daly in John Harte and Robert H. Socolow, eds., *Patient Earth* (Holt, Rinehart and Winston, 1971), p. 232.

11. Meadows *et al.*, *op. cit.*, p. 29.

12. J. W. Fulbright, *The Pentagon Propaganda Machine* (Liveright, 1970), p. 12.

13. Herman P. Miller, *Rich Man, Poor Man* (Thomas Y. Crowell Co., 1971), p. 157. For the alarming widening in the gap between rich and poor nations which is likely if we continue present trends, see Meadows *et al.*, *op. cit.*, pp. 42-44.

14. Gunnar Myrdal, *The Challenge of World Poverty* (Pantheon, 1970). p. 54.

15. Karl Mannheim, *Freedom, Power and Democratic Planning* (Oxford University Press, 1950), p. 15. For a more detailed discussion of economic and political alternatives, see Harvey Seifert, *Ethical Resources for Political and Economic Decision* (The Westminster Press, 1972).

16. Herman E. Daly, *The Stationary-State Economy* (Department of Economics, Graduate School of Business, University of Alabama, 1971), pp. 3-4.

17. For the extent of limitations in economic production and population that would be necessary, see Meadows *et al.*, *op. cit.*, Chapter 5.

18. Ezra J. Mishan, *The Cost of Economic Growth* (Praeger Publishers, 1967), pp. 85-86. Quoted in Rufus E. Miles, Jr., "Whose Baby is the Population Problem?" *Population Bulletin* (April 2, 1970), p. 10.

19. For further discussion of this problem, see Norman J. Faramelli, "Ecological Responsibility and Economic Justice," *Andover Newton Quarterly* (November, 1970), pp. 81-93.

12

THE ECONOMIC ALTERNATIVES

Joseph Spengler

Decision-making exists in a world of penalties and rewards, and the behavior of each decision-maker is dominated by his assessment and comparisons of these rewards and penalties.[1] In what follows I shall deal with issues in economic rather than in ethical terms[2] and hence in instrumental rather than in final terms reflecting a *summum bonum*. Two aspects of ethical principles, viewed as motives, influence my comments. First, ethical principles may have little effect upon some types of conduct. Second, ethical principles, unsupported by sanctions, are unlikely to be influential if they run too counter to an individual's behavioral orientations. I offer here several points for consideration:

• A man's wants cannot be infinite even if he be Croesus, since they are limited also by his physical capacity and by the time of which he disposes, both of which are quite limited and hence compel him to choose.

• For much of mankind what Luke reports Jesus as saying is pertinent in that they are condemned to low levels of consumption and hence are pressed to choose outlooks on life in keeping with their prospects.

• There does not, for any man, exist a stable, permanent scale of priorities; he is always in the position of choosing more or less of A and hence less or more of B, since he is always subject to budgetary, temporal, and physical constraints. What is considered prior turns on current situations.

• I find it difficult to give concrete meaning to the proposition that everyone have equal opportunity for access to the full range of available values. Everyone is subject to his own range of choice as well as to budgetary constraints, and these are necessarily reflected in the access allowed anyone to anything. Scarcity is the one overwhelming fact, the fundamental source of all social science as well as of our concern with commutative and distributive justice and equity.

• Given man's generally high rate of discount of the future, it is to be taken for granted that he generally prefers to let future genera-

tions shift for themselves. For example, even at 3 per cent, a dollar to
be had a century hence is worth only a nickel today, too little to
stimulate any current action. An individual may be motivated to include in his private welfare function his own children, grandchildren,
and possibly great-grandchildren, but seldom more. Moreover, if
conditions are improving, there will be less gound than ever for attach-
ing much weight to distant generations, since transferring funds to
their use is transferring funds from the less well to do to the more
well to do. Nor is the state well suited to intervene, since it is manned
so largely by people interested in the shorter run, especially in
getting reelected and hence in actions serving this purpose.

Population growth absorbs inputs that might otherwise be de-
voted to current consumption (including leisure) or to increasing
physical and non-physical capital per head and thereby elevating
the rate growth of average output. Increase in size of population
increases the amount of pressure exerted upon those elements in the
biosphere and homosphere which are in fixed supply or subject to
depletion. Population growth thus reflects desires to utilize inputs
one way rather than another. To this there is no income-increasing
offset after increasing returns have been exhausted as they have in
much of the world.

Harvey Seifert seems to suggest that it is advisable for numbers to
increase not merely until the marginal product of a population incre-
ment falls below its average product, but until this marginal product
coincides with its cost. This rule would imply a low wage and a low
average output. I would prefer to argue that in a free society further
population increments would be considered undesirable if they reduced *average* output or some comparable indicator below the otherwise attainable maximum.

Two considerations are in order here. First, in most underdeveloped countries, continuation of the current net reproduction
rate for another century will make their situation utterly hopeless—
e.g., about 25 billions in India, or about 32 per acre, and about 21
billions in Mainland China, or close to 9 per acre. Although reducing
the net reproduction rate to 1.0 by the early 1980's would permit
India's population to level off at 1,211 million, postponing this action
by 20 years would raise India's stationary population by nearly half
to 1,763 millions. It is very important, therefore, that net reproduction be reduced to the replacement level as soon as possible. This
is all the more important because today the demographic arrow like
time's arrow points in but one direction. Today, in the absence of

thermonuclear holocaust, there do not exist, as in the Middle Ages, forces that cut back populations that have come into being. Hence the stork destroys many options forever. The other point is that the problem in most of the world is not one of optimizing population size but of bringing population growth to a dead halt. Later on I shall refer to the qualitative problem, noting here only that, as Professor Seifert points out, growth in size of population as of family beyond a point is purchased at the expense of quality of population.

There are no effective alternatives to halting population growth in the underdeveloped world as in the advanced world, since getting the net reproduction rate to 1.0 takes time and since thereafter a population continues to grow for 60-65 years and increase by around 70 per cent before stabilizing. I agree with Boulding that use without using up one's stock is the key to enjoyment. Yet, I do not find much of a palliative for population growth in reducing avoidable obsolescence in advanced countries, nor do I anticipate much from planning at the international and the national levels. Agencies of the state at both levels are loaded beyond administrative and fiscal capacity, and remoteness from the underlying population greatly restricts the capacity of the state in a mixed, or even in a centralized economy, to achieve results. While a strong case exists for the heavy taxation of rentier income that is unproductively used, attempts at redistribution that increase consumption at the expense of production may work against policy objectives.

Excessive emphasis upon altruism as a basis for policy is self-defeating. Egoism is in the saddle. I find no "moral" obligation on the part of advanced countries to extend unilateral assistance to under-developed countries, or to "share" (i.e., give away some of) their resources or territory with others. Good grounds for political and economic sovereignty still remain. As a rule economists do not, as economists, recognize moral obligation as such in a world of transactions; what is called welfare, "charity," etc., may be expressed in terms of exchange. Sharing based upon the exchange of what are considered equivalents is what tends to make for increase in welfare as well as in stability.

The capacity of any one country to help any other is very limited; improvement depends in the main upon a country's own efforts— efforts which foreign assistance can proportionally complement if conditions are propitious. Foreign aid can weaken as well as benefit a receiver. It may accentuate population gowth or it may discourage indigenous activities. Moreover, unless effective steps are being undertaken to halt population growth and security is assured private investors, an advanced country has little incentive to extend aid to underdeveloped countries. However, given security of property, foreign private enterprise can contribute greatly to economic development in underdeveloped countries; and, given convincing evidence of a willingness to deal with the population question, developed countries may extend considerable technical, economic, and related assistance.

Unfortunately we live in an age when we can easily be swamped by unwarranted assumptions undergirded by rhetoric and sentiment. If we do not guard ourselves against this, we cannot achieve our objectives. Many problems are moral, insoluble through gadgets, and resolvable only through changes in man's behavior and institutions, especially in the underdeveloped world.

As Dr. Seifert suggests, zero population growth does not entail zero economic growth.[3] Indeed, a zero rate of population growth might be accompanied by nearly as high a rate of aggregate economic growth, should a population desire this, as that associated with a rate of population growth of one percent. The composition of output would differ, of course, and presumably make less demand per dollar of output upon the physical environment.

A zero rate of population growth should be easily attainable in the United States and similarly situated advanced countries. At present governmental policy is pro-natalist on balance. Parents of children do not bear all the costs of reproducing and rearing children, and in addition escape some externalities. This may or may not be preferable, but it does make for a higher birth rate. A considerable number of births are not wanted; many births are illegitimate, especially among non-whites. Presumably, were all unwanted births prevented, net reproduction would be around unity and the population of the United States would level off at close to 270-280 million by 2050 (if there were no immigration); with immigration of 400,000 per year, this number would be 320 millions and continue to grow. Of course, given a net reproduction rate of unity, it would be inconsistent to admit immigrants unless, as in Australia, they filled critical gaps in the labor force.

Satisfying the demand for the utilities associated with having children is quite compatible with a zero rate of population growth. Given a replacement rate of 2.11 children per woman who has completed the childbearing period, those with children could average something like 2.3-2.5 children, given that 10-15 percent had none.

The cohort of women 50 years old in 1969 and with 0-4 children had averaged only 1.8 children, a figure raised to about 2.4 if one included those with 5 or more children. The cohort of married women aged 35-44 in 1969 averaged about 2.65 children; those with 4 or less, about 2.32; those with 3 or less, about 1.92. The average for this cohort if all who had 4 or more children instead had had only 3, would have been about 2.1. In sum, with something like 30 percent of all women averaging one child or less and with the rest averaging 3, a population replaces itself, and all who are physically able and desire to do can have children.[4] This average could be higher if parenthood were confined to those competent in every respect to meet its obligations.

This brings us to a question properly raised by Professor Seifert. It is desirable that children be born into an environment suited to the development of their potentials, particularly since the family environment is so critical for children. Parenthood needs to be viewed as a privilege, not as a so-called right; currently it is treated as a right in virtual disregard of the "rights" of the very young. As remarked earlier, a considerable fraction of the births taking place—perhaps around one in seven—reportedly is not wantd, a finding somewhat complemented by the fact that (in 1968) 31.2 percent of non-white and 5.3 percent of white births were illegitimate.[5] Furthermore, with the survival into reproductive age of so many persons bearing undesirable genes, the composition of the gene pool is now affected adversely more than ever. Adverse physical and social environments reduce the probability that the potential of these children will be realized and that they will fit effectively into society. For example, in part because of wage and other barriers to employment currently imposed by trade-union, corporate, or government bureaucrats, disadvantaged persons find it difficult to obtain steady employment. Among these are mentally retarded children,[6] sometimes put as high as one in every seven or eight births, at least insofar as they are the product of, among other conditions, birth in poverty-ridden families.[7] Even when the physical environment is adequate, the social environment provided by parents may be deficient because parents are unable or unwilling to devote adequate time to rearing their children. Diseconomies of scale may become operative when children exceed three or four.

Seifert is correct in noting that less privileged components of our society as of foreign societies are not entirely happy about ecological and parallel proposals. Again there is the matter of choice, of alternatives, and this is much easier of solution in a society whose aggregate income is growing and which therefore can finance the proposals under consideration.

For reasons noted earlier I have less confidence than Seifert in the bureaucracy or in the Congress. As a rule, centralization of power deprives individuals and communities of the opportunity to choose among alternatives; the power of decision is surrendered to the Congress and/or the apparatus of state, both of which tend to be dominated by special interests and to be insensitive to the wants of the underlying population as well as indisposed ever to relinquish power gotten over the underlying population. Waste is ever the handmaiden of the state as Samuel Pepys long ago observed, and so is injustice. Witness the billions that flow as subsidies to special interests and the billions that are allowed to escape taxation while (as Milton Friedman points out) a person aged 65-72 years and on Social Security may be subject to a marginal tax rate of 100 percent or more. Since the state always has been and always will be a partial master, it is advisable that its role be limited and be confined to matters in respect of which it can be kept under strong pressure to remain impartial.

It is essential to keep in mind what the term optimum denotes. It denotes the maximum value of some indicator of per capita "welfare." The relation of this value to numbers turns on the *content* of the welfare indicator; and of the *sources* of this content, one, but only one, is size of population stable in form. Because of the propensity of men to quarrel about the *content* of an indicator to be selected for maximization, I believe it preferable that the problem be approached by inquiring whether an overwhelmingly positive case can be made for more population, more manpower, especially in a society in which more and more robots are being brought into use—even in the form of the remotely piloted vehicle designed to replace fighter pilots. After all, as noted earlier, it is always possible to increase numbers but not to reduce them. Given the suggested approach, much attention needs to be given to socio-political and economic mechanisms for arriving at answers and for settling upon how births are to be distributed.

Of great importance besides the matter of *how many* people is optimization of their distribution among regions and population concentrations. In some instances this aspect of the population problem is more important than small changes in number, since location has so much to do with the quality of environment. Furthermore, concrete answers are easier to come by, and policies having been decided upon, are easier to translate into reality.

1. The concept penalties is understood to include the opportunity costs of courses of action.

2. My basic ethical orientation has been influenced in particular by W. D. Lamont, *The Value Judgment* (Edinburgh: The University Press, 1955). See especially Chapter 6.

3. See my *Declining Population Growth Revisited* (Carolina Population Center, 1971).

4. The above estimates are based upon pp. 17, 27 of U.S. Bureau of the Census, *Fertility Indicators: 1970; Current Population Report*, Series P-23, No. 36, April 16, 1971.

5. *Ibid.*

6. Unsigned, "Retardation: Hope and Frustration," *Time* (May 8, 1972), pp. 51-55.

7. U.S. Bureau of the Census, *Characteristics of the Low Income Population 1970*, Current Population Reports, Series P-60, No. 81, November 1971, pp. 4, 66. Among families of 4 or more children, 21 per cent of the children lived in poverty; among families of 1-3 children, about 9 per cent.

PART II

THE MORAL RESPONSIBILITY OF GOVERNMENT

Government is basic to population policy, either through active intervention or through decisions not to intervene. Historically, governments have often become involved in the pursuit of demographic objectives—usually through attempts to stimulate additional growth. Today, there is more interest in exploring ways to decrease growth rates. A number of value questions are raised in this section which concern the propriety of any governmental role in relation to population matters.

Andre Hellegers' essay on "Government Population Planning and the Doctrine of Subsidiarity" borrows its central theme from a principle which is prominent in twentieth century Roman Catholic papal encyclicals. Dr. Hellegers, professor of philosophy and biophysics at Georgetown University, was deputy secretary general of the Papal Commission on Population and Birth Control and writes today out of an intimate acquaintance with current Roman Catholic teaching. However, he reminds us that the principle of subsidiarity, which suggests that one should not "transfer to the larger and higher collectivity functions which can be performed and provided for by lesser and subordinate bodies," is one that is also acknowledged by many non-Catholics. In effect, this principle places a burden of proof against referring problems to governmental planning. In the present context it raises the question whether decisions to create new life are always more properly the business of the family than of society as a whole acting through government. In reading Dr. Hellegers' essay, one should reflect upon the debate between those who regard state action in a field such as this as "demonic" and those who consider state action providing the greatest opportunity for man to shape his collective future. Douglas Sturm offers four critical comments in rejoinder out of a more optimistic viewpoint on government. A prominent Christian ethicist, Dr. Sturm is a professor at Bucknell University.

"Moral Consequences of Governmental Coercion" by Edward L. Long, Jr. is concerned with the question of how we should view the coercive aspects of official action in relation to the undesirable results of inadequate social regulation. The whole problem of voluntarism versus coercion is a difficult one in all political theory. Ethical analysis,

such as that embodied in this essay, must probe beneath the surface of the simplistic assumption that all coercion is bad and all voluntarism is good (or the reverse) into more refined judgments of the meaning of these two terms. Dr. Long, who is professor of religion at Oberlin College, has written a number of books on Christian ethics. His respondent, Rosemary Ruether, argues that he has neglected basic power factors at work in actual human history, thereby unwittingly helping to justify present oppressive power relationships. Dr. Ruether is a Catholic lay theologian on the faculty of Howard University and a widely read author of works of social criticism.

In "Government's Role in Changing Population Attitudes," former Senator Joseph Tydings (Democrat of Maryland) discusses the interplay between social problems and public opinion. This essay reflects Senator Tydings' own experiences with the politics of the population issue, and it is helpful to remember in reading it that he was himself a leading exponent of more active governmental policies while serving on Capitol Hill. Richard M. Fagley's paper expands upon a number of the issues raised by Senator Tydings, particularly in relation to problems of economic development in the underdeveloped areas of the world. Dr. Fagley, whose book "The Population Explosion and Christian Responsibility" was one of the first works on population ethics by a Protestant Christian ethicist, is an international affairs leader of the World Council of Churches.

13

GOVERNMENT PLANNING AND THE

PRINCIPLE OF SUBSIDIARITY

Andre Hellegers

In pronouncements of the Roman Catholic Church, the principle of subsidiarity is found in the encyclicals on social justice. It should be understood from the outset that, in that context, it has never carried the force or authority of a dogmatic pronouncement. It is, moreover, also a well known principle in political theory beyond the Roman Catholic context. The principle was first fully enunciated by Pope Pius XI in the encyclical *Quadragesimo Anno*, where it was defined in these words: ". . . it is an injustice and at the same time a grave evil and disturbance of right order to transfer to the larger and higher collectivity functions which can be performed and provided for by lesser and subordinate bodies." Calling the principle "most weighty," Pope Pius XI gave it its single most forceful statement. The principle is reaffirmed in subsequent encyclicals such as *Mater et Magistra* (where it is specifically referred to as "the principle of subsidiarity) and *Pacem in Terris* of Pope John XXIII.

In each case the encyclical affirms the dignity of the individual, insists on his freedom, and assigns to governments only such tasks as are required from them to ensure the common good with a clear view of the higher authority as servant, rather than as master, of the lower authority. The principle is viewed not only in the light of the relationship of individual man *vis a vis* government, but also in the light of smaller social units, such as the family, *vis a vis* larger social organizations. It favors decentralization in decision-making whenever it is possible without causing harm to the common good, which common good itself is interpreted as having to revert to the individual. At all times the individual human being is placed in the forefront, in his full dignity, and all the other discussion of the ethics of social decision-making is directed at protecting this individual dignity. It should be clear that the encyclicals are in no way to be seen as deemphasizing government's role in social planning. Rather they seek to bring out that in the decision-making process the higher authority should constantly keep before it the effects its decisions will have on the ability of the lower authority (or lesser organization) to maintain its individuality, freedom, dignity and exercise of responsibility. It seeks to protect maximally the dignity of the powerless as against the powerful. It is in the light of this understanding of the principle that this essay will discuss its possible relationship to actions of governments in population planning.

Having first discussed the nature of the principle it is next necessary to define basic terms. There is widespread confusion between the terms *family* planning and *population* planning. For purposes of this essay the terms have to be kept strictly separate. Family Planning is an activity carried on by husbands and wives and results in decision-making about the number of children they will procreate and when they will do so. While the term is now commonly interpreted as a decision *not* to produce a child at a given time, correct usage should recognize that the decision may precisely be to produce an additional child. Perfect family planning implies that families succeed in precisely *achieving* their *desired* family size. Population Planning is an activity carried on by organizations of various sizes, from local groupings to federal establishments. The planning may be for optimal accommodation of existing populations or for the achievement of populations of a given size by a given date.

Confusion between the two terms is readily understandable. Since populations achieved are the products of family planning (or absence of planning), organizations such as Planned Parenthood are sometimes thought of as involved in *population* planning. Actually their major activities are oriented towards providing contraceptive services for *family* planning. Should perfect use of perfect contraceptive services lead to an average achieved family size of four children, it is obvious that great population expansion would still occur. Thus it will be seen that the two terms are not necessarily identical, although the activities may affect each other. Clear separation of the terms will, however, be vital for an understanding of the thesis set forth in this essay.

Since the sum of family sizes constitutes population size, factors affecting the one affect the other. Without going into details it suffices to say that smaller *desired* family size is statistically associated to a significant degree with a number of social, economic, cultural and medical factors. Among these may be cited urban rather than rural residence,[1] increased education,[2] migration,[3] upward social mobility,[4] higher income,[5] lower infant mortality,[6] and, possibly, participation by women in the work force.[7] Moreover the rate of population growth is affected by the generational interval between mothers and daughters, and hence by age at marriage,[8] or rather age at reproduction. It is clear that most of these factors, associated with lesser desired family size, can be affected by government policies. It is precisely the multitude of interrelationships between desired family size (and hence population size) and factors affected by government policies which makes the application of the principle of subsidiarity to population planning so complicated.

Governmental programs in land use, in extending educational opportunities, in ensuring equal rights for women, in social security legislation can all affect desired family size. Each of such programs can in itself be scrutinized in the light of the principle of subsidiarity. Although the principle's purpose is to ensure maximum freedom of decision-making at the individual's level without causing harm to the common good, it is nevertheless clear that maximizing freedom in one area may not always be compatible with total freedom in another. Thus, for instance, in the area of waste disposal the free actions of one agent (e.g., a factory) may limit the freedom of another (e.g., a person wishing to swim in unpolluted water).

It should be realized that this does not make rigid application of the subsidiarity principle to population planning *impossible*. The principle does not require that government leave all decisions to each individual; it simply demands that there be no *unnecessary* curtailment or abrogation of free individual decision-making. Yet it is clear that real tension can exist between the desire to permit individual decision-making in two particular areas, once it is known that a decision in one area affects decision-making in the other. It may then become necessary to establish a hierarchy of values, one of which deserves the greatest protection in terms of maintaining individual freedom of decision-making. Other values are then assigned progressively lesser priorities. *It is the thesis of this essay that the primary value to be protected in population planning is the value of couples being able to achieve their desired family size.*

To describe the fundamental value in this way is to immediately recognize that tensions may exist between this choice and choices which might be made by others.

It should be recognized that the ability to achieve desired family size implies that the couple should have access to the information and to the methods to achieve this. Where this access does not exist government has a distinct duty to provide it. This statement by no means implies that *any* method of family planning is ipso facto morally acceptable. That, moreover, is not the subject of this essay. It is simply to say that to affirm the fundamental value and *not* to provide moral means to achieve it, is not a proper moral stance. Another fact to bring out is that to accept the fundamental value is neither to be pro nor antinatalist. Neither does it mean that governments may not try to enhance or slow population growth. It only recognizes that if government should do either, it should be done through mechanisms which maximally protect the fundamental value.

It will be clear that almost all the mechanisms available for inducing lesser desired family size described above would be acceptable to most of the population. The policies need not therefore be defended on grounds of population advantages only, but if the postulated primary value is accepted the policies become all the more defensible. Equally obviously the mechanisms are expensive since they largely involve methods of rectifying conditions of inequity and poverty. In this context it is of interest that throughout social teachings using the principle of subsidiarity, the encyclicals make special reference to the poor and their protection under the principle against the needless abrogation of their powers by the powerful.

From what has gone before it will be noted that it is granted that government has the right to induce decreased *desired* family size in times of excessive population pressure. Since the indirect method of doing so involves the expenditure of funds for social improvement, the question may be asked how this differs from offering a transistor radio to a man to induce him to undergo a vasectomy. Presumably he is free to reject the offer. Consequently superficial analysis might suggest that in both cases bribery is involved. This would be an erroneous conclusion. The planned inducement of lower *desired* family size does not demand a quid pro quo. It seeks *social* improvement from which lesser desired family size may flow, but allows dissent by individual couples who may remain impervious to the effects which such conditions seem to have on others. *They do not get excluded from the social improvements.* (This does not mean to imply that the author considers transistor radios to be a major social improvement.) It is the demand of a quid pro quo which makes the transistor-for-sterilization program so demeaning.

A further requirement for moral justification of programs to reduce desired family size through indirect mechanisms, with maintenance of the principle of subsidiarity, is that there be public information about the aim. This is to say that people have the right to know that the program aims at inducing lower desired family size, if that is one of the reasons for its introduction.

If the fundamental value is accepted it follows that government must budget the funds to produce the family planning methods which permit couples to achieve desired family size by methods compatible with their consciences. To acknowledge publicly that there is a population problem and then to refuse to support measures to develop the methods of family planning is to frustrate the applicability of the subsidiarity principle in population planning. *It is dishonest to suggest that economic development will solve the population problem without acknowledging that it will occur through the use of family planning methods, unless one holds that it leads to total sexual abstinence.* It is equally unjust to refuse to support research in family planning methods on the grounds that the knowledge gained may lead to the development of methods of which one disapproves. Both "natural" and "artificial" methods can only come from knowledge of basic reproductive biology which is common to the development of both. It will be similarly obvious that if a population problem exists, of sufficient magnitude to warrant action, and if the fundamental value is to be protected, then there is a duty to do that demographic research which maximizes the possibility of decreasing desired family size by finding the conditions conducive to it.

It may be argued whether there is any U.S. governmental *population* policy. It may equally be argued whether there is a U.S. *population* problem. It is not the purpose of this essay to discuss either question. It may however be said that the government, in various ways, has *implied* that there is a problem and that there is a policy. This would seem to follow from the appointment of population commissions, population committees, population centers, and civil servants with primary functions in the population area. The question is in how far government actions are presently in compliance with the principle of subsidiarity, once it has indicated by its actions that it considers a population problem to exist. A comparison of approximate budgets for the years 1971, 1972, and the proposed budget for 1973 is illuminating:

	1971	1972	1973
Family Planning Services	45,000,000	108,000,000	151,500,000
Contraceptive Development and Evaluation	18,200,000	28,400,000	30,000,000
Training	3,000,000	2,600,000	2,600,000
Center Core Support	300,000	1,500,000	2,500,000
Behavioral Science	6,100,000	5,500,000	6,700,000

It is immediately obvious that the services and the development of new methods are the areas upon which the government is concentrating. Activity in both is proper and is indeed required. Both in training of personnel and in core support of university centers more than half the funds are assigned to biomedical work. In countries with more equitable health care distribution systems the U.S. family planning services, designed for the poor, would never be funded under the name of population, but would be covered under standard universal health care. What is disturbing is that research support in the category called behavioral science is disproportionately small compared to that in the biomedical area. Yet this is the section of the budget from which must be derived the information about the magnitude and nature of a population problem, its antecedents and consequences—in fact the precise data on which all other programs are predicated.

If the analysis of this essay is accepted, it could be argued that present government action is in serious discord with correct application of the principle of subsidiarity. The action is overwhelmingly geared to direct action at the functional level of the reproductive system rather than at determining the social environment which will decrease desired family size. This could be said a fortiori of U.S. population activities abroad where the effort in terms of socio-economic assistance decreases, while that in the reproductive area increases. The morality of such an approach is seriously questionable.

The thesis is proposed that where a population problem exists government has the right to intervene in those functions which can not be carried out by individuals. In the course of such intervention the principle of subsidiarity is to be applied. Since many socio-economic variables affect desired and achieved family size, policies affecting each variable could be scrutinized in the light of the subsidiarity principle. Given that individual freedom in one area may be lost if it is not partially ceded in another, it is proposed that in the field of population planning a hierarchy of values be established, of which the ultimate one to be protected would state that "the principle value to be protected is that of couples achieving their desired family size." To follow this goal is not to cede the principle of subsidiarity since it does not acknowledge total freedom in all activities, but only demands that where individual freedoms are ceded the ultimate dignity of man is the value to be protected.

Seen in this light, present U.S. government action at home and abroad can seriously be faulted on grounds of insufficient social action and research, although this is not a condemnation of bio-medical research or establishment of family planning services, which are necessary. Totally condemnable would be the offering of goods in return for sterilization, since a direct quid pro quo is involved. The action of many churches is equally open to criticism. Largely the Protestant churches have uncritically followed any government approach. The Catholic Church's approach is open to criticism in other, equally serious ways. While recognizing population problems, and insisting that spouses are to determine the number of their children, it has fostered the notion that economic development will solve the problem without openly admitting that this can only occur through the use of family planning methods (unless it believes total sexual abstinence will result). The Catholic Church has been totally negligent in insisting that the government make available the funds to do the necessary research in reproductive biology and demography. It might even be argued that if it is convinced that economic development leads to smaller family size (and that this is not due to the use of total sexual abstinence, or of calendar or temperature rhythm as presently available), it is immoral to advocate economic development of the poor (as advocated in the social encyclicals) knowing that it will predictably lead to practices condemned in *Humanae Vitae.*

Informed Catholics may therefore find the existence of a real tension between the social encyclicals, like *Quadragesimo Anno* and *Populorum Progressio* and the marriage encyclicals *Casti Connubii* and *Humanae Vitae.* It is therefore the author's conclusion that Roman Catholic leaders have been seriously remiss by not taking the leadership in ensuring government expenditures so that their own socio-economic teachings will not lead to actions described as intrinsically evil. One may well wonder, knowing the consequences, how a Catholic should act today when he knows that to foster the teachings of *Populorum Progressio* will factually lead to practices condemned by *Humanae Vitae.* This is particularly so if one adheres to the tenet that sins in the realm of sex are objectively and automatically considered to be serious matters, while in the social realm they are not.

In the final analysis application of the principle of subsidiarity is quite compatible with activities of government in population planning, providing a proper hierarchy of values is established with the most important ones being preferentially protected and with some admitted loss of freedom in less important areas. It is, of course, recognized that theoretically a population problem could exist of such magnitude that even the postulated fundamental value might have to be ceded.

1. Bernard Berelson, "KAP Studies on Fertility," in Bernard Berelson *et al.*, eds., *Family Planning and Population Problems: A Review of World Developments* (University of Chicago Press, 1966), p. 662.

2. *Ibid.*, p. 663, 665.

3. Pravin M. Visaria, "Urbanization, Migration and Fertility in India," in *The Family in Transition*, Fogarty International Center, National Institutes of Health, Proceedings No. 3, 1969), pp. 277-280.

4. C. F. Westoff, R. G. Potter, Jr., P. C. Sagi, and E. G. Mishler, *Family Growth in Metropolitan America* (Princeton University Press, 1961), pp. 250-253.

5. R. Freedman, "American Studies of Family Planning and Fertility: A Review of Major Trends and Issues," in C. V. Kiser, ed., *Research in Family Planning* (Princeton University Press, 1962), pp. 295-309.

6. Maria Maraviglia, *Effects of Infant Mortality on Subsequent Fertility: A Regression Approach—Chile 1952-67* (M.A. thesis, Georgetown University, Dec. 1970), p. 18; and D. M. Heer, "Economic Development and Fertility," *Demography* (1966), pp. 423-44.

7. Judith Blake, "Demographic Science and the Redirection of Population Policy," in M. C. Sheps and J. C. Ridley, eds., *Public Health and Population Change* (University of Pittsburgh Press, 1966), pp. 62-67.

8. P. R. Whelpton *et al.*, *Fertility and Family Planning in the United States* (Princeton University Press, 1966), p. 65.

14

SUBSIDIARITY: FOUR CRITICAL COMMENTS

Douglas Sturm

There is a strong tendency in the policy sciences nowadays to stress the sufficiency of some combination of three factors for purposes of adequate decision-making and policy-formation. The three factors are behavioral research, operations analysis, and computer science. One of the most striking contributions Andre Hellegers has made in his paper on population planning and the principle of subsidiarity is to remind us of the relevance of the philosophical dimension in the process of policy formulation and implementation. The neglect of this dimension is an act of self-deception, for whether attended to or ignored, the philosophical dimension is ever present. Indeed, it could be argued that the problematic of much governmental and corporate policy in the modern world results from the assumption that the philosophical dimension is irrelevant. That assumption permits a form of narrow-minded dogmatism that equals or even surpasses the dogmatisms effected by ecclesiastics throughout the centuries. And, as anyone sensitive to the condition of modern man is aware, narrow-minded dogmatisms lead to the most horrendous forms of death, degradation, and destruction. On the other hand, to admit the philosophical dimension of policy is not only an act of honesty, of owning up to a factor that is actually present. It is as well to promote public debate at its most significant level.

There are four critical comments I wish to direct to Dr. Hellegers' paper. They deal, respectively with the principle of subsidiarity itself, the distinction between indirect and direct methods of population control, the notion of constructing a hierarchy of values, and the critique of the allocation of funds in the area of population control by the United States government.

First, the principle of subsidiarity is fundamentally an expression of the Thomist philosophical tradition. Its meaning, indeed even its very language, depends upon that particular philosophical framework. That there is a hierarchy of associations, that the highest associational authority is the state, that the dominant social purpose is the common good, that the common good is ultimately directed toward the enhance-

ment and fulfillment of the individual human person are all propositions that are characteristically Thomistic. So far as this is the case,
the principle of subsidiarity depends upon a perception of the world in
which the notions of substance and hierarchy are central.

Granting the fact that to Pius XI, the principle of subsidiarity is "a
fundamental principle of social philosophy, fixed and unchangeable,"
is it translatable into alternative modes of philosophical thought? Suppose one's basic perception of the world is more processual, relational,
pluralistic? This is a type of philosophical thought that is increasingly
invoked even within the Catholic community. From this alternative
perspective it is not so clear that there is a graded hierarchical order
among associations. It is not so certain that one can speak about higher
and lower authorities. It is not so fixed that there is a set of distinct
organizational forms each with its precise and proper function to fulfill. Without neglecting the question of propriety, which associations
fulfill which particular social policies may be partly a matter of convenience, partly a matter of historical context, partly a matter of leadership motivation, partly a matter of sheer tradition, partly a matter
of distribution of power. It is possible within the framework of this
alternative, indeed from my standpoint it is morally desirable, to maintain the highest regard for the dignity of the human person, relation-
ally and contextually understood, but to argue that the principle of
subsidiarity may actually delimit rather than expand the possibilities
for creative personal and communal action.

At the very least, it seems somewhat extreme to assert that the
assignment of tasks that "lesser and subordinate organizations" are
able to do to a "greater and higher association" is "an injustice," a
"grave evil," and a "disturbance of right order." In a small community, for instance, families are able to dispose of their own garbage.
Is it unjust and a grave evil for the borough council to establish a
community disposal service?

The second comment I wish to direct to Dr. Hellegers' paper has
to do with his distinction between indirect and direct methods of
population control. The indirect method depends upon a variety
of research data indicating a significant statistical correlation among
three factors: (a) desired family size, (b) certain demographic
factors, and (c) related governmental policies and programs. Thus,
for instance, (c) an extension of educational opportunities to a
wider population will lead to (b) an appreciable increase in the educational level of the society, and in turn to (a) a general desire for
smaller family size. Conversely, of course, (c) a retraction of edu-

cational opportunity (b) decreases the educational level and thus leads to (a) an overall desire for larger family size. Other relevant demographic factors and related governmental programs are suggested. The indirect method of population control, which seems to be presented as an extension of the principle of subsidiarity, would employ governmental programs based on such demographic correlations.

The direct method of population control, on the other hand, is apparently conceived by Dr. Hellegers to be morally inferior if justifiable at all. The one example of the direct method of population control presented in the paper is a governmental program offering transistor radios in exchange for vasectomies. Presumably more sophisticated examples would include tax subsidies or penalties, provision of contraceptive devices at governmental expense or conversely placing a high tax on contraceptive instruments, intensive educational and propaganda campaigns aimed at population control, etc.

There are several questions I should like to pose about the moral distinction between these two methods of population control. First, setting aside the possible use of coercive means such as compulsory sterilization or compulsory propagation, what is the real difference? In the instance of both methods, the location of ultimate decision-making is the person himself or herself. Thus the voluntary principle is not violated. Furthermore, both methods are directed toward the manipulation of patterns of desire. Thus one cannot decry one method as manipulatory and praise the other as non-manipulatory. According to Hellegers the difference rests in the fact that direct methods entail a *quid pro quo* and thus are demeaning. Depending perhaps upon the *quid* (!), this is difficult to comprehend, since in so many other areas of social and political policy direct methods are employed without any such hue and cry. Direct subsidies, tax benefits, G. I. bills are all direct efforts to manipulate the desires of people to fulfill policy. Are they demeaning?

Moreover, the governmental programs that can allegedly affect desired family size—e.g., land use, education, equal rights for women, social security—may be debated on their own merits, independent of their effect on population size. It would be a matter of serious decision to weigh their merits solely as independent variables in relation to population growth. The conflict might be vividly illustrated if, for instance, to increase population a government were to delimit educational opportunity, lower income, increase infant mortality, and put strictures on migration and social mobility. Would it not be the better course to approach the control of population in as direct a method as possible in order not to tie in these other areas of potential social improvement with population control?

Then, consideration must be given to factors not mentioned by Dr. Hellegers in assessing the relative merits of the two methods—the probability factor and the time factor. Which method increases the probability of effective and successful control? What is the relative time lag in instituting these two methods and their appreciable effect? One might hazard a guess that direct methods are, in the short run, more immediately effective, and indirect methods are more lasting though take a longer time to become effective.

The third comment is directed to the notion of constructing a hierarchy of values. Acknowledging what Berdyaev has called "the tragic and paradoxical character of the moral life," that is, the inevitable conflict persons encounter among freedoms, values, and policies, Hellegers proposed the establishment of a set of priorities or hierarchy of values. For that purpose, he asserts that "the primary value to be protected in population planning is the right of couples to achieve their desired family size." In general, it might be more reflective of the condition of man as well as more morally justifiable to suggest a continuing process of redefining value configurations rather than to support the construction of a hierarchy of values. This is not to deny the propriety or even the moral necessity of distinguishing more and less significant values. But it is to admit the propriety and moral necessity of respecting the personal, cultural, and historical dimensions of valuational patterns.

In particular, it is not clear why the right of couples to achieve their desired family size should be paramount in population planning or precisely what other values are to be subordinated to it. Given the indirect method, it would appear that education, women's rights, social and geographical mobility, concentrations of population, infants' health are to be considered as merely instrumental values or at best as subordinate values to the procreative desires of potential parents. However, the principle of subsidiarity by itself does not seem to entail this conclusion. Thus the moral force of the assertion of the valuational primacy of family planning is not at all clear.

The fourth comment deals with Hellegers' critique of the current policies of the United States government. Granting the right of government to use means to induce a decrease in desired family size, he quite rightly insists (a) that that policy be publicized clearly and forthrightly if adopted, (b) that government should support research in and the production and dissemination of family planning methods, and (c) that government should support research in the demography of desired family size. The last duty is particularly critical given a combination of the principle of subsidiarity and the indirect method. In this connection, Hellegers finds the United States government lacking, for a comparative analysis of the government's budget over a three-year period reveals a disproportionately large share of monies allocated for biomedical research and family planning relative to the small amount assigned for basic demographic studies. However, it should be clear that the validity of this moral critique depends on the validity of the principle of subsidiarity, the moral superiority of the indirect method of population planning, and the primacy of family planning as a model, all of which have been brought into question above.

More seriously, it should be noted that population experts argue that population growth is, at the present moment in the history of man, a global problem, not simply a national or local or familial problem. If so, perhaps it should be approached with a global perspective and on a global scale. Perhaps, while the principle of subsidiarity contains a germ of truth, it should be superceded by a principle that forces one to discern all particular decisions and policies within the full context of nature and history and that acknowledges the need to conjoin creative freedom intimately and essentially with universal responsibility.

15

TOWARD A MORAL CRITIQUE OF

GOVERNMENTAL COERCION

Edward LeRoy Long, Jr.

The control of coercive sanctions is the most basic function of statesmanship. Without such sanctions the state is helpless to perform many of its appointed tasks of protecting the health and safety of its citizens. Unless the sanctions are restrained the authority of the state turns bitter and its role ceases to be credible. Powerless officials cannot affect public policy. Officials who possess too much power or exercise it heedlessly turn the state from servant to ogre. The state often interposes its authority between men in order to prevent them from curtailing each other's rights; it just as frequently becomes a party of its own interest that threatens to curtail the freedoms of those over whom it rules. Pointing to the lessons about the state that can be garnered from the New Testament, John C. Bennett catches both sides of its role: "the Christian should take a positive attitude toward the order-creating functions of civil government because in and through them the providence of God is at work in preserving essential conditions for human life, and [at the same time he should note] that the state should be kept in bounds and not be allowed to usurp the place of God." [1]

The vigilance required to maintain both the power of the state to effect constructive social orderliness and the checks over that power which are important to the protection of the individual ought never to be relaxed. We cannot expect that it will be less important to keep these roles in balance when the problems to which the state must address itself include the population problem. The ambivalence surrounding the role of government may even heighten because the state will be called to act in ways broader in scope and more intimate in impact than has been the case with many of the problems dealt with by the state in the past.

The interplay between freedom and order has a double quality. In one sense these two realities stand in opposition to each other. Order is developed by limiting the freedom of men to do as they utterly please and the restraints upon individual license which every civilized order has found it necessary to impose do curtail freedom in one sense. But there is another sense in which the restraints of civil order become the instruments by which freedom is enhanced. Men who are bound by common allegiance to respect the same laws often find they can accomplish things—even enjoy privileges—that are impossible in isolation from each other or in the uncharted relationships of anarchy. At a leading university the Bachelor of Law degree is presented after the candidates are certified to the President as being ready to "aid in the shaping and application of those wise restraints which make men free." This intriguing phrase sets restraint and freedom in a symbiotic rather than a juxtaposed relationship. The art of government consists in no small measure of knowing when restraints curtail and when they enhance human freedom.

The alternative defense of and vituperation unleashed upon government, especially in America, suggests the ambivalence that attends every human effort to order social life. Those who see ways in which the power of the state enhances freedom will naturally look to it as an effective—perhaps the only effective—instrument for bringing the population explosion under control. Those who see the state as a potential instrument of repression, interfering with the private destiny of individuals or special groups, will be frightened by suggestions that the government should be given authority to control the intimate reproductive choices of individual couples. Both of these responses are understandable. Neither in and by itself monopolizes the truth or furnishes adequate wisdom for approaching this problem.

In order to speak intelligently about the consequences of governmental action it is important to bear in mind the various ways in which government goes about its work. Modern government is a complex enterprise. It controls social behavior and influences public policy by many means. The alternative strategies it employs involve different types and degrees of coercion. It is simplistic to think of the function of government as exercised through just one technique or the coercive features of government as equally present in all official actions.

The most traditional form of state control is the criminal statute. In some countries this is promulgated by authoritarian edict; in others by legislative action taken by elected representatives. The prohibition of certain acts (and in other cases, the required performance of other acts) becomes codified within a political jurisdiction as its criminal law. The state prosecutes those who are discovered in violation of its prohibitions or in default on its mandates. The requirements of criminal law are coercively sanctioned. The state deprives men of goods, personal freedom, and (in some countries, even of life itself) in order to compel obedience.

Criminal law should be made free as possible from ambiguity in meaning or arbitrariness in application. It is most legitimate when its prohibitions or expressed requirements apply to clearly identifiable actions. Criminal law should specify actions outlawed or required and not subject people to prosecution for merely looking suspicious or holding "wrong" opinions. To make law as compatible as possible with freedom also requires continual supervision over the methods of its enforcement. Selective, spasmodic, or arbitrary enforcement introduces unfairness into the law and should be minimized. The ideal of "equal justice under law" is sound, though we are increasingly aware how very far we are from its attainment because men's standing in the system frequently affects their treatment by it.

Ambiguity can never be removed entirely from either the enactment or enforcement of criminal law. Thus it should be enforced through judicial processes rather than by administrative fiat. Although violators of minor laws may waive judicial review without serious injustices accruing, no serious punishment should be meted out apart from adjudication. A free society must constantly battle the tendency of police to usurp the adjudicative and punitive functions covertly, as they sometimes do against the poor and defenseless. Moreover, the discretionary power residing in the office of the public prosecutor, although subject to many abuses, is a possible instrument for making the enforcement of law flexible in mitigating circumstances. While a prosecutor who uses his discretionary power to play favorites or to advance partisan or private objectives threatens the integrity of government, one who refuses ever to see a mitigating circumstance is usually too wooden to be a statesman with his office.

Statute law usually contains a clear specification of the prohibited or required act or duty. In contrast, administrative regulation often turns over the task of specifying requirements and prohibitions to the enforcing officials who are charged in more general terms with obtaining more social consequences. This permits such requirements or prohibitions to be adjusted to circumstances and to change as the conditions necessary to obtain a particular objective change, but it also opens the way for arbitrariness in the exercise of governmental power. There has been an enormous growth of administrative regulation in all phases of corporate life in the twentieth century. It is clearly tied with "Consciousness II," with the development of the corporate state, and with the effort to regulate social development by planning and political initiative.

The misuse of administrative regulation can be checked by judicial remedy, such as suits and injunctions—but these are of significance only for those who can afford legal and court costs. The under-privileged have more frequently turned to the local ward representa-tive of the big city machine to redress the misapplication of regu-lations, but the role of the local ward representative has been clouded by the spectre of corruption and by the movement of welfare functions to a larger political base. It may well be that the rise of public interest law will take the place of local dickering as the main device by which the general public safeguards its freedoms against the perversion of administrative regulation. In any event, unless counter-vailing forces grow in proportion to the increase in administrative regulation it will be difficult to balance freedom with order.

The licensing power of the state deserves special mention as a form of regulation. Licensing has many dimensions. In some cases it is designed to provide a screen test of competence before individuals are allowed to perform certain services for the public. But licensing can also be used to restrain the practice or extent of a particular kind of activity, and can become a serious instrument of restraint in the hands of unscrupulous politicians or those who would use the power of the state to serve particular interests. Much licensing is done by localized units of government and instances of corruption have fre-quently arisen in connection with it. Local units of government are not always, as some people argue, more satisfactory than wider jurisdictions because they are closest to the people.

The government can also use the inducement to achieve social goals. Inducements are not new. American railroads were built with their benefit and, later, the country's air transport system. Induce-ments may be as simple as the bounty payment to the local sports-man who kills unwanted species or as complex as the purchasing policies of a military complex upon which huge industries come to depend for their very livelihood. Inducements may discourage as well as encourage certain acts, as in payments under the soil bank programs for refraining from the planting of particular crops. Per-haps the most wide-spread inducement—the exemption for dependents under the income tax laws—has very special bearing on the population question. A system of guaranteed minimal income could have the same consequences unless special attention is taken to devise it otherwise. It is tempting to think of the inducement as the very opposite of coercion. It rewards certain behavior or accomplishment (or their omission) but doesn't punish. If coercion is equated with the power to punish, as it frequently is, then many inducements would seem to come "clean" of coercive features. But if understood as the manipulation of the parameters of possibility, then inducements may also be viewed as devices by which the government gets its way by affecting individuals. For example, if I do not have money for higher education, and if the government gives educational subsidies only for those willing or aiming to do military service (as in the service academies or through R.O.T.C. programs) then my freedom is limited even by the pattern of inducements. The inducement does not eliminate the problem of freedom vs. constraint, but rather redefines its character and calls for new sensitivity to detect the possibilities of its misuse.

A strong ingredient in the classical perspective of the American dream distrusts the capacity of the state to engage in the direction of social consequences. The role of the state in restraining unsavory conduct or protecting life and property has been more readily accepted than the role of the state in attaining socially desired objectives. The private sector has been accorded by the presumption of openness; its activities assumed to be more free of coercive factors than those of the public sector. This belief has persisted largely because individuals are assumed to have an essentially voluntary relationship to private enterprises whereas their obligation to government is considered inescapable and obligatory. Moreover, it has been assumed that the officials of the state are not as well-motivated as private business men to reduce costs and to operate efficiently and that therefore public enterprise is always inferior to private endeavor.

Karl Mannheim, writing in 1950, attacked this bias with the following observation: "Once we free ourselves of the bogey that whatever the state or its bureaucracy do is wrong and contrary to freedom, and that whatever others do is efficient and synonymous with freedom, we can squarely face the true issue. Reduced to a single phrase, the issue is that in our modern world everything is political, the state is everywhere, and public responsibility is interwoven in the whole fabric of scoiety. Freedom consists not in denying this interpenetration but in defining its legitimate uses in all spheres, setting limits and deciding the pattern of penetration and, last but not least, in safeguarding public responsibility and shared control over decisions. From this follows the importance of institutional control for a strategy of reform in a democratically planned society, and the need for a theory of power based on democratic principles." [2]

Mannheim argued that the sharp distinction which developed in the age of classical liberalism between "the state" and "the society" cannot stand the test of scrutiny. He pointed out that all social units— family, trade unions, voluntary associations, corporations, and the like—exercise power and thus potentially threaten to coerce people into certain activities. "It is meaningless," he wrote, "to assert that the fight for freedom consists in hampering central authorities as much as possible, and to call this goal freedom regardless of the possible chaos resulting from the unhampered action of lesser social units." [3] He pointed to the necessity of developing a democratic theory of power which was rooted in a solid empirical observation of the actual forms and the social setting of coercion wherever found. Rejecting both anarchism and power politics as abstract and ideological, he urged men to see that "power is present whenever and wherever social pressures operate on the individual to induce desired conduct." [4] Such pressures are not confined to the police powers of the state functioning as the enforcement sanction for criminal law codes.

Mannheim's view forces us to reconsider the premise that the privately organized society is the freest society. It demands a re-examination of thinking that assumes that any pressure exerted by the government is coercive while pressures exerted by private groups are legitimate aspects of the competitive interaction between autonomous agents. The laissez-faire doctrine is partly rooted in a belief that centralized planning and social administration won't work. One source of this assertion is a belief that a natural harmony or balance pervades an unregulated state of affairs and that this balance is upset by efforts to guide social policy by governmental action. In classical forms of this belief the pursuit of his own interest by each man is held to create an interplay of countervailing forces that protects the interests of all men. The self-regulatory aspects of a free market system are trusted to produce the common good. To be sure, classical liberalism was not blind to the fact that there are ways to circumvent the free market process by manipulating power within the private sector, and it postulated the need for governmental intervention in order to protect the very free processes in which it trusted. The anti-trust action is the logical outgrowth of this realization. It is also an illustration of the way in which controlled coercion may be an instrument for the maintenance of freedom.

Another complaint against social planning centers in the feeling that no one group—even the collective whole—has sufficient knowledge of the complexities involved to make planning fruitful. This observation is not to be dismissed as the raving of the "anti's" and it may have particular cogency as a warning of the complexities which must be considered in so grave a matter as demographic planning. Men who would exercise controls over the possibility of what might become life for other men—even when such controls are judged to be necessary in order to maintain an environment in which those who are born may find necessary sustenance and fulfillment—take upon themselves fearsome responsibility. Any group that grasps such responsibility in a posture of self-righteous arrogance and self-assured confidence is probably unworthy to have it; but it does not follow that such responsibility is therefore always to be eschewed. Omniscience is not a precondition of responsibility in planning even if failure to realize the very fragmentary nature of one's wisdom is a likely invitation to foolhardiness.

Bureaucratic elites assume arrogant postures in which the exercise of power is a substitute for competence, but this fault is not monopolized by public servants. The American suspicion of politicians has sufficient rootage in experience to make it plausible. It becomes misleading when ideological considerations turn it into a special scent for corruption or mismanagement in the public sector accompanied by a flagrant inability to imagine that similar shortcomings can be discovered elsewhere. Many people suppose that incompetence in the public sector is more onerous than in the private sector. You have to deal with the appointed tax collector but presumably you can go somewhere else to have your refrigerator repaired. In practice, however, this freedom of alternative choice is not nearly as absent in the one and as real in the other as popular imagination tries to make it. The development of licensing procedures and regulation of service functionaries under private control witnesses to the fact that we often turn to government to insure the freedoms that are presumed to inhere in optional arrangements under contractural law. We have not entirely settled for market freedom as a safeguard against incompetence.

The move to society-wide planning is no guarantee that special interests are denied privileges and exemptions. Even democratic governments are subject to bias and to a propensity to make rulings and policies that favor one group over another. The "public interest" is not a neutral matter the definition of which is quickly ascertained by detached analysis. Political planning does involve hemming and hawing between the concerns of contending parties and often creates policies in which bias can be charged. But public planning should be open planning in which men are free to contend for their views, to criticize the existing bias, and to plead for alternatives. Such openness is sometimes eclipsed by tricks and devices which provide perennial materials for the muckrakers to investigate. To argue that because some officials take bribes (often without mentioning who gives them) the use of all officials is therefore illegitimate is to look for some pure land where both corruption and existence disappear at the same time.

Freedom is full of risk, and the freedom that can be garnered by social planning is no exception to this rule. The risk can be reduced by shrewd design and constant vigilance, but it cannot be eliminated— least of all by some refusal to enter into the processes which produce it. A riskless world is a stagnant world and the greatest degree of certainty is often obtained at the lowest point of creativity. If the tyrant is afraid of the freedoms that go with democracy the anarchist blocks off the accomplishments that can come from controls. Neither accepts the contingencies that go with maturity nor understands the ambiguities that inhere in social freedom.

Coercive governmental sanctions are no stranger to aspects of human behavior that bear upon the demographic problem. The use of criminal law to prohibit birth control has been with us for considerable time. It is probably fair to say that the prevalent effect of governmental policy, especially in America during the last quarter of the nineteenth and the first half of the twentieth century, was strongly adverse to population control. A country with an open frontier, the appeal of which as a motivating image lasted far longer than the geographical reality, could hardly have been expected to have made its laws otherwise. At that time we needed people more than we needed space.

In England about a century and a half ago Francis Place, a labor leader who saw that limiting the growth of families could serve to make labor more scarce and thus drive up wages, wrote a treatise entitled *Illustrations and Proofs of the Principle of Population.*[5] It urged family limitation through birth control and described various contraceptive techniques that could be employed to achieve that end. Books on birth control and family limitation circulated in both England and America during the next fifty years. In 1872 a grocery clerk from Massachusetts was elected to Congress and his moral zeal was to have a profound effect upon the role of legal enactments for nearly one hundred years. Anthony Comstock, a director of the Society for the Suppression of Vice, introduced a code to curtail obscenity. As embodied in Section 1461 of Chapter 71 of Title 18 of the United States Code the use of criminal law was set strongly against dissemination about either birth control or abortion. Comstock's intentions were moralistic. He equated contraception with obscenity and succeeded in having an entire category of materials barred from the mails and severe offenses specified for violating this ban in order to protect the purity of the moral atmosphere.

During this same period the individual states were placing prohibitions upon the dissemination of birth control information and the use of contraceptive devices. These laws were felt to embody the moral standards general to the community. Many of them remained on the books even after the public temper ceased to accept them and many were never removed from the books by legislative repeal. Rather, their effectiveness was nullified by a series of court decisions. The last major such decision occurred in 1965, when the Supreme Court struck down a Connecticut statute forbidding the use of contraceptives on the ground that such a prohibition imposed an unconstitutional invasion of privacy upon individuals.

The reasoning of the courts was, as is frequently the case with judicial decisions, a response to a changing public sense of social need. This changing perception was created to a large extent by open challenges to existing laws and mores from crusaders like Margaret Sanger. She had witnessed the unnecessary death of a woman following a second self-performed abortion. A doctor, following both law and attitudes of the time, had denied the woman birth control advice even after noting that a second abortion would be fatal. Margaret Sanger's career is the story of devotion to beliefs despite legal restrictions upon their expression or practice, but it was not merely the law that confounded Margaret Sanger. A complex of public attitudes, induced in part by laws and in part by innate conservatism of both the clergy and the medical doctors of the time, was also at work. Court decisions are but one factor—painfully slow as perceived by some, woefully rash as perceived by others—in a matrix of complex social pressures that affect legal and social freedoms.[6] The courts would be powerless without the capacity of the state to compel obedience but they also limit that capacity and at times function to redirect the uses to which it is put.

There are several kinds of laws that either encourage or permit the growth of population. They include the rigid proscription of contraception, legal bans on abortion, and personal tax exemptions based without ceiling on the number in a family. Most of these laws were placed on the books when little, if any, recognition of population growth as a potential problem was imaginable. They were enacted when multiple children were deemed a temporal blessing because they provided additional hands to perform the chores. To be sure, the laws were not passed as part of a pro-natalist program. Moral (or moralistic) factors figured heavily in the bans on contraception. Abortion laws were passed for several reasons, including the protection of the foetus from unjustified destruction and as hygienic safeguards against medical practices too crude to be safe. The granting of exemptions for each child under the income tax laws was a perfectly reasonable thing to do in a culture dominated by expansionist outlooks.

We should not scorn those who developed policies in the past as Neanderthals who flouted known information in order to persist in policies generally recognized as unwise. Had government in those periods been more active in social planning it would have encouraged population growth and our situation might be more difficult today than it is. The expansionist mood was afoot—much that was good came from it as well as much that is problematic—but neither the mood nor its consequences were induced merely by harsh laws and stupid moralisms. To hope for different social consequences in our day does not require us to condemn the past from the viewpoint of the present nor to hold that it is full of colossal and avoidable blunders. We are required only to develop the insights and muster the fortitude to implement the directions we believe to be appropriate for our day.

Even though no explicit population policy based upon ecological considerations has been adopted by our country, there has been a considerable change in the role of law and policy toward those matters which bear, directly or indirectly, on the birth rate. In 1969 President Nixon went to Congress to propose the creation of a study on population growth and the country's future. The next year Congress enacted the Population Research Act of 1970 (P.L. 91-572). The provisions of this Act set up machinery for exploring how the demographic problem can be solved and resulted in the development of a Five-Year

Plan by the Department of Health, Education, and Welfare which foresees a role for government in the area of family planning.[7]

The HEW Plan contains this interesting passage: "By acknowledging the prime contribution of family planning services and population research to health, the right of every woman to control her own fertility and the right of every child to be wanted and physically and mentally well born are recognized. This concept is fundamental to human dignity. This plan delineates the steps necessary to accomplish this ideal." The formula that reads "the right of every woman to control her own fertility" allows for many interpretations. Read from one perspective it seems to say that women can bear as many children as they wish; read from the other it seems to say that they have a right—until now often denied them by the law—to control pregnancy by either prevention or termination. Moreover, by speaking of the child as having rights to be "wanted" and "well born" the report throws back into the arena of public discussion many considerations involved in defining such terms. Is a child, otherwise healthy, "well born" if there is insufficient room for it either within its immediate family (as might be the case now) or on the planet (as might become the case sometime in the future)? Is it sufficient to be "wanted" by the parents alone in terms of action or does "wanted" imply the willingness and capacity of the culture to give opportunity for the pursuit of growth and well-being?

Several studies stemming from the Congressional Act of 1970 were released in the spring of 1972. Prepared by the Commission on Population Growth and the American Future, which was chaired by John D. Rockefeller, 3rd, these reports conclude that no substantial benefits are to be derived from the continued rise of the nation's population. They also take a very favorable attitude toward the legitimacy of population control and toward abortion by choice—a fact that has rendered them very controversial. Certainly here is a revolutionary development in which a special commission working under the auspices of the very government that a hundred years ago made mailing of contraceptive information illegal now calls for widespread access to means of terminating pregnancy. In a few states there have even been changes in laws strictly prohibiting abortions. Laws that prohibit abortions except to save the health or life of the mother are only incidentally pro-natalist. They involve serious moral issues that go far beyond questions of population size. Even laws that grant the right to abortion on demand in the early weeks of pregnancy do not contribute in a sizable way to slowing population growth, despite the fact that they are sometimes believed to do so and often advocated by those concerned about the population problem.

There has been considerable discussion of ways in which governmental action should relate to the population question. This discussion is illumined, though its implications are not exhausted, by dividing the suggestions made by various people into voluntary incentives and obligatory requirements. Those suggestions relying upon voluntary actions are frequently classified as "family planning" and those calling for coercive mandates as "population control."

The voluntary incentives include a proposal by the Ehrlichs that we adopt a realistic exemption for the first two children of each family (in the neighborhood of $2,000 each) but allow no tax deductions for any children in excess of that number.[8] While this incentive would not materially affect those too poor to pay taxes nor those too rich to feel the differentials involved it could be modified to do so. Others have proposed the payment of bonuses to late or childless marriages. We have bonuses for veterans of war against enemies on the field of battle, why not bonuses for soldiers in the war against escalating population? These and many similar suggestions are premised on the assumption that the use of money as an incentive is less objectionable than the use of other sanctions but even this technique could be carried to the point where a government hedged all citizens into rigidly prescribed patterns.

Suggestions generally classified as compulsory include the proposal of Kenneth Boulding that each married woman be issued a permit to have 2.2 infants. These permits would be marketable, like stock warrants, and the unused portions could be bartered. The figure 2.2 represents the number of births that would result in an eventual halt to the population growth. It takes into account the fact that some women do not marry and others do not bear children if they do. If a country wanted to shrink its population rather than merely bring the growth to a halt it could lower the allowable births per woman. Another suggestion calls for the compulsory submission of one or both sexes to either chemical or mechanical contraceptive treatment that would make it impossible to mate unless the effects of the treament are counteracted.[9] A third example of compulsory population control would rely upon a penal code assessing a fine upon every male who fails to acknowledge infertilizing a female and refuses to sign a permit for an abortion, and upon every female who has become pregnant and gives birth to more than two children. Richard Bowers, founder of Zero Population Growth, proposed such a criminal code in September of 1969 as the only realistic way to stabilize the population.

It is not fully clear that all of these suggestions are technically feasible even if they would be politically acceptable. The debate between those who favor voluntary means of family planning (with the hope that such methods will control population size) and those who favor imposition of rigorous compulsory controls (on the ground that only the most severe compulsion can achieve the necessary demographic consequences) has been a complex amalgam of many strands in which the questions of values have been intertwined with much conjectual speculation about technical matters. The debate does not sort itself out easily into any simple set of rubrics.

"Alternative strategies recommended by those who seek a reduction in U.S. population growth range from voluntary family planning practices to coercive governmental action. The pattern of policy choices corresponds rather closely, as might be expected, to the sense of urgency with which each writer views the 'population problem.' Those who see ecological crisis nearly upon us tend to favor more draconian measures, such as putting sterilants in the water supply, while those who consider that we have not yet reached crisis levels favor building on existing motivation. For most of the measures proposed, predictions of success remain untried and speculative." [10]

Kingsley Davis has been one of the more explicit advocates of population control. Doubting that family planning will work he has called for more drastic measures. "The unthinking identification of family planning with population control," he writes, "is an ostrichlike approach in that it permits people to hide from themselves the enormity and unconventionality of the task." [11] Garrett Hardin has frequently raised serious questions about the adequacy of voluntary controls,[12] though he pleads for the most widespread possible employment of such controls in the hope that their success can stave off the necessity of coercive methods.[13] The Ehrlichs have stressed the possibility that compulsory methods will eventually have to be employed to cope with the enormity of the problem.[14]

Barry Commoner has expressed reservation about coercive approaches to the ecological and population problem. He has called Hardin's view of the problem of the commons, as developed in the editorial in *Science* for June 25, 1971, "faintly masked barbarism." [14] He warns against over-estimating the power of technology and the pressure of population growth, and suggests that too often "both technology and population growth take on the aspect of an autonomous, uncontrollable juggernaut, threatening to crush humanity beneath its weight. Understandably, the reaction is fear and panic, self-preservation becomes paramount; humanism is an early victim. One moves from a 'war on crime' and a 'war on poverty' to a war on people." [15]

Arthur Dyck has stressed the importance of freedom to human dignity, concluding that we cannot uncritically accept every compulsory measure even as a last resort. We must remember that the continuation of human life depends upon free and responsible exercise of the right to reproduce after our own kind. Overly coercive controls or prohibitions upon that right could rob humanity of its dignity. [16]

Perhaps the most sustained and passionate critique of calls for coercive means of controlling population has come from Richard Neuhaus. Neuhaus has been through the literature suggesting such controls, though he spurns the amenities of scholarly documentation and it is not possible in every case to check whether he has reported fairly the positions he castigates. But Neuhaus has taken a strong position against proposals that would control population growth by resort to stern coercive measures. His critique is not based solely upon a preference for voluntarism as against coercion, but upon a plea that the concerns of people, and particularly concerns about fairness and justice for the poor, be central. [17]

We have raised questions about both a laissez-faire policy in which every concern about demographic matters is declared beyond the ken or sphere of government action and also about proposals for the resort to harsh coercive measures advocated in a quasi-panic about survival. Even in the short time since concern about population has been part of the American consciousness the rate of births has taken a-not-insignificant drop and may further decline without the imposition of specifically coercive sanctions. Economic factors seem to have a very important effect on birth rates, which vary inversely with general affluence. The most effective way for the government to control birth rates may be to raise the standards of living for the wide base of the population. The growing concern of women for a more equal role with men in non-household affairs may have a decisive consequence for demographic patterns. In the third world family planning clinics have proven less effective in changing birth rate statistics than changes in economic and educational levels.

While we have argued that the government must have a concern about and play a role in the population problem we have suggested that its role should not become singularly decisive. The lessons to be learned from debates about the problem include the realization that

a single value orientation translated into official coercion can be dys-
functional and often oppressive. It was true in Comstock's day, when
his moral zeal resorted to the use of criminal statute to eradicate vice
from the body politic. It could become true in our day if those concerned about very different matters from Comstock should be tempted
by his methods to stamp out excessive population growth by resort
to the same zealous use of governmental coercion. To wed Zero
Population Growth to a zero sum theory of political dynamics would
be to head into a gruesome world.

Even though structures of law and order are important and necessary aspects of every civilization, and especially of civilizations in
which freedom is functional, the structures of government can never
be permitted to submerge every other vitality. The United Nations
was right in its declaration of 1967 to declare that the right to marry
and have a family should be protected without regard to race, national-
ity, or religion. But the Commission on Population Growth and the
American Future was also correct in pointing out that unless population growth is checked social freedom will be choked by fees, forms,
licenses, lines, regulations and red tape. Freedom cannot be protected
indefinitely by merely resisting one kind of inroad upon or danger to it.
Karl Mannheim was perceptive in suggesting that "the real task is
rather to substitute new control for ineffectual ones in order to eliminate waste, restore efficiency, give scope to foresight and . . . to do
all this without inhuman regimentation or needless interference with
the normal aspirations of the citizenry." [18]

If Mannheim is taken as portraying the government as the neutral
embodiment of the general will directed wholly toward the common
good by a process of rational political decision his vision will mislead
us. Extant governments are not paragons of benevolence, but embodi-
ments of class and racial and ideological interest that are at best
impure and often self serving. This is why it is crucial to keep
government under the restraints mentioned above and also to keep
countervailing vitalities, which the government is not at liberty to
eradicate, alive in every social order. The government is never, as
Charles West has observed,[19] to be trusted with the task of enforcing
a single overarching view of what is right and how people must live
in order to attain it. Against totalitarian claims the Christian will
always seek the legal protection of legitimate conscientious objection
and be prepared to exercise such objection even if it is not legally
protected.

We are living in a time when it is easy to become disillusioned with the integrity and adequacy of government to deal with human problems. But while contemporary experience should alert us to the difficulties that might attend public policy concern about the population problem, it should not blind us to the role which governmental actions can play in helping to direct affairs toward more constructive futures. Hedged by the proper constitutional restraints, kept within bounds by countervailing vitalities, and questioned by the ultimate right of every man to place his conscience before God, government can employ "those wise restraints which at least help to make me free."

1. John C. Bennett, *Christians and the State* (Charles Scribner's Sons, 1958), p. 35.

2. Karl Mannheim, *Freedom, Power, and Democratic Planning* (Oxford University Press, 1950), pp. 44-45.

3. *Ibid.*, p. 43.

4. *Ibid.*, p. 46.

5. Francis Place, *Illustrations and Proofs of the Principle of Population* (London: Longman, Hurst, Rees, Orme, and Brown, 1822).

6. For a study of the kinds of complex factors that can work to enforce a social/legal attitude see Kenneth W. Underwood, *Protestant and Catholic: Religious and Social Interaction in an Industrial Community* (Beacon Press, 1957).

7. Forwarded by Secretary Elliott L. Richardson to Vice President Spiro T. Agnew on October 12, 1971.

8. Paul R. and Anne H. Ehrlich, *Population, Resources, Environment: Issues in Human Ecology* (W. H. Freeman and Company, 1970), p. 252.

9. Edgar R. Chasteen, *The Case for Compulsory Birth Control* (Prentice Hall, Inc., 1971), p. 206.

10. Robin Elliott, Lynn C. Landman, Richard Lincoln and Theodore Tsuruoka, "U.S. Population Growth and Family Planning: A Review of the Literature," in *Family Planning Perspective II* (October 1970). Reprinted in Daniel Callahan, *The American Population Debate* (Doubleday and Co., 1971), pp. 197-98.

11. Kingsley Davis, "Population Policy: Will Current Programs Succeed?" *Science* (November 10, 1967), p. 739.

12. See especially Garrett Hardin, "The Tragedy of the Commons," *Science* (December 13, 1968).

13. See Garrett Hardin, "Multiple Paths to Population Control," *Family Planning Perspectives II* (June 1970).

14. Barry Commoner, *The Closing Circle: Nature, Man and Technology* (Alfred A. Knopf, 1971), p. 297.

15. *Ibid.*, p. 248.

16. Arthur Dyck, "Population Policies and Ethical Acceptability," *Rapid Population Growth: Some Consequences and Some Public Policy Implications* (Johns Hopkins Press, 1971).

17. Richard Neuhaus, *In Defense of People: Ecology and the Seduction of Radicalism* (The Macmillan Co., 1971). See especially Chapters 5, 7, 8 and 9.

18. *Mannheim, op. cit.*, p. 47.

19. See his essay in this volume.

16

GOVERNMENTAL COERCION AND

ONE-DIMENSIONAL THINKING

Rosemary Radford Ruether

Edward Leroy Long's essay, "Toward a Moral Critique of Government Planning" exemplifies the complex balancing act in which the ethicist becomes involved when he atempts to apply ethical principles to government functions. The reconciliation of contradictory tendencies often appear more as a verbal *tour de force* than a real symbiosis. To that extent the language of ethical balance often serves to conceal rather than expose the explosive forces which lurk under the surface and which, when exposed, make the whole analysis much more problematic.

The paper itself seems to be of two minds about the kind of society it is describing. On the one hand, there is that model of society which assumes a fixed system of social needs and individual desires which are in some moderate tension. Judicious application of coercion is necessary to bring constant readjustments to a system which otherwise would fall into that anarchy which destroys 'true freedom'. Within this balancing act of readjustment through coercion, the social planner threads his cautious way, leaning neither too far to the right, nor too far to the left, balancing optimal pluralism of choice against the minimum of that necessary coercion by governmental structures necessary to keep the system as a whole in concert. Yet this kind of rational calculus has, in recent times, revealed its darker face. We have a species of much this same kind of mentality in the coercion exercised by Messrs. Kissinger and Nixon in Vietnam.

The Vietnamese are regarded as having only irrational drives, rather than a moral consistency of their own. The government is regarded as an essentially benign, however "harsh," force for the curbing of "excess." The possibility of excess on the part of the government is recognized theoretically, but not in such a form as to allow a calling into question of the legitimacy of its coercive power at any point. Against that swarm called "the people," the benign force of government exercizes a graduated escalation. Each show of 'excess' on the part of the population calls for new and more stringent measures of coercion on the part of the government, until finally we reach the paradoxical conclusion of genocidal destruction of the Vietnamese people and land in order to "save" them.

Yet the ideological question with which Dr. Long chooses to contend in this paper turns primarily on the obsolete struggle between a conservativism suspicious of centralized government and a bureaucratic liberalism confident of its ability to know "what is best" for everyone. But it is precisely the last decade of American history which has demonstrated a transmutation of this struggle between the traditional libertarianism of small town America and "new deal" liberalism. The Republican party, which still affects to speak in the name of this small town libertarianism, has, in fact, fallen heir to the power structures of bureaucratic liberalism shorn of its earlier idealism. In command of dictatorial executive power over the greatest centralized bureaucracy in the world, Mr. Nixon now thinks in terms of naked power politics around the world, abandoning all pretence that this power structure fights on the side of those oppressed by local government. At the same time the executive's office becomes a huge propaganda machine for the mystification of the main stream with a veneer of "boy scout wholesomeness." In this situation of radical reversal of the traditional tensions between local and "big" government, it seems that an entirely new analysis is necessary.

What these recent shifts in the relation between traditional ideology and the actual functioning of governmental bureaucracy must teach us is the overweening capacity of mangement to become its own *raison d'être* and to form secondary structures of privilege and profit emancipated from any consideration of the common good or accountability to the general population, while maintaining an elaborate facade that contradicts this actual mode of functioning. Dr. Long's paper seems to be only partially aware of these post-liberal lessons of the demonic capacities of mass management. His essay still has one foot in the "end of ideology" perspective which blanks out the class bias of society.

But "end of ideology" thinking is precisely what Marcuse calls "one dimensional" thinking, which lacks a sense of transcendence from which the class bias of the dominant group can be critically appraised. For this reason it becomes the most ideological form of thinking since it blanks out all the critical factors which bias a government against domestic and foreign populations and presents the results to us as if this were truly the reality within which we are to make moral judgments. The basic ideological assumption of one-dimensional thinking is that the prevailing power structure does, in fact, represent "all the people" and has the interests of "all the people" at heart, in an equal and even handed way. Even though some levels of management—i.e., "the police"—may sometimes act in a strangely 'biased' way, there is some benign "father" above them who can correct this excess. It never becomes apparent that this peculiar malfunctioning of the police may simply be the crudest and most overt expression of the class bias of the government as a whole.

But it is hard to credit this model of representative government as approximating the reality of the government of the United States of America of the 1970's. This is a government which has abandoned any serious confrontation with domestic racism, which is overgrown on its police and military side, and which is engaged in massive counter-revolutionary activity around the world to maintain traditional elites and to prevent more popular governments from coming into existence. By ignoring the realities of this government's bias in favor of its own structure of political and economic privilege within the United States and around the world, we are presented with an unreal framework within which to analyse the possible effects of coercion in the area of population control which might emanate from this government. The actual factors through which any such programs of coercion would grow into an amoral monstrosity will then be perceived too late by those who have not been trained to look for such biases in their analysis of their own society.

All too late the exponents of benign bureaucratic liberalism will stumble, with great surprise, upon the fact that the very structures which they have created to guide the development of population for the general good have, from the beginning, been an integral part of the war of the rich against the poor, the war of colonial power against the third world, the war of men against women, the war of whites against colored. These factors might well explode the framework of Dr. Long's analysis. Most peculiar is the fact that there is not one word about the neo-colonialist relations between the United States and those countries of Asia, Africa and Latin America which are the objects of our counter-insurgency police and military training, in the service of maintaining our ecoonmic dominance. Any population programs created by the United States government today would inevitably fall within the framework of this neo-colonialist power relationship to these "over-populated"—i.e. economically dependent areas.

The revelation of the class bias of bourgeois society explodes the liberal mythology of atomic individualism and equality before the law. The 'poor' can no longer be seen as existing in the same position, politically, as the rich, except for the accidental factor of having less money. The class and racist bias of society upsets these assumptions, revealing that all decisions are structured, not for the benefit of all, but to perpetuate and enhance the power of a ruling class. How, then, in a class and racist society can one assume that any sanctions of government will not be used discriminatorily against those already in structures of dependency and coercion? One cannot do so without raising the question of a restructuring of such a society as a whole. This must start, not with an essentialist analysis of the nature of 'all government', but with a historical analysis of the situation of particular governments. To fail to look at the historical relations between a power such as that of the United States and colored and third world populations in terms of the racist and imperialist biases of the American ruling class is a serious oversight. An analysis of these elements as they would actually condition the structure of coercion toward these populations is not incorporated into Dr. Long's judicious analysis of the factors of the social equation. For this reason the attempt to arrive at the Aristotelian mean between extremes of freedom and coercion becomes hollow, because the presumed model of society as a description of any society, particularly American society today, is unreal.

Two traditions of thought, one stemming from Protestantism and the other from the Enlightenment, have tended to stultify the social imagination of liberalism. In the Protestant doctrine of the "two Kingdoms" government is regarded as the realm of the coercion of "sin"; not the realm of potential fellowship or grace. Any escalation of force against the "sinful" populace by the government can be legitimated if it is seen as necessary to preserve "law and order." At what point the law and order of a government becomes illegitimate because it is systemic disorder in favor of a ruling class cannot be raised within this framework. A moral struggle against constituted power in the name of a higher community of "love" is excluded as a possibility of human nature. Only "justice", not love, can be incarnated in social structures. What has happened here is that the parameters of necessity set up because of "sin" have become the parameters of what is now called "human nature." But this kind of "realism" has a tendency to sink more and more toward cynicism and a resigned acceptance of evil in government.

By an insufficiently dynamic view of those higher possibilities of human nature that might penetrate and transform the limits of the possible, one comes to settle more and more for brute force in the facing of a rising tide of "sin." By confining the limits of human nature to the balancing of egoism, one closes off critical thinking about the legitimacy of the present social structure and imaginative thinking about alternative possibilities. The static confrontation, typical of recent crisis theology, between sinful human nature and the transcendent creates a view that is good at knocking down pretences, but impotent to imagine the possibility of transforming the reality of moral calculations. The "is" becomes the necessary. One can repent, but not really redeem.

The second bias of liberal thinking was one which assumes a mechanistic view of society. Society is seen as a mechanism in which all parts work only if controlled from a directing center. This is the model of thought which came to dominate Western science with Newton, and which contemporary systems analysis sees as the height of realism and objectivity. Spontaneity or non-programmed response within the system is seen as a threat against the whole. But this bureaucratic centralism tends then to reduce the system as a whole to the lowest common denominator, both in terms of innovative methods and ethical insight. It is strange that those who are regarded as spokesmen for the ecological movement, such as the Erlichs, seem to be most addicted to this mechanistic model of control. It seems that the ecology movement has scarcely even begun to imagine a genuinely ecological consciousness that could be the foundation of a new harmony between man and nature. In his many volumes on social development, Lewis Mumford, has been a critic of this mechanistic view and a spokesman for an "organic" view that alone could be the foundation of an ecologically sound society. Mumford believes that we must approximate anew in society that spontaneity and self-regulation which produces harmony and balance in natural systems. Only in such organic forms of operation do freedom and regulation become identical. In organic systems regulation is intrinsic rather than extrinsic, and so it is experienced as freedom rather than coercion.

One approach to the meaning of this distinction might be offered by Hannah Arendt's small study *On Violence*. Here she suggests that violence and power are antithetical. Violence or external coercion is not the natural extension of legitimate power but arises with the breakdown of power. Power is that cohesion and self-regulation in a society that holds a significant consensus about values and life-styles. Coercion in such a society is low because there is a high degree of consensus about behavior which generates willing adherence to norms. Such adherence expresses an agreement between the individual and the social norms. Therefore, it is experienced as freedom rather than coercion. Even what appear to be very "coercive" societies, such as contemporary China, apparently can be perceived by the vast majority of those within them as "liberated" because of this communal *élan*.

When this intrinsic power begins to break down with the disintegration of such a consensus, then coercion comes in to force continued conformity to a style of life which is now viewed as good only by the ruling sector. But it is no longer spontaneously adhered to by many people in the community at large. Since the ruling class takes its definition of its own self-interest as identical with the common good, the rise of dissent becomes an occasion for increased coercion rather than a critical force that could transform the whole into a new consensus. Instead the whole system comes to rely more and more on force, until finally the government reaches the end of its capacity to coerce an unwilling population and the government breaks down altogether. No government can coerce more than a small percentage of the population. A broad base of voluntary assent to norms because they are perceived as conducive to the common good is then essential for the functioning of government.

Of all forms of human activity, reproduction is the least responsive to extrinsic coercion. It is the place where any external regulation is felt most directly as an unjust interference with personal freedom. It is well known that all methods of population control have little effect until a society reaches that point of development where the people themselves no longer see large families as necessary to an economy of scarcity and begin to adhere spontaneously to the preference for the small family. The schemes of population experts for escalating doses of coercion against a recalcitrant population bent on reproduction become actually absurd. Far from generating cooperation, such schemes would create that reign of total force against total resistance that spreads the collapse of community into a police state, unless conditions are already ripe for a voluntary change of preference in family size. But when this happens such schemes of control quickly prove quite unnecessary.

Thus if the ecologists really desire a new ethic of family regulation, they should put away all mechanistic concepts of coercion as their primary societal model. They should concentrate instead on imagining the ways of developing the world community as a whole toward more equitable distribution of the goods of the earth. They should seek that revolutionizing of society that will bring genuine equality of opportunity to oppressed minorities and that revolutionizing of the method of production so that the private sector no longer exploits the goods of the earth for profit regardless of ecological damage. They should begin to imagine that ecological society embued with a new consciousness that would build into its functioning the conservation and recycling of every commodity, rather than the present social economy of exploitation and waste. They should seek a society where the female half of the population is not artificially segregated in the suburban bedroom communities with insufficient opportunities for occupations beyond the domestic sphere. They should seek to overcome that disparity of development between the industrialized world and the third world which keeps the latter impoverished and dependent. By overcoming the social inequities that presently control the capitalistic system, they will find that the population problem will tend to take care of itself. Self-regulation and use of available contraceptive methods will arise as an integral part of a life style where the small family is preferable.

Without such changes, on the other hand, the schemes of coercion function actually as a method of trying to control the effects of lack of social development while refusing to deal with its real causes. The one-factored schemes of population control applied to minority or third world populations, in lieu of social revolution, become actually a part of a counter-revolutionary arsenal for maintaining present social inequities while attempting to repress their effects by force.

17

GOVERNMENT'S ROLE IN CHANGING

POPULATION ATTITUDES

Joseph D. Tydings

For the purposes of this paper, I am confining my thesis to the role of the United States Government in regard to changing population attitudes rather than the broader definition of any government's role. Quite obviously, the citizenry of our nation have a right to demand and expect a different and hopefully more enlightened and intelligent leadership than that provided by the Government of say Upper Volta or even Brazil or Portugal or the Soviet Union. Because of our system of "free public education" we are or should be uniquely able to separate the pragmatic "wheat" of good governmental policies proposed by leaders of ability and good will from the political chaff of the demagogues, religious zealots, and "baloney artists" who always seem to drift to government and politics in every clime. Then too, in the United States of America we have the protection of the "noblest instrument" yet devised to govern a nation and still preserve the dignity of its individual citizens—The Constitution of the United States and more particularly its first ten amendments and the Fourteenth Amendment.

Before one can really address the problem of what the United States Government's moral responsibilities are with respect to changing the cultural attitudes of our nation towards population policy, it is necessary to objectively review the likely effect of too rapid population growth on our nation and the world over an extended period. In addition to the problem of exponential rates of growth of our population, we must be aware of the related exponential decrease in water supplies, arable land, natural resources, not to mention the exponential increases in all types of pollution. One half of the people who have lived on earth since the time of Christ are alive today. The world population which at one time doubled in about 1500 years now is doubling in 30 years. It took the population of the earth almost 1600 years from the birth of Christ to double. It doubled again by the Civil War; it doubled again by World War II; and will double again by the year 2000. The sheer numbers of people suffering as a result of that growth staggers the imagination. Of the almost four billion persons alive on our globe today, two-thirds live in a chronic state of malnutrition. Almost 500 million face painful starvation. One half of the children of school age in the under-developed countries are not in school. In the developing countries the population doubling rate is not 30 years but less than 20. Honduras, for example, has that kind of a doubling rate with one half of her population 15 years old or below. She has about 15% of her population in the active work force; 15% producers and 85% consumers. She must maintain every school and build another; maintain every hospital and build another; train every teacher and doctor and nurse and train another every 17 years just to stay where she is today. No nation, rich or poor, can do that. So the gap continues to grow between the developed and developing nations and between the aspirations of peoples and their dismal realities. Against this picture I must admit to a certain revulsion when I hear that the population explosion is a myth, something we need not act on at this time.

Basically the rise in population has to do with decline in death rates. For hundreds of years death rates balanced birth with famine, pestilence and early mortality. Most deaths occurred before the child-bearing years. Only towards the 19th Century did these death rates turn down and continue to decline during the late 1800's and the early 1900's in Western Europe and the United States under the impact of emergent medicine, nutrition, transportation, sanitation, all the developing products of the industrialized and scientific society.

The recent summary report of the results of Phase I of the Club of Rome's Massachusetts Institute of Technoolgy project *"The Dynamics of Global Equilibrium"* is perhaps the most revealing, comprehensive and scientific survey or our diminishing natural resources and the factual limits of growth on this planet that has ever been compiled and disseminated. Dr. Dennis L. Meadows in his introduction to the *Limits of Growth* summarized the world problem, which is our problem, very succinctly when he said "for some four thousand years the condition of the human race has been characterized by growth and change, technological development has accelerated, natural resources have been depleted, our environment has been polluted at an ever-increasing rate, population has multiplied at least fifty fold and may double again within this century. Now there is evidence the growth may be occurring too quickly to permit adaptations by the planet's social institutions and its ecological systems. Growth cannot continue indefinitely on a finite planet. Sometime we will be faced with an inevitable transition from world wide growth to global ecological equilibrium. Because of the time delays inherent in social system change, decisions made today are already influencing the nature of that future equilibrium."

"The predicament of mankind is that we can perceive the individual symptoms and the components of these profound social and political problems. We are frustrated in our efforts to comprehend the total situation and develop global solutions."

The aspect of the MIT report which is the most profoundly disturbing is the exponential growth factor which the leadership of past generations and our generation has failed to grasp. Exponential growth is a geometric increase, as compound interest, whereas linear growth is an arithmetic line. The difference can mean a sudden and immense lurch upward.

The sobering result of the Club of Rome's unusual study basically is this: All of the factors which relate to the Limits of Growth on this earth, all of the forces—over-population, over-industrialization, declining amounts of arable land, dwindling natural resources, and increasing pollution are all changing exponentially. Each affects the other and is affected in return, combining a growing strain on our planet and our nation at a suddenly frightening speed. The MIT study goes on to show that our natural resources are being depleted exponentially even faster than the population grows because each year more of our citizens use more electricity, more automobiles, more gasoline, and more of the world's goods, etc. Succeeding generations use more and more natural resources per capita as they demand higher material living standards. The supply of some of our most vital resources will fall below demand shockingly soon. Nickel in 53 years; aluminum, 71 years; zinc, 18 years; silver, 13 years; gold, 9 years; petroleum, 30 years. We have been proceeding along our merry way lulled to sleep by static linear indices on the lifetime of our vital natural resources.

The figures, on our supply of arable land are equally sobering. These, at least we can compute to a nicety on our finite planet. The world contains just seven and one-half billion acres of "arable" land. The most fertile and productive half is cultivated already, most of the rest would cost too much to reach, clear, irrigate, and fertilize, however urgent the needs. With present yields (and it is important to remember that ten to twenty million people a year are now dying as a result of malnutrition) every living person needs at least one acre of tillable land to sustain him. Each "additional" child born will need that one acre, and in addition, based on present uses on this globe of ours, an additional fifth of an acre for housing, roads, waste disposal, power lines and industry. In the United States the amount of land required per capita is substantially more because our citizens consume a substantially higher amount of the finite natural resources of the world in order to live the "Affluent Life."

The final point which this significant report dramatized is the apparent suddenness of the limits of growth which we will reach because of our exponential growth processes. The point is dramatized by an old French riddle for children. The riddle or story describes a pond in Burgundy where a farmer grew catfish. He noticed one day a beautiful water lily growing. It was the type of water lily that doubles in numbers each day. It was a large pond and the farmer realized that if the lilies were permitted to grow unchecked they would completely cover his pond in seventy-five days, choking off in the process all other forms of life in the water including the catfish. For a long time, however, the multiplication of lily plants seemed so inconsequential that the farmer did nothing about it. He put off the time when he would start cutting back the lily plants until the day they would cover half the pond. What day would that be? On the seventy-fourth day, unfortunately! The farmer had one day to save his pond. That is the problem which should concern us with respect to the exploding population on our globe and in our nation: As the Rockefeller Report on *Population Growth and the American Future* advised, even a one-child difference in average family size makes an enormous difference over a decade. A century from now, with continued immigration, a two-child family average would result in a population of 350 million persons; a growth at the three-child level would result in nearly a billion. None of us would like to condemn our grandchildren to live in a United States with a billion persons.

Population stabilization is the only affirmative and visible handle for the world and the United States (which is the leader of the world) to avoid the catastrophic physical and social consequences which are the handmaidens of exceeding the limits of growth on our globe and in our nation. By slowing, limiting and eventually stabilizing population growth, we can begin the long road back to balancing this planet's and our nation's precious resources with the need and demand to support unnumbered human beings. At the moment, population is the only exponential growth factor we can bring under

control without cauing great suffering (as by say, food or water
rationing) or without using the strongest and most totalitarian
governmental strictures. In the words of the Rockefeller Commission
Report, "America must slow down or even stop its population growth
or face an increasingly contrived and regulated future."

The Commission on Population Growth and the American Future
(commissioned by the Congress and the President to study the problem of population and over-population in the United States) found
"no substantial benefits will result from the continued growth of our
population beyond that made almost unavoidable by the rapid growth
of the past. On the contrary, it is our view that population growth
of the current magnitude has aggravated many of the Nation's problems and made their solution more difficult. The Commission believes
that the gradual stabilization of population, bringing birth into balance
with deaths, would contribute significantly to the Nation's ability
to solve its problems although such problems will not be solved by
population stabilization alone. It would, however, enable our society
to shift its focus increasingly from quantity to quality. The Nation
has nothing to fear from a gradual approach to population stabilization. We have looked for and have not found any convincing economic
argument for continued national population growth. The health of
our economy does not depend on it, nor does the prosperity of business
or the welfare of the average person. In fact, a reduction in the rate
of population growth would bring important economic benefits, especially if the Nation developed a policy to take advantage of the
opportunities for social and economic improvement that a lower
population growth would provide. The Commission believes that slowing the rate of population growth would ease the problems facing the
American government in the years ahead. Demands for governmental services will be less than they would be otherwise and resources
available for public support of education, health and other governmental activities would be greater."

The most ominous inference rising from the Rockefeller Commission was the hint of danger from ever-increasing public regulations
and lessening individual freedom caused by headlong population
growth. "Imbedded in our traditions," it said, "is freedom from public regulation, virtually free use of water, access to uncongested unregulated roadways, freedom to do as we please with what we own,
freedom from red tape and bureaucrats. Clearly we do not live this
way now. Maybe we never did, but everything is relative. The population of 2020 may look back with envy on what from their vantage

point appears to be our relatively unfettered way of life." With the facts as presented by the Club of Rome's MIT study, the Rockefeller Commission and many other prestiguous scientific and sociological studies, our governmental leadership has no alternative but to move forward vigorously and forthrightly through the religious and political quicksand which surrounds the objective of stabilizing our Nation's population growth.

The highest traditions of political leadership in our "Western Democratic" form of government were expressed by Edmund Burke in his famous address to the electors of Bristol. On this historic occasion he refused to bow to the electors' parochial self-interest at the expense of the welfare of England even though it cost him his position in the British House of Commons. His words were: "It ought to be the happiness and glory of a representative to live in the strictest union, the closest correspondence, and the most unreserved communication with his constituents. Their wishes ought to have great weight with him; their opinion high respect; their business is unremitted attention. It is his duty to sacrifice his repose, his pleasures, his satisfaction, to theirs; and above all, ever, and in all cases, to prefer their interest to his own. *Your representative owes you not his industry only, but his judgment; and he betrays instead of serving you if he sacrifices it to your opinion.*"

Our population will undoubtedly stabilize voluntarily as the individual American citizen challenges the traditional assumptions that growth for its own sake is good and appreciates what is at stake vis a vis the quality of life both for the individual family and the society at large.

In order to create the climate necessary to achieve voluntary stabilization, it will be imperative, I believe, for the top government leaders of United States to enter into serious dialogue with religious leaders and others to attempt to educate them and to change cultural attitudes or traditions which are relics of bygone years. This is particularly true with the National Catholic Welfare Conferences; its top leadership in Washington, D. C. and across the nation has unfortunately failed to take seriously the problems of population growth other than to oppose constantly efforts in the Congress and elsewhere to provide the means for voluntary population stabilization. In a free democratic society, religious leaders should be a potent and effective moral force, willing to challenge the anachronistic dogmas of the past. That some religious leaders can is graphically shown by the recent heroic leadership of many brave young Catholic priests, Protestant clergymen, and Jewish Rabbis, in opposing the war in Viet Nam despite harrassment from the hierarchy and congregations of their own church. They were willing to challenge the validity of an immoral, senseless U. S. policy of involvement and war in Southeast Asia. They risked the ire, and criticism, and in some cases ostracism of their own church. This same intelligent, moral, and valiant leadership from the clergy in our greatest churches will be necessary to achieve population stabilization. Here as in the Viet Nam war issue, there is traditional opinion and policy which is based on a system of mores, customs, and logic which developed in the past (and may or may not have been valid then) but which is today a dangerously short-sighted anachronism.

Education looms as the principal tool in reviewing means for a government to effectively change cultural attitudes toward population policy or anything as delicate and sensitive. Here I think several of the recommendations of the Rockefeller Commission should be vigorously implemented. In order to prepare present and future generations to meet the challenges arising from population change, the Commission advocates the enactment by the Congress of a Population Education Act to assist school systems in establishing well-planned population education programs. In order to maximize information and knowledge about human sexuality and its implications to the family, it advocates a national policy to make sex education available to responsible community organizations, the media, and especially the schools; and similarly to seek to improve the quality of education for parenthood throughout our society. In short it proposes a massive education effort.

Strong leadership can and should be provided through public advocacy by the television and radio networks, newspapers, by governmental leaders, and by the adoption of a Congressional resolution confirming voluntary population stabilization as a U. S. policy. Our national governmental, civic, and business leaders should promote debate and serious dialogue on the issue and thereby bring out the facts and the problems to the American people. Given the facts, our citizens will reach the only judgment that rational persons can. They will realize that only by slowing, limiting, and eventually stabilizing population growth can we avoid the catastrophic physical and social consequences which are the handmaidens of "exceeding our limits of growth."

In a democratic system, no matter how intrepid or heroic its public leaders, they can only legislate and lead for a long period of time within the broad penumbra of of public opinion. Therefore, it is vital that "opinion leaders" in private groups, church groups, philanthropic groups, political groups, labor groups, civic groups, community groups, educational and cultural groups, sporting and environmental groups, all consider the *limits of our growth* a major item on our national agenda. Policies and laws are not adopted in a vacuum. They are accomplished only when the citizen consistituency is sufficiently enlightened or concerned to permit or demand them.

Basically, the policy of enabling all Americans, regardless of age, marital status, or income, to avoid unwanted births should be a vital national commitment. This policy should include the capacity of all Americans to realize their own preferences in child bearing and family size. In order to carry out such a commitment effectively we must increase the investment in research for improved contraceptives. We and the world desperately need a contraceptive which is foolproof, one hundred percent effective, which is logistically easy, which is reversible, and which is inexpensive. We need the means by which individuals particularly young women, women who are fifteen years of age and younger may control their own fertility and their own destiny. We should extend subsidized family planning programs. These programs should be built around Mother and Child Care clinics. Indeed the Rockefeller Commission sets forth a broad agenda of items to be followed in this area.

This country is fortunate by reason of its vast resources and relative "youth" to have more time than the rest of the world to move in this field of over-population and diminishing natural resources. If we wish to preserve the quality of life in this country for our grandchildren, we must move rapidly and immediately. We are condemned by the demographers' calculus to attempt to reach family unity size now (that is an average of 2.2 children per family). Even if by some miracle we achieve unity size tomorrow, our population will increase for another seventy years because we have so many women in a child-bearing age group of our population.

We need courageous leadership in government and in religion. Those who are elected to lead us have a moral responsibility in changing the cultural attitudes of our people towards population policies. Knowing the facts as they exist today, any other policy would be criminally negligent, not only for our generation but particularly for our children and grandchildren. The government must enter into dialogue with religious leaders and others in attempting to change these cultural attitudes. A democratic government has a responsibility to try to lead and to educate and change the values and attitudes of its people when the facts are clearly and strongly conclusive and particularly when the facts lead to the issue of the very survival of mankind.

18

TOWARD A BROADER STRATEGY

FOR REDEVELOPMENT

RICHARD M. FAGLEY

As a member of the U.S. Senate, Joseph Tydings gave sterling leadership in the Congress to efforts to encourage and to undergird responsible decisions by Americans in regard to the size of their families. His commitment to voluntary means in the pursuit of responsible family limitation marks him as one who understands the potential of democracy. I share his faith that husbands and wives, given an adequate knowledge of the facts and with full access to appropriate methods of family planning, will generally reach socially sound conclusions as to the spacing and number of their children. Indeed, I would go a step further. If the technocrats who distrust human nature could somehow prove that even well-informed couples will persist in exceeding parental norms congruent with quality of life and social well-being, I would still opt for more education rather than a multiplication of coercive controls. Truly human development cannot be achieved by governmental methods that deny the truly human in the men and women who are governed.

The right and in fact the obligation of government to help families gain the knowledge and means required for responsible family life is widely recognized by churchmen. The Beirut Conference of 1968 on World Development, sponsored by the World Council of Churches and the Pontifical Commission Justice and Peace, focused on the problems of the two-thirds world of poverty and associated ills, but what it said has wider application: "Christians should recognize not only the gravity of population pressures for development, but also the right of citizens to be enlightened by public authorities and the right and duty of these authorities, within the limits of their competence, to inform all citizens in regard to population problems and policies."

A primary task of government is to seek and to express a national consensus on population policy, a task finally under way in this country in the work on this question by the Rockefeller Commission.

Undoubtedly the governmental duty to inform all citizens includes the duty to enlighten religious leaders, as Mr. Tydings has argued. But judging from recent political sounds emerging from Washington on this subject, I suspect that churchmen at present may have considerably more to learn from each other than from politicians—at least in a campaign year. I have worked too long on these issues not to be aware how slowly benighted attitudes die in churches as in secular society. But I am also aware of and grateful for the expanding ecumenical consensus furthered by the major Protestant statements and by important Catholic statements, particularly *Gaudium et Spes* of the Second Vatican Council, and the broadening Judeo-Christian harmony in this area. In particular regions, this consensus has not yet become politically effective. But the trend is not to be mistaken.

Mr. Tydings touches upon government use of its tax powers to discourage large family patterns and thus reinforce its educational efforts on behalf of a sound population policy. Since it is virtually impossible to devise tax laws that do not have demographic implications, whether or not intended, it seems clear that when a national population policy has received enough consideration and support to be adopted, tax policies should generally harmonize with it. If the 'slanting' of taxes to favor small families is not to become excessive and cross the border between the voluntary and the coercive approach, it is obvious that this sector cannot play a major role. It seems to me particularly important that the weight of tax penalties should not fall on the children of large families.

A far more important sector for winning wider acceptance of a sound population policy is the task of helping to build better opportunities for the disadvantaged to achieve a higher quality of family and social life. Studies of differential fertility recognize the influence of a 'front' mentality as Van Heek called it, when minority groups or groups in conflict feel disadvantaged or threatened. The hostilities and frustrations of our ghettos and slum areas, and consequent suspicions that efforts to extend family planning have a genocidal intent, constitute a substantial obstacle to an adequate national consensus on population policy. The arguments that matter are not what is said but what is done to provide better job opportunities and better education related to them, better housing and better community facilities. Just as family planning efforts among the underprivileged peoples of the world need to be integrated with programs to emancipate women, with health and nutrition programs, with job-related training, and with new approaches to old age security, so such efforts in underprivileged sections of our own society need to be integrated with substantial action to overcome the disabilities of prolonged social injustice. Hope and social reforms to give it substance are enduring ways to achieve motivation for responsible parenthood. Fortunately, many minority group leaders are giving leadership in this area.

While the influx of the poor into the cities and the spread of urban decay pose major issues for the American future, I submit that greater dangers are posed by the sprawling suburbs of our affluent and middle class citizens. The conditions and life styles of the poor primarily hurt the poor; but the life styles of the affluent endanger the human environment and thus threaten everybody. In a generation in which 2½ billion people in Asia, Africa and Latin America are in process of doubling, it is not *per se* the possible addition in this spacious land of 100 million persons that gives most concern. It is our population growth in relation to unprecedented patterns of affluence, of expanding production, consumption, pollution, and waste. The interrelationship between the American population problem and that of the environment is central to a sound approach. For it is our profligate way of life that is the more urgent issue: even if zero population growth were a present reality, there would still be the massive problems of American injury to the human environment.

The 1972 Stockholm Conference has helped to educate public opinion on the scope of the perils created by Western man in heedless pursuit of rapid industrialization and ever-higher G.N.P. At least it helped reveal the tips of the lethal icebergs. These include the vast and wasteful use of irreplaceable resources, the doubling of energy consumption every decade in the most industrialized societies, and the basic thrust of such societies to expand production and consumption. As those who study the environment talk more and more of the need for a 'balanced' society, a 'stable' or 'equilibrium' society, or a 'steady dynamic society' (to quote René Dubos) in which improving the quality of life substitutes for quantitative expansion, the revolutionary implications become more evident. Maurice Strong, the Secretary-General for Stockholm, remarked:

"The environment issue is moving out of the motherhood stage to the point where it is now being seen as one of the most pervasive, profound and revolutionary issues that man has ever faced. It requires us to confront such fundamental issues as the possible limitations to growth, the purposes of growth, the control of technology, the utilization of the world's resources and distribution of its opportunities. It points up the need for new attitudes and values, a redirection of man's scientific and technological drives, a more balanced distribution of the world's industrial capacity, the widest possible dissemination of new environmentally sound technologies and changes in the organizations and institutions of society . . ."

Thus governmental efforts to promote a population policy for the United States need increasingly to be closely related to a broader *strategy for redevelopment,* a strategy for effecting step by step the hard transition to simpler and more modest ways of living, and the social and economic patterns congruent with such life styles and with the safety of our sadly imperilled environment. The promotion of a population policy to reduce fertility is important as an adjunct of a broader strategy of economic and social redevelopment and indeed as a palliative while the agonizing reappraisals required to achieve such a strategy are being made. But population policy by itself distorts the nature of the social crisis we face, and will not in any case get us very far towards a solution.

Even laymen in the field of politics can sense the massive obstacles which stand in the way of ideas which challenge basic assumptions of many decades of industrial and pre-industrial development. The notion of unlimited material progress has been fundamental to the American dream and cherished by the elites of most countries. To find a new dynamic for industrial societies means a long, hard uphill struggle. The "motherhood" stage of the environment question, in which most were of one accord, was indeed short. The comments now heard in Washington, Detroit, and so on, illustrate this fact. Is it really necessary to involve the question of population policy in such a complex and difficult issue? I think it is. Until we wrestle with social values and patterns, until we redefine the good life in terms that respect the claims of future generations, until we begin to flesh out the meaning of substituting improvement of the quality of life for quantitative expansion, we will lack the framework for properly judging optimum population levels for the longer range. Consequently, while recognizing the importance of short-range programs to restrain population growth, I see no acceptable alternative to tackling the more fundamental questions.

As far as the churches are concerned, it should not have required the testimony of the ecologists to remind us of the dangers of a false and flamboyant materialism which gets in the way of life that is truly human. It is high time that we cultivate appreciation of more genuine and moderate ways of living in greater harmony with nature. This is an abiding insight of the Judeo-Christian tradition.

Part III

MORAL ANALYSIS OF POLICY PROPOSALS

Governments are beginning to explore population policies of different kinds. For the most part, new official policies are quite limited and highly tentative. Experts on population are, however, considering a wide range of possible measures ranging from the very limited to the highly coercive. The essays in this section are by no means exhaustive of the significant policy proposals currently under discussion, but they illustrate some of the dilemmas we face.

In "Public Provision of Family Planning Information and Services," James Allen and Anne Raper present policy on the provision of family planning information and facilities and assess these from an ethical standpoint. Both authors are associated with the Carolina Population Center, Dr. Allen as a professor, Mrs. Raper as a research assistant. In this essay they deal with the question whether provision of services is unwarranted government interference, whether it is equitable to use tax dollars in this way, whether certain forms of family planning facilities (including provision for abortion and sterlization) should be financed in this way, and whether such information and facilities should be available to unmarried people including teenagers. Their answers are generally affirmative as is the response by George Contis, director of the Family Planning Division of the Office of Economic Opportunity.

A number of population experts advocate use of incentives to lower the birth rate. They argue that in many ways government already has created "pro-natalist" incentives of various kinds, including tax exemptions and, in some countries, family grants for children. Proposed incentives include a bonus for each year free of conception, withdrawal of tax exemptions, and incentives for late marriage. A related question is whether welfare programs ought to be limited to the first two or three children. From time to time it has been proposed that unwed mothers on welfare should be sterlized as a condition of continuing to receive welfare payments. The essay by Robert Veatch examines the ethical issues at stake in such policy proposals. Dr. Veatch is an associate of the Institute of Society, Ethics, and the Life Sciences and helped direct that institute's study on population ethics for the U. S. Commission on Population Growth and the American Future.

Edward Pohlman, in reply is sharply critical of the Veatch essay at a number of points—particularly at the point of his own greater sense of the urgency of developing incentive programs. Dr. Pohlman is professor of psychology at the University of the Pacific and author of a number of studies on population questions. His observations on incentive programs are partly an outgrowth of several years' work on population programs in India.

In "Population Criteria in Foreign Aid Programs," Philip Hauser deals with the question whether wealthy nations should withhold foreign aid programs from countries with ineffective population policies. The rationale for this kind of proposal (which has been made by such writers as William and Paul Paddock and Paul Ehrlich) is that such aid may be useless in the long run since the population explosion in such countries quickly undermines the benefit of the aid. Would such a policy be sound practically and defensible ethically? Should certain forms of aid be offered for countries without effective population policies while other forms of aid are withheld? What is the significance, in this connection, of the fact that population stabilization has tended to follow—not to precede—economic development? What are the implications of Garrett Hardin's proposal that wealthier nations with lower birth rates are, in this era, the stewards of civilization and that such nations must not let the rapid growth rate of the others undermine this civilization? In addressing these issues, Dr. Hauser writes primarily as a demographer, but with considerable ethical force as well. In addition to his widely recognized leadeship on population matters, he has served as a consultant to ecumenical religious bodies. In a reply, Richard Dickinson seeks to sharpen a number of the ethical issues further. A professor of Christian ethics at the Christian Theological Seminary, D. Dickinson has given particular attention to problems of world economic development.

Harmon Smith's essay "Eugenic Control and Population Policies" is concerned with the very old question whether official policies should regard genetic quality as a variable in limiting or encouraging births. The basic concept of governmental eugenic control is as old as Plato's Republic, but recent genetic research suggests all kinds of possibilities which need to be assessed ethically. To what extent should governmental policy require eugenically defective people to be sterlized? Should eugenically defective fetuses be aborted as a matter of routine? The underlying question addressed by this essay is whether moral distinctions among human beings can properly be made on the basis of their genetic inheritances. W. French Anderson's reply is from the standpoint of a genetic scientist. Dr. Anderson conducts research on Molecular Hematology at the National Institute of Health.

"The Public Regulation of Abortion" by Clinton Gardner addresses questions which are at this time of writing being debated vigorously throughout the United States. Should the present, generally restrictive abortion laws of most states be modified or abolished? What, precisely, is the status of the human fetus at various stages of its development? What are the moral rights of potential mothers, and what are their responsibilities? In her supplementary essay, Jimmye Kimmey resurrects the history of present regulations and argues that they did not originate primarily out of a concern for the fetus. Mrs. Kimmey is Executive Director of the Association for the Study of Abortion.

19

PUBLIC PROVISION OF FAMILY PLANNING

INFORMATION AND SERVICES

James E. Allen and Anne B. Raper

This volume has so far dealt with the problems of establishing population policy objectives and of determining the role or function of government in regard to the creation and implementation of formal and informal population policies. Now we must consider the moral implications and probable impact on the American public of one particular policy: The public provision of family planning information and services to all. At issue here is whether or not this policy is consonant with such fundamental American values as respect for human freedom, human dignity and individual fulfillment, and concern for social justice and welfare. The authors believe that it is. In order to make an analysis of a public family planning policy, resolutions of the following several basic issues will be sought.

What would making family planning information and services available to all without charge involve? There is evidence that making "comprehensive voluntary family planning services readily available to all persons desiring such services," [1] is emerging as an American value. In 1970 Congress enacted the Family Planning Services and Population Research Act. Both this act and the Commission on Population Growth and the American Future promote the idea that comprehensive family planning services should at least include information about and treatment for voluntary fertility control through contraception, pregnancy termination and sterilization.[2] How many Americans might be affected under these policies? Assuming that, as a matter of policy, all persons should have access to all these services with no barriers or inequities in service based on income, minimum age, marital status or color, Charlotte Muller and Frederick Jaffe have recently estimated between 1972 and 1978 as many as 26 to 36 million women will be in need of family planning services.

If such a policy were effectively implemented, what impact might it have upon the U.S. population growth rate and individual family size? The impact of having free family planning information and services readily available to the U.S. population would depend on the aggregate of all individuals' decisions about their own family size. While a real ethical gain would result from this type of policy, in maximizing the possibility of effective individual control over fertility, this is not necessarily a fertility reduction policy. For example, if an individual family desires a family size of two or more children their desire, as well as another family's desire for four or more children, could be fulfilled. Families might well use the services provided through this policy to plan for four to six children well-spaced to keep the mother healthy enough to bear and care for them. In the latter cases, a voluntary family planning policy would aid families in achieving large family sizes through child spacing. Thus this type of population policy may result in either an increase or decrease in average family size and, consequently, in the population growth rate itself. Thus the demographic, and, in the last analysis, the ethical impact of these policies is potentially neutral depending on the resulting average family size of American families. It seems likely, however, that if present trends continue, this policy may well have the impact of further reducing the U.S. population growth rate. That is, the U.S., along with many other developed nations, may possibly be approaching a period of incipient decline in population growth. Three reports—the 1970 National Fertility Study, a survey by the Census Bureau, and a compilation by the National Center for Health Statistics—indicate a sharp decline in the number of children women intend to have from 3.03 in 1965 to 2.53 in 1970.[3] Other fertility research in the U.S. shows that, regardless of socio-economic status, most Americans share a desire for a family of two to four children [4] and the present trend is still downward. A possible parallel to this can be seen in the example of Sweden, which is going through a similar demographic transition. Sweden has a number of voluntary family planning and health measures and while its present slow growth rate is due in part to industrialization, it is also due to the availability of free family planning services and to the desire for and use of these services.

Since the desire for smaller families is also occurring in the United States, a similar family planning program could provide the means for achieving this desire and for continuing or lowering the present population growth rate. The results of several studies on unwanted or unplanned pregnancies point to the need for such a program. For example, there is evidence that families who initially desired smaller families later experienced unplanned births. Bumpass and Westoff concluded from the data in the 1965 National Fertility Study that 4.7

million children born from 1960-1965 in all socio-economic groups were unwanted.[5] This amounted to one-fifth of all births and one-third of Negro births. Bumpass and Westoff note that "the percent unwanted increased rapidly by birth order: five percent of first births, 30 percent of fourth births and 50 percent of sixth or higher order births." For Blacks the rates of unwanted children were even higher: 12 percent unwanted first births, 44 percent of second births and 66 percent of sixth or higher order births. Among the poor or near-poor, 32 percent of the births were declared unwanted.[6] In addition to difficulties, in achieving desired family size, more than two-fifths of the "wanted" births between 1960 and 1965 were reported by the parents as being "timing failures." It seems reasonable to assume that access to free family planning information and services could help families to avoid number and timing failures and to achieve stability.

What impact might this policy have upon the quality of life for individuals and for individual families? Quality of life is a complex and hotly debated value issue about which individual judgments differ. In the view of President Nixon the effect of 61-115 million persons by the year 2000 may well be a lowering of the quality of American life. For example, in terms of individual economic survival, a family of 3-4 children will mean for many extending a sufficient but limited income far enough to keep above the poverty level, and for other families the same size may mean being unable to provide for themselves at all. Our view is that as a means to increasing the quality of American life voluntary family planning services and information should be viewed as a preventive health measure. Taking this view a number of improvements seem possible, including reduction of perinatal and infant mortality, protection of maternal health, improvement of children's physical, mental and emotional growth and development, prevention of unwanted births and their psychological and sociologocial effects, enhancement of family health and adjustment.[7] Each of these is a desirable step which should result in an improvement in the quality of the lives of our citizens. Since the average American family presently desires 2.5 children or less, presumably individual control over the number and spacing of children, together with improved and extended health care, could lead to significant reductions in maternal mortality and health complications.

We have already mentioned that an estimated 20-30 percent of births are unwanted in the U.S. The psychological and social consequences of unwanted births—legitimate and illegitimate—indicate that both the mother who bears the child and the child itself may be handicapped by their mutual misfortune. Psychoses and neuroses may be triggered by an unwanted pregnancy, to say nothing of maternal deprivation, parental rejection or over-protection and child abuse after the child is born.[8] It seems fair to assume that free, comprehensive family planning services would significantly increase the possibility that every child born is wanted and that many of the present serious psychological and sociological problems of child growth and development presumably related to present levels of unwantedness would disappear.

A national family planning program could affect the quality of individual lives in America in still another way: it could provide the opportunity for an increasing number of individual and family life styles. If fertility could definitely be planned, then individuals and families could plan other parts of their lives with greater certainty and less anxiety. Men could feel free to change jobs or careers and be less anxious about financial security if they did not have to support unplanned children; more women could follow the careers for which they trained or embark on new ones. Teenagers could survive their sexual explorations and avoid forced, unsuccessful marriages. Families could be more successful at building better lives for themselves as individuals and as members of a family group.

What effect would this type of government policy have upon individual freedom? There are some who see any type of governmental population policy as a threat to individual freedom—whether it be freedom to reproduce, the right to privacy or the liberty of determining the course of one's own life. However, one need not even appeal to a social conscience or the concept of mutual aid in order to find support for a national voluntary family planning program. It is voluntary, it does offer individuals the opportunity to make choices, it enhances individual freedom. This type of policy would enable people to determine when and how often they want to produce children and to select privately on the basis of the fullest possible knowledge which fertility control method they prefer to use.

The fear of governmental control of individual liberty takes its most extreme form in the Blacks' charge of racial genocide. This charge is legitimate because our present national family planning program has so far been aimed only at the American poor (which includes a disproportionate number of Blacks) and because elements in our society have considered proposals forcing fertility control, including sterilization, on welfare mothers. Blacks argue that better total health care as well as the eradication of poverty and racism in general, not family planning by itself, will improve the quality of Black life. Even though this paper does not consider a total medical care program, a family planning policy and program could still be utilized within this broader context. However, the Black charges of genocide may be met by offering a policy of free voluntary access to family planning to *all* Americans.

Furthermore, Blacks themselves sense the need for better family planning. Bumpass and Westoff have already shown that Blacks claim an even greater problem with unwanted children than whites (30-41% of the Blacks vs. 20-22% of the whites). Many Blacks are also aware that their maternal and fetal death rates are about twice that of whites (7.0 v. 2.0 per thousand and 25.1 v 13.3 per thousand).[9] These problems would be greatly alleviated by better access to family planning and good maternal and child health care.

Individual freedom need not be incompatible with national family planning, especially if it is voluntary. Sweden again provides us with an example of a country with a population policy that its citizens regard as beneficial rather than restrictive. Sweden has provided the opportunity for every individual to know how to space and limit the number of children by requiring sex education in schools and by offering contraceptive information and services through maternal and child health centers, community physicians and out-patient departments of women's clinics. Despite Sweden's desire for a higher population growth rate, the individual right to control fertility is considered more important. Thus Sweden is committed to the rights of individuals to plan their family size and to develop their own general life styles.

Should all forms of family planning services, including abortion and sterilization, be incorporated in this policy? Now we turn to specific family planning services about which there is a strong controversy: abortion and sterilization. On October 29, 1970, the APHA Executive Board made the following recommendation: "Abortion services are an integral part of comprehensive family planning and maternal and child health care. As such, abortion and contraceptive counseling and services should be available together."[10] In the same year the American College of Obstetricians and Gynecologists favored liberalizing abortion laws to permit abortion "if the addition of another child to the family would interfere with the health of the existing children or members of the family."[11] Then in March of 1972 the U.S. Commission on Population Growth and the American Future recommended that "present state laws restricting abortion be liberalized along the lines of the New York State statute," that "federal, state and local governments make funds available to support abortion services in states with liberalized statutes," and that "abortion be specifically included in comprehensive health insurance benefits, both public and private."

Abortion and sterilization are becoming increasingly more acceptable means of post conceptive control because sometimes contraceptives fail, people fail or the circumstances of life change. The predictability of these three variables make abortion and contraception complementary rather than competitive.[12] In the U.S. we have already noted that 20-50 percent of married couples will have at least one unplanned pregnancy. Abortion could provide the additional insurance necessary to successful family planning. Voluntary sterilization could represent additional family planning insurance; back in 1965 at least eight in every 100 couples not intending to have children elected this method.[13] Probably more couples would seek sterilization upon completing their family if there were fewer access problems. Although Utah is the only state in which sterilization is illegal, the Commission on Population Growth and the American Future found that "lack of any specific law in many states often leaves physicians in a climate of uncertainty where many fear civil or criminal liability for performing voluntary sterilizations." Frequently hospital sterilization committees or individual doctors restrict the number of these operations by imposing their own restrictions. Moreover, hospital and physician fees put sterilization out of the reach of the poor and the near-poor. Recognizing this problem, the Commission has advised that "all administrative restrictions on access to voluntary sterilization be eliminated" and that medical groups and associations promote the removal of existing restrictions. OEO has already lent support to voluntary sterilization by authorizing funds for vasectomies and tubal ligations.

In sum, sterilization and abortion, as integral parts of a national family planning program, could enhance the possibility of individual and family well-being and development and concomitantly enhance human dignity.

Should family planning information and services be available to unmarried people, including teenagers, as part of this policy? This question also provokes considerable controversy because of fears that such a program might "undermine the moral fibre of young Americans." Although there is increasing recognition of the extent of premarital pregnancy in the U.S. and of its adverse health and social consequences, in many communities, as reported in the Five Year Plan, "minors can obtain information and medical guidance in relation to sexual behavior and contraception only after they have had a first pregnancy—in or out of wedlock—even though the potential personal benefits to be derived from providing service to sexually active, unmarried minors are many.[14] This description leads us to consider six questions:

- What is the extent of non-marital pregnancy in the U.S.?
- What is the nature of this problem?
- Would a national family planning program offered to unmarried women actually have any effect upon illegitimacy rates?
- What are the moral problems in providing or not providing services for this group?
- What legal factors are involved in offering contraceptive help to minors?
- Is there any evidence of support for providing services for this group?

Teenagers appear "to be assuming a larger proportion of the births; from 40 percent in 1964 to 47 percent in 1967 of the out-of-wedlock births were to women under 20 years of age. . . ." The estimate is that in 1969, 84,000 school age girls bore an out-of-wedlock child.[15] The HEW estimate for the same time is even greater: 100,000 of the 300,000 illegitimate births each year are to teenagers.[16] Considering these numbers from another point of view, we find that 40 percent of all U.S. marriages involve teenagers and of these more than 50 percent of the high school brides are pregnant on their wedding day. The rate increases to 80 percent if the bridegroom is also a high school student.[17] If the number of unwanted births in the U.S. is to be significantly reduced, this group must certainly have fertility control information and services available.

One reason the size of this group is so large is that illegitimacy is not limited to any particular socio-economic class. Elizabeth Herzog found that a significant number of illegitimately pregnant teenagers consist of white girls from middle and upper income levels "who are relatively mature, upstanding and economically self-sufficient." [19] A Minnesota study supports her findings: 22 percent of the family incomes of unmarried pregnant girls were under $5,000, 57 percent were over $5,000 and about 19 percent over $10,000.[19]

What happens to these unmarried teenagers is both a health and a social problem. The health hazards a sexually active and unprotected minor faces, according to lawyers Pilpel and Wechler, include greatly increased risk of prematurity, stillbirth, perinatal and infant mortality and brain injury to the child born.[20] The fetal death ratio (stillbirths, miscarriages and induced abortions) has been ten percent to 50 percent higher for illegitimate pregnancies than for legitimate ones.[21] According to Dr. B. Simons, if the child should survive birth, he or she "stands a much higher than average risk of dying or being damaged through ignorance or neglect of the mother, or of being actually battered, burned, or starved." [22] Studies have also estimated increasingly higher rates of venereal disease among the 15-24 age group since the beginning of the 1960's.[23] The social problems that arise from illegitimacy are familiar: lack of educational attainment, limited jobs and income advancement, divorce [24] and separation and the possibility of poverty and economic dependency for parent and child.

The U.S. Commission on Population Growth and the American Future recently made the following report: "Toward the goal of reducing unwanted pregnancies and childbearing among the young, the commission recommends that birth control information and services be made available to teenagers in appropriate facilities sensitive to their needs and concerns." As significant as this change in public policy and in the liberalization of the laws mentioned above is the change in the attitudes of physicians themselves. Pilpel and Weschler again note that "two years ago the National Medical Committee of Planned Parenthood-World Population and the American Association of Planned Parenthood Physicians alone among physician groups recommended that doctors prescribe contraception for sexually active minors. Now this position is upheld by the American Medical Association (AMA), the American College of Obstetricians and Gynecologists, the American Academy of Pediatrics and the American Academy of Family Physicians." [25]

In sum, the benefits of an accessible family planning program to both individual teenagers and to society as a whole outweigh any moral prohibition against or punishment of sexual activity among unmarried people.

Is it equitable to use tax dollars for this type of policy, and is its cost justifiable in light of all our other pressing needs? The question of whether or not the spending of public funds for this type of policy is just arises because some groups within the population are officially opposed to the services, especially abortion. In particular, opposition comes from the Roman Catholic hierarchy and from some fundamentalist groups. However, these views tend more to be those of the church hierarchies rather than of their constituencies. In fact, most Catholics and Protestants today are more in agreement with each other about birth control than are Catholics and their official hierarchy. Based upon a study of Catholic conformity before and after the 1968 Papal Encyclical, Ryder and Westoff concluded that "the Papal Encyclical has certainly not effected the slightest reversal in the trend toward nonconformity and has probably not even slowed it down." [26] Furthermore, a survey made in 1971 by the Commission on Population Growth and the American Future indicated there is considerable support, including among Catholics, for a federal policy for family planning.[27] Eighty-three percent of the Catholics (87% of the total respondents) favored making birth control information available to all those who want it, 70 percent of the Catholics (74% of the total respondents) favored making birth control supplies available to those who want them, and 66 percent of both the Catholics and total respondents favored the government making abortion available to all women who want it.

Religious resistance to a national family planning program is becoming less and less. Yet, perhaps just as important in the consideration of public support is the U.S. policy of the separation of Church and State that posits that no one religious group has the right to impose its views on the majority. Thus our government, on these two counts, could be justified in spending tax dollars for such a program. The protection of minority rights in this case is assured by making actual use of such information and services entirely voluntary. Moreover, there would be no discrimination against minority groups because the information and services would be equally accessible and free to all parts of the population.

Support for such programs will probably increase once it is recognized that "the cost estimates do not represent wholly new expenditures for the U.S. Society." [28] Muller and Jaffe estimate that more than 85 percent of the total fertility-related health services, including maternal health care and pediatric care, are already financed through some combination of individual, public, and third party financing mechanisms, and public medical care programs. (One-fourth—about $1.7 billion in 1972—of Muller and Jaffe's total cost is chargeable to a voluntary fertility control program.) This figure can be placed in another perspective by noting that total U.S. health expenditures in FY 1971 were $74 billion and that the GNP was more than $1 trillion. Hence the cost of delivering healthy children and preventing unwanted pregnancies may be only about 2 percent of the nation's health bill, and about .2 percent of the GNP. Furthermore, Muller and Jaffe argue "about one-fourth of the total expenditures for the fertility control services would be offset immediately by fewer claims for maternity care alone stemming from the prevention of unwanted pregnancies and births." [29] Jaffe himself thinks that the 21 percent decline in the birth rate among poorer women in the late 1960's was primarily due to the "availability to the poor of better contraceptives" through increased Federal spending.[30]

Any truly effective and unbiased national family planning program will have to offer information and services free to any individual. The Commission on Population Growth and the American Future has already recommended how this should be done: "Public and private financing mechanisms should begin paying the full cost of all health services related to fertility including contraceptive, prenatal, delivery, and postpartum services; pediatric care for the first year of life; voluntary sterilization; safe termination of unwanted pregnancy; and medical treatment of infertility."

Finally, we must examine the question, "is the cost justifiable in light of all our other pressing needs?" Some may feel that the estimated per capita expenditure of $9-10 could better be spent improving our cities or in promoting business growth. Yet the benefits which would accrue to the American public from a per capita expenditure of $9-10 could directly and indirectly affect slum conditions, business growth, education and job potential, environmental conditions and a host of other public concerns.[31] The Commission on Population Growth and the American Future has observed "slower population growth can contribute to the nation's ability to solve its problems in these areas by providing an opportunity to devote resources to the quality of life rather than its quantity, and by 'buying time' . . . (to develop) orderly and democratic solutions."

Conclusion

Public provision of family planning information and services to all is an ethically desirable public measure which could improve the quality of American life. This policy could fulfill the basic goals recently recommended by the Commission on Population Growth and the American Future: "Creating social conditions wherein the desired values of individuals, families and communities can be realized; equalizing social and economic opportunities for women and members of disadvantaged minorities; and enhancing the potential for improving the quality of life." Finally, this type of policy would probably be more acceptable to the American public than more coercive measures because, as the Commission suggests, "it minimizes the changes to be adopted; and maximizes variety and choice in life styles, while minimizing pressures for conformity."[32] It supports individual decision-making and planning based upon knowledge of the various means of fertility control. In improving the possibilities for freedom and well-being among individuals and families as well as contributing to the solution of many of our national problems, this type of policy should, in our view, be viewed as both ethically sound and highly desirable for the American nation.

1. Family Planning Services and Population Research Act of 1970. Public Law 91-572, Sec. 2(1).

2. A stricture against using any of these funds for abortion services was, however, attached to the act.

3. Jack Rosenthal, "Population Growth Rate in U.S. Found Sharply Off," *New York Times* (November 5, 1971), pp. 12, 25.

4. Norman B. Ryder and Charles F. Westoff, "Relationships Among Intended, Expected, Desired and Ideal Family Size: United States, 1965," *Population Research* (U.S. Public Health Service, March, 1969).

5. The term "unwanted" brings up questions such as "by whom?" and "at what point?" Families, even individual husbands and wives, differ in their feelings about having an unplanned child. They may repress unwanted feelings or retroactively rationalize an unwanted birth as wanted. In addition, some studies of the numbers of unwanted children are becoming out-of-date because of increasingly effective contraception. In any case, the concept seems useful to at least point to a widespread dissatisfaction with fertility control efforts among some groups in our population.

6. Larry Bumpass and Charles F. Westoff, "Unwanted Births and the U.S. Population Growth," *Family Planning Perspectives* (October 1970), p. 10.

7. These improvements and the relationship between family planning and mental and physical health in general are discussed in Abdel R. Omran, *The Health Theme in Family Planning* (Carolina Population Center Monograph 16, 1971).

8. Edward Pohlman, *The Psychology of Birth Planning* (Schenkman Co., 1969), pp. 305, 327-28.

9. *Vital Statistics of the U.S., 1967*, Vol. 2, Part A, Sec. 1, p. 41 and Sec. 3, p. 5.

10. "Recommended Standards for Abortion Services," *American Journal of Public Health* (February 1971), p. 396.

11. Alan F. Guttmacher and Harriet F. Pilpel, "Abortion and the Unwanted Child," *Family Planning Perspectives* (March 22, 1970), p. 22.

12. Three developed countries, Japan, Hungary, and Britain, have liberal abortion laws, yet their declining birth rates are due to a combination of pre- and post-conceptive control of fertility. See D. M. Potts, "Post-conceptive Control of Fertility," *International Journal of Obstetrics and Gynecology* (November 1970), pp. 960-961.

13. Norman B. Ryder and Charles F. Westoff, *Reproduction in the United States, 1965* (Princeton University Press, 1971), pp. 130-131.

14. *Report of the Secretary of HEW Submitting Five-Year Plan for Family Planning Services and Population Research Programs*, prepared for the Special Sub-Committee on Human Resources of the Senate Committee on Labor and Public Welfare (October 12, 1971), p. 322.

15. Edith Garmezy, "Overview of Illegitimacy and the School-Age Pregnant Girl: The Minneapolis Response," *Illegitimacy, Today's Realties* (New York: National Council on Illegitimacy, 1971), p. 60.

16. Henry P. David, N. A. Hilmer, E. J. Liberman and P. R. Williams, "Behavioral Research in Population Planning," *Professional Psychology* (1970), p. 207.

17. Henry P. David, "Mental Health and Family Planning," *Family Planning Perspectives* (April 1971), p. 21.

18. Floyd M. Martinson, *Sexual Knowledge, Values and Behavior Problems: With Especial Reference to Minnesota Youth*, report based on a study conducted by the Department of Sociology, Gustavus Adolphus College, in conjunction with Lutheran Social Service of Minnesota (Gustavus Adolphus College, 1966), pp. 316, 326.

20. Harriet Pilpel and Nancy F. Wechsler in "Birth Control, Teenagers, and the Law," *Family Planning Perspectives* (1969) Several cases are cited.

21. "Trends in Illegitimacy in the United States, 1940-65," National Center for Health Statistics, Series 21, No. 15 (U.S. Public Health Service, February, 1968), pp. 17-21.

22. B. Simons et al., "Child Abuse—Epidemiological Study of Reported Cases," *New York State Journal of Medicine* (November 1966).

23. National Communicable Disease Center, *Morbility, Mortality, Annual Supplements*, Summary 1968, pp. 62-63; Summary 1970, p. 13.

24. "Divorce rates are highest among teenagers, three times higher than among marriages consummated between ages 21 and 45." David, "Mental Health and Family Planning," p. 21.

25. Pilpel and Wechsler, "Birth Control, Teenagers and the Law: A New Look, 1971," *Family Planning Perspectives* (1971), p. 43.

26. Ryder and Westoff, *Reproduction in the U.S.*, p. 213.

27. Gerald Lipson and Dianne Wolman, "Polling Americans on Birth Control and Population," *Family Planning Perspectives* (January 1972), pp. 39-42.

28. Muller and Jaffe, "Financing Fertility-Related Health Services," *Family Planning Perspectives* (January 1972), p. 8.

29. *Ibid.*

30. Rosenthal, *op. cit.*, pp. 1, 21. "Poorer Women" are those with family incomes under $5,000. There was an 18% decline for other women.

31. This is one of the main topics of a book entitled *Population Policy and Social Problems* the authors are planning to publish.

32. Memorandum from Jeannie I. Rosoff, Planned Parenthood-World Population, March 24, 1972, p. 2.

20

FAMILY PLANNING SERVICES:

AN INDIVIDUALIZED APPROACH

George Contis

The paper on the "Public Provision of Family Planning Information and Services" by James Allen and Anne Raper reflects their
optimism that family planning is an important solution to the problem
of population growth in this country. I am in agreement with them
on a great number of points. I would like to elaborate on some of
these and take issue with the authors at other points.

First of all, as advocates of family planning, it is understandable
that the authors believe that the downward trend of the U. S. population growth rate is a good thing and should continue. Is this a valid
assumption, however? While we talk about "optimum population
growth" and "stabilization of population," do we have any hard
statistics that support these suppositions? After studying the relationship of population and resources in India, can we say with great
confidence that overpopulation and a high population growth are the
basis of many of the national problems in the United States? After
listening to discussions on "optimum population," are we not reminded
of the endless medieval debates on "how many angels can dance on
the head of a pin"?

There are no statistics that demonstrate that one population growth
rate is more advantageous than another. Even though it is logical
that continued unlimited population growth may have detrimental
effects in the long run, the whole concept of population stabilization
needs far more critical analysis. In their paper, the authors use the
example of Sweden as a country whose population policy "promotes
the growth and social development of her population." There are
many factors besides Sweden's population policy that must be taken
into consideration. For example, Sweden has not been at war for
almost two centuries, and Swedes have practically no illiteracy.
Furthermore, there is increasing concern over the depopulation of the
northern third of the country, and the continued migration to cities
beset by urban problems. In other words, even in a country the size

of Sweden with all its natural resources, one cannot conclude that a slow growth rate is responsible for anything near a utopian life.

In my mind, the fundamental issue is not that there are too many people, but that the quality of life is not high enough for everyone. In saying this, I acknowledge that "quality of life" is difficult to quantify also. The authors define it in terms of reduced prenatal and infant mortality, better maternal health, and enhancement of family health and adjustment. They also define quality of life in terms of individualism and individual freedom. This is an important point to Americans, for it is one of the cornerstones of our way of life and our social, political, religious and economic institutions.

The point I am trying to make is this: let us not decry population as the single root cause of our failures as human beings and as a society. Rather, let us examine the various aspects of the population problem and identify those parts that have a detrimental effect on the quality of life of individual human beings. This is more a combined ethical and epidemiologic approach rather than a mathematical one. It is one that seeks to define what "unwanted pregnancies" are, and to whom they are occurring. It is a highly individualized approach to life that seeks out, in a humanized way, those persons whose lives are at risk for a possible disrupting experience.

This individualized approach to improving the quality of life is not unrealistic for the United States today. Given our systems of communication, transportation, health care and education we can focus our attention on reducing unwanted and unplanned pregnancies in a systematic but highly personalized way. Unfortunately for many countries of the world, a number of factors make it difficult for them to deal with the problem of rapid population growth in the same way. The awareness of population as an issue is not uniform throughout the world. Indeed, there is a spectrum of sophistication regarding this problem ranging from the rather enlightened attitudes of India and Pakistan to denial among some of the nations of Africa and South America. In addition, lack of resources, trained personnel and adequate facilities hamper many developing countries who are interested in doing something about rapid population growth. In the United States, it costs about $75 per patient per year to provide family planning information and a complete range of services. These services are usually provided through a network of hospitals, clinics and private physicians and a support staff of many thousands of professionals and paraprofessionals. Even so, only about half the poor women who want these services in the United States have received them since the program first began in 1966. Imagine then the problem facing developing countries that try to mobilize large scale family planning programs.

Inadequacies in the methods of contraception are an additional handicap. By now the drawbacks to the oral contraceptive and intrauterine device are well recognized. Few people would seriously considering operating massive programs offering these methods without adequate patient screening, follow up and other safeguards. In addition to being dependent on some form of medical supervision, most birth control methods are female oriented, thus narrowing participation in a program to only one of the sexes.

Allen and Raper touched briefly on the issue of genocide. This problem does exist, but is perhaps not as prevalent as some persons indicate. Project directors, particularly in predominantly black areas, have reported occasional confrontations with members (usually males) of various militant groups who are vehement in their denunication of family planning projects in their neighborhoods. Despite such threats, there is a solid basis of support for family planning among community black women who easily distinguish between a needed service and a new form of exploitation.

One issue that the authors did not discuss was the categorical versus the comprehensive approach to family planning. Up until now, the majority of family planning projects have been categorical—that is they have been somewhat independent of other health services. The argument in favor of this approach is that categorical projects permit a more focused effort when there are only limited dollar and personnel resources available. Proponents of the comprehensive approach view family planning as only one aspect of good health care. They argue that family planning may be used as an entry point into the health system, but that a family usually needs more than just this service. Furthermore, a community that is sensitive to the genocide charge may be unwilling to accept family planning services unless they are closely integrated with other social, health and welfare programs. While the comprehensive approach is far more expensive, the legislative trend in Congress indicates that family planning may well be assimilated into a larger health care system in the near future.

The introduction of a family planning project into a community brings other changes with it. Ideally, a federal agency should develop a systematic and logical plan of action, identify program priorities, allocate funds and people to the project, and then hope that the services offered will be to everyone's satisfaction. Obviously the ideal situation never develops; Instead numerous problems arise. For example, new funds coming into a community sometimes touch off controversy and a struggle to control the project. Compromises and trade-offs have to be made if the program is to have any chance of being instituted. Sometimes external pressure is brought to bear on federal and local officials, in ways that make it difficult for public servants to be even handed and cool tempered.

21

GOVERNMENTAL INCENTIVES:

ETHICAL ISSUES AT STAKE

Robert M. Veatch

In the best of all possible worlds there would be no government incentives to modify population-related behavior. Individual desired family sizes would collectively produce some mythical and commonly agreed upon optimum population size, growth rate, and distribution. In a slightly less utopian world individuals might not act voluntarily in common to meet commonly perceived goals even if it meant some personal sacrifice. Until that day, however, there will be individuals and institutions, governmental and private, who feel they must face the question of what should be done to modify human behavior to meet what is perceived as a population crisis.

There are really many population crises—many differing perceptions of problems related to population size, growth, and distribution. Some are disturbed by population, consumption of natural resources, rise in global temperature or carbon dioxide level. Others by urban crowding, noise, and decay. Still others by the depressing effect on economic growth or the destruction of open spaces and forest land. Differential growth might be producing changes in the gene pool or an increase in ethnic or economic groups labelled as being "less desirable" according to some often bigoted standards of value.

Public policy and ethical evaluation of governmental incentive programs will depend heavily upon which of these many population problems are considered significant. They will also depend upon just how grave the population "crises" are perceived to be. Finally they will depend upon the evaluation of alternative policies under consideration: provision of voluntary services, educational programs, changes in social structures and institutions. and other "involuntary" or more directly coercive program proposals.

Incentive can be defined most broadly as anything which induces or tends to induce behavior on the part of man or animal. This definition must, for our purposes, be limited in several ways. First, I shall discuss only those entities which are used *consciously* to induce behavior, in our case demographically related behavior. Secondly, I shall discuss only proposals to offer economic inducement or related material goods and services. Thus educational campaigns attempting to induce small families by teaching a new value system by an appeal to sacrifice for the common good will be excluded. Third, I shall limit the term incentive to those things offered for inducement in such a way that there is some modicum of freedom to reject the inducement. "Incentive" is on a continuum between fully free, voluntary choice and full coercion or at least it is used in ordinary language as if that were the case. We shall explore this further when discussing the ethical issue of freedom.

Within this definition we need a classification of incentives in order to examine the ethical implications of different types of incentive proposals. In developing this classification we shall comment briefly on some of the ethical implications, but withhold more detailed discussion until the next section of the paper.[1]

The Object Offered as an Incentive. The "object" used as an inducement may be monetary (cash, tax rebates, bonds, or social security bonuses). It may also be goods and services which are not directly monetary (medical services, maternity leaves, education, food, jobs, clothes, transistor radios, wedding costs, and even government favors, etc.). In Andhra Pradesh State in India, for instance, during 1969 a *sari* was awarded to each tubectomy adopter and a *lungi* (male garment) to each vasectomy adopter. In Ghana the same year the government decided to grant maternity leaves for only the first three children for an employee. Perkins reports a preliminary trial in the same country in which during the first and third weeks of the trial each woman contacted by field workers for a family planning program was offered gift coupons for a free two-pound tin of powdered milk for her baby and herself if she came for family planning within ten days. The second and fourth weeks no such offer was made. In the fifth week the offer was again made, and, in addition, the field worker having the largest number of points obtained by recruiting referrals and visitors to the clinic would obtain six tins of powdered milk.[2]

Money is a generalized medium of exchange. Thus the recipient has substantial freedom over what he will purchase (or give up if the incentive is negative), but monetary incentives also may have the impact of "monetizing" childbearing more dramatically—making the birth planning decision a "cold financial calculation."

Behavior to be Induced. There has been substantial debate over the appropriate forms of behavior to induce by means of an incentive program. Some, such as incentives to use temporary contraceptive methods—condoms, diaphragms, daily pills—are probably economically infeasible, and it would be difficult to confirm their use. Others, such as payments for periods of non-pregnancy would necessitate an administrative bureaucracy to carry out periodic physical examinations which would be administratively cumbersome, subject to corruption, and perhaps seen by many women as demeaning. Still others, particularly incentives for sterilization now emerging in governmental programs in countries such as India, South Korea, Pakistan, and Ceylon have a degree of finality about them that some find objectionable. Finally, some behavior which is the subject of incentive proposals is seen by some people as inherently morally reprehensible. Included certainly would be incentives for abortion. Incentives for IUD insertion and certain new hormonal steroid preparations [3] are questioned by those who classify agents which may block implantation as abortifacients.

Timing of Incentive: Immediate or Delayed. Ridker [4] has proposed that couples be given a bond which would be timed to mature at the time the female reaches menopause. Others, basing their proposals on the observation that one of the motivations to have children particularly in less developed countries is to provide for old age security, propose that social security bonuses be given to couples with few children. Delaying incentives avoids, at least in part, two major ethical problems. Impulse sterilization for quick cash is eliminated and, more important, the impact cannot be transferred to the children as readily as, for example, depriving couples who bear children of maternity benefits, milk, or cash.

Also, delaying incentives will not completely eliminate the transfer of effects to children. Children might otherwise be expected to provide old age support and might be blamed by the parents and other siblings for parents loss of bonds or social security. Still other proposals provide for continual incentives. Proposals for changes in the yearly tax structure to favor couples with few children or provide a surtax based on the number of children are of this kind.[5]

The Nature of the Recipient: Individual or Group. Pohlman [6] reports an experiment he directed in a vilage in India given the fictitious name of Rampur. As an experiment comparatively large incentives were offered for vasectomy. The village declined the offer obviously designed to produce pressure for vasectomy, but 100% of the eligible couples in another village adopted family planning mostly through vasectomy, in response to an offer of a village well. Else-where, Kangas proposes as part of an integrated incentive plan, re-wards to groups (extended families, clans, farmers clubs, cooperatives, etc.) and to entire communities for new contraceptors recruited, the percentage of contraceptors, postponement of the age of marriage, or lowered group birthrate.[7] "Solemn public ceremonies" to recognize groups meeting quotas and the establishment of vasectomy as a rite of passage, have even been suggested. Group pressure is the obvious objective of such proposals. This, however, could also raise serious ethical difficulties in the not to subtle psycho-social coercion which could result. Somewhat less apparent is the possible injustice of group incentives in that they would bring relatively greater pressure to bear on poorer villages, perhaps demanding group sterilization as the price for a decent water supply or health facility. The question of injustices in incentives which place greater burden on certain groups will be discussed more generally below. There is a potential advantage to group incentives over some individual incentive plans, however. Within any community only a fraction of total births need be pre-vented to reach policy goals. Group incentives may allocate those reductions in the community in a way that minimizes the total amount of individual sacrifice.

The Nature of the Recipient: Adopter/Diffuser/Provider. Pohlman [8] summarizes data for eight countries with incentive programs in 1968. Of these only four provide incentives for acceptors of vasectomy (India, Pakistan, South Kora, and Mauritius) and only three for acceptors of IUD's (India, Pakistan, and the U.A.R.) On the other hand all provide incentives to "finders," usually nonprofessionals from the community who recruit candidates for contraceptive services. Moreover, a third candidate for per capita incentive is the provider of the service, normally a physician. Diffuser incentives open the way for abusive deception as well as social coercion similar to that seen with group incentives. Payments to diffusers and providers must also be examined in terms of the resulting distribution of income within a country.

The Rate of the Incentive: Flat Rate or Variable. The size of the incentive for a particular type of demographically related behavior is usually constant: so much for a vasectomy, an IUD insertion, or a period of non-pregnancy, although there is no particular reason why this need be the case. The question of the rate of incentive opens the complex question of the just rate for incentives. Even flat rate in-centives may have a very different psychological meaning to different individuals. This is often offered as a positive argument by those interested in using incentives for eugenic purposes. They argue that welfare recipients and low-income individuals will be most persuaded by the incentive curbing births among a group they consider less desirable. One author proposed targeting an incentive scheme for poverty level families in the United States "because research funds are limited, one must start somewhere, and concern over 'pronatalist' welfare payments might make communities most willing to see poor families given somewhat balancing incentives encouraging small families." [9] The justice of such an impact is certainly open to question. The rate of an incentive could theoretically be structured to distribute the pressure to curb births in any manner. The target could be the desirable, the least useful, the most fertile, or there could be other basis of distribution. Variable incentive rates could also be used to equalize the psychological impact of the incentive. Such a proposal has been put forward by the author in a proposal of a sliding scale fee for each child in the form of an income tax surcharge linked to a progressive income tax rate.[10]

The Psychological Impact of the Incentive (Positive or Negative). We have defined incentives in such a way that they may be either positive or negative, i.e., they may be offered by the government to induce desired behavior or taken from the individual by the government if "undesired behavior" occurs. The difference may be primarily a psychological one. Giving a transistor radio to each male having a vasectomy could be conceived of as giving each male in the country a radio and taking it away if he is not sterilized. The difference between positive and negative incentives can be seen in terms of a perceived base line of normally expected relationships. Not all negative incentives are the same, however. In a strange twist of our psychological perception it is possible to conceive of removing a pronatalist positive incentive as being rather different from a directly negative act. Proposals to remove child care allowances or possibly pronatalist income tax deductions for children seem to envision two "base lines." One is current practice, but that current practice is seen as an addition over and above another base line determined without regard to children in one's family.

Even among direct negative incentives, however, there is an important difference. The main objection to negative incentives, in spite of the fact that they are in economic terms very similar to positive ones, may be that they impute blame. The individual will be required to pay a "penalty" for disapproved behavior. At this point it is crucial to make a distinction. Penalties must be distinguished from "fees." A penalty is appropriate for behavior which is directly disapproved, for speeding in one's car, damaging public property, or missing a mortgage payment. Fees are charged, however, for transactions where the behavior itself is in no way disapproved, yet somehow there is a cost which must be borne. There are two conditions when fees are appropriate. First, a fee may be charged when the government (or some other institution) bears a cost for providing a service. We pay car registration fees for maintaining the roads, water fees for public water systems, and golf course fees for maintaining the fairways. Secondly, fees are used to deal with what are sometimes called threshold problems. These are problems which arise when an individual act is in no way harmful, yet an aggregate of those acts above a certain threshold is considered bad.

With this classification of incentives before us we can now examine more systematically the ethical issues at stake in governmental incentive proposals designed to modify population-related behavior. After exploring the questions of freedom, general and individual welfare, honesty, and justice, we shall propose a set of ethical guidelines for evaluating incentive proposals.

Freedom. An "incentive," by definition, must be placed in the continuum of freedom and coercion. It is thus natural that ethical questions of infringement of freedom arise first when evaluating incentive proposals. While there are obvious limits to human choice, very few human beings seriously doubt that partially free choice occurs routinely in everyday life. At this phenomenological level there exists a continuum from voluntarism through persuasion, incentives, and outright coercion. If freedom is conceived of as the perceived opportunities to make choices among plausible options, incentives offered by the government may be seen as added factors or weights in the decision-making process. Sometimes these will be seen as limits on voluntary population-related decision-making. That is the nature of the freedom-coercion continuum. This might not always be the case, however. In some cases incentives may actually increase the number of options open to an individual. Here, however, the question must be asked if those options can best be increased by financial or other resources linked to population-related behavior, or whether it is more just to make those options available through governmental mechanisms independent of population.

While governmental incentives will be seen as deviating from the norm of full voluntarism there are other aspects of freedom which cannot be overlooked. Those who advocate aggressive policies in response to the various population problems are also concerned about freedom. They see population growth, size, and distribution limiting freedom—freedom to use a preserved space for agricultural, aesthetic, and recreational purposes, freedom from congestion, noise, and environmental deterioration. Of even greater moral significance, continued growth is seen as potentially infringing upon the freedom of future generations to make choices. In the most apocalyptic view the very survival of future generations is at stake. In evaluating the extent to which incentives infringe upon individual freedom these other dimensions of freedom must be taken into account.

Even though incentives exist on the freedom-coercion continuum, freedom is not the only ethical imperative. Coercive incentives must certainly be preferred to other policies which would be grounded in individual choice and voluntarism—voluntary infanticide, for instance, or for some, even voluntary abortion. On the other hand, certain directly and physically compulsory policies are not seen as morally intolerable—compulsory immigration restriction, for instance, in spite of the challenge of such policies to the American dream of a haven for the "tired, the poor, the huddled masses yearning to breathe free."

There are certain rights which are associated with the basic value we call freedom. Among these rights some are often judged of such significance that they are "inalienable." Such claims can be made only with extreme caution since it is clear that no two mutually conflicting "inalienable" rights can exist in the same system. The right to bear as many children as one wants is probably one which should not be considered inalienable, no matter how important that specification of freedom might be. On the other hand the right to bear some children may be much closer to the limit of inalienability, i.e. we will surrender this right only under the most extreme circumstances if at all. Thus an incentive which had such force as to prohibit any childbearing, particularly for those who have no children at all, would have to be judged most harshly.

Another related "right" is the right to retain the power to bear children. The permanence of sterilization makes it, especially for young adopters, relatively less acceptable on moral grounds as a behavior to be induced by incentive no matter that for the same reason it may be the most efficient for curbing population growth in certain empirical situations. Choices made solely for monetary reasons and for immediate financial "pay-off" which lead to sterilization which cannot be assumed to be other than permanent can hardly be said to be other than coercive.

Individual and Group Welfare. It is probably unfortunate that many of those developing incentive proposals are trained in economic and other social sciences which have a peculiar commitment to the normative ethical theory of utilitarianism as summarized by the classical Benthamite formula "the greatest good for the greatest number." There are two critically serious ethical objections to incentive proposals. One of them is that many incentive schemes do precisely claim that they may produce the greatest good for the greatest number while at the same time more clearly they may do rather dramatic and specific harm to certain individuals—the children who will be deprived of milk, medical care, education, or less directly, goods purchased with the money involved in monetary incentives. The utilitarian may quarrel with the conclusion that innocent children will, in fact, necessarily be harmed. But if he follows the traditional and simple form of the doctrine, he must be willing to argue, in principle, that the fact that certain individuals are harmed and harmed significantly is morally irrelevant provided the total good for the aggregate is served. That is, the utilitarian would say it is unfortunate that some children may suffer, but that is the price that may have to be paid if society is to survive or the general welfare is to be served.

That is an intolerable conclusion. The harming of innocent children is a rather dramatic, if emotional, potential consequence of incentive proposals. It is a "moral fact" which cannot be ignored even if the cost is a lesser total good for society. An ethical theory must go beyond a calculation of total good in a simple sense to include some provision for the ethical obligations such as truth-telling and justice. Exactly how this is done can be left open for our present purposes. The point is that the distribution of goods and harms, in this case disproportionately on the side of harm to innocent children, cannot be tolerated. We suggest the following guideline for evaluating incentive proposals: An incentive scheme for modifying population-related behavior will be considered ethically acceptable to the extent that, *inter alia,* it avoids harming innocent children.

This is not to say that all incentive proposals must thereby be rejected. One may argue that even though children may suffer the consequences of incentives which appear to be harming them, in the long run they, themselves, are better off. Parents and society in general so benefit by the beneficial consequences (economic development, environmental preservation, etc.) that the personal gain reaped by the children is greater than the short-range harm. This theoretically fits our guideline, but is a rather implausible case and difficult to demonstrate. A more plausible argument in defense of particular incentive programs would be that children do not, in fact, suffer even in the short run. Bond and social security bonus schemes attempt to delay the "pay-off" and thus avoid transferring the harm to the children, at least while they are young. This may be only partially successful, however. Parents who have large families may divert a portion of their resources to make up for the old age security they might otherwise have. Children, particularly younger siblings, may be blamed, consciously or unconsciously, by parents for the loss of their bonds and by the older siblings if and when they must provide old age security for the parents. At least as adults, offspring may be obligated to care for security-lacking parents.

Another method of attempting to protect the welfare of children who might be hurt by an incentive program is to establish minimal standards of health, education, and welfare for all children regardless of family size. If negative incentives or fees are used, the revenues could be earmarked, in part, specifically for such child welfare programs. This, of course, will remove some of the anti-natalist effect of the incentive, but it is highly dubious that incentives should encourage, let alone directly bring about, depriving children of the necessities of life anyway. It might be possible to design properly structured incentives which would provide for at least minimal welfare for children and at the same time have an impact on the behavior of their parents. While no proposal will ever fully escape the potential of transfer of effect to children, any incentive scheme must be designed so that it will minimize such effect and eliminate any possibility that minimal welfare will not be provided. It does not appear that this has always been a prime consideration in incentive plans and programs.

The ethical significance of monetizing of childbearing is a more subtle question which may be considered an aspect of individual and group welfare. Those who are involved in planning incentive programs make the psychological observation that there may be feelings of guilt over accepting cash for vasectomy or limiting the number of one's children.[11] The ethical correlate of this question is whether these feelings of guilt are grounded in the ethical judgment that reducing such childbearing choices to economic transactions profanes values and obligations which should be beyond financial consideration.

That is to say an ethical judgment must be made to determine whether those guilt feelings are "justified" or whether they merely reflect cultural conditioning which is best overcome.

But we cannot overlook the fact that childbearing decisions have always had major financial implications and have always been monetized. In an agricultural economy offspring are in some cases an economic asset as they might be in areas where child labor is acceptable. On the other hand there is a tremendous cost in raising a child. In less developed countries the estimates of the economic value of an avoided birth is hundreds to thousands of times greater than the typical incentive. The poor, and in many cases the not-so-poor have often had to restrict for financial reasons the number of children they had. In this sense an incentive program, particularly one linked to child health and welfare programs may not increase the monetization of childbearing decisions at all. Developers of incentive schemes must deal with their more pervasive ethical dimension more directly and avoid those proposals which force excessive attention to monetary consideration or are, in reality, nothing more than plans to buy procreative powers at public auction.

Truth-telling. One of the obligations which we have suggested that goes beyond the simple calculation of the greatest good for the greatest number is the obligation to openness and honesty in announcing the intentions of a public policy. On the administrative level, the problem is indicated by the report that five percent of the men in the Srinivasan and Kachirayan study did not really possess information about the vaesctomy they had had. This is a particularly serious problem in programs which offer incentives to finders and others who are not directly the adopters to the techniques of the program. There is also a need for openness and honesty in the development of the program itself. J. Daniel Loubert has proposed a "National Family Support Program" for the United States as a means of providing a monthly subsistence allowance for each child in the U. S.[12] In order to prevent the proposal from actually being or being interpreted as being pronatalist he incorporates a fertility control incentive into his plan. While this is apparently an above board attempt to develop a child subsistence program, others have seen it as a model for developing a fertility control program which can pass in the guise of child welfare support. Suggestions have been made that for such programs the fertility control aspect could be kept in the background and perhaps introduced at a minimal level at first, to be gradually increased as the public becomes adjusted to the plan.

It is this kind of close-to-the-chest hidden agenda which leads to a public credibility gap which jeopardizes all incentive programs and leads to the camel's nose arguments against even the most incidental fertility control incentives. Another version is the provision of international aid to countries who will accept population limitation aid under the guise of development of demographic study centers, health care programs, research or educational training.

Justice. We have said above that one of the two critically serious ethical difficulties with incentive proposals is the potential harm to innocent children. The second is that of the potential injustices in the generation of pressures to reduce family size below the desired level. As long as there is a need felt by some to reduce population size or growth below individual desires there will be a question of justice. What constitutes a just incentive? Or to phrase the question somewhat differently, what constitutes a just distribution of children in a society?

Justice is not a simple ethical concept, but a complex of differing principles of distribution each seen as appropriate to certain contexts and goods to be distributed. There are at least nine different bases of distribution each of which might be considered just under certain circumstances.[13] A list of these principles includes flat equality, equality in proportion to some objective measure of use or interest, need, desire, effort, ability, willingness to serve society, need of society, and past harm done by society. To make matters more complicated it is clear that distributing one good according to one principle can be exactly the same as distributing another according to another principle. Distributing food according to need will tend to distribute happiness or relief from suffering equally. There are many goods which are candidates for a just distribution in an incentive program. These include such things as income, the right to bear children, burdens on parents or children, and specified necessities of life.

Probably the most obvious distribution principle for an incentive program, one which is often adopted intuitively and without ethical examination, is that of equal or "flat-rate incentives to all without regard to any social considerations; i.e., each acceptor receives an equal amount of money or goods. Each vasectomy acceptor receives 4.0 rupees; each woman visiting a family planning clinic receives one two-pound tin of milk, etc. Yet, it should be clear that an equal distribution of money, materials, or services to all may often result in a very unequal distribution of the psychological pressures put on individuals to change their population-related behavior. A tin of milk is a very different thing for a mother with starving children and the wife of the country's prime minister.[14]

For some this is accepted quite consciously as one of the virtues of incentive schemes. The greatest pressure is placed on what is considered to be the least desirable elements in society. To use the categories developed above *children* are distributed according to the principle of the *need of society* or the cost to society. One author, in defending a flat rate yearly bonus of $600 for not having children argues: "Best of all, it would act on a eugenic basis. The reward would be most effective in the poorest and least educated and least forward-thinking part of our population: those that are usually dependent, those that require social security and unemployment compensation (the least employable usually have the biggest families) would benefit [sic] the most. We could dispense with some of these awards, and let the burden of financing the family fall on the bonus for not having a child." [15]

Another author argues in defense of his proposal for licensing babies: "Furthermore, to the degree that intelligence is heritable and correlated with income, upper-income couples will be more able to pay the price and to afford larger families, hence natural selection will play a socially beneficial role rather than the damaging one to be anticipated from a policy of exhortation." [16]

The elitist character of arguments for incentives, especially those which are based upon cutting off of welfare payments, government housing, and other benefits which are specifically limited to the poor, cannot be denied, yet many seem to put forth proposals with an honest ignorance of their class-biased impact. Nevertheless how, in a multi-class society, can the differential impact on different classes be denied? Specifically, flat-rate incentives must be assumed to have their greatest impact on the poor and thus, until proven otherwise, be judged unjust.

It is my view that, especially for something as central and significant to human beings' religious, cultural, and ethical values as childbearing, no one group or class should bear a disproportionate share of the burden in reducing the explosive rate of population growth. Using the categories from above we should focus on burden as the thing to be distributed, and that burden should be distributed equally. Stated in the form of a guideline for evaluating an incentive scheme: An incentive proposal for modifying population-related behavior will be considered ethically acceptable to the extent that, *inter alia*, it distributes the burden equally. This is quite specifically to reject those incentive proposals which single out particular groups, such as the poor, as the ones who will carry the entire load of reducing an undesirable rate of growth. By saying that "burden" should be distributed equally we are also saying that other things, including specifically the number of children per family, may be distributed unequally.

The other plausible candidate for a just distribution is that children (or a minimal number of children) per family should be distributed equally. This alternative principle of justice underlies proposals which begin offering incentives, particularly negative incentives, after the Nth child. N children (usually two or three) is considered a reasonable or "fair" number to which each couple is entitled. Before examining the arguments against N-child proposals let us state in somewhat more detail the case for distributing the burden, rather than the children, equally.

It is clear that children have different values to different individuals just as those conditions in the environment which some consider threatened by population growth or size have differing values. It is those who value population-threatened things in the environment relatively more and children relatively less who are most eager for population growth to be curbed. Thus such a person is, in effect, saying "I want others to give up something they value greatly and I happen to value relatively less (i.e., children) so that I can enjoy something I value relatively more (e.g., open spaces, quietude, high standard of living, etc.) ." It seems only fair that those who have a value system which emphasizes population limitation should bear at least an equal share of the burden in the enterprise when they are asking others to give up that which they value most in order to achieve something which those others value relatively less.

Beyond this basic ethical argument that all must share in the common task, especially those who value the goal of population limitation relatively more and children relatively less, there are specific problems with N-child proposals, problems which cast further doubt on their ethical acceptability. These problems can only be enumerated here:[17] First, N-child proposals will, at least by implication, create a norm of no more than N children per family. This rigid norm could unjustly create hardship for children born after the Nth. Second, psychological burdens and guilt may be attributed to children and parents, even if, especially for children, they were in no way responsible for births beyond the Nth. Third, an N-child norm may suggest that the N-child family is socially preferable when evidence for such is hard to come by and, in fact, a mixture of large families and small families may be preferable. Fourth, policies which encourage a *universal* N-child family rather than an *average* N-child family will tend to stagnate the gene pool. All of these arguments must be placed along side the point made above that an N-child norm would place great burdens on some while others would be asked to contribute nothing to curbing the population explosion. We are thus forced to conclude that those incentive programs which are universal rather than limited to N-child situations are more just.

It can be seen that the total amount of burden produced will be less with a proposal which has as its goal N as an average family size rather than a universal N family size This is so because the burden (and therefore probably the size of the incentive) for some to refrain from having a second or third child which they were uncertain about anyway may be less than the burden of a couple which strongly desires four children to refrain from having the fourth. Thus even for those who use the classical utilitarian formula of "the greatest good for the greatest number" N-child proposals must be questioned.

The principle of justice creates grave difficulties for incentive proposals. Can an incentive be found which overcomes these objectives? The answer is yet to be found, but it seems to me not to be an impossible task, at least in principle. Elsewhere I have tried to formulate one such proposal.[18] Only the general ideas can be summarized here. First, we shall limit our comments to possibilities for the more developed countries. Then we will offer a few possible modifications for less developed areas.

Having ruled out flat-rate incentives as unjustly discriminatory against certain groups until they can be proven otherwise, we must search for a sliding-scale incentive, specifically one which will distribute the burden equally. The task would be the same whether or not one restricts incentives to procreative behavior after the Nth child, but we have argued that this would be less acceptable. It seems ethically and politically impossible to adopt a system of positive sliding-scale incentives which would generate equal amounts of pressure on the rich and poor. This would require much greater incentives for the rich and, almost certainly, would be rejected. If any just incentive scheme is to be found at all, then it seems to us it must be in the form of a progressive sliding-scale fee. Such a fee would have to be progressive at the rate which would place equal burdens on all members of society. In the United States the income tax has this as its objective even though we are all aware of the imperfections and injustices which exist. Thus we have suggested that, for the United States, a surtax on a just form of the progressive income tax would constitute a starting point for a just system of fees.

An income tax surcharge related to childbearing might be called a "child welfare fee." If a portion were earmarked for provision of education, health care, and a minimal standard of welfare for all children, many of the problems of harm to innocent children may be minimized. Other portions of the fee might be used for contraceptive research, child health and child development research, and other services not now provided. A "child welfare fee" which would be an X percent surtax on one's income tax would thus simultaneously provide for the welfare of children and serve as a progressive sliding-scale anti-natalist incentive. The exact percentage could be regulated to meet these common goals.

The details of such a proposal would indeed be immensely complex and even then injustices might remain. Several adjustments or refinements would have to be made. I have argued, for instance, that the effect of an incentive should not be limited to immediate economic gain or loss. The child welfare fee surtax could be charged (at a proportionally smaller rate) for every year the child is a minor. This would have the added advantage of minimizing the desire by couples who know their income will rise sharply to rush to have their children while in a low tax bracket. Perhaps a combination of 10X percent surcharge during the year of the birth (possibly coupled with government provided maternity and child care) and X percent surcharge for remaining years while the child is a minor could be developed. To further guard against planning births for an advantageous tax year, the surcharge might have to be based on the average of several year's taxes.

The question arises of what about those who pay no tax anyway. Several consideration are relevant. First, for the poorest, if an economic incentive were to have any impact on their procreative behavior at all, their dire economic condition would already have provided very strong anti-natalist pressure. Monies from the child welfare fund might appropriately be used to provide birth planning services and education to those in this group who are bearing children out of lack of knowledge of or access to birth planning information and services. Beyond this a guaranteed minimal annual wage which would lift the poor beyond the most dire conditions of poverty may be a more urgent-moral imperative in any case. This would have the interesting possible side effects of bringing all into tax paying status and in addition might in some cases carry the anti-natalist effects of a rising standard of living. These need not be the purpose of such a program, however. In a situation with relatively few in the non-tax paying group the demographic need is proportionally smaller in any case.

What about developing countries, however? In some cases a relatively large proportion do not pay any form of governmental support based on a progressive rate which attempts to distribute burdens equally. In any society, whether more or less developed, it is extraordinarily difficult to develop any just population policy when the conditions of society are extremely unjust. Certainly there are very strong and discriminatory de facto economic incentives presently at work which force many poor to have fewer children than they consider ideal. We have argued that a positive flat-rate incentive (or any flat-rate incentive) is unjust to the extent it cuts across different socio-economic classes and thereby has a different psychological impact on different individuals. Within one socio-economic group, however, this problem would not arise. If all of a country's population, for instance, received the same psychological impact from a given monetary or non-monetary incentive, there would be no justice problem of this type. When the vast majority of a country's population constitutes one such group, might it be possible to develop small positive incentives which would have their impact within that group in combination with a progressive, sliding-scale positive incentive such as a surtax which would provide for a just distribution of the burden among those of different economic means? Such an arrangement could be viewed as shifting the "base-line" for the sliding scale incentives. Particularly if the positive incentive were designed to have symbolic value and to overcome inertia rather than to pressure individuals into behavior they would not otherwise have an interest in, such a combination of positive and progressive sliding scale incentives might be the most feasible arrangement in the less than utopian world of exploding population.

This discussion of the ethical implications of incentive proposals to modify population-related behavior has assumed that the ethical rights and obligations related to freedom, individual and common welfare, truth-telling, and justice are complex. Throughout we have suggested guidelines for evaluating incentive proposals. Collecting these at the conclusion of the paper will serve as a summary. In the paper we have argued that if an incentive program to induce population-related behavior is to tend toward being judged as being ethically acceptable among other things:

- It should preserve freedom by avoiding incentives which are, in effect, coercive.
- It should avoid harming innocent children.
- It should minimize the monetizing of childbearing.
- It should avoid forcing population-related decisions primarily for purposes of immediate financial gain.
- It should avoid deception both in its announced intent and in its administrative procedures.
- It should distribute the burden of change in population-related behavior equally rather than limiting it to one class or group.
- It should avoid flat-rate incentives until such incentives can be shown to be nondiscriminatory.
- It should apply to all childbearing decisions equally rather than being limited to decisions after the Nth child.

1. In developing this classification and in the discussion of the ethical implications we have drawn on several previous discussions of incentives for population related behavior. Among the most extensively used have been the study prepared for the Commission on Population Growth and the American Future, by the Program on Population and Ethics of the Institute of Society, Ethics and the Life Sciences, *Ethics, Population, and the American Tradition* (Hastings-on-Hudson, 1971, 3 vols.); Edward Pohlman, *Incentives and Compensations in Birth Planning* (Carolina Population Center, 1971); Everett M. Rogers, "Incentives in the Diffusion of Family Planning Innovations," *Studies in Family Planning II* (December 1971), pp. 241-48; Bernard Berelson, "Beyond Family Planning," *Studies in Family Planning* (February 1969), pp. 1-16; and International Planned Parenthood Federation, *Incentive Payments in Family Planning Programmes* (London: 1969).

2. Gordon V. Perkin, "Non-Monetary Commodity Incentives in Family Planning Programs: A Preliminary Trial," *Studies in Family Planning* (September 1970), pp. 12-15.

3. Sheldon J. Segal, "Beyond the Laboratory: Recent Research Advances in Fertility Regulation," *Family Planning Perspectives* (July 1971), p. 19.

4. Ronald G. Ridker, "Synopsis of a Proposal for a Family Planning Bond," *Studies in Family Planning 43* (June 1969), pp. 11-16.

5. Bob Packwood, "Incentives for the Two-Child Family," *Trial Magazine* (1970), pp. 13, 16; Robert M. Veatch, "A Proposal for Taxing Childbearing: Can It Be Just?" Working Paper Series, Institute of Society, Ethics and the Life Sciences (Hastings-on-Hudson, 1971).

6. Pohlman, *Incentives and Compensations*, pp. 83-85.

7. Lenni W. Kangas, "Integrated Incentives for Fertility Control," *Science* (September 25, 1970) p. 1281.

8. Edward Pohlman, "Mobilizing Social Pressures Toward Small Families," *Eugenics Quarterly* (1966), pp. 122-127.

9. Pohlman, *Incentives and Compensations*, pp. 48-49.

10. Veatch, "A Proposal for Taxing Childbearing."

11. Edward Pohlman and Kamala Gopal Rao, "Some Ethical Questions About Family Planning and Cash Incentives," *The Licentiate* (1967), p. 238.

12. J. Daniel Loubert, "A National Family Support Program: A Summary Statement" (mimeographed, 1969).

13. I have developed this in greater detail in "Justice and Population Policy," in *Ethics, Population, and the American Tradition*, a report of the Institute of Society, Ethics and the Life Sciences Program on Ethics and Population (1971), pp. E-35—E-49.

14. Documentation of the disproportionate impact of incentives on the poor comes from the data reported by Repetto. He points out that in one government hospital in Madras City, 57 percent had a monthly income of less than Rs. 50 (U.S. $6.65) and 96.1 percent earned less than Rs. 100 (U.S. $13.50). Although one would have to know class income levels of the general hospital patient population for accurate comparison. Repetto concludes that "lower class preponderance is beyond dispute." As for educational level, 44.7 percent were illiterate, 92.8 percent had completed eighth standard or less. See Robert Repetto, "India: A Case Study of the Madras Vasectomy Program," *Studies in Family Planning* (May 1968), p. 13.

15. Raymond B. Cowles, "The Non-Baby Bonus," in Garrett Hardin, ed., *Population, Evolution, and Birth Control: A College of Controversial Ideas* (San Francisco: W. H. Freeman and Co., 1969, 2nd ed.), pp. 339-340.

16. Bruce M. Russett, "Licensing: For Cars and Babies," *Bulletin of the Atomic Scientists* (November 1970), pp. 17-18.

17. A more detailed argumentation is presented in my paper "An Ethical Analysis of Population Policy Proposals," in *Ethics, Population and the American Tradition*, pp. 0-22—0-23.

18. Veatch, "A Proposal for Taxing Childbearing: Can It Be Just?"

22

INCENTIVES: NOT IDEAL, BUT NECESSARY

EDWARD POHLMAN

Dr. Veatch's paper on governmental incentives shares in criticisms that can be leveled at the entire symposium. Inevitably, the papers as a group reflect the collective biases of the participants. These participants are primarily (1) Christians, (2) Americans, (3) capitalistic in orientation, (4) biased toward individualism and freedom, (5) white, (6) affluent, well-fed, well-doctored, and (7) representatives of the 1970's rather than the 21st Century or the 23rd. It would be arrogant for this symposium to seem to be handing down verdicts about the ethics of population—for the whole world.

There is another broad criticism: that "ethicists" and related academicians represent a somewhat biased perspective on ethics. The American Christian truck driver or dentist, or the Bangladesh Christian coolie or beggar, may have ethical insights and convictions different from those of the Christian labelled as an "ethicist." To become an "ethicist" requires peculiar characteristics—writing, scholarly study, perseverence in advanced degree work, financial resources for such study, perhaps special personality tendencies. While these are nothing but laudable, they do result in selection and screening.

These considerations need to be borne in mind in what follows.

Please imagine that this symposium is being written on the day I was born, January 30, 1933. FDR is today celebrating his first birthday after election as U.S. President. Adolf Hitler is today installed as chancellor. Across the Western intellectual world a growing alarm is felt over the population crisis. The crisis: not enough babies. Here are the titles of some of the articles published within the last three years, 1930 to the present. "Britain's Big Birth Slump."[1] "Race Suicide in Germany." "The 'More Babies' Drive in Italy." "German Alarm at 'Birth Strike'." "Where are the Children?" "When Population Ceases to Grow." "World Suicide by Birth Control." "Our Dying Families." "Will Birth Control Lead to Extinction?" In the next few years there will appear, "Malthus was Wrong," "The Vanishing Briton," "The Twilight of Parenthood."

Last year, 1932, an ingenious suggestion was made by an economist,

Professor Joseph J. Spengler.[2] He suggested that if Detroit had to
sell an automobile for $200, Detroit would soon stop making cars
since it cost much more than that to produce them. Parents, similarly,
had to be adequately remunerated if the nation expected them to keep
rolling out babies. So, an incentive scheme. Interestingly, the eminent
economist Spengler is still alive and busy at Duke University in 1972.
In the late 1960's he shamelessly recommended incentives to cut down
on births, with no reference to his earlier work. And most recently he
came out with a monograph titled *Declining Population Growth
Revisited*.[3]

Spengler's work represents the curious yo-yo, the zig-zag, the yin
and yan of alarms over too few or too many babies in Western
countries. We have had both pro-natalist and anti-natalist incentive
schemes.

All this sneering sarcasm aside, I believe that population growth
will prove to be a growing problem, particularly in the developing
countries. I believe that if unbridled population growth did enough
harm, and if incentives were able to avoid much more harm than they
caused, then they would be ethically justified. The hark-back to the
1930's was just to remind ourselves that if incentives can be justified
only by a bona fide crisis, then we need to check fairly carefully to
be sure we are facing one. For the 1930's saw their Ehrlichs of
underpopulation, their alarmists and hucksters, and many of the titles
quoted above were works by respected professors. It is impossible to
make an ethical valuation of governmental population incentives as
some sort of monolithic global category; there are myriad possible
incentive programs with very diverse ethical implications. It is difficult even to begin to discuss aspects of the topic without a
foundation in the jargon of population incentives, and in some of the
major schemes usually proposed. This foundation is appropriately
given in the first third of Robert Veatch's paper. Veatch has done
a good job of giving an overview of incentives but I have a couple of
small quibbles. Veatch cites my monograph as recommending that
an incentive scheme be "targeted" to poverty level families in the
U. S. For balance, I wish he had quoted the whole paragraph instead
of portions of one sentence. Unquoted portions speak of a "proposal
to *start* with poverty level families" (italics added) and say that
"Over the long run, ideally, the program should be as available to
the rich as the poor." Another quibble is with the statement, "In
less developed countries the estimate of the economic value of an
avoided birth is hundreds to thousands of times greater than the

typical incentive." This sentence is set in a context which makes it seem to apply to the economic values to parents themselves, whereas the estimates refer to economic values to society. Secondly, the lower limits on the estimates are in the range of scores, not hundreds—e.g., Rs. 600, or 20 times a vasectomy incentive of Rs. 30, which is not atypical.

The present paper is not a systematic statement of my views on the ethics of incentives; chapters published elsewhere come far closer to that.[4] All I shall try to do here is to make a few stray criticisms of Veatch's discussion of ethics of incentives. In general that discussion seems very strong. It shows a constant and sophisticated awareness of two sides on many points. Repeatedly, however, the choice between two sides seems to be made on nearly arbitrary grounds and then regarded as sacred. I agree with the paper that in an ideal world incentives would not be necessary. Hopefully they will never be necessary at all; they are not ideal. But they seem to me on a continuum between an extreme of complete laissez-faire concerning family size, and the extreme of outright coercion, such as compulsory abortion, birth control chemicals in the drinking water supply, sterilizing all males at puberty after they have put sperm into a frozen bank for their future use as regulated by the government, and so on. I believe incentives are ethically more acceptable than outright force. Actually we do not have enough research on incentives, enough carefully analyzed field experience, to know whether or under what circumstances this or that incentive scheme would yield this or that effect on population growth.

One central figure in the Veatch paper is the innocent child mentioned at least once per paragraph in each of the nine paragraphs of section 2. An incentive scheme, we are told, should avoid harming innocent children. Presumably it is ethically acceptable for an incentive program to harm children if they are guilty children. Seriously, "innocent" here means that under the system, children suffer for their parents' wrongs. Parents are offered financial benefits if they keep families small, some fail to do that, and so they have less resources and their children lose out. As one who was born and reared and worked in India and Pakistan I have seen a lot of children malnourished, starving, dying, disease-ridden, going without education and medical attention, living in squalor. They were innocent victims, not victims of incentive programs. Without wanting to jerk tears by what Veatch admits is "a rather dramatic, if emotional, potential consequence," I submit that there are circumstances and countries where continued unchecked population growth will have rather disastrous consequences for innocent children. If incentives could avoid these consequences, they might be justified, perhaps even as the lesser of two evils.

In a monograph on ethics and population, Daniel Callahan[5] seemed to be saying, if I may translate very loosely, that if things got bad enough population-wise, then theoretically under those extreme circumstances incentives aimed at limiting families to, say, two children would be justified. Does Dr. Veatch agree with this? It was never clear to me. In discussing innocent children, Veatch does consider possible ways in which incentives might be just even if they did some harm to these innocent children. But this justness would in each case require that in some way the harm done those children was balanced out for *those particular children*. There is no provision mentioned for the possibility that if one group of children was harmed a little bit by an incentive scheme, and other totally different innocent children were helped a lot by it, this would be just. Veatch rejects a simple Benthamite notion of the greatest good for the greatest number. But is there *any* amount of good done for a huge number which would justify a small amount of harm done for a few? As a ridiculous extreme, if cutting off my little son's right arm would cure all the cancer and all the birth defects of all the other children in the world, would it be just to cut off his arm against his will? In my view, society would be justified in imposing incentive schemes that did some harm to some innocent children, if they did enough good to other children. Avoiding all harm to innocent children is a good ideal, but not an absolute.

Probably the innocent children are of more interest as a dramatic discussion topic than one of practical consequence. In any politically practical, sensible incentive scheme, the amount that a parent would lose because he had too many children and did not get an incentive would rarely if ever change a child noticeably. At one time, Julian Simon[6] argued that incentives would so boost the economy of an entire developing nation, by reducing population growth, that everyone would profit economically. Those families who stayed small and received the incentives would profit most of all, but even those who got no incentives and were taxed to pay for the incentives of the others would still find this loss more than offset by the economic advancement of the nation in which all shared. In the lovely unspoiled world in which we lived before fiendish incentive schemes were suggested, children were being hurt all the time by parents who failed to get out of bed to find the condoms, or failed to take their pills. Incentives might motivate some parents to avoid births that would otherwise be a terrible economic burden to those parents and to their older brothers and sisters—the innocent siblings. Incentives might avoid some deeply unwanted births—thus the innocent children saved from harm might be the ones never born, saved from the harm of parental hatred and rejection.

Designing an incentive scheme is like planning a Utopia, painting a picture, or rearing your son: you become terribly ego-involved in the process, you fall in love with what you have produced, blind to its faults. In the 1930's economist Spengler designed a pro-natalist incentive scheme; in the past decade dozens of authors, including myself, have designed anti-natalist incentive schemes. When they write about their own darling schemes, the inventors write with a sort of benevolent dotage; they point out faults of other schemes and see few in their own. They are fascinated with cute little details and incidental benefits of their scheme. Much of Veatch's paper is hard-hitting criticism of the ethical problems of incentive schemes. But I was disappointed to see that Veatch finally got seduced by the same siren as the rest of us: he designed his own incentive scheme. In so doing he fell from heaven, lost the Olympian objectivity of an ethicist, and became a mere mortal with a scheme in hand.

As one who has examined most of the schemes and decided that his own pet is not as good as some others, I fear that Veatch's scheme is not particularly outstanding. He agreed with me that positive incentives have better psychological appeal than the negative schemes of taxes. Yet he proposes a negative approach, although calling the surcharge supertaxes "fees." Surely the public would see the fees as tax increases, despite their pious varnish. Veatch sets up the guideline that a program should not harm innocent children, yet his scheme might well do some such harm, as much harm as many other schemes.

Veatch rejects the idea of the same flat rate tax to all as unjust, and concludes that it "seems ethically and politically impossible to adopt a system of positive sliding-scale incentives which would generate equal amounts of pressure on the rich and poor." But he apparently feels that it *would* be possible, ethically and politically, to adopt a system of *negative* incentives that would generate equal pressure on rich and poor. He speaks loftily of "a surtax on a just form of the progressive income tax." There are two nasty assumptions made. One is the politically naive one that the U. S. Congress might be induced to revise the income tax laws so that the percentage of taxes for each income bracket would be just what Veatch considers just. This is not about to happen. Many rich people pay no taxes; the reality is that this will continue, so some rich families would pay no surcharge child fee for their large families. The second point is that even if Veatch's mythical "just child welfare fee" could be legislated, the psychological pressure on various individuals would never never be the same even for all the people of a given income bracket, who perceive the same objective tax rate differently. And to imagine some near-homogeneity across social class lines and income brackets, some near-homogeneity in the pressure of fees, is fanciful. Veatch keeps telling us his scheme isn't very good but he describes it with fascination. Actually it is not a bad scheme; the point is it is just not dramatically superior, ethically, to the many other schemes Veatch finds ethically repugnant. The Commission on Population Growth and the American Future, to which this scheme was submitted, makes no mention of it in its report.

I have a great faith in the powers of the intellectual to rationalize in support of his preconceived notions. When one reads the Veatch paper over again knowing that eventually the paper is going to wind up plugging for a particular incentive scheme, in this retrospect some of the arguments that seemed puzzling earlier make sense as rationalizations leading toward a specific goal.

Specifically, the arguments for the wickedness of a fixed-rate incentive or fee or tax and the virtues of a "progressive sliding scale" with Congress playing the God-like role of deciding justice—those arguments are not so compelling as to lead to the flat assertion of superiority for sliding scales that is made. Similarly, the arguments for the evil of schemes that aim to limit family size to N children are not so compelling as to lead to a flat assertion that such schemes are inferior. After all, no one is talking, in discussing incentives, of sheer force that limits families to two children. Instead the incentive seeks to mold behavior to this norm, recognizing that it will often be unsuccessful. In practice I cannot see where Veatch's scheme— which is to charge the fees from the very first child right on, apparently—is basically different. In either case the incentives work on the third, fourth, fifth etc. child; the difference is that the evil N-child schemes do not come into play concerning the first or second child, whereas the righteous schemes do. Why this makes N-child schemes evil is unclear, since Veatch has indicated he feels that the right to have at least some children is more near to an inalienable right than the right to have all one wants. So why is a scheme that starts before even the first child, superior to one that waits until a couple of kids before it begins to work?

In general those of us who play the role of ethicists need to beware of using our own idiosyncratic reasoning, colored by our subculture and experience, to arrive at somewhat idiosyncratic conclusions about right and wrong—and then pontifically sharing standards with the multitudes as if they were absolutes.

Some of the "obvious" points in Veatch's paper need to be doubted. He refers condescendingly to elitism. Is elitism always bad? If I have any control or influence over a group of mentally retarded parents who very much want to reproduce children, I shall try to discourage them in ways that are elitist. One cannot throw out this illustration by saying retarded people are less than human and hence do not deserve full human consideration. It is not a matter of clear dichotomies between human and non-human, but of degrees of human-ness. Other things equal I believe children are better off if they are not born hemophiliacs, diabetics, stupid, club-footed or given to constant headaches. Similarly I believe there are some home environments superior by far to others. Where one draws the line between nosy elitist interference in parents' rights to reproduce whatever kinds of people they are, and a considerate protection of unborn generations, is open to some dispute. But I think there should be a distinction between elitism in the sense of exterminating living individuals in gas chambers or treating them as inferiors, and elitism in who is encouraged to procreate or discouraged therefrom. Today the key word in population is quantity; in the past at times it has been quality (eugenics); and ethical concerns may include a concern for the quality of the children who shall be born.

Two points to be mentioned briefly, elaborated in detail elsewhere: What happens "naturally" is often artifical, very artificial indeed. An example is the myriad financial constraints on childbearing that already exist, or the way children are penalized "naturally" by their parents' actions and mistakes. Secondly, there is a danger of feeling that if we do nothing we are not responsible; that the only ethical danger is when we actively intervene in the "natural scheme of things." An example is the feeling that we must not have N-child incentive schemes that pay flat rates, if they do any harm to innocent children. It is at least imaginable that while public opinion and expert opinion block incentive schemes because they interfere with nature in ways that hurt innocent children, even more harm is being done to innocent children by "natural" events that might have been averted—the natural event of a population flood, avalanche, forest fire, apocalyptic scourge.

Now I take you to the centennial of my birth: the year is A.D. 2033. A conference of 21st-century ethicists happens to be gathering to discuss population ethics. They are mindful of that Manressa conference some 60 years back. In the light of the development and perspectives of 2023, what evaluation can be made of the papers, the thinking, the discussion of 1972? How provincial, how broad-gauge, how time-bound, how forward-looking?

1. Edward Pohlman, ed., *Population: A Clash of Prophets* (New American Library). References for the titles listed in the paper are found in Section I.

2. Joseph J. Spengler, "The Birth Rate—Potential Dynamite," *Scribner's Magazine* (July-December 1932), pp. 6-12.

3. Joseph J. Spengler, *Declining Population Growth Revisited* (Carolina Population Center Monograph 14, 1971).

4. Edward Pohlman, *Incentives and Compensations in Birth Planning* (Carolina Population Center Monograph 11, 1971), and *How to Kill Population* (Westminster Press, 1971).

5. Daniel Callahan, *Ethics and Population Limitation* (The Population Council, 1971).

6. Julian L. Simon, *The Value of An Avoided Birth: A Reply to Enke* (University of Illinois, mimeographed).

23

POPULATION CRITERIA IN FOREIGN AID PROGRAMS

Philip M. Hauser

Consideration of foreign aid policy as it may be affected by population criteria requires prior consideration of population trends and prospects and of the factors which underlie them. In fact, without first gaining the perspectives which such prior consideration provides, it is not even possible to ask the right questions in respect of foreign aid policies and programs.

The failure to begin with a sound understanding of population facts, retrospective and prospective, has indeed led not only to the raising of wrong questions but, also, to providing wrong answers for policy purposes. Among such wrong questions are those posed by William and Paul Paddock, Paul Ehrlich and Garrett Hardin, who in varying forms ask whether foreign aid should be given to nations without effective population policies; whether the "triage principle" from military medical practice should be applied by the economically advanced nations in providing aid to the less developed countries; and whether the more affluent nations are not the "stewards of civilization" who must not permit the less developed countries to undermine this "civilization." [1] Among the wrong answers are those set forth by those authors, out of good intentions and in good faith, when they propose a negative answer to the first question and affirmative answers to the other two. Two types of population perspectives must be assimilated to deal comprehensively and effectively with population criteria in the administration of foreign aid. First are those which arise from an understanding of "the social morphological revolution"; [2] and second, those which flow from an understanding of the facts about population control, past and present. [3]

Man, as the only complex culture-building animal on this planet, has generated three population developments closely interrelated with technological change which have profoundly affected his attitudes, values, institutions and behaviorisms. These, in easy to remember language, may be termed the population *explosion*, the population *implosion*, the population *displosion* and the *technoplosion*—elements of the "social morphological revolution."

The population explosion is perhaps the only one of these population developments which is widely understood. It refers, of course, to the remarkable acceleration in population growth in the economically developed countries during the three centuries of the modern era and in the less developed countries, containing over two-thirds of mankind, mainly since World War II. The facts of the population explosion indicate that at the present rate of growth (approximately two per cent per year) it is not unlikely that world population could reach seven billion by the end of the century, little more than one human generation from now. Assuming this number, the present trends would result in the developing nations having a population of 5.4 billion by 2000, whereas population in the developed nations would be 1.6 billion.[4] Thus the increase in the population of the developing countries in the thirty years from 1970, almost three billion persons, would be about as great as the total population of the world in 1960—the product of all man's reproductive activity from the beginning of his time on the earth! Nothing is yet available in the way of concrete evidence to indicate that present efforts to dampen birth rates and growth rates in the developing countries will materially change this outlook—although there is much evidence of wishful thinking on this matter.

The population implosion refers to the increasing concentration of people on relatively small portions of the earth's surface, a phenomenon better known as urbanization. This is a development much more recent than the population explosion—dating largely from mid-nineteenth century. It must be recalled that man did not even achieve fixed settlement until as recently as the Neolithic Era, some 10,000 years ago, nor did he achieve sufficient technological and social organizational development to permit agglomerations of 100,000 or more until Greco-Roman civilization. Cities of 1,000,000 or more were not achieved until the beginning of the 19th Century, and it is only since that time that it has become possible to trace world urban development.

Using the criterion proposed by the United Nations for urban (20,000 or more persons) little more than two per cent of the world's peoples were urban in 1800. At the present time, although the results of the census in and around 1970 have yet to become available on a world-wide basis, world urbanization is at a level of about 37 per cent, 66 per cent in the economically advanced areas and 25 per cent in the developing areas. By the end of the century, according to the latest U. N. projections, more than half of the people in the world may be living in urban areas, 81 per cent in the developed areas and 43 per cent in the developing areas.[5] Should this come to pass, it could be accompanied by the most profound change in human values and in the way of life that mankind has ever experienced.

The population displosion refers to the increasing heterogeneity of people who share not only the same geographic locale but also, more and more, the same life space—social, economic and political activities. By heterogenity is meant diversity by culture, language, religion, values, ethnicity, race and life style. Since the end of World War II, this trend has been accompanied by the "revolution of rising expectations." In consequence, this generation is the first in man's history in which there are virtually no societies in the world which do not insist on freedom and independence if they have not yet achieved them; and there are virtually no minority groups in any nation which do not insist on equality of opportunity and which do not possess the vision of egalitarianism in a pluralistic society.

The population displosion is harder to quantify than the population explosion and implosion. Yet it is clear that with the shrinking of the earth by reason of technological advances in transport and communication that diverse peoples have had more contact and interaction within the past century than in probably all previous history combined. Moreover, although diverse peoples shared the same geographic area is antiquity, not until after the revolution of rising expectations has diversity generated intense inter-group conflict throughout the world on the present unprecedented scale.

The technopolosion refers to the accelerated pace of technological innovation flowing from the rapidly growing fund of scientific knowledge and increased capital inputs. Especially important has been the great expansion in the use of non-human energy, which in the economically advanced countries, has also largely displaced the use of animal energy. Also especially significant in its impact on the way of life have been the advances in means of transportation and communication.

The population explosion, implosion, displosion and the technoplosion are interrelated. The explosion has fed the implosion and both have fed the displosion. The technoplosion has been both antecedent and consequent to the other developments. These developments, which together make up the social morphological revolution, after Emile Durkheim's discussion of "social morphology," are transforming the world from the "little community," to use Redfield's terminology, to the "mass society" to use Manheim's phrase.[6] The consequences of these developments may be summarized by stating that man has created a 20th century demographic and technological world in which he is still trying to learn how to live—and thus far not too successfully. Moreover, the consequences of these developments are manifest both in the high levels of living in the economically advanced nations and in the chaos which afflicts the contemporary world, not excepting the United States. An understanding of the impact of the social morphological revolution, still underway, is prerequisite to dealing with the role of foreign aid and, for that matter, most contemporary problems.

At the present time the world has, belatedly, become aware of the importance of facing up to the implications of the population explosion but has not yet achieved as much awareness of the role of the population implosion and displosion in generating other problems which sorely affect mankind. Yet, it is almost certain that the problems created or exacerbated by the implosion and displosion will create more human misery during at least the remainder of this century than the problems produced by excessive fertility and growth. Furthermore, the problems associated with the implosion and displosion are inextricably interrelated with those of the explosion and must enter into any consideration of foreign aid policies as affected by population criteria.

The social morphological revolution has precipitated unprecedented problems. Generated by the population explosion are such problems as the race between population and food production raising the specter of famine; problems of environmental degradation given present attitudes and practices in respect of air, water, waste disposal and the use of natural resources; and the obstacle that rapid population growth poses for the aspirations of the less developed countries to achieve higher levels of living.

The population implosion has precipitated or exacerbated most of the problems subsumed by the "urban crisis" in this nation as well as throughout the world. The urban crisis encompasses a wide range of problems—environmental, physical, personal, social, economic and governmental. "Urbanism as a way of life" is essentially the transformed life in the mass society which in the economically advanced nations has been accompanied by increased productivity and higher levels of living, on the one hand, and, on the other, many forms of personal and social disorganization. In the developing countries urbanization has not necessarily been accompanied by increased productivity and higher levels of living. On the contrary, urbanization has more often been the result of their colonial heritage which produced urban agglomerations as entrepots between the colony and the mother country—a function which has tended to become minimal with the disintegration of empire; of refuge flows of population because of unsettled conditions produced by wars and internecine strife; and of sharply reduced death rates after World War II which increased rural population more rapidly than the soil could support it. Whereas urbanization in the economically advanced areas was the result largely of the pull of economic opportunity as well as social lure, in the developing nations it was more the result of the push of population from the overburdened rural countryside—the transfer of rural poverty to the urban setting.

The population displosion, by reason of the revolution of rising expectations, has increased inter-group tensions to the point of overt conflict throughout the world. Examples are the bitter guerilla warfare in Northern Ireland; the conflict between the Punjabis of West Pakistan and the Bengali of East Pakistan, now Bangladesh; the communal uprisings between Chinese and Malays in Malaysia; the tribal conflicts in Africa; the black-white confrontation in the Union of South Africa, Rhodesia, England and the United States.

Many of the problems generated by the social morphological revolution have served as barriers to economic development and they not only are traceable to the population explosion but have also been the product of the implosion and displosion. By reason of the differential impact of the social morphological revolution and especially of the technoplosion, wide gaps in productivity and levels of living have arisen which serve as the basis for differentiating the economically advanced from the developing nations. Moreover, since the end of World War II, despite increasing efforts of the more affluent nations to help the less developed countries bilaterally and through the U. N. and the Specialized Agencies, the gap between the have and have-not nations has been increasing. This is the setting in which the role of U. S. foreign aid policy is now being examined.

A review of population trends, of reductions in fertility which have been effected, and present efforts to control fertility permits the following significant generalizations which are presented without elaboration. They have been well documented elsewhere.[7]

• Contemporary rates of population growth for the world as a whole and especially for the developing areas could not possibly have been sustained for long periods in the past.

• Contemporary rates of world population growth, especially in developing nations, cannot possibly persist for very long into the future.

• In the long run any rate of population increase would exceed the carrying capacity of the earth. That is, in the long run zero growth is inevitable.

• There has never been a population which having acquired education and higher levels of living did not reduce its birth rates. Unfortunately, the converse of this proposition is also true. The world has yet to witness a population mired in illiteracy and poverty that has managed to reduce its fertility.

• In the economically advanced countries the birth rate declined even though government, the church, the medical profession and the "establishment" in general were opposed to it. It remains to be ascertained whether in the less developed countries the birth rate can be significantly reduced when the government and the establishment in general has this as an objective.

• In the economically advanced countries the birth rate was reduced before the advent of even the "traditional" methods of contraception, before the development of modern medicine, before the availability of birth control clinics. It remains to be seen whether the vastly improved methods of contraception and abortion will be effectively utilized by the less developed countries.

• There have as yet been no examples of populations in less developed countries which have managed to initiate a reduction in fertility by means of a family planning program. The often cited examples of the "success" of family planning programs—Taiwan, South Korea, Hong Kong, Singapore—experienced decreases in fertility before significant family planning programs were mounted. Birth rates declined in these areas for apparently the same reasons as in the economically advanced areas—namely, increasing education, levels of living and modernization.

• In the developing nations which have invested heavily in family planning programs over considerable periods of time as, for example, India and Pakistan, little more than 10 to 15 per cent of "eligible couples" have been reached and birth rates have not materially come down.

• Such declines in fertility as have occurred in the less developed countries have been very slow and not susceptible to accurate measurement over short periods of time. Nor is there any evidence to warrant the expectation that this situation will change appreciably in the forseeable future.

• There is mounting evidence that present major family planning approaches are plateauing at fertility levels still incompatible with effective or rapid economic development. In Taiwan, for example, not more than 25 to 30 per cent of the "eligible couples" are restricting family size and a large proportion of these are using methods not recommended by family planning agencies. In Korea there is also evidence of plateauing. In both countries the birth rate is projected to turn up under the impact of changing age structure resulting from post-war baby booms; and in both countries further declines in fertility may depend more on increasing modernization than on family planning activities.

• About 81 per cent of the population in developing nations, according to the Population Council, are now living in countries with national policies which promote or do not interfere with family planning activities.[8]

• In the economically advanced countries fertility reduction followed incentive and motivation to reduce family size. Birth rates were brought down by relatively primitive methods. In the less developed countries even the most modern methods of contraception and widespread availability of the methods are not, in the absence of motivation and incentive, being very effective in actual fertility reduction.

• The basic question in respect to fertility control is whether birth rates in developing nations can be reduced before modernization including education, higher levels of living and the breaking of the "cake of custom," liberation from the traditional order, are achieved.

The combination of perspectives derived from an understanding of the social morphological revolution and past and present experience in the control fertility permits now the raising and answering of more relevant questions than have yet been made explicit about population criteria for foreign aid.

Population and Foreign Aid Policy

United States foreign aid policy had its origin in the post-World War II world in which the need for closing the great gap between have and have-not nations was perceived as prerequisite for achieving world peace as well as in response to overdue humanitarian motivations. The Charter of the United Nations laid great stress on the importance of improving the levels of living of the impoverished peoples in the world, and the programs of the United Nations and of the Specialized Agencies have increasingly sought to assist the less developed countries to achieve their national aspirations to eliminate widespread poverty with its accompanying syndrome of malnutrition, disease, squalor and low productivity. United States foreign aid policy, while not without political motivation engendered in large part by the "cold war," was aimed at providing various forms of assistance to developing nations as were the technical assistance programs of the United Nations and the Specialized Agencies and the assistance programs of other affluent "donor" nations.

Because of the controversial and emotional character of policies embracing fertility control and insistent opposition to such policies by the Roman Catholic Church and sporadically by some Communist nations, only relatively recently has it become possible openly to consider and discuss population factors as essential elements in development programs, either in the U. N. family of agencies or in the United States and other donor countries. Most of the concern about population in relation to economic development has, however, been focused on high fertility and growth rates while, in general, little attention has been paid the impact of the population implosion and displosion on development. It is for this reason that proposed "population criteria" for continued U. S. foreign aid involve only birth rates and growth and the efforts of developing nations to decrease them. Yet the consequences of the implosion and displosion may be just as closely related to development as that of the explosion in many areas.

Since most of current consideration of population factors in relation to development focuses on birth rates, growth rates and their consequences, it should not be surprising that recommendations have been made for the United States not to provide assistance for development to the less developed countries which do not "effectively control" their fertility and growth. Perhaps the most extreme position in this respect has been taken by the Paddocks, who assume that "the exploding populations in the hungry nations combined with their static agriculture make famines, in many, inevitable." [9] Furthermore, they assume that "the timetable of food shortages will vary from nation to nation, but by 1975 sufficiently serious food crises will have broken out in certain of the afflicted countries that the United States will be "the sole hope of the hungry nations" and that this nation "will not have enough wheat and other foodstuffs to keep alive all of the starving," it will be necessary to make decisions on which nations it will or will not help.

It is at this point that the Paddocks propose the "triage" principle as necessary and practical.[10] They point out that in military medicine when the number of wounded is larger than available medical facilities can treat they are divided into three categories: the "can't-be-saved," the "walking wounded"—those who can survive without treatment, those who can be saved by immediate care. Military medicine then concentrates on the third category and ignores the other two. The Paddocks propose the same principle and approach be applied in helping nations with food shortages. This proposal by the Paddocks and also in varying degrees as it effects all foreign aid, by Ehrlich and Hardin is defective in at least two respects—one, technical and the other moral.

On the technical side the proponents of this policy stance fail to recognize that it is not posible, in the present state of knowledge, effectively and accurately to divide the nations of the world into the three categories of potential development as "can't be saved," certain to survive without help" and those which "can be saved." Nor would it help much to use the criterion of attempting to control population growth because about 81 percent of all the people in the developing areas already live in nations with national policies to dampen fertility and growth rates, and the list of such nations, which continues to grow, may soon embrace practically all the population in the less developed countries. Furthermore, if the criterion is made "effective" control of fertility and growth, none of the developing nations qualify. For up to this point in history no developing nation has managed to reach the level of about one percent per anum growth of the economically advanced nations and the latter, even at this level, are still faced with excessive growth threatening the quality of life even if not threatening survival. The report, *Population and the American Future,* recently issued by the "Rockefeller Commission," and not fully accepted by the President, points to the problems that confront the United States even with its present relatively low growth rate. With the exception of a few countries in the world nations have not yet achieved stabilization. The exceptions include only Japan, England and Wales, France, Denmark, Norway, West Germany, Hungary, Sweden and Switzerland, which have experienced fertility at or near replacement level for a decade or more, although much of this experience accompanied the depression decade of the '30s or catastrophic events of war and revolution. Thus, if "effective population policies" is to be the criterion, there are very few nations in the world which would qualify and none of these are less developed countries.

Another technical barrier to classifying nations by the criterion of "effective population policies" is the problem of measuring the impact of family planning programs over relatively short periods of time. Even if an initial triage determination is made, it may well take at least a decade, and probably more, to achieve enough lowering of the birth rate and growth rate with available programs to be accurately measurable by available techniques of demographic analysis. Thus, initial erroneous classification could persist as a result of which some nations which might have had the potential for population control remained unassisted while others received assistance without living up to expectations. It would be difficult to make a case for equity or fairness in such circumstances.

Next, and most important as a technical limitation in attempting to apply the criterion of "effective" population control as a prerequisite to foreign aid, is the assumption, a naive one, that low fertility and growth is the only population factor prerequisite for development. Other population factors may well be much more significant in determining success or failure in induced development programs such as the extent and impact of the population implosion and the population displosion. Balance in urban-rural population distribution and the consequences of urbanization in particular settings may be at least as significant as the growth rate in affecting the potential for development. Similarly the consequence of the population displosion, if manifest in overt communal conflict, may be a greater barrier to development than excessive fertility or growth as indicated by such examples as the Biafra revolt in Nigeria and the conflict betwen West and East Pakistan.

Moreover, many factors other than population factors affect a nation's potential for development. These could include the presence of a pre-Newtonian or post-Newtonian outlook; the way in which power is exercised by the elite; mechanisms for the allocation of resources and the distribution of income; the extent of political corruption; motivation to work; cultural values and priorities; and the ability of the nation to mobilize itself for collective action. Any one of these and other factors could, at least in the short run, be more important than excessive population growth rates or the other population factors as barriers to development. In fact, some of these types of factors also affect the ability of a nation to control its population growth. In short, a major technical deficiency in the proposed population criterion for foreign aid lies in its failure to adopt a holistic approach in which the population growth factor is evaluated in the context of all other relevant factors and given, not necessarily the major weight in the final determination, but the weight that it may actually merit.

There are also moral questions involved in proposing the population criterion for foreign aid. One is made explicit by the position Hardin has taken in stating that the economically advanced nations should regard themselves as "stewards" of civilization and as such have the responsibility of preserving the "civilization" of the developed nations. The obvious ethnocentric character of this posture requires no elaboration. Suffice it to say that if the value system of the United States with its present national and international priorities is to be taken as the standard of "civilization," it is at least a moot question of whether "civilization" is worth saving.

Another moral question lies in the attempt to cut off foreign aid on the basis of the population criterion, admittedly because there are limits to the aid the United States or any of the donor nations can give. The cutoff point, however, could vary considerably with different patterns in the allocation of national resources. Is it a high moral obligation not to give foreign aid to a country with an ineffective or non-existent population growth policy so as not to threaten the present allocation of resources to the military—in the United States and in the world as a whole? When, at the present time, the world is expending well over $200 billion a year for military purposes, it would seem not unreasonable to propose that such expenditures be decreased before setting cutoffs of foreign aid whatever criteria are used.

Finally, if it be morally aceptable to apply the triage principle to developing countries should it be equally applicable to minority groups within the United States? At the present time the birth rates and growth rates of blacks, for example, is relatively high and their levels of living relatively low. If blacks and other minority groups do not achieve "effective population policy" should the majority white population regard itself as the "steward" of American civilization and refuse to aid minority groups on the assumption, if not the hope, that disaster will overtake them to bring about eventual extinction? Or since minority groups in the United States are becoming increasingly troublesome in their insistence on equality of opportunity because the revolution of rising expectations has not bypassed them, do white Americans as "stewards" have the obligation to hasten the extinction of relatively poor, uneducated and rapidly growing minorities? The absurdity of applying the triage principle in foreign aid policy, even assuming there were a way to do it which was sensible, is brought home, hopefully, when transferring the principle to the domestic scene. The triage principle may be a necessary evil in military medicine. But it is neither technically sound nor morally acceptable applied to the contemporary developing world.

As indicated earlier, the Paddocks, Ehrlich and Hardin, while well motivated and undoubtedly sincere, do not seem to possess the basic perspectives which emerge from an understanding of the social morphological revolution and retrospect and prospect in regard to population. They have asked wrong questions and given wrong answers. They have done so in large part because of their simplistic approach both to population and development problems. Although the seriousness of excessive population growth and of environmental degradation and potential food shortages cannot be denied the application of their proposed population criterion as the basis for foreign aid is both professionally unsound and morally reprehensible.

It is the wrong question to ask whether high fertility levels and excessive population growth obstruct economic development and, if so, whether foreign aid should be denied if nations do not have an effective population policy. Although an affirmative answer to the first part of this question is correct, a "yes" answer to the second part, for the reasons indicated, is not. The correct question, assuming the present policy to provide foreign aid to developing countries is continued, is "How can foreign aid be most effective given the total situation in a given country?" The answer to this question involves consideration of all factors affecting development including, of course, population factors and not fertility and growth levels alone. Since the amount of foreign aid does have a limit, it is necessary to make choice of amounts, nations and programs. In making these choices, however, it is to be hoped that the proposed population criterion of "effective population policy" will not be the dominant one in the choice of nations but rather only one criterion among others, other population factors as well as other factors—cultural, social, economic and political. By "political" it is to be hoped that the criterion will not take the form of utilizing foreign aid as an instrument in the "cold war."

Similarly the question of whether the triage principle should be applied in extending aid to developing nations is the wrong question; and the affirmative answer is the wrong answer. For both technical and moral reasons, as indicated, the triage principle is inapplicable and reprehensible. The correct question is "What proportion of the world resources and especially of the resources of affluent nations should be mobilized for assistance to developing nations?" And the answer involves not only a comprehensive consideration of the total situation in an individual nation but, also, a comprehensive consideration of the total amount and all sources of foreign aid. Certainly foreign aid as now administered not only by the United States but, also, by the other donor nations and combinations of nations, and by the United Nations and the Specialized Agencies is often competitive rather than complementary, haphazard rather than planned, and wasteful rather than efficient. More effective planning, coordination and efficiency would make the foreign aid dollar do better work. More significant in formulating an answer to this question is the need to examine the present pattern of priorities in the allocation and utilization of United States and total world resources. The question of decreasing present expenditures for the military should certainly be considered a prior question to the applicability of the principle of triage. If this be considered an impractical question and an affirmative answer utopian, it is in order to insist that the assumption of the possibility of an effective population policy in developing nations is at least as impractical and the assumed affirmative answer at least as utopian.

The United Nations has proposed, in connection with the "first development decade," the allocation of one percent of GNP of the affluent nations for aid purposes. The United States, although it contributes far more than any other nation, has by no means reached the one percent level. Should this nation do so even at the expense of shorter Cadillacs and fewer multiple color TV set families? Needless to say, if this nation faces up to the need for a change in present national priorities, there is need to consider the needs of the poor (disproportionately minority groups) within its own boundaries, as well as its obligations and responsibilities abroad.

Finally, the third erroneous question posed is that relating to the responsibilities of the economically advanced nations as "stewards of civilization." This ethnocentrically oriented question and affirmative and equally ethnocentric reply is given by the Paddocks, Ehrlich and Hardin. The more relevant and appropriate question is "What targets should be set for achieving higher levels of development, social as well as economic, for mankind as a whole?" The answer to this question involves an evaluation of the social and economic situations not only in the developing countries but, also, in the economically advanced nations. Certainly there is much that is wrong as well as much that is right in America, despite the loud and often vulgar pronouncements of American flag-waving jingoists. In the evaluation of what is desirable and what is undesirable for the transmittal to future generations there would be reason to study and note variations in national priorities among the more affluent nations as well as differences between the economically advanced and developing nations. For example, the United States has national priorities which give it a very high income per capita but a relatively low expectation of life at birth, in contrast with the Netherlands whose national priorities give it a high expectation of life at birth but a lower income per capita.

Moreover, since infinite growth is impossible within finite limits, by axiom, mankind must face up to the reaching of limits to material growth involving utilization of natural resources and measured by GNP, as well as limits to population growth. Unless this basic fact is recognized the affluent nations, as "stewards of civilization," may be preserving a wasteland planet on which neither economically advanced nor developing nations can survive.

The setting forth of world social and economic targets will involve the best of minds and unprecedented world-wide cooperation. Although it is an activity not immediately in the offing, there is increasing evidence that exacerbating world problems may force it upon mankind— if man does not have the prescience to anticipate the need for such activity. In any case, further consideration of this problem is beyond the scope of this essay. Not beyond scope, however, is consideration of population targets—defining "population" in the broad sense discussed above rather than as restricted to fertility and growth levels. In attempting to relate population factors to development it is a prerequisite to have targets in mind—feasible and achievable. Such targets should include all aspects of population and not be restricted to fertility and growth.

The population growth rate must, of course, be considered a major factor in planning for economic development. It is not necessary to elaborate the reasons for this statement. Suffice it to say that it has conclusively been demonstrated that rapid population growth can be, and in most developing nations is, a serious barrier to increasing per capita income.

In consideration of desirable growth rates the question of "optimum" population size and growth rate inevitably arises. Yet, the "optimum" is always necessarily a function of the value criteria applied in its determination. The economic optimum (or more accurately optima) is not necessarily the same as the social optimum (or optima) and both are variables depending on the value yardsticks used. The quest for "optimum" population size quite apart from the arbitrary character of any optimum agreed upon is in a fundamental sense a quest equivalent to that for "the Holy Grail" in King Arthur's time; that is, it is a futile quest with little, if any, relation to reality. The question of what is the optimum population for the world or any subdivision thereof must be regarded as another erroneous question. This is so because not only is it highly unlikely that consensus could be reached in an effort to answer the question but it is, also, unlikely that much could be done about it, realistically, even if a consensus were achieved. It is certainly unrealistic to asusme that it is feasible to strive for an optimum population size well below an already attained size. That is, it is unrealistic to assume that any nation in the contemporary world would deliberately set out greatly to diminish its present size.

A more realistic approach to the problem of population size flows from recognition of the fact that zero growth is inevitable on this finite globe. Much attention has recently been paid to the Meadow's (et al.) study, *The Limits of Growth*,[12] with special authority attached to the study because it involved the use of the computer. Actually that there is a limit to population growth was widely publicized by Malthus towards the end of the 18th Century, a conclusion reached without the use of a computer. That there is such a limit needs no empirical research for validation. It can be taken as a mathematical axiom that infinite growth is impossible within finite limits. In this age of space exploration there is no longer any question about the finite limits of this planet and, therefore, about the inevitability of zero growth. But zero growth as a short run target is impossible short of extreme methods not likely to be acceptable or successful. In the longer run, although there is no question but that zero growth will be reached,[13] there is considerable question about whether it will be achieved by nature or by man, and if by man, by relatively rational and desirable or by irrational and undesirable means. If achieved by nature, it will be by increase in the death rate through some combination of famine and pestilence—forces to which Malthus referred. If achieved by man through relatively irrational and undesirable means it would result from war, homosexuality, cannibalism and the like. In respect of war it may be observed that up to this point in history the military has been relatively inefficient in the sense of having had relatively little impact on total world population. During World War II, for example, the bloodiest of wars thus far, world population increased by 200 to 300 million. With the advent of the hydrogen bomb, however, there is now no doubt that the military could become an effective instrumentality for the control of world population growth.

If zero growth is achieved by man by relatively rational and desirable means, it will involve three types of programs often confused although they are quite different. They are conception control, birth control and population control. Conception control refers to all means by which conception is prevented—behavioral, mechanical, chemical, physiological and surgical. Birth control involves abortion as well as conception control. Population control involves policy and program concerned with all components of population change, fertility, mortality and migration, and the social, economic and political milieus which affect them. At the present time only the economically advanced nations have achieved substantial control of fertility and growth and, although they are still well above zero growth levels, they could, however, achieve stabilization by doing a little more of what they are already doing. The developing nations, with over two-thirds of mankind, exercise relatively little control over family size and do so mainly by means of abortion. Their efforts at family planning may be interpreted not only as efforts to control family size but also to substitute conception control for abortion. No nation yet has achieved population control in the sense defined above. Perhaps the recent comprehensive report of the Commission on Population Growth and the American Future may help to set the United States on this path.

Given the inevitability of zero population growth the more relevant question than that of optimum size or growth rate is the more specific and realistic question, namely, "Given the present situation in any nation, what are alternative paths to zero growth and which one (or combination of paths) is a feasible and desirable one?" The report on *Population and the American Future* outlines criteria for paths to stabilization or zero growth which are also applicable in varying degree to the less developed countries. The criteria discussed include the following:

• "a minimum of fluctuations" from period to period in the number of births;

• zero growth should be achieved at "a lower rather than a higher level";

• "moderate changes" in patterns of marriage and childbearing;

• an average number of children of about two children per couple in the United States (in countries with higher death rates a higher average would produce zero growth). The average could, of course, be achieved in ways involving combinations of marriage patterns and number of children for individual families.

It must be emphasized that zero growth could not actually be reached until about 70 years after the replacement level of children per couple is attained. There is, thus, no quick, short-cut to zero growth short of the catastrophic. Moreover it has been shown by Coale and others that too precipitous a turn downward in birth and growth rates may produce problems as difficult as those which are being avoided.[14] It is desirable, then, to set targets for growth rates aimed at reaching zero growth which are feasible and attainable.

Targets should also be set for other population objectives. Population targets in addition to including desirable pathways to zero growth should aim at: continued lowering of mortality and diminution in differential mortality generated by differences in socioeconomic status; reasonable control of immigration and emigration; rational population distribution, urban-rural, metropolitan-non-metropolitan and regional, including attention to eco-systems; increased equality of opportunity for diverse population groupings by elimination of discriminatory attitudes and practices towards minorities; and increased quality of population as affected especially by opportunity for education and the acquisition of skills. A comprehensive set of population targets of this type, the details of which also fall outside the scope of this essay, and all aspects of which can effect development, further point to the absurdity of singling out the birth rate and growth rate as the only population criterion applicable to foreign aid.

At this juncture of world history aid to developing nations of adequate magnitude and with effective coordination and impact may be the safest and cheapest if not the only path to the closing of the gap between the have and have-not nations and world peace and order. The United States, by far the most affluent nation in the world, has an especially significant role to play in furthering the development of the less developed countries. Because the resources available for foreign aid are not without limit this nation will necessarily have to make choices in respect to the amount of air, the nations to be aided and the specific programs that are to be effectuated. In making these choices population factors must certainly be among those which are considered but they are not necessarily the only factors involved. Furthermore the utilization of population factors involves more than consideration of birth and growth rates.

The proposed population criterion for the granting of foreign aid—namely, "effective population policy" (meaning effective fertility control)—would impose a simplistic and irrational prerequisite for giving assistance. The application of the "triage" principle is neither technically feasible or morally acceptable. The assumption that the economically advanced nations are the "stewards" of civilization and have the obligation to preserve civilization at the expense of permitting the extinction of developing nations deemed to be beyond salvation is both ethnocentric and blind. It is necessary to raise and to answer more fundamental questions than have been raised by the Padocks, Ehrlich and Hardin to help guide United States foreign aid policy. Some of these question and answers have been considered. They point to the need for more comprehensive understanding of barriers to development, more carefully planned and coordinated aid programs, and, most of all, to the altering of world and national priorities so as to increase, by a significant degree, the resources available for foreign aid.

1. William Paddock and Paul Paddock, *Famine—1975!* (Little, Brown & Co., 1967); Paul Ehrlich, *The Population Bomb* (Ballantine Books, 1968), pp. 159-163; Garrett Hardin, "The Tragedy of the Commons," *Science* (December 13, 1968), pp. 1243-48; and Garrett Hardin, "Nobody Ever Dies of Overpopulation," *Science* (February 12, 1971), p. 527.

2. For an elaboration of various aspects of "the social morphological revolution" see Philip M. Hauser, "The Chaotic Society: Product of the Social Morphological Revolution," *American Sociological Review* (February 1969), pp. 1-19.

3. For elaboration see Philip M. Hauser, "World Population: Retrospect and Prospect," *Rapid Population Growth: Consequence and Policy Implications*, National Academy of Sciences (Johns Hopkins Press, 1971), pp. 103-122, and sources cited in Note 7.

4. United Nations, *World Population Prospects* (United Nations, 1966), pp. 23.

5. United Nations, tables prepared in late 1971 (in press).

6. Emile Durkheim, *The Rules of Sociological Method* (The Free Press, 1938), p. 81: Robert Redfield, *The Little Community: Viewpoints for the Study of a Human Whole* (University of Chicago Press, 1955); Karl Mannheim, *Man and Society in an Age of Reconstruction: Studies in Modern Social Structure*, trans by Edward Shils (London: K. Paul, Trench, Trubner, Ltd., 1955), p. 61.

7. These are conclusions reached by writer and set forth in following articles: Philip M. Hauser, "Family Planning and Population Programs—A Book Review Article," *Demography* (1967), pp. 397-414; Philip M. Hauser, "Non-Family Planning Methods of Population Control," in Nafis Sadik *et al.*, eds., *Population Control*, proceedings of the Pakistan International Family Planning Conference at Dacca (Islamabad: Pakistan Family Planning Council, 1969), pp. 58-66; Philip M. Hauser, "On Population Problems and Population Policy," *Sociological Focus* (Fall 1970), pp. 63-78.

8. Population Council, "Population and Family Planning Programs: A Factbook," *Reports on Population/Family Planning* (Population Council, June 1971), p. 4.

9. William Paddock and Paul Paddock, *op. cit.*, p. 205.

10. *Ibid.*, p. 206.

11. e.g. Gunnar Myrdal, *The Asian Drama* (Twentieth Century Fund, 1968). See Philip M. Hauser, "Cultural and Personal Obstacles to Economic Development in the Less Developed Areas," *Human Organization* (1959), pp. 74-78.

12. Donella H. Meadows *etal.*, *The Limits to Growth* (Universe Books, 1972).

13. For elaboration see Philip M. Hauser, "Non-Family Planning Methods of Population Control," *loc. cit.*, p. 58.

14. Ansley Coale, "Should the United States Start a Campaign for Fewer Births?" *Population Index*, 34:4, pp. 467-474.

24

DEVELOPMENT IN GLOBAL PERSPECTIVE

RICHARD D. N. DICKINSON

My basic reaction to Philip Hauser's paper is one of deep appreciation. He deals directly with a fundamental issue ("should United
States foreign aid be contingent upon effective population policies in
the potential recipient countries?"), puts the question in the context
of both technical information and moral principles, and achieves this
with remarkable lucidity. More concretely, I find myself in agreement with the general thrust of his argument, and with several of his
key propositions. I am always annoyed by critics who, when they
cannot find dramatic disagreements with an author, feel obligated to
chide him for what he omitted. Without implying that Hauser should
have written the paper my way, or that he should have included more
points in his already rich paper, my remarks may be understood as
complementary.

Moral Ambiguity. My first observation reveals a professional de-
formation as an ethicist. Hauser contends that to use the criterion of
"effective population policy" is neither workable nor moral. It is immoral, he says, for basically two reasons—its ethnocentricity and its
refusal to consider America's own priorities. Important as these two
observations are, I believe that the issue of morality has to be
seen in a broader framework. Other criteria may be adduced for judging the morality of a decision. Does it impose on others standards
which one is unwilling to accept for oneself? Does it unilaterally impose values on others? Does it take advantage of weak or exposed
nations? Does it promote anxiety, ambivalence and anomie in the
recipient country by inculcating heteronomous values? Does it attempt
to win commitment to certain values by introducing extraneous advantages and considerations? To answer such questions adequately requires an assessment of whether there is a tolerable consonance between
means and ends.

Aid is not and cannot be neutral. The withholding of aid is not and
cannot be morally neutral. Strings are attached to all aid; they may be
loose (positive inducements for family planning) or tight (coercive
constraints on foreign aid). Some ethnocentricity is inevitable. My

argument with Garrett Hardin is not that he wants strings (to be a good steward of the best values he knows in life), but that he defines those values in the particular way he does. Similarly, to affirm the goal of zero population growth is a culturally conditioned objective, as are the means one approves for attaining this objective. There are times when I think that more, rather than fewer, strings ought to be attached—especially strings related to the movement toward social justice in many countries dominated by a small privileged elite. (In passing we might observe that one possible advantage of a foreign aid program conditional upon a "local" effective population policy is that it would help to avoid our trampling in with an aid program for which there was no local enthusiasm.)

In short, the question of the morality of certain forms of aid is related to a systematic and critical examination of what an aid program is designed to accomplish. In the final analysis, the question of morality is pushed back to a systematic and critical examination of the intellectual presuppositions behind the whole aid endeavor. Giving foreign aid its best construction, it is primarily concerned with "development," "humanization," "liberation" in its fullest sense.

Perception of Development. What I find most egregious in the suggestion that American foreign aid should be conditioned upon effective population policies is not only the technical problems with applying such a policy, nor the ethnocentrism implicit in Hardin's approach. Obviously these are enormous difficulties; in themselves they should preclude a foreign aid program predicated on that principle. I would carry the argument further to the level of what we intend to accomplish with foreign aid and what we mean by development (if one can use that term any longer). Much contemporary discussion of the population problem dichotomizes the problem between population pressures and ecological limits. Hauser's insistence on seeing the problem of population "holistically," moves in the right direction, but there is something almost too casual in his passing remark that the population implosion could be "accompanied by the most profound change in human values."

To pit ecological limitations against population pressures connotes a hypnotism with quantitative measurements of development. How often do we hear that the 4% growth rate of the majority of poorer countries is halved by the increase in population? This tends to suggest that consumerism would be acceptable were it not for the unfortunate limits of the earth. It implies that if we did not have an ecological problem (or a population problem), we would not have any value problem. Today's cultural revolution is more profound than that. That cultural revolution poses profound questions about the insidious warping of values through the very technological preoccupation which has inculcated this quantitative, manipulative way of thinking about value. Today's ecological and population crises confront us through quantitative limits with the question of qualitative meaning. These quantitative limits remind us that the human question has always been the quality of human relationships rather than the acquisition and having of goods—that goods and services (health, education, leisure, as well as things) are humanizing only to the extent that they liberate men to affirm others as ends and not means to one's private goals. Certainly the prospects of massive under- and unemployment in the next decades will force the value and human dignity issue upon us in irrepressible fashion. This deeper element was implicit in many of Hauser's remarks, but I am more comfortable when it is made explicit.

A corollary is that development must be perceived as promoting self-reliance and interdependence. Foreign aid progams can be assessed by the degree to which they foster these human values; it is successful to the extent that it helps people to become subjects of history (conscious co-creators of their own and our corporate future) rather than objects of other people's decisions. The means-ends problem is crucial here. If foreign aid is understood as a process for contributing to such creativity and liberating responsibility, it would be ironic and paradoxical if the conditions of aid were unilaterally decreed by the potential donor. Such a unilateral policy would not only engender hostilities and resentment. At a deeper level it would perpetuate dependencies on others and alienation from self, rather than contributing to responsible moral decision-making in the "recipient" country. The means would militate against the desirable ends—telling a man he can be free as long as he accepts your way of defining his freedom and accepts your way of achieving it.

Another basic difficulty with the proposal to make foreign aid conditional upon effective population policies is that it defeats a global perspective on development. Hauser rightly contends that through the population "displosion," communications and travel have shrunk the earth, changing the values and perceptions of people within it. One could say that the earth-culture mass has become more dense, and the frictions caused by this densification more intense. While we have been preoccupied with the friction between the "socialist East" and the "democratic West," the new "North-South" dynamic has quietly taken over as a dominant factor in international affairs. That this new and dominating friction has not yet been perceived is evident, not only in the atrophy of our foreign aid program and the Vietnam and Latin American fiascos, but also in the incredible obtuseness of the President devoting half of his announcement in 1972 about the mining of Haiphong harbor to plead with the Russians not to overreact! It is infuriating for the peoples of the Third World to be told time and again, implicitly or explicitly, that they are simply pawns in the dividing up of the world by the two great super-powers. Peoples of the Third World increasingly stress that they are fighting against not only political colonialism and economic neo-colonialism, but also against cultural imperialism.

My point is simply that development must be seen as global partnership, but both our institutions and our attitudes militate against that partnership. The Pearson Commission talked grandly about "partnership for development," but the rich are either so oblivious to, or contemptuous of, the institutional patterns and cultural values of the poor countries that the phrase is a mockery. In the present international, inter-racial and inter-cultural context, to demand that foreign aid should be given only to those nations which comply with one's own cultural standards will be perceived as the intolerable arrogance it really is. It will exacerbate rather than improve prospects for global partnership.

Indirect population policies. Hauser's masterful resume of the salient facts of our experience so far in population control is worth volumes of statistics. One point stands out above the rest, *viz.* there is no clear evidence that top-down population planning programs, with or without external pressures, have worked until the people are ready to accept planning on other, broader grounds ("increasing education, levels of living and modernization, . . . liberation from the traditional order"). If top-down family planning programs fail when under the aegis of one's own government, there is little prospect that pressure from another country (especially from a superpower suspected of trying to lock the poor in their inferior position) can help.

Yet we cannot leave the discussion at that point. We must move beyond Hauser's paper to ask, "if family planning and zero population growth are desirable goals, urgent goals, how can foreign aid be used to foster these objectives without undermining the overall objectives of development?" Hauser's paper rightly suggests that many development programs only indirectly related to population policies can have a major impact on the achievement of family planning. But which ones? That he does not give us more guidance on alternative styles of aid is not a simple oversight, and certainly not a blindness on his part. Rather, I believe it reflects the fact that our ideological preoccupation with direct action to curtail conceptions (as the quick, simple and obvious remedy for an overriding problem) has kept researchers from doing the more sophisticated and complex analysis required. It is always the case that research needs are defined by the way the affluent perceive the problem. If one wishes to be cynical and sermonic, he could claim that we were blinded by our cultural arrogances—we believed that rational people, once they knew the options, would opt for birth control. The problem as we saw it, therefore, was how to produce and distribute quickly and cheaply enough instruments for them to exercise their rational option.

A major task for the years just ahead is to detour around the present question of whether aid ought to be related to effective population policies, and address the issue of *what kinds* of aid will achieve zero population growth and effective population policies—starting yesterday! Should we concentrate on literacy programs, especially those which, in Paulo Freire's term, "conscienticize" the masses to belief in their own worth, dignity, freedom and responsibility? Or should we emphasize programs which are, on the surface at least, more neutral from a value perspective? This has been urged by some who argue that health and health education are relatively neutral, and therefore preferable for aid programs. We simply don't know enough about what inputs are going to be most productive, partly because we have not asked the question, as Hauser points out, in broad enough terms.

Since there is a paucity of scientific data to support any particular indirect population program, we must make up with courage what we lack in knowledge. My own hunch is that far more attention to rural literacy and conscientization processes in development (especially among women and disenfranchised groups) are a promising first step. Yet it would be utopian to believe that governments, either in the Third World or the other two worlds, could tolerate the threat of an aroused and conscienticized mass. Among other advantages, such a policy or concentration would help to rectify the myopia (a shortsightedness which we Westerners have encouraged) of many development plans with industrialization and urbanization, notwithstanding the fact that about 60% of the Third World's people live in rural areas, and one of their problems is under-employment. I believe that no population policy can work until the rural masses are brought consciously (politically, economically, culturally and psychologically) into the dynamics of their own society. Development theory and practice have failed abysmally on this count.

Beyond Foreign Aid. I concur wholeheartedly with Hauser's appeal for more foreign aid, and that it is absurd to talk of limited resources demanding hard choices between countries when our foreign aid program has been so scandalously feeble and distorted. Hauser said politely that as a nation we have never attained the 1% of GNP principle which has been so widely endorsed. He did not say, however, that presently we give only about two-tenths of 1% of GNP, and that we have tried to use even that amount to intimidate the poor to vote correctly in the United Nations. Nor did he have time to refer to a number of other striking anomalies in the foreign aid picture. It is noteworthy that UNESCO recently announced that it is preparing a report which calls into question the utility of the whole foreign aid program of the past ten years.

My problem, however, is not at that level, even though there must be many significant revisions in present foreign aid strategies, either multilateral or bilateral. What must be clear is that foreign aid—even at 1%, 2% or more—is a relatively small part of the development picture. We must not be hypnotized with aid from above. Hauser's paper addresses only aid policy. Clearly, three additional areas of impact upon the Third World must be reviewed critically as well: trade patterns and policies which currently widen the gap between the rich and poor; international fiscal policies and controls which keep the weaker nations vulnerable, even in international agencies like the International Monetary Fund; and inadequately restricted multinational corporations which often do great harm to poorer countries despite the shibboleths of "industrialization," "employment," and "economic prosperity." These powerful institutions and patterns of relationships, backed by ideological assumptions about the good life and how it is attained, dominate the world scene. They have far more influence on world development than do foreign aid programs, important as those aid programs are. Global development will require not only sacrificial giving of our surplus, and not only a reduced rate of growth and/or consumption; it also will demand basic re-thinking of some of the fundamental world economic relationships. Foreign aid is only one piece in the puzzle.

Confirming the Disadvantages of the Poor. The Christian community always (at least theoretically) had a special concern for the poorest and most vulnerable segments of society. There is no moral justification to insist that the poor, many of whom have no "effective population policy" should be confirmed in their poverty by refusing them aid. One could argue that it is just such countries which, if they want assistance, should receive it first. Further, given the fact that 72% of the people of the Third World live in countries where there is a population policy (a figure distorted by India, with her 570 million), a number of the remainder live in countries where, on the basis of present national boundaries, natural resources and population figures, there is no immediate urgency for a policy (at least a birth control policy). Should we conclude that if such a country does not think it needs a population policy, it either does not deserve or does not need any other type of assistance? That is a vapid conclusion.

Too Many People vs. Too Much Control. Is quality of life compromised more by having too many people, or by having too much direct governmental control—especially if that control stems from another country and culture? While I appreciate the distinction made by Hellegers between population planning and family planning, I believe the two issues tend to merge on this point. The case against too much direct governmental interference in family planning is argued from a variety of premises: the inviolable right in natural law for parents to determine the size and condition of their family; the principle of subsidiarity which stresses the primacy of the family in determining family size; the doctrine of "orders" which tends to separate and divorce functions of state and family; the principle of free man continuously creating himself (corporately and individually) in existential anxiety, hope, freedom, risk and responsibility.

When Skinner asks whether contemporary man can afford freedom, Toffler asks how much freedom a man and society can stand, and Fromm notes man's retreat from freedom and responsibility, one is tempted to argue that strong governmental population policies are mandatory. Yet man becomes human (individually and corporately) by exercising ambiguous freedom and accepting the consequences of that freedom. I believe that, in terms of foreign aid policies related to such a crucial and sensitive area as population policy, society should err on the side of freedom rather than overt constraint.

This brings us full circle, back to the basic postulate of Hauser's paper, *viz.* that as we move vigorously in the direction of zero population growth and qualitative planning, our policies of ends and means push us back to basic questions of value and meaning. Foreign aid programs cannot be separated from a broader perspective on the population problem.

25

EUGENIC CONTROL AND POPULATION POLICIES

Harmon L. Smith

"Eugenic" translates literally as good beginning, or good origin, or good creation. The term is technically employed, however, to signify attempts at recombination of existing genes by directed control of conception through such means as parental selection, parthenogenesis, and artificial insemination. More specifically, eugenic engineering entails both *negative* eugenics (breeding *out* certain undesired traits) and *positive* eugenics (breeding *in* certain desired traits). For the purposes of this paper, "eugenic control" means the regulation of government, by some superordinate authority, of human hereditary origins to a purposive direction of human reproduction which can be called "good." We are therefore concerned less with day-to-day decisions which are called for by particular cases than with describing a more or less "settled course" for the expression of socio-political wisdom and prudence. The focus of this paper is thus on policy rather than procedure.

Others can detail the present state of genetic technology and the operational limits of our capacity to control the "good origins" of *Homo sapiens*. Our task here is to review the general features of eugenic control and to inquire into the wisdom of alternatives and the morality of options. At the outset, let me say that I see no *prima facie* reason to exclude any of the methods currently available to us for modifying our species or controlling our genetic future as potential means for eugenic control. Thus, a state-sanctioned population policy which intends to provide a "good beginning" for our species could, except for compelling contraindications, employ eugenic, genetic, or euphenic engineering or all three. But we are not objectively concerned, in consideration of eugenic control and population policies, with such matters as artificial insemination, *in vitro* fertilization, cloning, chimeras, and cyborg-androids.

It is arguable that an inquiry into eugenic control and population policies is appropriate and timely in the measure to which the two-million-year evolution of our species as a humanly *un*directed process is now nearing its end. We are accumulating much of the technology which will allow us to direct the further evolution of our species in distinct and intentional ways. Of course, to claim that does not venture to propose the particular shape which the future product may take; it only alleges that we increasingly possess the means to control the process which produced us.

Genetic and population policy formation, however, is ineluctably future-oriented and that awareness deserves early rather than late consideration. By the choices which we are now able to make, we will shape the destiny of future generations; and, at least to the extent that this is so, we will reflect our sense of obligation toward them. To be sure, there are certainly discrete ways in and by which we ourselves, together with our immediate progeny, stand to benefit (or not benefit) from choices we make now. Even so, the rhetoric of virtually all the urgent "causes" of our time—diplomacy, population, and environment are obvious examples—clearly points to doing or not doing certain things, or taking this rather than that course of action, because it is hoped and supposed that the future will thereby be made peaceful or safe from overpopulation or free from pollution. All of these are variant (or perhaps ingredient) ways of describing a "good life" which we ourselves may not live to see. Any eugenic program aimed at a "good origin" must therefore calculate the ways in which it will also issue in a "good end."

There is surely no physical sense in which the future can make these kinds of claims upon us. Yet we have acknowledged (maybe the power of our own rhetoric has overcome us) an obligation to future generations which somehow obliges us to do *now* what we think will promote a "good creation" for them *then.* Thus immediate eugenic choices, while important in their own right and deserving of their own integrity, will bear most lasting consequences when appreciated in view of future generations, some of whom are not merely "yet unborn" but (depending upon our decisions) may be "never to be born."

But how meaningfully can we speak of our obligation to future generations and simultaneously honor acknowledged responsibility to ourselves and our immediate families? It is a good deal easier to achieve consensus on general rather than specific points; so a rudimentary beginning might frame future humane obligation in terms of a present duty to provide, both now and in the not-yet, for the extension under optimum circumstances of freedom, justice, community (or the general welfare), and perfection (or the secure possibility for development and achievement). These values can be commended initially because they are the ones which have historically sustained the civilization which now possesses the possibility of depriving the future of them. But, beyond that, these values also appear to constitute, in our own cultural ethos, the legitimate legacy we can conscientiously commit to the future.

Few, if any, among us would seriously challenge the claim that we have an obligation to produce, guarantee, and engender conditions conducive to and congenial with such a "good life" for both present and future generations. What can (and probably will) be argued with both reason and passion is what "good life" means. This positive obligation—whatever its eventual meaning—is joined by a negative duty which is to refrain, insofar as we can identify the ways, from harming future generations. To acknowledge this negative duty is important, I think, if only because doing so tends to temper our (sometimes less than adequately informed) zeal for positive manipulation of the future. The particular conditions which we choose as a legacy for the future are, at best, informed guesses because we cannot predict with certainty or precision what future generations themselves will regard as the "good life." Correspondingly, we can only make educated guesses as to what they will regard as a bad legacy. At the pragmatic level, it may be easier to decide what we will *not* do—for many of the same reasons that it is ordinarily easier to say what we would rather *not* be done to us.

The current arguments *pro* and *contra* eugenic control are, as I understand them, grounded in tacitly opposed assumptions. On the one hand it is argued that the expense of large numbers of defective people is too great to bear and that we are therefore obliged, in consideration of the survival of society, to make a pragmatic judgment as to the kinds and numbers of defective people we can reasonably be responsible for. On the other hand it is urged that "defective" is logically an arbitrary and relative category and that in consideration of the survival of value we are faced with an *a priori* ethical judgment, grounded in theism, which respects the inviolability of human species life and surrounds it with sanctity. The further implication of these respective assumptions, it is widely supposed, is that the former indicates a policy of more or less rigorous controls while the latter would leave the choices of human reproduction very much *laissez-faire*. Neither of these assumptions need be, of course, mutually exclusive of the other; but each one does tend to locate the preeminent criteria for decision-making in particular interests which, in conflict with the other, would be governing. Both assumptions are, however, largely mistaken in my opinion—one for reasons of fact, and the other for reasons of value.

Of the 46 chromosomes contained in a fertilized human egg, 23 are inherited from the egg and 23 are inherited from the sperm. Thus, if there were only 23 differences between the genes in the two sets of chromosomes in the father and only 23 differences between the genes in the two sets in the mother, each of them could potentially produce 2^{23} (or 8,388,608) genetically different sorts of eggs and sperms. Through random fertilization we then have the possibility of yielding 70 trillion genotypes—a figure that would roughly correspond to approximately 2300 generations of the present population of the entire world. The incredible mathematical possibility of gene combinations therefore renders talk about "progressive eugenics" enormously problematic at the theoretical level.

In addition to these facts, more than 1000 "defects" have been identified in man and are now known to be genetically transmitted and controlled; and that number is being added to daily. I am told that we presently possess effective *in utero* tests, principally amniocentesis and blood analysis, for a very small percentage of these. We know what the likelihood is for appearance in the general population for some of these (e.g., 3% for cystic fibrosis and 20% for diabetes mellitus); and we also know that mating pairs who have autosomal recessive diseases run a statistical risk of producing offspring that is calculated to be 25% homozygous affected, 25% homozygous normal, and 50% heterozygous carrier. We are not always careful, however, to distinguish between population risk and mating pair risk: the population risk of phenylketonuria is 1/40,000, but the mating pair risk for a carrier couple is 1/4.

Each of us, moreover, is likely to carry 5 to 10 defective genes among our underterminated but large number of genes; and that fact alone indicates how it is that 1% of live births are grossly defective, that another 1% are born with a defect serious enough to prevent marriage or holding a productive job, and that still another 4-6% of live births are abnormal in some way.

Given the social values which are operative in our culture, I have no doubt that "defective" people represent a great expense. But two considerations should make us cautious about advocating a population policy which is predicated upon either negative or positive eugenic control. The first is demographic and refers to patterns of breeding which are a critical component of the incidence of disease: the dispersal of populations by greater mobility, together with an increase in genetic information, will tend to result in fewer incidences of particular diseases. The second relates to concepts and information which are requisite to purposive programming: we are not yet very far beyond a rudimentary aspect of sophistication in either knowledge or technique for positive genetic manipulation.

The principal assumption underlying arguments *contra* eugenic manipulation is mistaken for reasons of value. To suppose that *all* human species life is of equivalent value is functionally naive; we do treat different people differently, and that different treatment derives from the different attributions of worth which we assign. To be sure, these attributions are most appropriately made with reference to the subject whose value it is, and not by a subject who is arbitrarily or capriciously imposing his value upon another.

But even this way of understanding relational value is aware that communities of persons unavoidably confront us with competing neighbor-claims; and that larger, the more *im*personal contexts (e.g., scarcity of resources, limits of effective procedures), also influence and shape our ordinary understandings of duty and worth. On the battlefield, triage is the medical corpsman's method for making this discriminating moral judgment; in the genetic counselor's office, the availability (e.g., insulin for diabetes) or unavailability (e.g., in Lesch-Nyhan syndrome) of effective therapies or controls is usually the presiding criterion for advice in the presence of conflicting values. To acknowledge these circumstances is, in the last analysis, no more than honest confrontation with our creaturely and finite limits.

Moreover, we need to understand clearly that *we* make these attributions, even if they are thought to be grounded in a particular understanding of God and of his intention for man and the world. Nor is it any longer credible that nature's way is God's way, or that human mastery over human life and death verges on the demonic. Our knowledge of the ways things work, of consequences we could not earlier foretell, of the relativities of history, of cultural conditioning, and all the rest, make us wary of abdicating responsibility for *doing what we can do* to alleviate pain and suffering and disadvantage. Conversely, it is arguable that we have an obligation to engineer the best possible auspices for a "good life," an obligation which includes the refusal to take inordinate risks.

What is at stake, then, is not a general prohibition towards manipulating our species life but a careful and compassionate regard for only doing what we can do responsibly. *For the most part,* and in consideration of the *present* stage of our genetic knowledge and technology, this may (and I think it does) mean "don't do anything, just stand there." But there are aspects of our present knowledge and technology which may (and I think they do) deserve to be acted on; so that, in view of the varieties of values in this mix, what we are called upon to do is to make discriminating judgments. Neither technological romanticism nor technological cynicism will serve us well for either present choices or future consequences.

In times of political and social evolution (such as our own!), the tendency is for a society to move precipitately on incomplete evaluations of data. The widespread introduction of hexachloriphene into toilet articles is an example, as was the nationwide use of DDT. The subsequent tendency is to over-react when these chemicals are found to be deleterious; or, as in the case of dispensing with phosphate detergents in order to avoid water pollution, to *hope* for a cure rather than provide one. We are learning, bit by bit. But it is arguable that what we know is *comparatively* trivial, that the basic elements of population genetics are unknown to us, and that therefore we should not act on any *general* population policy until and unless we have the facts more comprehensively in hand. Meanwhile, what shall we do with what we know?

On the one hand, we know that we do not know enough about some things yet to venture decisions which might include an irreversible component; so we need to know more. The only genuine problem here is how, simultaneously, to expand medical and scientific knowledge and to protect the dignity and security of persons. This is not, however, a new problem in principle; and we have more or less managed successfully in the past to honor both values. Indeed, they are not even mutually exclusive in the measure to which medical experimentation is sponsored by humane interests, and human well-being is guarded and extended by advancements in medical knowledge. Still they cannot always be harmonized, and deciding when and where that is the case can go a long way toward acknowledging where the priorities lie. If these two highly desirable goals should sometimes appear to be incompatible, I have no doubt that experiments and the expansion of knowledge should be subordinated to the dignity and security of persons. We do not yet fully know, for example, the long-range consequences of a population policy calculated to erase a single genetic (e.g., sickle cell anemia or Favism) defect. Perhaps more animal experimentation, or modeling, or something else will provide better clues than we now have. Good; let's get on with it. Meanwhile we may do more lasting genetic, and human, harm than good by rushing precipitately to a population policy which would immediately foreclose extension of those genotypes in the gene pool. The expansion of knowledge thus provided might constitute an inordinate risk to human well-being.

On the other hand, we do know *some* things about which we can make some choices. Genetic counseling is perhaps the clearest instance of our present attempts to act responsibly on what we know; although it deserves noting that genetic counseling is also a case of professional privatization which needs to be opened to public exposure precisely in order to disseminate what we know, to acknowledge a pluralism of values at stake in it, and to invite discriminating opinions from a variety of professional competences. To this point—and maybe because it is relatively novel and still more or less "under wraps"—there is no general or explicit policy respecting genetic counseling, with the result that different institutions employ different protocols and different personnel. There are certain inequities unavoidable in the nature of that situation; nevertheless the purposes of genetic counseling are fairly well agreed upon; to advise prospective parents of the genetic condition of a fetus and/or to advise them of the stitistical risks of a genetically problematic pregnancy, and to ascertain their wishes by assisting them to work through the implications of their identified genotypes. Not infrequently, but less defensible in the absence of tacit assumption about the "quality" of life, genetic counselors sometimes also influence the decisions of prospective parents with respect to which pregnancies should be terminated and/or discouraged.

More than forty disorders can be diagnosed with different certainties by chemical analysis of amniotic fluid and cells and examination of the morphological characteristics of chromosomal patterns. Among these are galactosemia, mycopolysaccharidosis, erythroblastosis fetalis, hemophilia, muscular dystrophy, phenylketonuria, cystic fibrosis, adrenogenital syndrome, branched-chain ketonuria, Gaucher's disease, cystinosis, glucose-6-phosphate dehydrogenase deficiency, Marfan's syndrome, Lesch-Nyhan syndrome, Pompe's disease, orotic aciduria, sphingomyelinosis, phytanic acid storage disease, homocystinuria, Wilson's disease, and chromosomal disorders such as Down's syndrome, ploidy of the X and Y chromosomes and others. Altogether, that is an impressive list considering the relative novelty of amniocentesis and the techniques for analysis. It is not by any means an exhaustive list of chromosome or enzyme defects, but it is evidence that we do know some things about which we can now make some choices. Those choices are principally three: we can elect to terminate pregnancy (in cases, let us say, of cystic fibrosis which is, among Caucasians, the most lethal genetic disease of childhood); or we can attempt to manage the disease (in cases, let us say, of phenylketonuria); or we can accept the defect and try to make the best of it (in cases, let us say, of Down's syndrome). In anticipation of future recurrence of similarly problematic pregnancies, elective sterilization offers an additional (but not remedial) option. Each choice carries its own particular cost—to parents and society, in money and sentiment, and a variety of other ways. The central questions which any population policy that implements eugenic control must address are who will make these decisions and upon what predicates?

Not only theologians and ethicists, but also scientists and physicians, differ in their opinions on this point. Some would advocate an almost automatic decision for abortion, when one or another of these diseases is diagnosed *in utero,* sometimes together with a recommendation for sterlization; others would just as passionately argue that none of these defects is adequate warrant for termination of fetal life or sterlization of carriers; and still others would insist upon reserving these awesome decisions to those who are most immediately and lastingly affected by them, namely, the prospective parents. If our obligation to both the present and the future is to conserve and extend freedom, justice, community, and perfection, the last of these options seems to me preferable to either of the first two.

Significant evidence has been developed through birth data to indicate that pregnant women, age 40 and older, run a very high statistical risk of carrying a genetically problematic fetus. Down's syndrome, for example, is prone to occur in approximately 2% of such fetuses. Thousands of amniocenteses have resulted in minimal maternal and fetal morbidity and mortality, although there are potential complications which make the procedure more than casual. In view of the evidence, it is probably appropriate to advise amniocentesis as a more or less "routine" procedure for women who are 40 years or older, or those who have already borne one diagnosed genetically defective child, or who fear some extrinsic damage (via x-ray, for example). This advice, however, is best kept just that: an intra-professional convention is preferable, in the nature of these cases, to government policy. And, given the information which amniocentesis provides, the prerogative of prospective parents to decide whether to terminate the pregnancy deserves to be honored and guarded.

There may be an emerging consensus in our culture as to what constitutes distinctively "human" or "personal" life, or what is minimally requisite to achieving that status in our species. So we are concerned for public education, adequate housing, sufficient nutrition, political participation, parks and playgrounds, music and literature, and all those other components which make life human. And we are also interested in redefining death in order to know and agree as to when further possibility of life recovery has been exhausted, when artificial prolongation of vital life becomes arrogant and fanatic, when the needless extension of life amounts to a contemptuous and forbidden torturing of it, and when mechanical and instrumental means of death-deferment may be terminated. Moreover, we want to know when and under what circumstances a fetus is so terribly disadvantaged (whether by familial circumstance, genetic inheritance, or whatever) as to be deprived of even the prospect for development and achievement. But how much and what kind(s) of housing, education, nutrition, and the rest, are "adequate" or "sufficient"? And what cerebrocortical function is "minimum"? And at what point (perhaps anencephalic?) is an organism of our species so personally and publicly disadvantaged as to be personally and publicly worth*less*? We are grappling with these questions because we have not yet achieved a consensus; and until we do, I think it would be disastrous to establish and implement a population policy which treated these questions as though they had been answered.

Meanwhile, however, decisions—some of them life-and-death—cannot be indefinitely postponed until the emerging consensus becomes articulate. I have argued in another context that in terminal cases of irreversible illness or irremediable injury the final decision(s) affecting the management of the primary patient are probably best left to the informed and compassionate judgment of those whose love for the patient most reasonably and compellingly serves his best interest and well-being. That moral logic seems also appropriate to eugenic control: decisions affecting the "good origins" of our species are, in view of our present knowledge and technology, probably better left to the informed and compassionate "parents" of a genetically problematic fetus than to some other state-enacted population policy. Although some states have enacted compulsory sterilization statutes for certain classes of "defective" citizens, the rationale for that action would be inapposite in the cases we are considering *unless* "gentic defect" were combined with "mental incompetence." We are not yet prepared, I think, to undertake major application of either positive or negative genetic bio-engineering; and until we are, some of our most noble and altruistic goals for our species will be temporarily thwarted. Still, that seems to me (despite the pain and disappointment and frustration that will attend it) a price worth paying, and one which is hopefully proportional to the "good life" thereby secured.

Compulsory, or even coercive, programs for eugenic control infringe upon long-cherished reproduction freedoms. Affluent, middle-class majorities can reasonably be expected to resist imposed regulation and/or foreclosure of such choices; but given the current situation with minority groups and the disadvantaged, both nationally and internationally, it may be more important to anticipate response from these populations. The "liberalization" of abortion laws has already been suspected and feared as another weapon in the white man's arsenal for genocide. The feelings and conflicts engendered by a program of eugenic control, which would employ compulsory abortion or sterilization, are potentially bitter and far-reaching and so politically and socially undesirable as to erode the very quality of life which such a program (ostensibly) would undertake to conserve and extend. The fundamental conflict is between the relatively private well-being of families and offspring and the relatively public welfare of the general population.

There is too much uncertainty shrouding heredity, too much ignorance of the etiology of too many mental diseases and physical defects, and too little social gain at too great a social cost to warrant any compulsory program of either positive or negative eugenics. On the other hand, a eugenics program which would require amniocentesis for every pregnant woman age 40 and older, and provide counseling to all persons for whom reproduction is or may be genetically problematic, would employ responsibly what we now know while simultaneously guarding some of our most cherished and honored civil and personal liberties.

A recent Associated Press dispatch (29 April 1972) quoted Dr. Carey Bostian's caution against allowing science to be shackled because of fear that immoral men would make improper use of new discoveries: "I believe," he said, "the promises of the new genetics far exceed the perils." Whether Dr. Bostian, a distinguished geneticist at North Carolina State University, intended what I interpret, I do not know; but his statement seems to me an appropriate opinion at all three points of its emphasis: (1) "I believe" acknowledges that, at this stage, we can only express confidence or faith that this, rather than some other, course or outcome will be pursued and secured;

(2) "promises" not fulfillment therefore best describes the present stage of genetic technology; and (3) the hope that "promises . . . will far exceed the perils" is doubtless one which we all share. Still, it deserves saying as plainly as possible that our situation at present is one of belief-promise-hope, and while these are crucial for shaping the destiny of genetic manipulations it would be foolhardy to suppose that they are accomplished fact-fulfillment-reality.

Both scientific and humanistic disciplines will continue to accumulate explicit knowledge, expand understanding, and gain increasing mastery of the world and its creatures. If it is still arguable in some quarters whether this is how it *should* be, I think it beyond reasonable doubt that this is how it *will* be. It is therefore all the more urgent that the struggle for mastery be accompanied by an awareness of tragedy, an acknowledgment of the mystery of the reality of overwhelming human suffering. To deny tragedy and mystery, to become desensitized to finitude and anguish, is to forfeit part of what I take to be the essential meaning of *humanum* and, perhaps eventually, to mutilate irreparably our own best self-understanding.

26

EUGENIC POLICY AND THE HARD DECISIONS

W. French Anderson

Harmon Smith's fine paper has contributed several insights with which I am in immediate agreement. He points out that "we are accumulating much of the technology which will allow us to direct the further evolution of our species in distinct and intentional ways . . . . By the choices which we are now able to make, we will shape the destiny of future generations." But he also adds that "we cannot predict with certainty or precision what future generations themselves will regard as the 'good' " life. Nor do we know what the end result of an attempt at genetic manipulation would be. Even if all our motives are well-intentioned, we might very well do more harm than good to future generations by any attempted regulation of population genetics at this time. "What is at stake," he writes, "is not a general prohibition towards manipulating our species life but a careful and compassionate regard for only doing what we can do responsibly." In the meantime, we must acquire the knowledge necessary to make wise and correct decisions. "The only genuine problem here is how, simultaneously, to expand medical and scientific knowledge and to protect the dignity and security of persons." Aside from protecting the dignity and security of persons, governmental regulations regarding eugenic control and population policies should not be enacted until our state of knowledge is sufficiently advanced that such policies can be made wisely.

I agree in principle with Professor Smith in all of these statements. However a certain number of governmental regulations already exist. In many states there are laws restricting the marriage of individuals who possess certain genetic abnormalities; there are laws on sterilization procedures and on abortions. Even if one agrees with Professor Smith that the best policy is that of no compulsory restrictions, how would he translate this policy into the present world? Would he freeze all laws as they now exist? The New York abortion law as it is? The state marriage laws as they are? And so on. Would he advocate the repeal of all present laws relating to population policies? In view of the fact that there is already governmental restriction in the area of population policy, what are we as "careful and compassionate" observers to do?

Let me be more specific. As Professor Smith correctly points out, prenatal diagnosis of genetic defects by means of amniocentesis is now a most important and exciting new area of genetic medicine. If a serious genetic defect in a fetus is detected during pregnancy, should the parents be allowed to choose voluntarily to terminate the pregnancy by means of a therapeutic abortion? Should this procedure be available on request to all married couples in our country? We can discuss the general principles of eugenic control and population policies very eloquently and for a very long time. But to the doctor who must counsel young couples and who must manage the infant born with a genetic defect, the immediate question is this: What are the present legal restrictions, including federal, state, and local, concerning therapeutic abortion? I find Professor Smith's eloquent discussion limited when faced with the situation of a mother who chooses to have her pregnancy terminated because a fetus is proven to be grossly defective in utero. Principles are fine, but what do we do about the present very real situations that many of us must face daily? Prenatal detection of genetic defects is a most significant advance towards eugenic control. Do we as physicians, theologians, parents and human beings want this procedure carried out or not? Do we support therapeutic abortion, or not? Does Professor Smith (and this audience) support the right of a mother to have a therapeutic abortion when her fetus has been proven to be defective? If he does, what is his attitude towards those regions of the country where such a procedure is not now legal? If he maintains that the law should be changed, then he is going against his stated position that we should not rush into changing population policies.

Let me make clear that I do not mean to put Professor Smith "on the spot." My objective here is to emphasize that as a physician I cannot always sit back and debate the issue in a detached manner. I must face the young couple who have one defective child and who fear another. General principles are of little use to them. They face very specific decisions and their decisions are enormously influenced by the laws of their locality. I agree with Professor Smith that this couple ought to have the right to make the decisions concerning their own offspring, but what should be done if the local laws prevent this?

Next, I would like to bring up several fairly important points for clarification. Professor Smith lists twenty or so disorders which can be diagnosed in utero by means of amniocentesis and subsequent tissue culture and biochemical analysis. Once a defect is detected, he states that three choices then exist: first, to terminate the pregnancy; second, to attempt to manage the disease; or third, to accept the defect and try to make the best of it. Although I do apprecitae that Professor Smith is only attempting to classify the choices. I must caution against giving each choice equal weight. Specifically, one should consider adopting the third "choice" only with great hesitation. Although it might be the most humane course of action, it is only with great trepidation and soul-searching that a physician would counsel a parent to accept the defect and not try to correct it. Professor Smith's point, of course, is that there are some defects (such as Down's Syndrome) in which the fundamental error cannot be corrected and where a parent might decline extensive surgery which would help, but in no way cure, the child. I would feel less strongly if as an example, Professor Smith had used polydactylia, i.e., extra finger(s) or toe(s). In this latter case, one could easily "accept" the condition and live with it, rather than to have the extra digit amputated. There are cases, of course, in which the defect is so severe that the decision is made not to manage the disease at all, but rather to allow "nature to take its course." This situation actually defines a fourth category, since such a case does not involve trying to make the best of the defect.

A second point about which I would take mild issue with Professor Smith is his statement that genetic counseling is "a case of professional privitization," that it is "more or less under wraps." This is not true; on the contrary, it is the wish of every genetic counselor that genetic principles be widely known and understood. Young couples seldom consider genetic problems until they have already had a child with a serious defect. Geneticists have always pleaded that prospective parents read about and understand the principles imparted in genetic counseling. I would also take some issue with the statement that advice from a genetic counselor is "less defensible" when parents are directed towards the termination of a pregnancy. In the situation where a given baby would have a syndrome from birth characterized by irreversible blindness, mental retardation, spasticity, seizures, pain and suffering, and who would die within months, I feel that it is completely correct to encourage the parents to make the decision that the pregnancy should be terminated. If the mother does not want to terminate her pregnancy, then this should be her right regardless of the personal feelings of the physician. There are those, of course, who maintain that it is immoral to terminate such a pregnancy; that this poor baby who has suffered a tragic and pitiful mistake of nature "deserves" to have a chance to live, I have heard outstanding theologians argue this position. But I would agree with Professor Smith in asserting that loving and compassionate parents should make the decision concerning whether their defective infant should come to term. If the parents do want to terminate the pregnancy but they feel great anxiety in being totally responsible for this fateful decision, then I believe it is not just the right, but rather the responsibility, of the physician to support the decision of the parents. It is very difficult to do the "right thing" in situations such as this. The physician finds himself "playing God" at times and this is a most uncomfortable position. Nonetheless, these times do exist and physicians must do the best they can in any given situation.

Thus, while I find this a thought-provoking paper and agree entirely with the principles Smith has stated, I find it difficult at times to apply these principles in the real world. I do not know the correct answers to the many moral and ethical questions that have been posed here, but I do feel that continued open discussion of these difficult questions is essential if society is to reconcile the new advances in genetics with its collective conscience.

27

THE PUBLIC REGULATION OF ABORTION

E. Clinton Gardner

In *The Morality of Abortion,* John T. Noonan, Jr., identified four forces which contributed to the dramatic changes in attitudes toward abortion during the decade of the 1960's.[1] First was the desire for professional automony on the part of trained physicians who believed that the discision to abort was basically a medical decision which should be made by those who are medically competent. Second was mounting pressure to provide efficient means of population control in view of the critical growth in world population. Third was the revolt against all traditional codes of morality and the demand of sexual autonomy. Viewed in this light, abortion as a final means of controlling pregnancy represents the maximization of the freedom of women to determine their own sexual behavior. Fourth was a related trend in contemporary culture, *viz.,* the desire for rational control over one's future, including one's environment as well as one's personal and family life.

This more permissive attitude toward abortion in our American ethos quickly manifested itself in a demand for less restrictive abortion laws in the various states. At the beginning of the sixties the existing statutes allowed only for therapeutic abortions. In order to qualify for such an abortion the operation had to be performed on the basis of medical or psychiatric indications to preserve the life or, in a number of states, the health of the pregnant women. In some states the life and/or health of the latter was interpreted broadly by judicial opinion to include mental as well as physical factors. In a similar manner, in those few states where the law did not expressly permit therapeutic abortion the courts tended to read this exception into the law.[2]

In the early 1960's the American Law Institute proposed a Model Penal Code which, if enacted into law, would permit a licensed physician to perform an abortion "if he believes there is a substantial risk that continuance of the pregnancy would gravely impair the physical or mental health of the mother or that the child would be born with grave physical or mental defect, or that the pregnancy resulted from rape, incest, or other felonious intercourse."[3] The last named category was intended to include "all illicit intercourse with a girl below the age of 16." The Model Penal Code also carried the stipulations that a justifiable abortion must be performed in a licensed hospital, except in case of emergency when hospital facilities are not available and that it must be recommended by two physicians who certify in writing the circumstances which in their opinion justify the particular abortion.

The proposed Model Penal Code of the American Law Institute gave focus and impetus to the movement to liberalize the restrictive laws of the various states on abortion. In part, such efforts have been aimed at the reform of the existing laws; in part, they have been directed toward the removal of abortion from the area of criminal law. By the end of 1971 more than one-fifth of the states had modified their statutes to include a broader range of legal indications for abortions.[4] Three states—Alaska, Hawaii, and New York—had enacted statutes permitting abortion-on-request under certain prescribed circumstances pertaining to the performance of the act by a licensed physician or surgeon in approved hospitals or other facilities (Alaska and Hawaii), the length of pregnancy (in New York, the first 24 weeks; in Alaska and Hawaii, before the period of viability of the fetus), and domicile requirements (in Alaska, 30 days; in Hawaii, 90 days).[5]

It is not my purpose to trace the variations in the existing statutes or to describe in detail the changes which have been effected in the recent reforms which have been enacted in a number of states. Such a task would prompt a paper in itself, and it would also require the skills of a specialist in the field of law. The purpose of this essay is rather to identify some of the ethical issues involved in the current debate over the public regulation of abortion and to propose an alternative approach to these issues based upon responsibility rather than upon "natural rights." Nevertheless, a brief look at the directions which abortion reform legislation has taken in this country in recent years will help to focus attention upon some of the ethical issues in the debate over abortion legislation in their present context. Roy Lucas summarizes these developments in terms of five trends.[6] First, at least five states have enacted statutes permitting abortion in order to protect the woman's physical or mental health. Secondly, at least six states now specifically provide for the termination of pregnancies caused by rape, and three of these also authorize abortion in the case of incest. In the third place, four states permit abortion where there is a strong probability of fetal deformity or mental retardation. A fourth kind of change has been the specification of residence requirements upon patients in order to be eligible for an abortion. Finally, legislative reforms in at least three states have included time limitations for the performance of abortions. Such restrictions have been based upon an effort to bring the law into conformity with a medically informed understanding of the development of the fetus and the dangers which an abortion poses for the woman during the later stages of pregnancy.

Speaking generally, the abortion reform legislation which was enacted in this country during the sixties represented a removal of legal barriers to abortion and a reliance, instead, upon the woman's choice and the physician's judgment. As a whole the reformed abortion statutes also constituted an effort to overcome the ambiguities of the older laws through a more specific definition of the provisions of the law itself. By the end of the sixties there was a mounting demand not just for the reform but for the abolition of all abortion laws. The reasons for this change continued to be essentially those cited by Noonan: the professional autonomy of physicians, the demand of women for greater freedom and control over their sexual behavior, the desire of rational planning for one's future, and population control.

All of these movements operated within the context of a growing pluralism in contemporary life. Significantly, however, the advocates both of reform and of abolition of abortion legislation have generally assumed that abortion is at best a "lesser evil," an "unhappy choice that one would wish to avoid." [7] Doubtless, different persons (including physicians, lawyers, theologians, ethicists, and others involved in the shaping of public opinion on this subject) would, if pressed, give different reasons why they reject abortion as an ideal alternative to the continuation of pregnancy under any circumstances. Some would doubtless do so for medical reasons; others, for theological, religious considerations. But the fact that abortion is generally considered as at best morally ambiguous is evidence in itself that it is an ethical issue and not merely a question of positivistic law or personal convenience.

The campaign for the liberalization and/or abolition of abortion laws has given rise to a number of new counter-groups and organizations opposed to abortion on demand. Among these anti-abortion groups are the Value of Life Committee (Cambridge, Massachusetts), Right to Life committees in many communities throughout the United States, the Solid Rock League of Women (Houston), the Coalition for Life (California), Chance of a Lifetime (Washington), Birthright (largely female groups in Washington and Atlanta), Women Concerned for the Unborn Child (Pittsburgh), and Citizens Concerned for Life (Minnesota). In general such groups lobby against the liberalization of abortion legislation, and they also seek to spread anti-abortion propaganda. Their membership cuts across a wide range of religious views and includes Roman Catholics, members of the Greek Orthodox Church, fundamentalists, a sizeable number of liberal Protestant theologians and ethicists, and Orthodox Jews. Those groups which have traditionally opposed abortion on religious grounds have found new allies from among those who have recently become alarmed by the moral consequences of the changes that are taking place both in abortion legislation and also in the new permissiveness toward abortion in the name of individual rights.

In the course of the controversy over the liberalization of abortion laws, a number of issues have emerged and a number of important gains have been made toward a better understanding of these issues. For example, there is greater awareness of the dated character of the prevailing abortion laws which were enacted before the advent of modern medicine and before the full-fledged development of pluralism in our society. These laws were written, moreover, before the problems of population growth and the threat to man's environment had become urgent isues and before the new consciousness of women's liberty had emerged. Debate over the existing abortion laws has also resulted in a clearer understanding of the inequities in the application of these laws to the rich and the poor in our society. Similarly, it has issued in a greater realism concerning the limits of law as an instrument of moral control particularly in a society which is increasingly pluralistic and secular. Recognition of this fact has pointed to the need for a new consideration both of the function of law and' of the relationship of law to sectarian morality.

Hopefully, with the identification of the issues at stake both in the public regulation of abortion and in abortion itself the discussion may now move into a more constructive stage. Recognition of the need for fuller examination of the whole range of issues which are raised by abortion is widespread. Unfortunately, however, it is still difficult to renounce appeals to rhetoric and the use of labels which pre-judge the issues which need to be re-examined. To call abortion "murder," for example, is to foreclose any real examination of what abortion is and how it differs from the intentional taking of human life after birth. Likewise, simply to argue on the basis of the unexamined assumption that a fetus is a child or a person is to refuse to take seriously the question as to whether a fetus may differ from a person after birth.

In *The Morality of Abortion,* John T. Noonan, Jr., forcibly argues that the basic issue at stake in the debate about abortion is the question, "What is Man?" Yet this issue of the meaning and nature of our humanity is generally overlooked by the advocates of more permissive attitudes and policies relating to abortion. The answer which Noonan gives to this fundamental question may be summarized thus: human life begins at conception and the fetus possesses equal rights with all other human beings. This in essence is the position of the Roman Catholic Church. This answer does not mean that all abortions are absolutely prohibited. It does mean, however, that the fetus is inviolable and that abortion can never be justified on the ground that it is good for the fetus itself. In cases of the conflict of human life with human life, however, there is the possibility that an abortion may be permissible. Moral theologians in the Catholic tradition deal with such cases in terms of "direct and indirect consequences" and in terms of the principle of "double effect."

The case which Paul Ramsey builds against abortion is closely akin to that of Roman Catholicism.[8] Ramsey argues along two lines, one genetic and one theological, to demonstrate that human life begins at conception and that from that point onward the fetus places the same claims upon the community as human beings who have been born. On the one hand, he appeals to a genetic description of the development of the fetus in order to maintain that the beginning of human life might be located at any one of the following three stages: (1) conception (when the unique genotype originates), (2) implantation/segmentation (when it is irreversibly determined whether there will be 1, 2, or more individuals), or (3) the early development of the fetus (from the time when brain activity and/or heartbeat first appear or when all of the essential organic formations are present or when spontaneous movement of the fetus may first be detected). Modern genetics may thus give a demonstrable biological answer to the question which theologians have been forced to answer only in speculative terms, viz., when does human life begin? The most persuasive answer, Ramsey believes, is that human life begins at the sequential beginning of it, viz., at the moment of impregnation when a new genotype comes into being bearing its distinctive genetic code. One might, however, also place the beginning of human life at one of the other stages in the development of the fetus. In any event, Ramsey suggests abortion legislation such as that proposed in the Model Penal Code should take the fetus and its process of development into account. The early stages of the development of the fetus are more critical in the determination of the human quality of life than is either quickening or birth; hence, if the sanctity of human life is to be protected, it should be protected "in its beginning" and not in its later stages only.

Despite the vigor with which he presses his argument for the humanity of the fetus based upon genetics, Ramsey confesses that this argument is in the end basically irrelevant for Christian ethics. "Having begun with all these distinctions and theories about when germinating-life becomes human," he writes, "it is now necessary for me to say that from an authentic religious point of view none of them matters very much." [9] Thus Ramsey turns from genetics to theology to build the real case, from the standpoint of religious faith, for the dignity and sanctity of human life from its earliest stages. The argument from genetics is based upon the assumption that the sanctity of life rests upon something that is inherent in the embryo or fetus from a particular stage of development onward. From the standpoint of religious faith, however, the value of human life is grounded in creation, Ramsey declares, and more particularly in the relationship of human procreation to the creative action of God. Thus "sanctity" is bestowed upon human life by reason of its relationship to the divine will in calling human life into existence through the procreative act. "*Sub specie Dei* human procreation is pro-creation," he writes, and this means "procreation in God's behalf." [10] Thus, from its beginning nascent life shares in the "blessing and sanctity and protection which God places over all human lives." Nascent life participates in the covenant relationship in which man stands with his fellowman. With Barth, Ramsey holds that embryonic life shares fully and equally in that dignity and "respect" and sanctity which all men possess by reason of their common humanity. For this reason nascent life places equal claims upon society for the same charity and respect and protection as does human life after birth.

Assuming as he does, then, that the fetus is fully human, Ramsey is unable to conceive of any argument that could really justify abortion which would not at the same time justify infanticide. Indeed, most arguments for the termination of pregnancy are stronger arguments for infanticide than for abortion, he believes, since the uncertainties of the medical indications would be greatly reduced. Ramsey does not, however, reject abortion in every instance any more than do Roman Catholic theologians. Like the latter he, too, appeals to the distinction which Catholic moralists make between *direct* and *indirect* abortion. While it is never permissible directly and primarily to intend the death of a fetus, it may be permissible to abort the latter in order to save the life of the mother if the fetus is the "material aggressor" in mortal conflict between the two.

In the two positions to which we have referred thus far, viz., the traditional position of Roman Catholicism and that of Paul Ramsey, the sanctity of human life includes equally that of the fetus from its beginning; and abortion is permissible only as a secondary and indirectly intended consequences of action aimed at the preservation of the life of a mother or, if the life of the mother is in irremediable danger, that of the fetus itself. But clearly other theologians and Christian moralists who also recognize the sanctity of human life are led to different perceptions of the claims of nascent life in its initial stages and to more permissive attitudes toward abortion on a variety of grounds. It has been noted, for example, that Ramsey appeals to Karl Barth's understanding of the "respect" that is due even to "germinating life" because of its relationship to God.[11] On account of the relationship which embryonic life bears to the Creator and also to the Giver of eternal life, God commands its protection.[12] This is the "direction" of the Divine command; the protection of all human life is the line along which the Divine command always moves. Hence, abortion is forbidden unless it in itself becomes the "ultima ratione in its surrender and sacrifice."

Since human life is not an absolute value, there is the possibility that the destruction of fetal life may in certain "exceptional cases" be not only permitted but even commanded.[13] Such exceptional cases are very carefully circumscribed by Barth, and they come into consideration only after proper attention has been given to the inviolability of all human life insofar as such inviolability is in keeping with the requirement to protect life. The exceptional case arises only when absolute adherence to this principle results, one might say "indirectly," in a greater destruction of life. Instances of the exceptional case include those pregnancies in which both the nascent and the maternal lives are faced with well-nigh certain death unless the former is destroyed, but they also include pregnancies in which the only viable choice is that between the life or health of the mother, on the one hand, and the fetus, on the other. As compared with Ramsey, the distinctiveness of Barth's position is two-fold. It lies, first of all, in the provision which Barth makes for the possibility that an abortion may in a particular instance be an act which is commanded (and therefore a duty) rather than simply permitted. Barth's position is also distinguished from Ramsey's by the possibility which the former envisages that abortion might be commanded even in certain rare instances in which the health of the mother would be seriously threatened by the continuation of a pregnancy.

Other Protestant ethicists whose attitudes toward abortion are more permissive, or at least less rigid, than those of Noonan, Ramsey, and Barth also recognize that nascent life is in some sense human and therefore sacred. James M. Gustafson and Harmon Smith, for example, defend abortion on broader moral grounds than the writers whom we have been considering. Nevertheless, they insist that it is at best only a bad and therefore morally culpable act. Such a judgment seems to imply that embryonic life has *human* value and that it therefore places some *human* claims upon society to protect it. Thus Harmon Smith concludes his analysis of "Abortion and the Right to Life" in *Ethics and the New Medicine* with the judgment that while abortion is not murder, "it can, and ought always to be considered a *genuinely regrettable* alternative to unwanted pregnancy." [14] In a similar manner, James M. Gustafson draws an analogy between the concept of the just war in Christian ethics and abortion in his description of "A Protestant Ethical Approach" to the latter. Gustafson writes: "As the morally conscientious soldier fighting in a particular war is convinced that life can and ought to be taken, 'justly' but also 'mournfully,' so the moralist can be convinced that the life of the defenseless fetus can be taken, *less justly, but more mournfully.*" [15]

Up to this point we have been attempting to show why, from a religious point of view, the most fundamental ethical issue in abortion is that of the sanctity of human life, including human life in its initial stages. This question is basic because it focuses attention upon that set of claims which are most completely overlooked in the movements to make abortion a private matter between a woman and her physician, to make it a matter of medical judgment only, and to reduce it to utilitarian considerations of social consequences. But even among those who acknowledge the sanctity of human life including nascent life, there is considerable disagreement about the implications of this religious view. Theologians and moralists differ with regard to the *specific* claims which nascent life places upon society to protect it. They differ, for example, as to whether all forms of human life from impregnation to the grave place equal and identical claims upon society for protection. Theologians and moralists who recognize the dignity of all human forms of life also differ among themselves as to the absoluteness of such claims and the proximate ground upon which these claims rest. Noonan and Ramsey tend to speak of certain rights which are absolute and which are bestowed upon all human life from the time of conception onward. Others tend to interpret such claims in more relational terms and thus set them in the context of a *community of claims*. Barth does this in principle although he strictly limits the application of this concept in practice. James M. Gustafson and Harmon Smith allow for a greater relativization of these claims by placing them in the context of many other claims and values. In this connection it should be noted that many Roman Catholic writers—notably Daniel Callahan,[16] for example—have employed a similar relational concept of rights in their approaches to abortion and have therefore rejected the more rationalistic interpretation of the doctrine of "natural rights" associated with traditional Catholic moral theology.

What conclusions, then, can be drawn from the claim that all human life has dignity and worth which are ultimately grounded in the relationship which it bears to the Creator? What are the implications of this fundamental conviction for personal decisions concerning the termination of pregnancy and also for the public regulation of abortion?

It is the thesis of the present paper that these questions can be responsibly answered only as they are raised in the context of *a community of claims* rather than in a context of autonomous rights, whether of physicians or of women or of society as a whole. Whether we will it so or not, the decisions which we make in our individual freedom do affect the destinies of many other lives which share in our common humanity. This is the covenant relationship in which we stand in our given created existence. Seen in this context, there are many claims which each life places on those upon whom it is dependent for fulfillment. These claims are not always the same because the needs in which they are grounded differ. Protecting the sanctity of human life means recognizing the different needs as well as the different capacities of life in its different stages of development from the formation of the genotype to death. It means giving different valences to many different interrelated values and needs—physical protection; the need to be wanted; the need for physical, emotional, moral, and spiritual nature—at different stages of human development and awareness. Responsibility means taking all such needs and claims into account and seeking to fulfill them to the fullest extent possible in the community of all mankind out of the motivation of neighbor-love.

Responsibility is also concerned with the consequences of any decision relating to abortion and not with the motivation of Christian charity only. Moreover, it is concerned with the totality of the con-

sequences involved in the choice and not with the preservation of life
in isolation from all other claims for human fulfillment. In order to
differentiate between the claims which human life makes in its
earliest stages of potentiality and those which it makes when it arrives
at the stages of consciousness and self-awareness, a distinction should
perhaps be made between "humanoid" and "human" life. Such a
distinction could not be absolute, but it would call attention to the
differences which do in fact exist between embryonic life and a
"child" or a "person," differences which account for the fact that an
intentional termination of pregnancy is commonly differentiated from
murder, including infanticide as well as homicide.

When the sanctity of life is considered in terms of a community of
claims rather than from the perspective of autonomous rights, the
question arises as to whether an abortion may ever be defended as
being good for the fetus. It is usually if not universally assumed by
theological ethicists that abortion can never be justified as being
good for the fetus. Such a conclusion would be obvious on the basis
of an exclusively biological understanding of nascent life. However,
if the needs of the fetus are understood in relationship to the tragic
consequences of extreme physical deformity, brain injury, and inevitable hunger, emotional starvation, and rejection, charity might
under these circumstances lead to a responsible decision for an abortion
for the sake of the fetal life itself. Obviously such a decision would
only be justifiable in the sense that it were the lesser of several evils,
but it would be justifiable as a charitable although tragic response to
the claims of nascent life itself.

In view of the approach to the moral issues in abortion decisions
which has been outlined above, the questions of a woman's right to
have an abortion on request and that of the freedom of a physician
to decide whether or not to perform an abortion exclusively on medical grounds can be treated briefly for present purposes. The "sanctity of life" means not only the recognition of the claims of nascent
life; it means also that consideration must be given to the claims
which other individuals and/or groups place upon each moral agent
and also upon society. These claims include the claims of the mother,
the father, other children whose welfare might be affected by the birth
of a particular baby, and society as a whole. Here the whole range of
social, economic, and population questions come into view, and they
must be taken into account. The basic point which needs to be made
once again in regard to the demand for laws permitting abortion on
request is this: these values confront the moral agent primarily as

claims, and they cannot be ethically understood primarily as rights of individuals who personally desire *these* values for themselves. The self and other moral agents are *responsible* selves in their freedom, not autonomous selves.

Two fundamentally different but related issues are involved in the demand for laws permitting abortion on request. One is the legal issue of woman's civil liberties; the other is the personal ethical issue of the values and duties and responsibilities which are at stake in the exercise of that freedom. To be sure, the legal issue also has an ethical dimension, for it poses the question of the claims of nascent life which might be jeopardized by granting a pregnant woman absolute control over the destiny of the fetus for life or for death. But the legal issue does not in itself predetermine what decision a particular woman will make regarding a particular pregnancy. The issue of civil liberties is an issue of public policy; the question of the individual's use of such liberties is a matter of personal ethics. Both, however, are fundamentally questions of claims rather than autonomous rights. Viewed in this light, rights for the self are based upon duties or claims with which the self is confronted. Rights are limited by the needs and claims of others; thus, they are never absolute.

As it is generally propounded, the argument for abortion on request rests upon the assumption that a woman has a fundamental right to control her own body, including the right to decide unilaterally whether or not to terminate a pregnancy. Such a right, it is alleged, is an essential requirement of her dignity and freedom. This position fails to take adequate account of the need to protect whatever claims the fetus, the father, and society may have in the abortion decision. It does, however, call attention to the crucial position of the woman in whatever decision is finally made whether within the law or outside of the protection of the law. It represents a recognition also of the *claims upon the woman herself* (claims of other children which she may have for education and food and emotional support, claims of the father and others who are in various ways dependent upon her, claims of unborn generations in the face of mounting population and ecology crises). In order to protect the woman's freedom to make a responsible decision in the light of all of these competing claims, the existing laws in most states need to be made much less restrictive. Such a reform of excessively restrictive laws is needed both out of consideration for the dignity and freedom of women and also out of consideration for nascent life itself in view of its dependence upon the mother for its nurture and development. It is needed for the protection of the sanctity of life. This does not mean, however, that no laws are needed either for the protection of woman's freedom or for protection of the fetus in its later stages of development or for the safeguarding of the interests which society has in the protection of nascent life.

The argument that an abortion is essentially a medical procedure and that a physician should have the freedom to decide whether or not to perform an abortion entirely upon medical grounds raises basically the same kinds of questions as the argument that a woman should be able to secure an abortion on request. Obviously, the surgical procedure in an abortion is a medical procedure, but merely to assume that this is all that is involved is question-begging.

If we assume that nascent life places any claim upon society for its protection, this responsibility falls upon all members of the community who participate directly or indirectly in decisions related to the termination of such life. Just as the woman needs to have her freedom to make a responsible decision recognized and protected, so the physician should be given similar freedom and protection. Such freedom, it should be emphasized, is for the sake of responsibility first of all, and most directly, to the woman seeking professional medical help; but it is also freedom for the sake of responsibility toward particular fetuses for conscience' sake. Hence the physician's right to refuse to perform an abortion should be protected. Beyond this, however, the claims of fetal life, the claims of the father, and the interests of society provide additional elements which enter into the formation of a responsible decision with such an interlocking network of consequences as abortion.

The interests of society constitute still another issue in the public regulation of abortion. Here the basic question may be stated quite briefly: Does the practice of abortion diminish the value or sanctity of human life as a whole? Does it threaten to diminish the dignity and worth of each member of society?

On the basis of the distinction made earlier between the claims of "humanoid" (potentially human) and "human life," it seems necessary to conclude that the sanctity of human life would be more adequately protected by the adoption of less restrictive abortion laws. Protecting the sanctity of human life means protecting the quality of life for each human being. It includes protecting the freedom of women to be responsible in their decisions to bear children. It includes providing physical and emotional and spiritual nuture for every child. It includes commitment to abolition of poverty and war. Evils such as these, rather than abortion, are among the evident, certain de-humanizing forces in our society. After an exhaustive study of abortion in a number of countries, Daniel Callahan found no empirical evidence to substantiate the claim that permissive abortion laws do in fact undermine the worth of human life. He wrote: "The uniqueness of the abortion situation—where it is a question of potential human life (increasingly but gradually actualized as it develops)—means that it is all but impossible to extrapolate from attitudes toward fetal life attitudes toward existing human life . . . . In short, it cannot be said how the life of those already living would be harmed by the taking of the life of the unborn." [17] Edward Shils similarly declares: "There are many good reasons to regret abortion or the necessity for it—effective contraception would be much more satisfactory—but I think that for our purposes it should be said that the principle of the sanctity of life of the individual as an individual, or the life of the lineage as the lineage of separate organisms, is not infringed or affronted by abortion in the earlier stages of pregnancy." [18]

Thus, there does not seem to be any warrant in empirical data for prohibiting abortion in order to protect the value of human life. This does not imply, however, that society's interest cannot and should not be protected through the enactment of *regulatory* laws rather than prohibitory legislation. Examples of such regulative statutes would be laws preventing the destruction of nascent life in its later stages, laws making adequate counseling services and hospital facilities available to all women seeking abortion, and laws requiring that abortions be performed only by qualified physicians.

Discussion of the interest of society in the public regulation of abortion has already raised the question of the function and limits of law in a pluralistic society. It should be noted, at this point, that the public interest is served by safeguarding the freedoms of the members of society to follow their consciences so long as this freedom is consistent with the common good. In a pluralistic society the public interest is nurtured by private, voluntary groups, including religious groups. Such groups nourish the dignity of our common humanity in so far as they preserve and transmit their heritages of religious faith and responsibility to God and one's fellowman according to conscience.

From the standpoint of Christian ethics, the ideal solution to the problem of abortion as a method of dealing with unwanted pregnancies would be the recovery of the religious bond between sexuality and responsibility for procreation represented in monogamous marriage. While every sexual act would not intend procreation, it would nevertheless take place in the context of a relationship in which the sacredness of sex was acknowledged, the mystery of creation was recognized, and responsibility for the creation of new, human life was accepted in a community of loyalty symbolized by monogamous marriage. This aim and this strategy is good within the context of the Judaic-Christian tradition, but it cannot be imposed by law upon society as a whole as the solution to the problem of abortion because we live in a pluralistic, secular society. It is, however, a profound contribution of the religious community to the sanctity of life in society as a whole.

But, beyond this, it must also be recognized that abortion is like-wise much too stubborn a problem to be dealt with in such an idealistic way even in the religious community, for even here unwanted pregnancies do occur and here the same reasons for permitting abortion occur which arise in secular society. The problem raises the question of the priority of claims in dealing with an issue that is characterized by conflicting claims. Hence, the church must deal with the prob-lem of abortion at two levels, viz., that of the individual and that of public policy. The thrust of the present paper has been to argue that the prohibitory and highly restrictive abortion laws which are presently part of the criminal statutes of most states in this country should be replaced by laws which are regulatory and permissive within certain broad limits.

Our purpose has been to identify and clarify some of the ethical issues involved in the public regulation of abortion, not to develop a model law. The latter is a task for lawyers, a task which needs to be informed by ethical reflection upon the values and claims which the law is intended to serve. As Norman St. John-Stevas points out, law and morality are closely related. The law both reflects and preserves the moral consensus of society. It not only gives expression to the general moral consensus at a particular time; it also serves a pedagogical function in so far as it molds and nutures attitudes and values by giving public sanction to particular norms. Many values and many claims are at stake in the public regulation of abortion. Among these are the rights of the fetus, the rights of the individual woman seeking an abortion, the rights of other members of her family, the professional integrity of physicians, and the claims of society as a whole.

In its final *Report* (March, 1972) the Commission on Population Growth and the American Future has set forth the position that abortion should be included as one element in a comprehensive health care system, although it should not be considered a substitute for birth control. It is regrettable, however, that in its recommendations the Commission follows the liberalized New York State statute (New York Penal Law 125.05) too uncritically and thus fails to give adequate attention to the *regulation* of abortion.

The majority of the Commission held "that women should be free to determine their own fertility, that the matter of abortion should be left to the conscience of the individual concerned, in consultation with her physician and that states should be encouraged to enact affirmative statutes creating a clear and positive framework for the practice of abortion on request." Both health and ethical considerations, however, indicate that the provision in the New York statute for abortion within the first twenty-four weeks of pregnancy needs to be revised downward to take into account the developmental stages of embryonic-fetal life such as the first signs of brain activity, the beginnings of heart-beat, and the stage of "viability." [19] In medical terminology, the induced termination of pregnancy prior to the twentieth week is called an *abortion;* after that date it is referred to as a *premature delivery.* The significance of this distinction in medical practice as well as other stages in embryonic-fetal development, should be taken into account in statutes regulating abortion, not only for the sake of the fetus itself but also for the safety of the woman and for the protection of the sanctity of human life.

In addition, greater consideration needs to be given to the quality as well as the availability of sex counseling, contraceptive information programs and services, and pregnancy and abortion counseling services than either the Commission's Report or the New York statute provides. Unless such services are made available in a manner which is consistent with a proper respect for both the freedom and the integrity of persons seeking an abortion, such persons are dehumanized and the sanctity, or dignity, of human life is thereby demeaned through "shameless exploitation" and manipulation. In short, without adequate regulation, illegal abortion mills tend to be replaced by legalized abortion mills.

The following statement on abortion by the Council for Christian Social Action of the United Church of Christ can be commended as an example of the kinds of considerations which should be taken into account in the revision of existing abortion laws. The formulation of the revised statutes themselves is the proper task of lawyers and legislators in the field. The Council's statement reads as follows:

"The Council for Christian Social Action in recognition of the urgency and seriousness of the abortion problem in the United States, adopts the following:

"A responsible position concerning abortion should be based on a consideration of the rights of the individual woman, her potential child, her family and society, as well as the rights of the fetus.

"Many present abortion laws are neither just nor enforceable. They compel many women either to bear unwanted children or to seek illegal abortion regardless of the medical hazards and suffering involved. By severely limiting access to safe abortions, these laws have the effect of discriminating against the poor.

"While there is wide variation in theological and scientific views as to when personal human life begins, a majority of experts as well as of the general population would probably agree that such life should not be interrupted during the last months of a normal pregnancy except for the most serious reasons (such as physical or mental health of the mother, abnormality of the fetus, incest, or rape). At the same time, an increasing number of persons find it difficult, if not impossible, to attribute anything more than the potentiality of human existence to the embryo in its early stages. A wise law will recognize these realities, repealing legal restrictions on physician-performed abortions during the early months of pregnancy and permitting the physician to determine the applicability of more limited criteria thereafter. The right of physician or patient to refuse abortion on moral or medical grounds should in any case be respected.

"The Council calls upon the churches of the United Church and their members to involve themselves extensively in programs which would support the repeal of overly restrictive abortion legislation and to expand their ministries of counsel and concern to all women who have problems related to unwanted pregnancies. We also encourage the expansion of programs of sex education and the wider availability of information and service relating to contraception.

"To implement the foregoing policy statement, the Council calls the foregoing action to the attention of the Social Action Committees of the several Conferences of the United Church of Christ and urges the appropriate CCSA staff to work closely with the Conference Committee to promote—in cooperation with the Conference Health and Welfare Committees—new programs and strengthen existing ones in support of legislative change in the area of abortion." [20]

From the perspective represented in the present paper, this statement constitutes a basically responsible approach to the public regulation of abortion. Legislative reforms along the lines which it suggests would provide adequate protection for the developing claims of the fetus, including premature births, and for those of society than a wholesale repeal of abortion laws. They would also provide protection to the mother as well as guidance to the physician in making provision for the termination of pregnancy in its later stages on account of grave medical, psychological, or social considerations. In addition, such legislation would protect the freedom of both the physician and the patient to refuse an abortion on moral or medical grounds. Finally, the revised laws recommended by the Council would greatly advance the cause of social justice by removing abortion in the early stages of pregnancy from the criminal code and equalizing access to this option through public provision and support of abortion services, including counseling and hospital facilities. In all of these ways regulative laws are necessary for the implementation of social justice. Such laws are needed to balance the rights of freedom with the claims of responsibility in the context of community.

1. John T. Noonan, Jr., ed., *The Morality of Abortion* (Cambridge, Mass.: pp. ix-xvii.

2. See the *Reporter on Human Reproduction and the Law* (Boston: Legal-Medical Studies, Inc., 1971-), p. I-A-1.

3. *Ibid.*, pp. I-B-73.

4. *Ibid.*, pp. I-A-1.

5. For a list of state statutes pertaining to abortion, see RPTR. HRL., pp. I-B-1 ff.

6. Roy J. D. Lucas, " Laws of the United States," in Robert E. Hall, ed., *Abortion in a Changing World*, Vol. 1 (Columbia University Press, 1970), see especially pp. 130-133.

7. Cf. John D. Rockefeller, III, "Abortion Law Reform—the Moral Basis," in Robert E. Hall, *ibid.*, pp. xviii, xx. See also Edwin M. Schur, *Crimes Without Victims* (Prentice-Hall, 1965), p. 62: "Although no responsible student of the subject approves of abortion as a positive good, many argue that often it is a lesser evil than the sacrificing of the mother's life or health."

8. Paul Ramsey, "The Sanctity of Life in the First of It," *The Dublin Review* (Spring 1967), pp. 3-23. See also Ramsey's essay, "Reference Points in Deciding About Abortion," in John T. Noonan, Jr., *op. cit.*, pp. 60-100.

9. Daniel H. Lobby, ed., *Life or Death: Ethics and Options* (Seattle: 1968), p. 70.

10. *Ibid.*, p. 74.

11. See Karl Barth, *Church Dogmatics*, III/4, trans. by A. T. Mackey *et al.* (Edinburgh: 1961), p. 416.

12. *Ibid.*, pp. 397-98.

13. *Ibid.*, pp. 420-21.

14. Harmon Smith, *Ethics and the New Medicine* (Abingdon Press, 1970), pp. 17-54. Italics added.

15. John T. Noonan, Jr., *op. cit.*, p. 122. Italics added.

16. Daniel Callahan, *Abortion: Law, Choice and Morality* (Macmillan Co., 1970).

17. *Ibid.*, p. 475.

18. Edward Shils, "The Sanctity of Life," in Daniel H. Labby, *op. cit.*, pp. 2-38.

19. Cf. Paul Ramsey, "Reference Points in Deciding About Abortion," in John T. Noonan, Jr., *op. cit.*, pp. 60-100. See especially pp. 69-70.

20. *Social Action* (March 1971), pp. 36-38.

28

THE NEGLECTED HISTORY OF ABORTION LAW

Jimmye Kimmey

Clinton Gardner has quoted with approval the judgment of the Council for Christian Social Action (United Church of Christ) that a law "repealing legal restriction on physician-performed abortions during the early months of pregnancy and permitting the physician to determine the applicability of more limited criteria thereafter" would "provide a basically responsible approach to the public regulation of abortion." I, too, can agree with this wholeheartedly. Rather than attempting to criticize Gardner's paper I shall therefore supplement his discussion.

It may be particularly useful to look briefly at the history of public regulation of abortion as it bears directly upon present law. Until quite recently it was thought that under common law abortion was permitted until quickening but forbidden thereafter. It has now been demonstrated persuasively, however, that the common law did not, in fact, forbid abortion at any stage in pregnancy.[1] Whether we accept the earlier view of the common law right or this later, more expanded view we are still left with the question of what prompted legislatures to begin to regulate what had so long been unregulated. In an earlier article, Professor Means examined the legislative history of the adoption of New York's law in 1830 and found that the motive for its passage was what we would now call a concern for public health. The legislative purpose was to protect pregnant women from the danger to their lives imposed by abortion since at that time any surgical intervention placed the woman's life in much greater danger than childbirth did. Professor Means also demonstrated that concern for any supposed rights of the fetus was foreign to the secular thinking of the Protestant legislators of the time.[2] The emphasis changed somewhat in the 1860's and wording of the abortion laws passed then and later betrays a desire to use the law to enforce a particular view of public morality. These Comstockian laws did not, however, evince any concern for the rights of the fetus or any belief that a fetus should be given the protections due to persons under the constitution.

A century later, beginning in the mid-1960's, the movement for abortion law reform can be seen, in part, as a movement to restore legislative protection of public health in this area. The forces which John Noonan identifies as contributing to the changing of attitudes toward abortion (as summarized by Gardner) are not quite those that I would emphasize. One dramatic event in the early '60's sensitized the public to this problem—that event was the Sherri Finkbine case. Mrs. Finkbine had taken thalidomide early in pregnancy for insomnia, and had subsequently learned of the possible danger to her fetus from that thalidomide. She arranged for an abortion in her home state but pressure from the local Catholic and fundamentalist clergy forced the hospital to withdraw its permission. Mrs. Finkbine then went to Sweden where an abortion was performed and the fetus was found to be grossly deformed. Meantime, the details of this case were front page news for quite some time and many people who had before not questioned the justice of the restrictive abortion laws found themselves in sympathy with Mrs. Finkbine's desire for an abortion.

Before that case had time to fade in memory, a rubella epidemic broke out in the United States. By that time (1964) the damage that rubella could do to a fetus in early pregnancy was beginning to be widely understood. The result was that many women demanded and got legal abortions, but tens of thousands of others were prevented from taking that step and either had illegal abortions or ran the risk of delivering defective infants. Public perception of the restrictive laws as unreasonable and unjust was, therefore, reinforced.

Two other general social changes formed the background which made the '60's a propitious time for abortion law reform. One was the civil rights movement. Long before (if long is a word one can use for so recent a development) the neofeminists began to discuss women's rights with respect to abortion, the idea that women should not be dictated to in so personal an area of their lives was accepted within abortion law reform groups as a right which no state could abridge. That sentiment gained strength from the large movement for the recognition of civil rights of oppressed and disadvantaged groups.

Another general change which contributed to the strength of the movement was the growing willingness to accept human sexuality and honesty in discussing it. Whether this was, as Noonan phrases it, a revolt against all traditional codes of morality or whether it was a revolt against doing one thing while saying something else is at least open to question. But there is no doubt about an acceptance of greater openness in talking about sexual matters. This made the abortion law reformers' job easier in the sense that abortion became a problem which could be discussed in meetings and in the media as well as in private.

While the early 19th century move to regulate abortion by law did not spring from any concern over the possible personhood of the fetus, that concern is the basis for most of the present opposition to abortion law reform. Gardner's remark that "this issue of the meaning and nature of our humanity is generally overlooked by the advocates of more permissive attitudes and policies relative to abortions" is one I would, with respect, take issue with. We do examine the question "What is a human being?" but our answer often simply is not the Roman Catholic answer. Many of us do not accept as factual the belief that the pre-viable fetus is a human being possessed of equal rights with all other human beings. Even when we do believe that the pre-viable fetus is a human being the point most abortion law reformers make is that in the face of such conflicting beliefs the law should stand aside so that individuals can exercise their own conscience in this matter.

In one of the American jurisdictions in which individual conscience can be exercised in this matter, the results for public health are beginning to be clear. In New York City—where state law makes abortion on request possible through the first 24 weeks of pregnancy— the results have been excellent. A February 20, 1972 report from the New York City Health Services Administration includes the following details:

• The proportion of first-trimester abortions has continued to grow, from 68.6% in July-September 1970 to 79.1% in July-September 1971.

• A five-year decline in the maternal mortality rate, inclusive of abortion-related deaths, has accelerated since the new law went into effect. In 1971 it reached an all-time annual low of 29 deaths per 100,000 live births—compared to 53 in 1969 and 46 in 1970.

• The infant mortality rate has also reached a new low, from 24.4 deaths per 1,000 live births in 1969 to 21.6 in 1970, to 20.7 in 1971.

• Incomplete abortions—those which hospitals see after abortion has begun elsewhere—also seem to be declining, a possible indication that the new law is reducing the number of criminal abortions. In ten municipal hospitals, incomplete abortions (both induced and spontaneous) averaged 480 a month for July-December 1970, 350 a month for January-June 1971, and 199 a month for July-December 1971. It is assumed the drop is the result of fewer criminal abortions since the number of spontaneous abortions is likely to remain relatively steady.

• The death rate continues to decline. Between July and December of 1971, four deaths occurred in New York City associated with abortions under legal auspices, out of 109,372 abortions. The death rate for that final six-month period was 3.7 deaths per 100,000 abortions. This was down from 5.3 during the first six months and 4.4 during the second six months. The cumulative death rate for the first 18 months under the law is 4.3 per 100,000.

• The other index of safety, the complications rate, has also been steadily improving. For the period July-December 1971, the overall complications rate was 5.7 per 1,000 abortions—the lowest for any six-month period so far. For the first six months the rate was 12.4 per 1,000, and for the second six months it was 6.4 per 1,000.

With respect to out-of-wedlock birth, an April 25, 1972 report from the Health Services Administration stated that "out-of-wedlock births in New York City declined from 31,903 in 1970 to 28,036 in 1971—the first year-to-year decline since 1954 when data on such births began to be recorded."

In New York, and in other jurisdictions where abortion is available on request, the resultant impact in the area of human freedom is not subject to statistical analysis but is none the less real and important both for the persons involved and for a society that has some commitment to that freedom. It is only in a situation of free choice that the moral decision is present.

1. Cyril C. Means, Jr., "The Phoenix of Abortional Freedom: Is a Penumbral or Ninth-Amendment Right about to Arise from the Nineteenth-Century Legislative Ashes of a Fourteenth-Century Common-Law Liberty?" *New York Law Forum* (Vol. XVII, No. 2, 1971), pp. 335-410.

2. Cyril C. Means, Jr., "The Law of New York Concerning Abortion and the Status of the Fetus, 1964-1968: A Case of Cessation of Constitutionality," *ibid.* (Vol. XIV, No. 3, Fall 1968), pp. 411-515.

PART IV

THE MORAL RESPONSIBILITY OF
RELIGIOUS COMMUNITIES

Religious bodies have access to the thinking of millions of people on fundamental value questions. A very large proportion of mankind is consciously related to religious communities of one kind or another. Does this fact impose moral responsibilities upon the leadership of those communities in changing attitudes toward population problems? Do religious institutions have any peculiar moral obligations growing out of their own traditions? Roger L. Shinn's essay on "Religious Communities and Changing Population Attitudes" addresses such questions while taking cognizance of the difficulty of generalizing from the wide diversity of actual religious groups. A professor of Christian ethics at Union Theological Seminary, Dr. Shinn is a widely read author on social questions.

The four essays which follow Shinn's are written by scholars and religious leaders who are equipped to deal with its central questions from Protestant, Catholics, and Jewish perspectives. The longest of these, Arthur Dyck's "Population Problems are Moral and Religious Issues," takes issue with Shinn at a number of points while also presenting a sharp contrast with a number of the other writings in the volume. One example of this is his use of the words of a black woman to illustrate the feelings of impoverished people who resist family planning programs. These words, and Dyck's interpretation, can be contrasted with somewhat contradictory viewpoints from Jessma Blockwick and Evans Crawford. Dr. Dyck is professor of population ethics at the Harvard School of Public Health and a member of the Harvard Center for Population Studies.

David Feldman, Richard A. McCormick, and Evans Crawford explore different angles of the responsibility of religious groups. Rabbi Feldman is a Jewish scholar and a leading authority on the implications of Jewish tradition for birth control. Dr. McCormick is a prominent Roman Catholic moral theologian who teaches at the Bellarmine School of Theology. Dr. Crawford, a black scholar, is Dean of the Chapel at Howard University.

29

RELIGIOUS COMMUNITIES AND

CHANGING POPULATION ATTITUDES

Roger L. Shinn

Religion complicates most human problems. Hence problem solvers often prefer to wish it away. Or they hope to co-opt it for their purposes. But religion is stubborn. It is not easily ignored or co-opted. Whatever else it may be, religion is an expression of deep human impulses, not readily channeled into prescribed programs. It can be more creative and more destructive than social planners would desire.

All this is obviously the case in the problem of population. At the beginning of 1970 James Reston of the *New York Times* wrote about the "developing campaign for population control" that "This is a subject in which the Government and the young and the poor have a common interest. . . . For once, the Nixon Administration and the university student leaders, and men of all races and parties, *though alas not yet of all religions,* have a unifying challenge and topic of debate. . . ." [1] Since writing this, Mr. Reston has probably learned that racial and economic factions are not so easily united on this issue as he thought. But he is correct in pointing out that religion often gets in the way of solutions to social problems. Hence reasonable, idealistic people sometimes hope for the erosion of traditional religious commitments. But that deceptive answer has its own problems, including its reliance upon convictions that themselves need questioning.

The simplest basis for meeting population dangers is a utilitarian ethic that combines rationalism and hedonism. Almost anyone can think of population policies that will reduce suffering and make life easier and more pleasant. An elite, prepared to move "beyond freedom and dignity," might conceivably design a behavioral engineering to ease the human race through its troubles—a dream as old as Plato and as new as yesterday's newspapers. But religious ethics intrude strangely into reasonable visions of survival and harmony. A utilitarian ethic does not easily encompass religious commitments that lead some to choose celibacy and others to accept poverty for the sake of a large family. Religion characteristically questions normal assumptions about happiness, sometimes exalting suffering over happiness and sometimes redefining happiness in ways that jar the social consensus. Hence it is necessary to examine the meaning of religious commitment as it relates to pressing social issues.

Anybody who discusses religious and human values involved in the controversial issues of population already makes some assumptions. For the sake of honesty and clarity I should state my own. I think it is utterly evident that this planet cannot sustain an infinite growth in population. At some stage Zero Population Growth is not merely desirable but is necessary. My judgment is that the time of urgency is now. The alternative to intentional actions is to let disaster bring its own cruel "solutions" to the problem. The ethical issue is not whether population will be restrained; it is whether people will restrain it through actions consistent with humanity's most profound moral sensitivities or through inhumane or catastrophic methods.

However, I cannot agree with Claude Levi-Strauss, the French anthropologist, who says that "the only real problem facing civilization today is the population explosion." [2] Oppression, war, and social injustice are real problems. Frustrations of people struggling for human authenticity in the face of dehumanizing systems are real. Seductions by affluent societies that bribe people into subservience are real. If population is "the only real problem," any answer is better than no answer. If there are many human problems, the choice of answers to any one of them cannot be separated from the other problems. Some conceivable answers to the population crisis are as bad as the crisis. Some such traditional answers are infanticide, genocide, and starvation. Other seemingly benign answers—for example, mass painless compulsory sterilization—may strike intolerable blows at human dignity. The ethical acceptability of all answers depends upon deep convictions and feelings about human nature and destiny. Such convictions and feelings are usually called religious.

Religion is a mixed bag. Its assertions may be unenlightened, dogmatic, or destructive. But they may call for questioning of widely prevalent assertions of any society. Psychologist Gordon Allport in his classical study, *The Nature of Prejudice*, has shown well why the religious impact on any social problem is likely to be diverse. Religion, he says, "usually stands for more than faith—it is the pivot of the cultural tradition of a group." As such it becomes "a rallying point for all sorts of irrelevancies." [3] The situation becomes complicated because it is not easy to sort out the irrelevancies from the fundamentals of faith; one man's faith is another man's irrelevancy. And faiths, even in their most basic convictions, do not always agree with each other. Hence an understanding of the relation between religious communities and population attitudes is hard to come by—even if, as in this paper, we look only at the dominant religious traditions of the west.

The conflicts of religious teachings, noted by James Reston, may lead to an impasse. If clashing religious commandments—for example, on birth control—are dogmatic formulations, each resting on unassailable authority, there is little to discuss. But such conflicts are not common. Rarely do religious communities try to validate ethical teachings by sheer reference to authority—of Bible, of Vatican, of Synod, of majorities. Usually reasons are given to vindicate teachings. And reasons lend themselves to discussion.

Sometimes reasoning appeals to factual evidence. If there are arguments about the world's actual population, about growth rates, about statistical projections of present tendencies, evidence can help to resolve the disagreements. Questions like the relationship between population and starvation or between crowding and health are harder to settle factually, but evidence at least bears on the questions. People of differing religious commitments can compare evidence and sometimes modify their judgments on concrete issues. Most religious communities have changed some of their judgments about population in the last century, and one reason has been the weight of convincing evidence that there is a genuine emergency. In the last analysis, however, a concrete ethical position rarely if ever rests on factual evidence alone. If there are such things as bare facts, isolable from all valuations, such facts do not add up to ethical commitments. Any ethic of population rests on some root assumptions about the *meaning* of sex, of procreation, of the biological continuity of a family or community, of contraception, of social goals. The root assumptions can only partially be verbalized in propositions. Often they are expressed in myths and symbols, in sensitivities that affect perception, in loyalties and commitments.

In such cases ethical discussion includes two aspects. (1) Communities in ethical controversy may find that they share fundamental commitments. If so, they may investigate the reasoning and evidence that lead to opposing conclusions. They may ask whether old commitments today demand new conduct. For example, the same loyalty to posterity might call for a high birthrate in an age of high infant mortality and a low birthrate in another age. Such an issue is discussable, and people may change their minds without abandoning their loyalties. (2) Discussants may find that their root commitments actually differ. Such differences are still discussable, but are not easy to resolve, because there is no court of appeal transcending root commitments. Change of such commitments requires more than discussion. It requires new experiences, often shattering and transforming experiences, that revise persons' perceptions of reality.

Ethical conflicts among religious communities are especially stubborn because such communities constantly remind people that concrete judgments do rest upon root commitments that may not lightly be betrayed. Enlightened humanitarians often grow impatient with religious controversies—as often they should. Social problems may be more easily soluble if people forget their ultimate commitments and settle for utilitarian expediency. But the root commitments are not to be treated frivolously. Their destruction, unless it is part of a conversion to a richer faith, means the destruction of something important in the meaning of persons and communities.

In a time of changing ethical convictions—as our time surely is—the facile response is to take pleasure in the erosion of outworn faiths and ethical laws. A more profound response is to ask what may have been precious in the old commitments and how their deepest meaning may call for new behavior.

One widely shared religious commitment today is to the value of persons or to human dignity. Jewish and Christian faiths find this value, and the sensitivity behind it, imbedded in the Bible. But they recognize that secular humanists and people of non-biblical faiths frequently share this commitment. Human behavior repeatedly betrays the commitment. But the basic motif, once let loose in the world, is hard to stifle. Its acceptance does not lead to unanimity on the ethics of population, but it makes ethical differences discussable.

The formal ethical teachings of the principle religious communities of America are rather easy to locate.[4] Such formal teachings may not always reveal the ethical dynamics at work in those communities, but they are fairly good clues. No major religious community in North America now teaches that it is the consistent duty of men and women to produce large families. Traditional Judaism and Christianity often assumed large families were a blessing and a sign of divine approval, and through most of the centuries of their history these faiths had little awareness of a population problem. But these religious communities know that "new occasions teach new duties" and that responsible parenthood may call for family limitation.

Of the major North American faiths, Roman Catholicism has had the most explicit doctrines on this issue and has, in some respects, been most resistant to change. But Catholic teaching has moved significantly in a short time. A generation ago most Catholic moral theology taught that the primary purpose of the sexual act was procreation, with love and companionship as a secondary purpose. Furthermore many Catholic moralists taught that every act of sexual intercourse, to be moral, must intend procreation. Now no prominent Catholic moral authority teaches those two propositions.

Many Catholics, however, have been disappointed in the traditionalism of the Vatican, especially in Pope Paul's encylical, *Humanae Vitae* (July 25, 1968). While acknowledging conjugal love as "a very special form of personal friendship, in which husband and wife generously share everything," the encyclical maintains that every sexual act "must remain open to the transmission of life." Therefore, although it permits the "rhythm method" of limiting reproduction, it maintains the Roman Catholic ban on contraceptives. In this stand the Pope rejected the advice of his own Papal Commission on Birth Control, which by a 70-14 vote advocated approval of contraception.[5] In an immediate response Father Charles Curran of Catholic University in Washington led a group of Catholic theologians to draw up a statement supporting Catholic couples who might decide that "artificial contraception in some circumstances is permissible and indeed necessary to preserve and foster the values and sacredness of marriage." Something over 700 theologians signed the statement. Later (Nov. 15, 1968) the Catholic bishops of the United States issued a pastoral letter, "Human Life in Our Day," concurring with Pope Paul that contraception is an "objective evil," but granting that circumstances might reduce guilt and that personal conscience might differ from the papal judgment.[6] The French bishops made a stronger endorsement of freedom of conscience.

By this time, it is probably accurate to say, most Roman Catholics in the United States do not feel moral inhibitions about using contraceptives. Some still do. Many more do in other parts of the world. And, while many Roman Catholics have given serious thought to the world's population problem, the formal teaching of the church has only begun (in Pope Paul VI's encyclical, *Populorum Progressio,* 1967) to face the issue adequately.

Protestant doctrine is harder to define, because its teaching authorities are diverse and scattered. But one would have to look long and hard to find any moral objection to family planning, aided by contraception, in contemporary American Protestantism. It was not always so. Protestants, criticizing Roman Catholic efforts to keep legislation against contraceptives in Massachusetts and Connecticut, were often embarrassed to learn that it was their Protestant forebears who put that legislation on the books. Indeed, the change in Protestant beliefs about contraceptives is rather recent. The shift of stance in the Anglican communion between the Lambeth Conferences of 1920 and 1930 was one of the major episodes. By the present, however, most Protestant denominations have deliberately and clearly endorsed family planning and contraceptives as part of responsible parenthood. The change came about through a combination of factors. One influence was the traditional Protestant emphasis on the responsibility of personal conscience. Another was the general relaxation of old moral inhibitions as rising secular forces undermined past authority. Still another was the recovery of an authentic biblical and doctrinal tradition (see below).

Many Protestant groups have gone beyond the issue of family planning to address directly the threat to human values in the population explosion. Both the National Council of Churches and the World Council of Churches have taken up the issue. (These are councils of Protestant and Eastern Orthodox churches, but on this issue they function primarily as Protestant councils.) Several denominations have adopted positions on population. The United Methodist Church, for example, has emphasized "the moral necessity of adopting the small-family norm as an essential principle for stabilizing the size of the population," and has declared that "families with more than two children contribute to the population explosion" ("Population Crisis Resolution," April 25, 1970).

The Jewish community since ancient times has esteemed the family highly and has often regarded a large family as a divine blessing. Judaism has no tradition exalting celibacy. It has long celebrated the sexual joys of marriage, which have not needed justification beyond themselves. At the same time Judaism has taught the duty to marry and to procreate, but that duty can be fulfilled with a small family. Given these basic themes of the Jewish tradition, modern contraceptives have generally been acceptable in the Jewish family ethic. On the other hand, rabbinic teaching has not given much emphasis to the population problem. There are plausible reasons. In most of the world the Jews have been a minority, often persecuted, sometimes nearly decimated. Obviously they were not threatening the world with overpopulation. It should be added that many Jewish scholars, especially in the social sciences, are thoroughly alert to the population explosion and concerned to find answers to it. If they do not claim to speak for Judiasm, they do not feel that their concern for population in any way alienates them from Judaism.

Formal religious belief does not always guide behavior. One obvious reason is the familiar human gap between ideals and practice. Another reason is that religion, as we have already seen, is a complex and subtle aspect of human experience, only partly represented in verbalized teaching. To the extent that religion influences people and communities in their perception of the world and their emotional responses to situations, its effect is probably more significant than its specific ethical statements. Hence we should not expect the brief survey of ethical positions above to correspond precisely to the conduct of people in religious communities.

There are, of course, some discernible connections. In the United States the general assumption, which appears to be roughly accurate, is that Catholics tend to want and have larger families than Jews, with Protestants somewhere between the two. The position of Catholics on the scale might be expected from the traditional ethic of the Roman Catholic church on sex, procreation, and contraception—although the moderate size of most Catholic families confirms the findings of various polls that most Catholics do, in fact, approve contraception.

The tendency of Jewish families to have rather few children does not necessarily follow from, but is consistent with Jewish ethics. The absence of moral inhibition against contraception makes possible the combination of esteem for the conjugal relationship with the small family. But other cultural factors have had their influence since the time of the Old Testament appreciation of large families as a divine blessing. Insofar as the Jewish people, especially in the United States, tend to be more urban, more educated, and more professionally oriented than the general average, their small families are consistent with general demographic tendencies. Furthermore, the high Jewish regard for the family and the concern for the education of children reinforce the tendency to small families.

The Protestant place in the middle of the scale may have less to do with Protestant faith and ethics than with the traditional relationship of Protestantism to "middle America," in the many meanings of that perplexing term. A few Protestant groups are notable for large families. But in general the ethical acceptance of contraception encourages the limitation of family size, while the wide assortment of Protestants (urban-rural, vocational, and educational) means that Protestants in general are not likely to deviate much from the general demographic norms of the society. (Black religious communities are in some ways a special case. See the discussion below.)

Even though these few generalizations about the religious communities are possible, more detailed investigation shows some surprises. To take a single example, it is reported that in 1963 U. S. Baptists had a higher fertility than U. S. Catholics.[7] The difference is certainly not a consequence of formal religious teachings. It is more easily understood on the basis of the difference between a dominantly southern rural and northern urban religious community. The relevance of religion is less its formal ethical teaching than its embodiment in cultural traditions and valuations.

The same case is even more evident on an international basis. For example, Jewish attitudes are more pro-natalist in Israel—for obvious historical and cultural reasons—than in the United States. Roman Catholic demographic data vary widely in different parts of the world. The facts are equally discomforting to those Catholics who think that official church teaching ought to make a difference and to those anti-Catholics who would like to blame Catholicism for the population explosion. As one study points out, "the historic transition from large to small families in the West began in two Roman Catholic nations—France and Ireland."[8] The French decline in birth rate, starting about 1820, took place despite pro-natalist policies of both church and government. In Europe today birth rates in predominantly Catholic countries are barely distinguishable from those elsewhere. And, as is frequently noted, "birth rates are lower in Belgium, France, Italy, Spain and Portugal than they are in the United States."[9]

Latin America, of course, has a very high birth rate, and here the Catholic Church probably could make a difference if it chose to try vigorously. But Catholicism is not the chief determinative factor. Latin American birth rates are comparable to those in many non-Catholic regions of Africa and Asia. The common factors are not religion but poverty and inadequate education. One study indicates that Latin American women who attend Mass frequently have slightly fewer children than merely nominal Catholics.[10] Again and again the data suggest that mothers and fathers, given moderately favorable educational and cultural situations, know how to make up their own minds in relative independence of formal church teachings.

Such information might lead to the conclusion that religion deserves little of the credit or blame for exploding population and that

those who are concerned about population might better turn their
efforts in other directions. But such a judgment is too glib for two
reasons. First, religious groups are conspicuously active in various
controversies about public policy in many parts of the world. They
influence their adherents and bring pressure on government in such
controversial areas as sex education, contraceptives, abortion, and the
relation of foreign aid to population policies of other countries. And
they exercise strong influence on some families. Second, religious influences, as I have already argued, work less through the formal
teachings of the churches than from the ways in which religious attitudes and symbols affect people's self-awareness, purposes, and
perceptions of their worlds.

Therefore it becomes important to examine some of the basic religious commitments and beliefs that influence human behavior. In
the remainder of this paper I shall try to do that. The effort requires
a change in method. My references will be chiefly to experiential and
theological aspects of religion. In dealing less with data and more
with meanings, I inevitably lose some "objectivity," but gain—I
hope—something in depth perception. At any rate, a discussion that
avoids this area of inquiry misses the main point of religious ethics.

The relation of sex to procreation does not need much explaining.
In some imaginable futures of increased artificial insemination, cloning,
and test tube babies, old explanations may need changing. But for
the present a few of "the facts of life" are evident enough.

The status of sex is not evident in anything like the same way.
There are, indeed, many meanings. One such meaning compares the
delights of sex to the burden (personal and social) of child-bearing.
Of course, sex is not simply delightful; it may be predatory, satiating,
revulsive. And child-bearing is not simply burdensome; it may be a
joy. Some women have endured the burden of sex for the sake of
the delight of child-bearing. Thus no one meaning encompasses the
variety of human experience of sex. Nevertheless, a generalization is
possible: people, by and large, want sexual activity more often than
they want procreation. If, as some see it, the lure of sex is nature's
—or God's—way of coaxing mankind to do its duty of continuing
the species, the method has by this time become over-effective.

The religious meanings of sex have, in many human cultures, shown
three dominant facets. First, there is the sheer joy of the sexual relation as an expression of personal intimacy. Second, there is the
creativity of sex, symbolized by but not limited to its role in pro-

creation. Third, there is the daimonic (to use Rollo May's term) —
the mysterious, self-transcending, ecstatic quality that, in its paradoxical union of the creative and the destructive, makes impossible
the trivializing of sex.[11] However diverse the meanings of sex have
been, human cultures have characteristically surrounded it with some
restraints and tabus. In humanity sex is relatively free from the
instinctual controls that govern it in other species. Humankind, aware
of its power and of its predictable consequences, has sought to direct
its energies.

Sometimes people, frightened or distracted by sex, have emphasized
its vicious possibilities or, in a passion for spirituality, have deprecated
its material, fleshly quality. Such attitudes were rather common in the
Mediterranean world in which Christianity developed. Some traditions came to depreciate sex. They could not renounce it (unless as
a special vocation) because they saw it as part of God's purpose for
continuing the human race. But they might maintain that its alluring
non-rational power was a consequence of sin and that its only moral
justification was the purpose of procreation. That tradition I have
already noted above.

There were always counter-currents in the Christian tradition, and
modern history (including the population explosion) has done much
to release them. The religiously significant thing is not that the
churches are abandoning their sexual ethic but that they are redis-
covering it. The most significant interpretation of the sexual relationship in the Old Testament, repeated by Jesus in the New Testament,
describes the joyful union in "one flesh" of husband and wife, with no
hint that procreation is needed to give the union moral justification
(Genesis 2:24, Mark 10:7-8). In recent decades Protestantism and
Catholicism alike have come to renewed appreciation of this heritage,
which Judaism had never forgotten. Even the conservative ethic of
Humanae Vitae acknowledges the importance of sexual love.

Such a meaning of sex signifies that contraceptives can be accepted
as liberating of conjugal love and in no way shameful. Such is now
the understanding of most Jewish, Protestant, and Catholic ethics.
But Catholic teaching remains divided on the issue, with *Humanae
Vitae* still condemning the use of "artificial" methods of birth control.
Many Catholics answer that just as such "artificial" techniques as
medicine, surgery, and sanitation preserve lives that would "naturally"
be lost, so artificial contraceptives heighten human control over procreation to the advantage of the dignity of mankind.

Contraceptive innovations obviously have social "side effects."

They not only liberate marital love; they remove inhibitions to extra-marital sexual expression. One reason for resistance to them is that they threaten the moral tradition that the proper expression of sexual love is within marriage. The secular society, disturbed by the rise of illegitimacy and the "epidemic" of venereal disease, frequently debates whether to encourage the use of contraceptives through education and to make them more easily available to all people including youth.

A religious community might judge that, to whatever extent tradi-tional ethics depends upon sanctions that can now be avoided, such ethics deserve to be modified. To the extent that the moral tradition had other grounds, its validity is unimpaired. An authentic moral tradi-tion does not need extrinsic props. Religious communities might, in fact, welcome the opportunity to build their ethic on intrinsic grounds. Probably the moral situation is not quite so simple as that judgment would imply, because the fabric of any social morality is a rather deli-cate weaving of many personal and cultural influences. Perhaps few people would be honest or generous or humane if the culture provided no extrinsic reinforcements. But the fact is that humanity can now separate sexual activity from procreation, not only in specific instances but on a consistent basis; and religious communities will learn to live with the possibility of that separation. In doing so, they may learn more clearly than ever before what they really mean by and expect from the sexual relation.

The fact that a hedonistic sexual ethic and the trivializing of sexual pleasure are now more feasible does not mean that they are ethically desirable. The three facets remain real: joy in sexual intimacy, crea-tivity, and the daimonic. The ethical task of the religious communi-ties will not be to preside over the erosion of their traditional commit-ments but to rediscover the meaning of those commitments in a radically new social situation.

Most persons and communities have a desire for some kind of continuation of themselves in future generations. Such a desire has often been ethically altruistic. It has meant a willingness to forego im-mediate enjoyments, often to make sacrifices, for the sake of genera-tions yet to come. The desire for fulfilment in posterity is a strong theme in biblical religion with its promises of blessings to the present generation and to its "children's children." To a small community, whose survival was threatened by hostile neighbors, there was en-couragement in the hope that the descendants of a patriarch would be as the sands of the sea.

The same desire prevails among many peoples throughout the world. In times of high infant mortality it was reasonable that parents might want many children in order to have some assurance that a few would continue the family line. For this reason it may be that the reduction in infant mortality, which is immediately a major cause of the population explosion, will in time persuade many of the world's families to desire fewer children. Such is the reasoning of Roger Revelle, Director of the Center for Population Studies at Harvard University and one of the most ethically sensitive of demographers.[12]

Once again the easy answer might be an erosion of the religious concern for future generations and its replacement with a hedonistic ethic of enjoyment. But again the deeper responsibility of the religious communities is to rethink the meaning of their own commitments. When they do so, they frequently come to two ethical conclusions.

First, a valid concern for posterity is not limited to biological offspring. The heightened contemporary concentration on the nuclear family has meant that many parents find their fulfilment in their own immediate children, seeking every competitive advantage for their own at the expense of others. Tribal and racial groups have often done the same. A more imaginative ethic might enable people to take satisfaction in the children of their cousins, of their neighbors, and of the world. Much of the attraction of communes in the counter-culture is a reaction against excessive preoccupation with the nuclear family. Christians should find this ethical change congenial to their own loyalties, since they have always believed that "the household of God" is constituted by faith rather than biological kinship and that the community of mankind is made up of many ethnic communities.

Second, the legitimate concern for posterity has little to do with quantitative reproduction. Here the wisdom of the European and American Jewish community is helpful. More than most faiths Judaism has emphasized the continuity of the ethnic community and the family, but it has learned that its concern for its offspring is best expressed by maximizing their opportunities rather than their numbers. The time has come for mankind to make the same discovery. The ecological crisis is heightening human consciousness that the present generation's responsibility to the future requires stabilization of population. In fact, the emerging ecological ethic frequently asks contemporary humanity, in effect, to grant a vote to future generations in the determination of present policy decisions. Thus the authentic religious concern for future generations requires some changes in the traditional pro-natalist ethic that once embodied that concern.

Contemporary discussions of population are usually skewed by suspicions deeply rooted in social grievances and injustices. Attempts to cope with the dangers of rising population come through to some groups as threats.

The facts are that, by and large, the economically poorest societies and social groups within societies experience the fastest population growth. When wealthy people tell poor people about the perils of population, the poor hear the message as one more trick of the rich. A characteristic pattern appears in most international discussions of the issue. A white Westerner states the case for limiting population. An Asian, African, or Latin American replies that the real problem is social justice and that population is simply a diversion that the exploiting nations use against their victims. The Westerner replies that no matter what is done about social justice, exploding population intrenches poverty and jeopardizes the future. His respondent answers that no matter what is done about population, social injustice keeps many people poor. There is an irrefutable logic on both sides, but often neither side hears the other. So long as the arguments go on in a context of ideological clash, they appear as weapons rather than as truths.

The case is overwhelming that economic advances in developing countries cannot raise the standard of living if population rises as fast as production. Furthermore no conceivable economy can sustain people into a long future if populations continue to double every 20 years, as is now the case in some of the most impoverished areas of the world. But such information is not convincing if it comes from prosperous foreign elites who symbolize imperialism and exploitation. Their sincerity is also called into question by their habits of consumption. The United States, whose six percent of the world's population consume about 40 percent of the world's resources,[13] cannot gracefully warn other people that their population is outrunning resources.

Problems of justice and distribution cry for solution. So does the population explosion. Increasingly the economically poorest societies are recognizing that population growth frustrates their own efforts to help themselves. Recent discussions in the World Council of Churches have developed an atmosphere of increasing trust, enabling citizens of many societies to examine candidly issues of both population and international injustice.

Within the United States ideological factors related to race and class are relevant. In particular, black people are suspicious of white people who exhort them to control their population. They may even accuse the whites of plotting black genocide. Again some actual facts are useful. It is often said accurately that the black birthrate is measureably higher than the white birth rate. It can also be said, "At given social levels Negroes and whites generally have similar rates of fertility." [14] The black sociologist, Nathan Hare, writes: "Although the black birth rate is higher than that of whites, that is not true among women married to college trained men, where white women bear more children than do black women.[15] In a non-polemical situation it is possible to investigate the relation of fertility to poverty and education among all racial groups. Such investigation might help many people to act intelligently in their own behalf.

The difficulties of working toward some regulation of population in a distrustful world become evident in an illustration. Suppose Zero Population Growth were to become effective on a uniform, world-wide basis. Obviously this will not happen; social processes are not so rationalized. But the hypothesis shows the nature of the problem. A consequence would be the permanent stabilization of present statistical ratios among various ethnic and national groups. Some would regard this as a freezing of themselves into a permanent disadvantage. American black people would forever be 11 or 12 percent of the U.S. population. The Indians who once dominated this continent would be frozen as a tiny minority. White people might be less worried to be forever a minority in a world of color, since they have found methods more effective than numbers to assert themselves. But in many parts of the world minorities, living among hostile neighbors, would feel even more insecure than now.

Justice might suggest some adjustments in the uniform stabilization—allowing some groups, who have suffered discrimination, to expand. For example, world wide Jewry might deserve some opportunity for expansion in consequence of its losses in the Nazi holocaust. But no body of judges would be wise enough, no collective bargaining process sophisticated enough to work out the meanings of justice.

The example, of course, is artificial and unreal. But it points to real problems. It suggests that answers will come as various social groups discover that their own interests call for limitation of population. And possibilities of a world wide answer are commensurate with possibilities of international understanding and trust.

The population crisis raises in new forms one of the oldest and most perplexing of all human problems—the relation of personal freedom to social responsibility. This, one of the perennial issues of religious ethics, has never been more acute than today. Technology has made mankind more interdependent than ever before; yet alienation of persons from meaningful community and social structures is a world wide phenomenon.

Both freedom and social responsibility are fundamental religious values. Ideally they find their richest meaning in interaction; practically they often conflict, and society imposes constraints on freedom. How do people relate their craving for authentic selfhood and freedom to the demands of social systems? The question of population, in which social needs impinge upon the most personal of human decisions, is an acute example of the universal issue.

Until recent years the themes of voluntary family planning and sound population policy were usually conjoined. The assumption was that if people had the number of children they really wanted, the population problem would take care of itself. Increasingly that assumption meets challenges. The new argument is that family planning is not enough, that a social policy is required, that compulsory limitation of reproduction will become necessary because people usually want more children than are good for the society. Parents do not perceive a third child as a threat to society; but when the third child becomes normative for families, the threat becomes momentous.

No public population policy will be easy to carry out, especially in a time when society is withdrawing from its past efforts to control private sexual behavior. It is, of course, possible that society might say to its members, "Your sexual behavior is your own business, but your reproductive behavior is public business." But how can limitations on reproduction be enforced? Imprisonment of parents of infants is self-defeating. Fines might have some effect, but the poorest cannot pay fines and the moderately poor cannot pay them without becoming poorer—to the detriment of their innocent children. The only sure method of enforcement now available is compulsory sterilization or abortion, and these are deeply offensive, morally and religiously, to a great many people.

Furthermore, any coercive ethic in the area of population reinforces the distrust and hostility that some minorities feel against the social system. The black community, for example, has learned to suspect planners who impose elitist solutions upon ghetto residents who have little voice in determining their own destiny. At the First National Congress on Optimum Population and Environment (Chicago, 1970), the Black Caucus walked out in protest against "oppression of individual freedom" involved in some proposals at the Congress.

For the immediate future, in any case, control is not a live option in most societies. It is impossible without overwhelming public support, and such support cannot be achieved by coercion. When the overwhelming public support is available, compulsion may be unnecessary. Philip Hauser, Director of the University of Chicago Population Research and Training Center, says: "The fact is that decreases in fertility in what are now the economically advanced nations were achieved completely on a voluntary basis." [16] That gives some hope for the future. The problem remains that the world never before experienced the emergency that it faces now; future solutions must come faster and among greater varieties of people than in the past.

There is some help in the realization that life is never a choice between total freedom and total social control. Even now, there is no sheer freedom to reproduce without limit. The starvation that haunts some societies is not voluntary. Economic pressures are not voluntary. Shortage of housing is not voluntary. Taxation is not voluntary. Society, either through deliberate governmental regulations or through its even more pervasive institutions and attitudes, exercises pressures on people as they make decisions about reproduction. Such pressures will continue. We may expect them to become more intentionally and explicitly ordered with reference to a public population policy.

One considerable help from medical technology may be the development of a long-term contraceptive that would function so that a deliberate act would be required to accomplish procreation instead of (as at present) to prevent it. One factor in the population problem is careless spontaneity with unintended consequences. A single slip-up can undo a careful intentionality that functions 99 percent of the time. It is conceivable that some day young people will receive inoculations against fertility as routinely as they now take polio shots and that conception of children will require a deliberate medical step to revoke the standard inoculation. It is also conceivable that there will be "conscientious objectors" to such procedures. The development of such a possibility is a technological issue; its use and its consequences for human behavior are moral and religious rather than strictly technological issues. Technology frequently opens up new moral possibilities and redefines moral questions. It does not remove the necessity for moral decision.

The most profound contribution of religious communities to the population problem may be in the development of an ethic of responsible freedom. To the extent that they succeed, the harsh alternatives of irresponsible freedom versus social compulsion disappear.

The fundamental religious reason for limitation of population is a concern for the dignity of human life. Such a concern puts quality of life above quantity. Instead of the processes of nature, which in the past produced a high birth rate and a high death rate, it invokes human purpose, limiting birth rates but offering increased opportunity to those born. However, at some points the same concern that prompts population control may reject some methods for achieving this end.

Perhaps the most fundamental test case for the religious conscience today is abortion. It is one common method of limiting population in many societies. Although people may prefer other methods, it is often the method of last resort. When other methods fail, either because of technical inefficiency or human carelessness, abortion can overcome the omission. But abortion is not the same as prevention of conception. It is the destruction of embryo or fetus that, in normal expectations, would within a few weeks or months be born as a living infant. Hence religious communities often regard it as a violation of the sanctity of human life. For purposes of the present discussion, the issue concerns only the morality of abortion as a method of population control. This is not the same as the issue of therapeutic abortion where the life or health of the mother is at stake. It is not the same as the issue of the legality of abortion; it is quite possible to repect the morality of abortion, yet want the question removed from the criminal code, as does Robert Drinan, S.J.[17] The moral issue under discussion is the judgment of religious communities about the morality of abortion as a means of birth control.

Until quite recently it could be said that the dominant position of Jewish, Catholic, and Protestant religious communities strictly opposed abortion as a method of birth control. Roman Catholicism had the most rigorous and precise doctrine, judging abortion to be the destruction of human life. Protestantism and Judaism were more open to therapeutic abortion for grave reasons, but were far from acceptance of abortion as a legitimate method of birth control. The official position of Roman Catholicism has not changed. Individual Catholic theologians and philosophers may vary from the official position in softening the moral prohibition against abortion, but one would have to look long and hard to find a Catholic leader who advocates abortion as an ethically desirable component of population policy. The wide acceptance of contraception by Catholic theologians does not mean a similar acceptance of abortion.

Since Judaism has no centralized teaching authority comparable to that of Catholicism, the moral judgments of the Jewish community are harder to define. Authorities on Jewish moral law indicate that Judaism has never agreed with Roman Catholicism that abortion is the taking of a human life, but that Judaism's reverence for the potential human life of embryo or fetus means that abortion is permissible only for grave reasons. This basic teaching has not changed, although many Jewish people have become more permissive in their attitudes toward abortion.[18] In the 1972 controversy over the State of New York's permissive abortion law, the Rabbinical Council of America (Orthodox) attacked the law, while the New York State Federation of Reform Synagogues defended it.

It is in Protestantism that the most spectacular changes have taken place. A generation ago Protestant theology (e.g., explicitly and emphatically in such giants as Karl Barth and Dietrich Bonhoeffer) opposed abortion except when the life of the mother was threatened. Many Protestant denominations and councils of churches took the same position, often endorsing therapeutic abortion (in contrast to what they frequently thought to be the Roman Catholic position) but maintaining serious moral opposition to any more general practice of abortion. Within only five or ten years the reversals of old positions have been dramatic.

In most cases population policy was not the issue. Frequently churches (e.g., the General Synod of the United Church of Christ in 1971) have not endorsed abortion, but have asked for freedom for women to make decisions, unrestricted by laws that are "neither just nor enforceable."[19] Legislation, it is often pointed out, has never prevented abortions for the rich, but has made them impossible or exceedingly dangerous for the poor. On such grounds a church might endorse repeal of the prohibitions against abortion without deciding the theological and ethical issues in abortion itself.

The most abrupt change among Protestant groups has come in the United Methodist Church. In 1962, as Arthur Dyck points out, that church took the stand that "Protestants are second to none in condemning abortion" and, in particular, that "abortion ought to have *no* place in planned parenthood."[20] By 1970 the General Conference endorsed abortion upon request, subject only to "procedures of standard medical practice." Even more important for the issue under discussion was the fact that the stand was adopted as part of a Population Crisis Resolution, thereby seeming to endorse abortion as an important part of population policy. The action was denounced by some prominent Methodist theologians.

The current ethical arguments over abortion illustrate well the initial assumption of this paper—that religion complicates ethical issues. A utilitarian ethic can show rather easily that abortion, whether for personal reasons or as a calculated component of a population policy, can increase pleasure and decrease pain among humankind. Religion, insisting upon the sanctity of human life, requires a far more difficult judgment without providing an unequivocal answer. Is fetal life really human life? What does the dignity of the person mean for the rights of the fetus as compared with the freedom of a woman to make her own decision?

The strictest position opposing abortion holds that the fertilized ovum already partakes of the sanctity of human life. At fertilization an utterly unique human being is genetically complete and on the way to maturation. Such a position might mean that the "morning-after pill" and even the IUD are abortifacients rather than contraceptives, since both probably do not prevent fertilization but halt development or attachment. The problem raised by such a position is whether a fundamental ethical decision can rest upon such minute evidential distinctions.

The position endorsing abortion argues that the fetus is not a person—that personhood in its ethical meaning does not appear until birth. It is birth that establishes the personal independence of the infant. This position has problems like those of its opposite. Skeptics ask whether birth—admittedly an event of some importance—really confers personhood, when it is obvious that independent heart and brain activity have been going on long before birth and that surgery might have brought a healthy individual to birth well in advance of actual birth.

The disappointing thing about the present discussions of abortion in the religious communities is not the change from past positions—since change may mean ethical progress—but the rather slight attention to basic ethical issues as compared with the major attention to expediency. There are exceptions. Daniel Callahan's book, *Abortion: Law, Choice and Morality*,[21] is the work of a Catholic philosopher who has departed from the tradition of his church, but who still examines issues with moral seriousness. His style of inquiry, whether or not one concurs in his conclusions, might serve as a helpful model to religious communities examining their own minds and consciences on this and similar issues.

Any effort to deal with the real and urgent issues of population in any part of the world soon runs into some strong convictions of religious communities, as these convictions appear either in the formal teaching of the communities or in the cultural norms and feelings of their members. Often the rational crusader will resent the resistance of religious communities to his own ethics; he may wish for the erosion of religious traditions. The critic may be quite justified in opposing some influences of the religious communities. But he will often be wiser to examine the basic assumptions behind the specific teachings. He may find ethical sensitivities that a not-very-sensitive world needs, and he may find his own ethical assumptions unveiled and challenged.

The religious communities, however, will not serve the world of their own commitments well by simply repeating traditional injunctions. They will do no better by adjusting easily to the drift of contemporary history. They can fill a helpful role only as they continually re-examine both their commitments and the possible new meanings of those commitments in an ever-changing world.

1. James Reston, "Washington: Who Said 'Love Makes the World Go Round'?" *New York Times* (January 21, 1970). Italics added.

2. Claude Levi-Strauss, interview, *New York Times* (January 21, 1972).

3. Gordon Allport, *The Nature of Prejudice* (Doubleday, abridged Anchor ed., 1958), p. 415.

4. Arthur J. Dyck has done a valuable documentary study, *Religious Views and United States Population Policy* (Hastings-on-Hudson: Institute of Society, Ethics and the Life Sciences, 1971). His research is part of the Documentary Studies prepared for the Commission on Population Growth and the American Future. Although printed for private circulation only, it has been fairly widely distributed, and I have not judged it necessary to repeat or reproduce Dyck's research. Most of the data in Part 2 of this paper, unless specifically annotated, come from Dyck's study.

5. John A. O'Brien, "Birth Control and the Catholic Conscience," *Reader's Digest* (January 1969), p. 3.

6. *The Catholic World* (January 1969), pp. 146-7; *America* (November 30, 1968).

7. See Arthur Dyck, *op. cit.*, p. 46. Dyck cites Gavin Jones and Dorothy Nortmann, "Roman Catholic Fertility and Family Planning: A Comparative Review of the Research Literature," *Studies in Family Planning* (October 1968), pp. 1-27.

8. *Population Profile* (Population Reference Bureau, Inc., July 1969), p. 4.

9. Frank W. Notestein, Dudley Kirk, and Sheldon Segal, "The Problem of Population Control," in Philip M. Hauser, ed., *The Population Dilemma*, sponsored by the American Assembly (Prentice-Hall, 1963), p. 132.

10. *Ibid.*, p. 5. The study was made by the United Nations Latin American Demographic Center (CELADE) and Cornell University.

11. Rollo May, *Love and Will* (W. W. Norton, 1969), *passim.*

12. Roger Revelle, preparatory paper on "Technology and the World Population-

Hunger Problem," for National Consultation on Technology and Human Values, convened by the National Council of Churches, Chicago, May 2-4, 1967, p. 11.

13. Estimates vary upward and downward from 40 percent. I have picked the moderate estimate used by Robert S. McNamara, President of the World Bank, in an address to the Board of Governors of the Bank. See *New York Times* (September 29, 1970).

14. Notestein, Kirk, and Segal, "The Problem of Population Control," *op. cit.*, p. 168.

15. Nathan Hare, "Black Ecology," *The Black Scholar* (April 1970), p. 7.

16. Philip Hauser, testimony to a Senate Committee, *Population Crisis*, Part 2, 1967-68 (U.S. Government Printing Office, 1968), p. 492.

17. Robert Drinan, S. J., "The Right of the Fetus to be born," *The Dublin Review* (Winter 1967-68), pp. 365-81.

18. Arthur Dyck has summarized the evidence, *op. cit.*, pp. 47, 57-62.

19. Minutes of the Eighth General Synod of the United Church of Christ (June 25-29, 1971), pp. 131-32.

20. Arthur Dyck, *op. cit.*, pp. 49-50.

21. Daniel Callahan, *Abortion: Law, Choice and Morality* (Macmillan, 1970).

30

THE PROBLEM OF MOTIVATION

Richard A. McCormick

In a way that is characteristic of him, Roger Shinn has refused to snatch a cheap advantage for polemical or propaganda purposes. Rather he lays out the problem in the luxuriance of its complexity and urgency and misses very few folds and turns in the process. That is why it is so difficult to disagree with him. Specifically, I would agree with Shinn's basic contention that religious influences work much more profoundly through the attitudes and symbols which affect people's self-awareness and perceptions than through formal teachings. For example, popular eschatology has much more to do with social involvement and apathy than the encyclical *Populorum Progressio*. Furthermore, I believe Shinn is both accurate in his assessment and fair in his attitude in dealing with the questions of contraception and abortion in the Catholic community. Finally, I believe he has correctly identified the five root commitments that a population policy is likely to bring into play or to confront, though I am not nearly as clear as he that these commitments trace as heavily to religious or faith loyalties as he seems to suppose.

Because Shinn's paper is so carefully and well done, I am driven to an arduous and perhaps futile search for points where he may have left something more to be said. The gist of Shinn's paper is that rational critics of religious influence on population attitudes must examine and deal with the basic assumptions behind specific attitudes and techniques. Similarly religious communities must re-examine their commitments in a changing (here, rapidly overpopulating) world to discover the possible new meanings of these commitments. I certainly agree with this wise and balanced invitation. But there are, or could be, suppositions behind it which I think need more thorough ventilation if this coming to grips with basic commitments is to avoid the utilitarian traps to which the American pragmatic spirit has proved so vulnerable. I am not at all sure that Shinn makes these suppositions; indeed, I am rather sure he does not. But at least very many who discuss population policies and religious commitments are likely to do so. This justifies their mention.

First of all, Shinn suggests that root commitments, at least as customarily formulated, should constitute a center of concern in the present discussion of population. With no desire to challenge this assertion, I would like to suggest that to put the problem in this way is to have hastened by what might be a more immediate concern; popular realization of the existence of a population problem. Concretely, Shinn writes: "At some stage Zero Population Growth is not merely desirable but is necessary. My judgment is that the time of urgency is now." I wonder how many Americans would share that judgment, at least at the level of personal decision. At least very many Americans would not concede that there is a problem. Hence to face the problem in terms of basic commitments will appear to many to challenge these commitments *unnecessarily*. Strategically this could cause resistance and counterproductive resentment. If people are convinced of the utter urgency of a situation, they will generally tolerate a qualification of services and even rights. Rationing during a war which has widespread public support is an example. The more immediate problem, therefore, is one of communication and persuasion. The two-child family as an ideal has been proposed before people realize the urgency of the problem. For this reason it could be a good example of bad planning, a concrete symptom of the isolation and bureaucracy of the intellectual community.

If it is true to say that many people do not realize the dimensions of the population problem, then it is important to isolate the factors responsible for this. I would list the following. First there is the problem of the imagination. In an era of widespread jet travel and TV, people see millions of acres of untilled and uninhabited land. They know of the untapped resources of jungles, tundra, and oceans. It is simply hard to make clear to such people that we are running out of space and resources. Secondly, Americans have an all but limitless confidence in the capacity of science and technology. They have seen so many "miracles" achieved, so many obstacles overcome that they know that if science really got as serious about this problem as about the war, the whole picture would change. Thirdly, there is a seemingly intractable individualism of outlook where social responsibility is concerned. If our attitudes, values and priorities allow millions of our own fellow citizens (to say nothing of people from other countries) to wallow in poverty and to suffer injustice, then to expect such people to yield their comforts and commitments for future generations has overshot the problem.

Fourthly, demographic statistics and projections remain for most people dazzling elaborations from the gnosis of an elite. Much as we may dislike it, many people retain a lingering suspicion of and even cynicism about statistical and demographic calculations. They have experienced too many instances of statistics wrenched to yield a favorite thesis. Finally, there is the erosion of confidence in government and government planners. Americans increasingly associate bigness and bureaucracy with bungling and inefficiency, with narrow national self-interest and self-serving political motivation. "Population policy," suggesting as it does something national in scope and management, is in advance guilty by association.

When these factors operate in combination they result in a people which very generally does not sense a population urgency, and not sensing an urgency this people not only does not reexamine its root commitments, but even resents and resists approaches to them. Shinn hints at this when he says that "for the immediate future, in any case, control is not a live option in most societies. It is impossible without overwhelming public support and such support cannot be achieved by coercion."

The second supposition possibly operative in the invitation to reexamine root commitments in light of population pressures touches motivation. The supposition is that once people *realize* there is a population problem they will adjust their own personal decisions to this fact. One hates to be a cheerless pessimist but I think we must face the fact that motivation begins to have an impact only when it is too late. In other words, the public support to which Shinn refers will come only when individuals are personally affected by the problem. And that is too late.

Philip Hauser states: "The fact is that decreases in fertility in what are now the economically advanced nations were achieved completely on a voluntary basis." I have no doubt that Hauser is correct. But the voluntarism which achieved reduced fertility was associated not with population policies, but with family choice—the quality of worldly existence desired by the couple. Indeed population considerations were widely regarded as all but unrelated to personal decisions. Writing in 1964, the Catholic moralists Ford and Kelly stated: "Up to this point we have not mentioned the population problem as a factor in the morality of periodic continence. The reason is that as a practical matter demographic considerations of a general kind have little to do with the prudential judgment the average Catholic couple in this country is called upon to make as to the size of their family. Statisical considerations as to population increases, whether national or world-wide, play an insignificant role (and rightly so, in our opinion) in the formation of such a judgment." (*Marriage Questions*, 456) Later they note that "the matter of procreating or not procreating involves immediate personal and social factors in family life which would almost always outweight general demographic considerations in arriving at a prudent Christian decision." (458)

Perhaps attitudes have changed somewhat in the past several years. But it can be doubted that this change is very widespread or very deep. The motivational problem still remains. The very fact that decreases in fertility were achieved on a voluntary basis and that the values which operated to stimulate reduced fertility were personal and family values suggests that only when individuals are affected personally will they allow population considerations to enter their motivational field. This is not a call for coercion. Rather it is a reminder that coercion will be avoided ultimately only if the values which motivate voluntarism are expanded beyond those associated with the term "family planning." There is, in my judgment, nothing in Catholic tradition or teaching to prevent such expansion.

31

THE PRAGMATIC SPIRIT OF JUDAISM

David M. Feldman

Roger Shinn's excellent paper touches upon realistic aspects of the population control problem. The point he makes, to begin with, that religion "gets in the way" of utilitarian answers to problems, is well-taken. Speaking for the Jewish component of the Judeo-Christian tradition, my response is based on an awareness that this Jewish component—with the unique emphasis it places on the "be fruitful and multiply" imperative—is even more of an obstacle.

True, even the classic Jewish sources, formulated against the background of a world innocent of the population explosion, recognize that other imperative defined by Dr. Shinn, whereby "new behavior" is dictated by the same value commitments in new circumstances. Responsibility to posterity, or to the "dignity of life," means that it is just as selfish or reckless to overbreed as it is to refrain from "fulfilling the mitzvah" of procreation. One Rabbinic author, writing in the 1940's but basing himself squarely on all the traditional and classic Jewish sources, in fact used the imagery of the world-as-a-spaceship (a phrase not coined until the 1960's) to define the Jewish legal position: If Spaceship Earth threatens to reach the finite limits of food production and accommodation of its inhabitants, legal and moral responsibility dictate that the procreational imperative be set aside.

But this resolution of the moral conflict is remarkable in that it overrides another principle, one not mentioned in Shinn's paper. That principle is the faith postulate that "the Lord will provide" or, in its Talmudic formulation, "He that giveth life, giveth food." This reliance upon Providence or the Divine Scheme of Things can be more operative a principle than any abstract consideration for "the dignity of life." The pious Jewish community may indeed be sensitive or sensitized to the moral necessity of population stabilization, but may still believe that any intervention in God's affairs is not just a violation of natural law, it is foolishly unnecessary. Moreover, deliberate intervention to determine the size or the timing of one's family does offend against a sentimental fatalism of even the less pious. Yet, such "theology" is just not supported by the legal imperatives of Jewish religion. There is a delightful Rabbinic story, according to which a man balked at giving charity because, he said, people are poor and that must be the way God wants it; he was told to act as if there *were* no God and to do what must be done to help. In that pragmatic spirit, Jewish law requires contraception when the wife's health is threatened. Abstinence violates the essence of the marriage; "reliance on miracles" to protect health or life is forbidden; contraception is therefore mandated. Similarly, the welfare of existing infants who might be adversely affected if a nursing mother becomes pregnant again also dictates contraception for that mother. We are bidden to set aside the entire Torah for the sake of preservation of life or health, and the faith principle of God's providence is no more in conflict there than it is when recourse is had to any other medical procedure or safety precautions. One could go further, in fact, and point out Jewish legal attitudes favoring contraception in other than medical indications. For example, motherhood need not, according to traditional legal decisions, be more highly valued than wifehood or womanhood, when these goals clash. The very existence of such legitimate attitudes in the otherwise pro-natalist Jewish religion is highly significant for purposes of our present discussion.

But there is another kind of exception to the data presented by Dr. Shinn. Acknowledging the pro-natalist tendencies of the Jewish tradition, and even the right of the Jewish people to make up for losses, Dr. Shinn points, on the other hand, to the many Jewish scholars who are active as proponents of zero population growth. "If they do not claim to speak for Judaism, neither do they feel that their concern for population in any way alienates them from Judaism." Indeed, the relative and absolute decrease in birth rate in the U. S. reported for 1971 encompasses Jewish families as well, who may have in fact reproduced at a rate lower still than zero growth. Yet, the Hasidic community is an exception to this trend, as it is an exception to all trends. Separatist and extreme in their religious observance, the Hasidim continue to have large families, and they do so as a kind of militant gesture, a deliberate act of survivalism. If the general Jewish community has a theoretical right to make up for physical losses, the Hasidim go much beyond that. They have accepted for themselves the *actual* right to make up not only for physical but for *spiritual* losses as well. They see Jewish assimilation and secularism all around them, and they seek—consciously or unconsciously— to counteract this phenomenon by a positive strengthening of their numbers.

The acceptance by the Hasidim of marital sexuality as requiring no additional justification is, by and large, similar to that of the rest of the Jewish community; their abhorrence of contraception is probably no more or less than that of other people. But the sense they have of being a beleaguered minority, or a group charged with the sacred mission of perpetuating their life and culture, is far stronger than any similar sense among any other group or subgroup. The important point for our purposes is that they are acting and will continue to act on that premise.

And yet, again, Shinn's allowance can be said to be more generous than needed. He would grant "worldwide Jewry" the "opportunity for expansion in consequence of the losses in the Nazi holocaust." This, despite the implications such an allowance carries for other groups and their resistance to being frozen at minority status. But "worldwide Jewry" has never been interested in "expansion"—only in survival. Survival may not require expansion. Ancient Israel was told (Deuteronomy 7:7) that it entered the Covenant "not because ye were more in number than any people—for ye were the least in number." Minority status has never been scorned by the Jews; we have served our historic purposes as a minority, and our concern is not to change that status but to arrest any diminution and to survive in health. A poignant passage from the Daily Prayer Book illustrates:

> *Guardian of Israel*
> *Preserve the remnant of Israel*
> *Let not perish Israel*
> *Who proclaim "Hear O Israel"*

A newborn child is named after a deceased parent or grandparent so that continuity, not expansion, be guaranteed. It is no less than remarkable that the Biblical imperative "be fruitful and multiply"— which, on the face of it sounds so expansionistic—was interpreted by the Talmud as requiring, for Jews, that each couple give birth to at least one son and one daughter. Thus, the couple "replaces" itself and continuity is assured.

I would say, then, to Dr. Shinn: for the *State* of Israel, Jewish numbers are important. There, Jews must remain a majority so the State can retain its Jewish character; else the Zionist dream is mocked and aborted. "Worldwide Jewry," however, needs not expansion but survival—though this, too, means we must make up for losses. In this respect, the Jewish community differs both from the majority and from other minorities.

32

THE RESPONSE OF BLACK CHURCHMEN

Evans E. Crawford

A special agony of choice and commitment is posed by population discussions for Black churchmen. Practically all of our articulate laymen would tend to regard population concerns as a dilemma that exist, like Myrdal's *An American Dilemma,* in the minds of white people. The reality of that attitude, both within themselves and as a shared attitude in their community, must be seen as a basic fact in the situation of the Black church and the Black community. But there are other realities in the Black community which indicate a concern for life and liberation. Such realities suggest that the real issue with which we, too, must confront the population discussion is not so much in whose minds it is as in whose misery it is recorded and reflected. Perceived this way, it is impossible to be unconcerned with expanding population if that promises to intensify oppression. If the bells are felt to be tolling for society, the chances are that they are tolling for us too. Consequently, just plain self interest, if nothing else, suggests a basis for our sharing in the discussions of the population problem.

If we are to share in the discussions, however, we need a challenging word which is native to our own sensitivities, substance and soul. One of Jesus' sayings, spoken while experiencing agonizing choices of commitment after his own new experiencing of wholeness, may have possibilities for us. The saying is an inclusive but also a human word— open to the full range of ultimacy and thus neither an "either-or" nor a "both-and." The saying, as originally spoken, was "Man shall not live by bread alone." It needs to be reinterpreted for application to population issues. In this context it becomes "Man shall not live by breeding alone." Several dimensions of this reinterpretation challenge the Black community in the exercise of ethical imagination.

First, it contains and highlights the values of human dignity we share as a religious commitment. Our victimizing experiences have included being considered as property in slavery and then as problems mostly since that time. Consequently, our claims on human dignity are more deeply grasped in spite of barriers to humanity.

Second, the words "man shall not live by breeding alone" permit sex to have meaning for man rather than man being understood to exist for sex. In one sense this is a judgment upon the way the slave society made slave breeding a business and any family life an impossibility. The words expose the extent to which Black Americans themselves have been the victims of population control. They suggest a basis for judging the proper issues in family planning or population planning. Certainly they provide bases from which to assess self-righteousness in ethical discussions on population problems.

Third, relating this interpretation permits discussions on population issues to consider concerns with genocide more in prophetic than in polemical terms. It reveals the issue to be defined not simply in terms of numbers but in terms of quality. To be sure, there are stages and situations where group, community, perhaps tribes must consider survival a necessity, but in the light of this word, choice is possible without coercion or ultimacy.

Fourth, the interpretation "not by breeding alone" permits the embrace of children and others who are not related biologically. It confirms the possibilities in the large and extended type family, so long considered to be without value. With life open to more abundant meaning, the focus on quality and opportunity which Roger Shinn has mentioned become relevant to the Black community.

With these as a kind of "working formulation," I wish to make a couple of observations on Shinn's essay. In his discussion of social justice he seems to suffer a failure of imagination. Perhaps this is merely a matter of deciding to leave the agenda open for others to exercise the ethical imagination. It was on that basis that I undertook to apply my own formulation; and, indeed, it was while reading Shinn's paper and particularly while wrestling with a felt dissatisfaction with his discussion on social justice that this formulation opened up for me. The ethical imagination needs to be informed by two insights. First is Lionel Rubinoff's argument that the abuse of power requires attention to the exercise of an imagination for evil as the pathway toward the development of an imaginative critique of power. His book *The Pornography of Power* reveals the value of this approach in exposing the use of so-called scientific studies of social problems that function more to entertain than to establish a foundational critique or solution of problems. This is a dimension which ethical inquiry into population concerns should not overlook. The other point is our need to consider the human image as a separate area for discussion. Discussion of population issues should particularly take into account George Kelsey's claim in *Racism and the Christian Understanding of Man* that racism is a faith, a search for meaning whose political plan of action suggests geoncide. Such analyses clearly suggest the importance of more penetrating discussion of social justice as it relates to the population question.

33

POPULATION PROBLEMS

AS MORAL RELIGIOUS ISSUES

Arthur J. Dyck

There are two major ways in which moral and religious beliefs enter into the discussion of population: first, in the evaluation of the nature and consequences of population dynamics; secondly, in the evaluation of population policy. I shall discuss Shinn's essay under these two headings.

At the very outset of his essay, Shinn quite rightly notes that "anybody who discusses religious and human values involved in the controversial issues of population already makes some assumptions." For the sake of honesty and clarity, Shinn states some of his own assumptions. First, he assumes that this planet cannot sustain an infinite growth in population, and hence, at some stage zero population growth is necessary. With this assumption, one cannot seriously quarrel. But Shinn adds to this judgment that "the time of urgency is now," and that "the alternative to intentional actions is to let disaster bring its own cruel 'solutions' to the problem." Thus for Shinn, "the ethical issue is not whether population will be restrained; it is whether people will restrain it through actions consistent with humanity's most profound moral insensivities or through inhumane or catastrophic methods."

Unfortunately Shinn does not tell us what kind of crisis is posed by population growth. It is puzzling that he avoids any substantive discussion of what justifies this judgment. To decide that there is a population crisis, encourages and justifies serious consideration of population policy proposals that would have the effect of greatly curtailing liberty or of perpetrating social injustices. In the name of self-defense, a society will tolerate or even encourage involuntary conscription and martial law. In short, it is not an ethically indifferent matter to assume that there is a population crisis. And religious communities have something to say about how we make such a decision.

Since Shinn's essay only hints at the kinds of consequences associated with current population growth rates, it will be necessary to assess the catastrophies that Shinn could reasonably have in mind. The

assessment that there is a population crisis is usually made by associat-
ing population growth with one or the other of the following three
phenomena: 1) environmental deterioration; 2) famines and starvation; 3) economic deprivation and poverty. Let us examine the
relationship between population growth and each of these three types
of catastrophies.

Population Growth and Environmental Deterioration. Environmental deterioration can be seen as an imminent threat to human
survival. Paul Ehrlich in *The Population Bomb* [1] sounds the alarm:
our environment is sick; the disease is over-population. The remedy
is population control to achieve zero population growth rates, using
coercive methods as necessary. But Ehrlich's reasoning is too simple.
Our environment may be sick, but zero population growth will not by
itself cure its ills. Roger Revelle in a testimony given before the Reuss
Committee, a Congressional Committee on Conservation and Natural
Resources, made the following analysis:

"The lack of utility of any simple correlation between environmental
deterioration and population growth can be demonstrated by calculating the size of the population of the United States which, with the
same per capita income and dirty habits as the average U.S. citizen
in 1965, would have produced no more pollution than the country
experienced in 1940.

"Other things being equal, the number of automobiles and the
amount of gasoline and paper consumed would have remained about
constant over the quarter century if our population had declined
from 133 million people in 1940 to 67 million in 1965. To maintain a
constant flow of sulfur dioxide in the air from electric power plants, the
population would have had to decrease to only 40 million people.
Presumably the amount of nitrogen fertilizers would not have increased,
if all but 17 million Americans had reemigrated to the homes of their
ancestors. Only 17 million people in the country would use the same
amount of nitrogen in 1965 as we used in 1940. The national parks
would have remained as uncrowded in 1965 as they were in 1940 if
our population during the interval had gone down from 130 million
people in 1940 to 30 million people in 1965, instead of going up to 195
million, as, of course, it actually did.

"These unlikely speculations emphasize the uncertainties of the relationships between population, gross national product, and the quality
of life, of which environmental deterioration is one aspect." [2]

From this analysis we can discern that pollution is a way of life and
must be attacked in its own right. Clearly, we cannot accept this way

of life as the price of affluence. Wherever environmental deterioration is a *present* danger, the behavior that causes it must be immediately curtailed. Furthermore, if environmental deterioration is an inevitable by-product of affluence, then we must not urge non-affluent countries to reduce their population. The present argument for asking non-affluent countries to reduce their population is that such a reduction will stimulate economic development. If, then, affluence and environmental deterioration inevitably accompany each other, environmental deterioration will increase as populations decrease. Nothing we have said should be misconstrued: although population growth does affect the quality of our environment, no one can show that environmental deterioration of crisis proportions is presently a function of sheer numbers of people. In any event, no nation can solve the problems of pollution simply through reductions in population.

Population Growth and Starvation. Another dire prediction in some population literature is that of widespread famines. *Famine 1975* is what the Paddocks claim.[3] The favorite example of the famine prophets is India. Fortunately for this much maligned country, Indian scholars themselves have studied famines in India. These studies reveal that famines in the 19th century were due to genuine shortages of food; in the 20th century they occur because people do not always receive in time the food that is available and/or they cannot pay for it.[4] Food supplies in India continue to increase at a faster rate than population growth. There is currently enough food in India adequately to nourish its citizens.[5] There is another reason why people presently starve. In some localities the manner in which infants are fed contributes to a relatively high infant mortality rate due to insufficient nutrition. This cause of death could be curtailed by spreading the knowledge of the nutritional needs of infants.[6] We know that high rates of infant mortality, maternal death, and generally lower life expectancies occur in the United States because of malnourishment. Malnourishment in the United States is clearly a problem of social injustice, not lack of food.

Again we do not wish to be misunderstood. An indefinitely growing population in any region of the world would overtake its potential food supply. Our point is simply that there is no current necessity for people to starve because of the unavailability of food. Experts differ as to when time would run out for feeding the population of the world at its present growth rates.[7] At the same time, as we shall note later, there are good reasons to believe that present growth rates in many countries will decline.

Population Growth and Poverty. The relationship of economic gains and population growth are very ambiguous. We know that rapid population growth can and has been accompanied by increases rather than decreases in per capita income. India is an example of this. Furthermore, respected economists have argued that population growth may be construed as an incentive for economic development insofar as it brings in its wake increased motivation, imagination, and productivity.[8]

At the level of making decisions for one's family, it is not at all axiomatic that a large family is an economic liability. In many countries there are situations where children are a source of farm labor and of security in one's old age. Under these circumstances, it would be grossly unjust and unrealistic to expect people to assume that economic benefits accrue from reducing the size of their families. The claim that "no matter what is done about social justice, exploding population entrenches poverty and jeopardizes the future" is hardly the irrefutable logic that Shinn says that it is. Let us consider what children mean to the poor, and what would happen if involuntary poverty were eliminated or greatly reduced. Here is how one black woman from Roxbury describes what a new child means for poverty stricken mothers, to the men in their lives, and to their other children:

"The worst of it is that they try to get you to plan your kids by the year; except they mean by the ten-year plan, one every 10 years. The truth is, they don't want you to have any, if they could help it. To me, having a baby inside me is the only time I'm really alive. I know I can make something, do something, no matter what color my skin is, and what names people call me. When the baby gets born, I see him, and he's full of life, or she is; and I think to myself that it doesn't make any difference what happens later, at least now we've got a chance, or the baby does. The children and their father feel it, too, just like I do. They feel the baby is a good sign, or at least he's *some* sign. If we didn't have that, what would be the difference from death? Even without children my life would still be bad—they are not going to give us what *they* have, the birth control people. They just want us to be a poor version of them only without our children and out faith in God and our tasty fried food or anything.

"They tell you we are 'neglectful'; we don't take proper care of the children. But that's a lie, because we do, until we can't any longer because the time has come for the street to claim them, to take them away and teach them what a poor nigger's life is like. I don't care what anyone says: I take the best care of my children. I scream the ten comandments at them every day, until one by one they don't forget them. (You can ask my minister if I'm not telling the truth.) It's when they leave for school, and start seeing the streets and everything, that's when there's the change; and by the time they're 10 or so, it's all I can do to say anything, because I don't even believe my own words, to be honest. I tell them, please be good; but I know it's no use, not when they can't get a fair break, and there are sheriffs down south and up here the policemen, ready to kick you for so much as breathing your feelings. So I turn my eyes on the little children, and keep on praying that one of them will grow up at the right second, when the school-teachers have time to say hello and give him the lessons that he needs, and when they get rid of the building here and let us have a place you can breathe in and not get bitten all the time, and when the men can find work—because they can't have children, and so they have to drink or get drugs to find some happy moments, and hope about things." [9]

Not only is it unjust to ask women like this and under these circumstances greatly to curtail births, but it is also the case that once such women are released from the bonds of poverty and social inequity, they can and do voluntarily have small families of slightly more than two children. College educated black women have the lowest birth rates of all college educated women in the United States. It is fallacious to assume that you can have "exploding population" regardless of what is done about social justice. Shinn himself cites with approval the demographic fact that lower infant mortality has been associated with lower birth rates. Lowering infant mortality in the United States requires the implementation of social justice.[10] In this instance also social justice would enable and encourage people to have small families. The distrust that blacks in this country feel for those who urge the curtailment of birth rates will be merited so long as those who wish to see less poverty and lower birth rates refuse to make social justice their first and foremost concern.

Our conclusions then with respect to the relationship between population growth and dangers to the human species, such as environmental deterioration, starvation, and poverty, is that none of these dangers, however immiment, ensue directly from present population growth rates. The concern over space and the use of space in a finite world, also a genuine concern, is again something that is not solved simply by a decrease in numbers. However, it is the finitude of space that does make zero population growth at some point in the history of the world a necessity. This means that decreasing population growth and considering policies by which this is to be accomplished are worthy of our concern and reflection. But as we have tried to show, there is no justification for fanaticism or haste when considered reflection would better serve us.

Not only does Shinn assume that there is a "population crisis," but he also assumes that the appropriate response to it is to decrease population growth. Now to some that may seem to be a self-evident assumption, but it is not. This assumption depends upon how one defines the "population problem."

After a survey and an analysis of the various problems that have been called population problems, Ralph Potter notes that all these analyses can be summarized in the following definition of the population problem: "In certain parts of the world, the pressure of population factors of size, rate of growth, or distribution, is so severe that it may prove impossible to develop or maintain a level of resources necessary to sustain a good life for all persons through time." [11] Potter's formulation contains four elements or variables each of which can be the focus of what to do about the population problem: (1) level of resources; (2) rate of population increase; (3) sustaining a good life; (4) the persons who are to enjoy the good life. A policymaker concerned with solutions to the population problem can be concerned with any one or more of these four variables. Policy can be aimed at either: (1) increasing the level of available resources; (2) decreasing, halting, or reversing the rate of population growth; (3) redefining what is necessary to sustain the good life; or (4) limiting the range of access to the good life by excluding some and by denying the requirement that the full measure of resources to sustain a good life must be available for all persons through time. Stating the alternatives more crudely, and using the banquet metaphor first coined by Malthus and later used by Pope Paul at the United Nations, population policymakers have the options of: (1) increasing provisions at the banquet; (2) inviting fewer guests; (3) requiring those who come to the banquet to take a smaller share; or (4) excluding some now or over time from access to the common table.

The debate between Malthus and Engels was a debate over options one and two, Malthus claiming that unless fewer guests are invited, the banquet of life will be marred by starvation, war, and pestilence. Engels saw the proper response to population growth as one of providing an increasing amount of goods more fairly distributed. Shinn

does not depict, as a matter of population policy, Jewish and Christian
concern for alleviating poverty and increasing equity. It is one of
the ironies of history that official Roman Catholic and Marxist
thought agree in calling for population policies that will increase the
world's goods and increase the degree to which they are equitably
distributed. Shinn's essay simply does not recognize these responses
to population growth. His essay, therefore, is misleading in characterizing the nature and scope of population policies.

Since Shinn did not take into consideration the possibility of changing what is considered requisite for the good life as a population
policy, his essay nowhere mines the rich lode of religious reflection
on this worldly asceticism. The Christian tradition wrestles with
the relationship of the Christian to material goods, and the weight
of that tradition surely does not make it evident that contemporary
economic definitions of the good life are either ideal or morally
acceptable.

That Shinn should neglect the fourth option for population policy
is not surprising, for it seems quite patently unjust to exclude some
people from life's goods. But if the resources of the world that are
essential to human survival are irreplaceable in the long run, then
at some point there will be a future generation for whom there is no
banquet table. If one makes the assumption that human survival is
not possible over time, then even zero population growth will not
secure the future. Nothing will. And one is left to decide how many
generations we are morally bound to include in our division of a finite
amount of goods over time. Shinn gives no indication as to whether
his projected catastrophies do or do not make reflection on this
option a necessity. In religious terms, it is a question as to whether
the creation of a new earth will at some time be our only hope for
what Shinn calls "continued fulfillment in posterity."

Once we become aware of the four fundamental alternatives for
coping with the population problem, the moral and religious nature
of this problem is even more evident. Not only does our understanding of it entail what we think the good life is and what we
think is just, but we are also confronted with the necessity to rethink our fundamental notions concerning the nature of human beings. Malthus took the view that the only constraints upon human
reproduction other than war, famine, and pestilence, were to be
found in what he called moral restraint. One of the questions confronting us, as it confronted Malthus, is the extent to which human

beings will voluntarily curtail birth rates through some form of moral restraint.

As Shinn notes, there are those within religious communities who already speak of the sin and selfishness connected with having more than a certain number of children. At the same time, there are those who connect sin and selfishness with having sexual relations without children, or in deliberately having considerably fewer children than one can provide for. We have within religious communities of this country those who tend to see human sin exemplified in the all too prevalent tendency to have very few, if any, children. Now if sin is a pervasive human tendency, it would seem that population growth has an uncertain future. The danger to the human species would be that of extinction through selfish indulgence. To some this may seem like an utterly ridiculous point of view. Whatever you think of it, there is no way of escaping the question as to whether in fact the values placed upon childbearing and childrearing are, as many allege, culturally and religiously conditioned. For if in fact childbearing and childrearing and the extent to which they occur are largely culturally and ideologically induced, then motherhood can die and so can the human species.

I rather think that some of us, in a shallow way, assume that the desire to bear and rear children will go on no matter what we do, while at the same time thinking that we can or even should "liberate" women from the role of motherhood. From a theological standpoint we cannot have it both ways. Pragmatically, it may be the case that we can have a stable society encompassing some women who are deeply committed to motherhood and its satisfactions, and other women who view motherhood as demeaning or unworthy of their talents. But how do we know whether this is possible? A more important question is whether it is morally acceptable to view motherhood as something from which women ought to be liberated. If motherhood is not simply a culturally induced and regulated phenomenon, but rather a deeply rooted, biologically inbuilt desire, as in many other animals, then it is cruel to try to deprive women of this role or to berate them for their devotion to it. In his discussion of the separation of sex and procreation, Shinn does not tell us how important procreation is either for him or for the religious community. He does expect religious communities to sanction it, but does not reveal the grounds on which they will or ought to do so. It would be helpful to know what particular traditional commitments in the area of sex Shinn has in mind and what form he thinks they ought to take when he claims that, "the ethical task of the religious communities will not be to preside over the erosion of their traditional commitments, but to rediscover the meaning of those commitments in a radically new social situation."

Shinn is unclear, perhaps undecided, with respect to the larger question as to whether zero population growth will be voluntarily achieved and achieved in time. He cites the belief that voluntarism cannot possibly qualify as a viable population policy. At the same time, he takes cognizance of, but is not confronted by, the demographic fact that the substantial decreases in fertility that occurred in affluent nations were achieved on a totally voluntary basis. His unresolved uneasiness is expressed in his claim that "future solutions must come faster and among greater varieties of people than in the past." Since Shinn's assumptions regarding the relation between human nature and reproduction are not specified, we do not know whether his uneasiness is so deep that he would not be consoled by recent estimates that the demographic transition in a number of non-western nations is now occurring much more quickly than it ever did in affluent western nations.[12]

Shinn's indecisiveness about the efficacy of voluntarism may contribute to his rather unsatisfactory treatment of how we should view proposals to achieve population control through coercion. His arguments against compulsion, such as resort to compulsory sterilization and abortions, is that they "are deeply offensive, morally and religiously, to a great many people." This is surely a shaky defense against coercion. Shinn himself notes that it would be misleading to consider abortion morally acceptable were it generally thought to be. What we would like to hear from Shinn, and from religious ethicists generally, is why it is morally wrong to implement a policy of compulsory sterilization and abortion.[13] The moral status of voluntary sterilization and abortion as population policies should also be aired. Shinn is quite right in considering voluntary abortion as a debatable candidate for inclusion in any population policy, but he does not give us any clues as to how to debate the issue. On coercion he leaves us with the feeble assurance that "for the immediate future . . . control is not a live option in most societies." This implies that it may become an option in the foreseeable future, and if this is so, then it is time now to decide what kinds of population policies are on Shinn's terms inhumane.

Shinn is always eager to consider a variety of views, but he should not present patent nonsense without comment. When the Methodists claim that any couple that has more than two children is contributing to the population explosion, they are uttering a falsehood that is morally pernicious, especially for couples with more than two children. No society can replace itself if no couples have more than two children. Death and sterility have not been eliminated as human realities. Surely also the Methodists would not expect every woman either to marry or to have at least two children. Church statements of this sort can only alienate the faithful and the thoughtful, and make a laughing stock of the churches' efforts on behalf of responsible parenthood.

I have always been able to learn something from Roger Shinn's essays, and in conclusion I wish to summarize the contribution of his essay. Shinn's major thesis is that religion quite rightly complicates any of the decisions that are and will be made concerning population policy. Religion's role as a complicating factor is justifiable because it often expresses the deepest values and aspirations of human beings and at the same time enhances rather than thwarts the moral sensitivities of a society.

Again quite rightly Shinn has reminded us that no religious community can be indicted for contributing directly by reason of its teachings to high birth rates. Indeed, we can only agree with his claim that "the most profound contribution of religious communities to the population problem may be in the development of an ethic of responsible freedom." In fact, the Jewish experience in the United States, of placing a high value upon marriage, motherhood, and the family, while keeping the birth rates low, is a case in point.[14]

Shinn's essay provides a stimulus to the task of re-examining the traditional commitments of religious communities. Just as these religious communities "will not serve the world of their own commitments well by simply repeating traditional injunctions," they will do no better, Shinn reminds us, "by adjusting easily to the drift of contemporary history." Shinn's essay provides some good reasons why this re-examination of religious commitments and their possible new meanings is worthwhile.

1. Paul Ehrlich, *The Population Bomb* (Ballantine Books, Inc., 1968).

2. Roger Revelle (testimony), *Effects of Population Growth on Natural Resources and the Environment.* Hearings before the Reuss Subcommittee on Conservation and Natural Resources (U.S. Government Printing Office, 1969).

3. William Paddock and Paul Paddock, *Famine—1975!* (Little Brown & Co., 1967).

4. B. M. Bhatia, *Famines in India: 1860 to 1965* (New York: Asia Publishing House, 1967).

5. Private communication, Roger Revelle. There has been a general increase in per capita food supplies in the world between the mid-1930's and the mid-1960's. See President's Science Advisory Committee, Panel on the World Food Supply, *The World Food Problem*, 3 vol. (Washington: The White House, May 1967). The total number of malnourished people may be smaller than it was 30 to 40 years ago. See Roger Revelle, Paul Ehrlich, "New High Priest of Ecocatastraphy" *Family Planning Perspective* (April 1971), pp. 66-70.

6. J. B. Wyon and J. E. Gordon, *The Khanna Study* (Harvard University Press, 1971).

7. Roger Revelle, "Projected World Population and Food Production Potentials," *The Land-Grant University and World Food Needs* (University of Illinois College of Agriculture).

8. Harvey Leibenstein, *"The Impact of Population Growth on Economic Welfare— Non-*traditional Elements," *Rapid Population Growth: Consequences and Policy Implications* (Johns Hopkins Press, 1971).

9. Robert Coles, *Children of Crisis* (Atlantic-Little Brown, 1964), pp. 368-9.

10. Non-Whites in the U.S. have nearly twice the infant mortality rates and nearly four times the maternal death rates of their white counterparts.

11. R. B. Potter, "The Simple Structure of the Population Debate: The Logic of the Ecology Movement." *Ethics, Population and the American Tradition* (Hastings-on-Hudson, The Institute of Society, Ethics and the Life Sciences, 1972).

12. Dudley Kirk, "A New Demographic Transition," *Rapid Population Growth: Consequences and Policy Implications, op. cit.*

13. Some of the moral issues raised by sterilization are discussed in A. J. Dyck, "Population Policies and Ethical Acceptability," *Rapid Population Growth:Consequences and Policy Implications, op. cit.* Some of the difficulties of abortion as a policy are discussed in A. J. Dyck, "Perplexities for the Would-Be Liberal in Abortion," *The Journal of Reproductive Medicine* (June 1972), pp. 351-4.

14. A. J. Dyck, "Religious Views and United States Population Policy," *Ethics, Population and the American Tradition, op. cit.*